'Hughes's book is destined to become a seminal text in the fie
aging change. Not only does he capture all of the main then
with change in a highly reader-friendly format, he also seric
ness" of change in both an intellectual and entertaining wa;
book!'

James McCalman, *Professor of Leadership Studies,*
Portsmouth Business School, University of Portsmouth, UK

'The fields of leadership and change have been waiting for *Managing and Leading Organizational Change.* This excellent book provides and inspires throughout, providing radically fresh perspectives on numerous aspects of managing and leading change for academic and practitioner audiences alike.'

Sarah Fidment, *Subject Group Leader, Organisational Behaviour/Human*
Resource Management, Sheffield Hallam University, UK

'There are many books on change management but this is a must-buy because of its emphasis on the lived experience of change and the centrality of organizational process, emergence and voice. The "one size fits all" solutions of the consultancies is made obsolescent by this sophisticated, contemporary approach and its apposite cases.'

David Weir, *Professor of Intercultural Management, York*
St John University, USA

'A refreshing and welcome addition to the organizational change literature. This critical text challenges what we think we know about organizational change in an insightful, engaging and enjoyable text, a must-read for any scholar in this field of study.'

Richard Jefferies, *Lecturer in Management, University of the*
West of Scotland, UK

'This exceptionally well written book brings a much needed critical perspective to one of the most misunderstood issues in management. In challenging some of the most totemic figures and established ideas in the field Mark Hughes has written a book that I highly recommend.'

Dennis Tourish, *Professor of Leadership and Organisation Studies,*
University of Sussex, UK

Managing and Leading Organizational Change

Organizational change impacts upon all organizations regardless of size and sector. In this unique organizational change textbook, important ongoing debates about managing change and leading change are combined, giving a broader perspective that encourages readers to engage with both management and leadership. In combination, management and leadership insights inform how organizations are changing and how we can make a positive difference in such processes of change.

Managing and Leading Organizational Change speaks both to the applied and practical aspects of organizational change, as well as questioning the research and evidence base of organizational change practices. Chapters begin with real-world insights, followed by coverage of the major theories. The ongoing nature of these debates is signposted through the inclusion of questioning sections with research case studies showcased.

This textbook will be particularly beneficial for final year undergraduates and postgraduates studying organizational change, strategic change, change management and change leadership modules.

Mark Hughes is Reader in Organizational Change at the Brighton Business School, University of Brighton, UK.

Managing and Leading Organizational Change

Mark Hughes

Routledge
Taylor & Francis Group

LONDON AND NEW YORK

First published 2019
by Routledge
2 Park Square, Milton Park, Abingdon, Oxon OX14 4RN

and by Routledge
711 Third Avenue, New York, NY 10017

Routledge is an imprint of the Taylor & Francis Group, an informa business

© 2019 Mark Hughes

The right of Mark Hughes to be identified as author of this work has
been asserted by him in accordance with sections 77 and 78 of the
Copyright, Designs and Patents Act 1988.

All rights reserved. No part of this book may be reprinted or
reproduced or utilised in any form or by any electronic, mechanical,
or other means, now known or hereafter invented, including
photocopying and recording, or in any information storage or retrieval
system, without permission in writing from the publishers.

Trademark notice: Product or corporate names may be trademarks
or registered trademarks, and are used only for identification and
explanation without intent to infringe.

British Library Cataloguing-in-Publication Data
A catalogue record for this book is available from the British Library

Library of Congress Cataloging-in-Publication Data
Names: Hughes, Mark, 1962– author.
Title: Managing and leading organizational change / Mark Hughes.
Description: Abingdon, Oxon; New York, NY: Routledge, 2019.
Identifiers: LCCN 2018014882 | ISBN 9781138577404 (hbk) |
ISBN 9781138577411 (pbk)
Subjects: LCSH: Organizational change—Management. | Leadership.
Classification: LCC HD58.8.H8343 2019 | DDC 658.4/06—dc23
LC record available at https://lccn.loc.gov/2018014882

ISBN: 978-1-138-57740-4 (hbk)
ISBN: 978-1-138-57741-1 (pbk)
ISBN: 978-1-351-26596-6 (ebk)

Typeset in Sabon
by codeMantra

Visit the companion website: www.routledge.com/cw/hughes

Contents

Tables

Author biography

Dr Mark Hughes is a Reader in Organizational Change in Brighton Business School at the University of Brighton. Mark taught organizational change to MBA students for many years. He currently teaches on the Business School's MSc Managing Change and Innovation. The main focus of his work for the Business School is the facilitation of change related management/leadership development inside private/public service organizations. Mark's monograph *The Leadership of Organizational Change* published by Routledge in 2016 reviewed studies of leading change and transformation over the previous 35 years. Mark is a member of the Editorial Board of the *Journal of Change Management* and regularly writes and reviews for academic journals.

Preface

University academics engage in three activities in particular; teaching, research, and scholarship. Teaching is concerned with disseminating existing knowledge and textbooks are usually associated with this activity. Researching is concerned with gathering new knowledge, whereas scholarship is concerned with critically interpreting existing knowledge. However, as universities are increasingly evaluated on their teaching and research, scholarship invariably becomes marginalised.

I have chosen increasingly to engage in the critical interpretation of existing knowledge as a scholar. I enjoy questioning what we know (or think we know) about organizational change. I respect many organizational change researchers and I have drawn knowingly and extensively on their research in writing this textbook. However, for myself, it is more meaningful to critically examine the organizational change research literature in order to differentiate the good from the bad and the ugly literature.

I was told for too many years that 'research' had established that 70 per cent of all organizational change initiatives fail. In undertaking scholarship, I established for myself the spurious nature of the 'research' invoked in support of this popular myth (Hughes, 2011). I was surprised by what I found (discussed further in Chapter Seventeen) but equally encouraged to continue doing scholarship. More recently we have been told that 'research' suggests that we need change leaders, rather than change managers and that these change leaders will deliver successful change. I spent 18 months undertaking scholarship into the leadership of organizational change (Hughes, 2016a) and once again the myth was not substantiated by what we know. Kotter's (1996/2012) 'research' account of leading change has been cited over 6,000 times by my fellow academics. However, undertaking scholarship gave me the confidence to question the many favourable citations about this 'research' and to challenge the myth of leading change/transformation through eight generic steps (Hughes, 2016b).

I hope that you will join me and engage in your own organizational change scholarship. This textbook contains all the ingredients that you would expect from an organizational change textbook, but equally, it could have been called *The Organizational Change Scholar's Cookbook*. I have taken a risk in commencing with organizational change myths, rather than reassuring you with certainties. However, in moving into an unknown future through change, we are always in the realm of uncertainties and myths despite all the assertive organizational change rhetoric. Scholarship works through acknowledging and questioning myths and in this way encourages further questioning.

Most chapters follow a common structure acknowledging the applied nature of studies and the major theories but also questioning what we know. Most chapters showcase research case studies. However, these are not the normal fictitious cases or organization authorised cases. These are the cases from academic journals which inform my own scholarship. They have been significantly edited in being developed into textbook case studies with the addition of questions. They are based on the research of their authors and I do hope that you will be sufficiently engaged to visit the original source of these cases. In encouraging you to join me in organizational change scholarship, most chapters conclude with a section on navigating the literature. This should help you delve more deeply into the literature in critically interpreting what is known about organizational change. We all continue to experience organizational change whatever we do, wherever we do it. We urgently need more organizational change scholars willing to intelligently question the nonsense too frequently espoused in the name of managing and leading organizational change.

Mark Hughes
(Brighton Business School)

References

Hughes, M. 2011. "Do 70 Per Cent of All Organizational Change Initiatives Really Fail?" *Journal of Change Management* 11(4): 451–464.
Hughes, M. 2016a. *The Leadership of Organizational Change*. London: Routledge.
Hughes, M. 2016b. "Leading Changes: Why Transformation Explanations Fail." *Leadership* 12(4): 449–469.
Kotter, J. 1996/2012. *Leading Change*. Boston: Harvard Business School Press.

Acknowledgements

I thank my close family: Derek, Sheila, Stuart, Clair, Rob, and Beth for all of their loving kindness.

It is all change at Brighton Business School (BBS). The Founding Dean Aidan Berry retired, but he is still very fondly remembered. My work at BBS with organizations increasingly takes me away from the campus and out into the slightly more real world. Stephen Reeve and Chris Matthews have initiated and orchestrated these wonderful organizational change adventures and my working life would have been very grey without their companionship and camaraderie. Also, I appreciate my office buddies Paul Grant, Catherine Matthews and Vicky Richards who help to maintain my sanity in a higher education environment increasingly lacking sanity. I thank Bernard Burnes for travelling the extra mile literally and metaphorically a few years ago, an act of kindness which enabled positive changes in my academic life. I do like to road test my thinking at academic conferences and I have encountered the right balance between theory and practice at British Academy of Management conferences in recent years. Thank you to Ashley Braganza, Anne Clare Gillon, Richard Jefferies, John Mendy, Joanne Murphy, and Siva Sockalingham for making the recent BAM conference at Warwick such an enjoyable and special experience for myself. In terms of road testing my thinking, thank you to the many managers and leaders who have proved to be critically constructive audiences for drafts of these chapters. There are too many to mention everyone, but a big thank you to Adrian Kerr and his team doing such valuable work in Northern Ireland and Clive Dodds and his team enabling change on our railways.

I am always aware that the publisher has a team of people, who help to realise a book project. I am looking forward to handing over to them the final manuscript as I write this. I have enjoyed interacting with Judith Lorton, Lucy McClune, Natalie Tomlinson, Francesca Hearn and Rosemary Morlin at Routledge and thank them for helping me to realise this project.

Finally, in writing the acknowledgements I like to acknowledge the musicians who have kept me company on the long journey to publication. As I write this *The Orb* are doing a set in my study and I have regularly been accompanied by *Explosions in the Sky* and *Ennio Morricone* this time around. However, it is *Godspeed You! Black Emperor*, who still really orchestrate my emotions through encouraging quiet revolutions, quiet refusals, and self-determination.

.

Part I

Introduction

Chapter 1

Myth-understanding organizational change

Introduction and chapter questions

In a contribution to a recent organizational change book – *What academics, consultants and managers really think about change* (Burnes and Randall, 2015), Buchanan (2015) a highly respected emeritus professor themed his chapter around eight organizational change myths. His observations were based upon his work as a researcher and his experience in senior organizational roles. He effectively highlighted eight myths which although being most certainly wrong still endured. Many schools of thought and perspectives will be presented in this textbook. However, highlighting and working with myths, as well as, on occasions debunking organizational change myths will provide the unifying theme, for example:

Do we need change leaders, rather than change managers?
Do employees always resist organizational change?
Do 70% of organizational change initiatives really fail?

In answering these questions, we sensibly review the evidence, enabling us to offer informed and evidence-based answers to the questions. However, organizational change myths informing these questions reflect ongoing debates with regard to theories and practices of organizational change. Avoiding and marginalising organizational change myths may miss the origins of organizational change debates, underestimating factors currently and in the future influencing organizational change theories and practices. This view will be explained further in this chapter as it informs subsequent chapters.

   When you begin to engage with myths and myth-understandings you quickly appreciate that one person's myth may be another person's myth-understanding. The global consultancy Accenture (2016) published a report *Turning Change Upside Down: How New Insights are Changing Old Assumptions,* and highlighted four change management myths they wished to dispel.

Myth 1: Too much change, too fast, is destructive.
Myth 2: Change causes organizations to go off track.
Myth 3: Performance dips during the early stages.
Myth 4: People need to understand change before committing.

Their report drew upon 15 years of consulting experience as they challenged faulty assumptions encountered when consulting. In place of these myths they encouraged organizations to focus on the following performance drivers: leadership, process, vision and passion. Their message was very effectively crafted and more persuasive than most academic accounts of organizational change, although academic evidence in support of their so-called myths will be offered later in the textbook.

Parry (2011: 57) writing about the common association between leadership and organizational change acknowledged that they were inextricably intertwined and that 'organizational change has become an interest for organizational consultants more so than for empirical researchers'. There are many more books and articles on practitioner or conceptual scholarship than on theoretical or empirical scholarship. Much of the practitioner work is case study-based and anecdotal and not rigorous in its conduct. This acknowledgement introduces dilemmas central to this chapter and to this textbook.

In universities, we rightly privilege theoretical/empirical scholarship over practitioner/conceptual scholarship as Parry (2011) implies, but given the proliferation of practitioner literature don't we need to engage with such literature in order that anyone studying organizational change can fully understand the debate? Put another way, if we completely avoid prevalent myths characterising organizational change are we comprehensively understanding organizational change theories and practices?

In this textbook, the four assumptions highlighted by Accenture (2016) as myths will be challenged, raising issues for this field of study and you the reader. One person's myth might be another person's myth-understanding. There is no consensus, but this textbook will help you to navigate the mythical nature of organizational change as a field of study enabling you to make your own choices about the most appropriate theories and practices of organizational change. Although the title of this chapter refers to 'myth-understanding', you will not find this term in any dictionary. The term seeks to acknowledge the mythical nature of organizational change and the potential of myths to inform and misinform organizational change theories and practices. The related terminology of stories and storytelling is acknowledged in the next section.

In terms of the structure of this chapter, initially, it is necessary to understand myths and their wider influence on societies and organizations, before considering why and how organizational change myths occur. Acknowledging such myths has the potential to inform and misinform your studies and equally the potential to inform and misinform the practices of organizational change practitioners. Many organizational change myths are integral to particular chapters with these myths highlighted and the chapters in which they are addressed signposted. The chapter is organized around the following questions:

- How is organizational change myth-understood?
- What are the implications of myth-understandings for organizational change practice?
- What are the implications of myth-understandings for organizational change literature reviewing?
- How are organizational change myth-understandings addressed in this textbook?

How is organizational change myth-understood?

In beginning, to engage with organizational change myths, it is informative to consider how myths in general are understood. Mann (1947) referred to myth as the foundation of life and as a timeless schema and Armstrong (2005) in the preface to *A Short History of Myth* writes about myths being universal and timeless stories, reflecting and shaping our lives, in that they explore our desires, our fears, our longings, providing narratives what it means to be human. She goes on to explain how myths have played a central role in societies throughout human history. However, during The Great Western Transformation (1500–2000), belief in mythos was replaced with belief in logos. Logos reflects the logical, pragmatic and scientific mode of thinking favoured today. However, as Armstrong (2005: 31) warns 'mythology often springs from profound anxiety about essentially practical problems, which cannot be assuaged by purely logical arguments'. This is highly applicable to theories and practices of organizational change, which inevitably raise anxieties through attempting to engage with uncertain futures. However, before applying myth-understandings to organizational change, it is necessary to clarify related terminology. Gabriel (2008) has encouraged greater engagement with myths, stories and narratives in organizational settings; consequently his definitions of key terminology are favoured (see Table 1.1).

Table 1.1 highlights close relationships between narratives, stories and myths. In the literature cited in this chapter, authors do not always precisely differentiate narratives, stories and myths. As Brown et al. (2009) note, there is not a consensus around differentiating stories and narratives from myths. However, what Table 1.1 helps to differentiate, is the everyday nature of organizational storytelling from the more powerful symbolism of myths. It is the relationships between such myths and organizational change on which we now focus, relating myths and related concepts to organizational settings.

Movva (2004) in discussing myths as a vehicle for transforming organizations highlighted Stephens and Eisen's (1998: 219) account of the significance of myths in our day-to-day life.

> Myth is the story that we tell to explain the nature of our reality. It is a whole picture constructed out of the particular pieces of our attitudes and beliefs. Myths become our touchstones to what is 'real' and what is 'important'. They encompass the most basic, fundamental, and ultimate. They are the 'truths' to which we look when trying to decide how we should conduct our lives, what we should actually do, and how we should think and feel.

In this way, organizational documents such as annual reports, strategic change plans and vision statements have mythical properties. The forward-looking aspirations they encourage may not be completely evidence based, but these aspirations particularly for their authors are real. Berglund and Werr (2000) highlighted two basic managerial

Table 1.1 Defining narratives, stories and myths (Gabriel, 2008)

Narratives are then viewed as particular types of text. Unlike other texts... narratives involve temporal chains of interrelated events or actions, undertaken by characters. (Gabriel, 2008: 194)
Stories are pithy narratives with plots, characters, and twists that can be full of meaning. (Gabriel, 2008: 282)
Myths are narratives that carry a powerful symbolism, are capable of generating strong emotions, and have a profound effect on our thoughts and actions. (Gabriel, 2008: 191)

myths legitimising managerial practices; the rationality myth and the normative/pragmatic myth. These myths have a long history emanating from central western dichotomies of:

thought vs action,
theory vs practice,
objective vs relative and
nature vs culture.

Already we can locate Parry (2011) and Buchanan (2015) cited earlier on the left side whereas Accenture (2016) reflect thinking on the right side. If you asked the authors, I am sure they wouldn't see it as black and white as this, but these dichotomies help us to appreciate debates central to organizational change particularly thought versus action and theory versus practice. The first myth, the rationality myth is aligned with the left-hand side with expertise and techniques firmly anchored in modern beliefs in rationality. Formalised knowledge is praised for offering hard and objective truths. It is the central myth in organizations and businesses with managerial decision making regarded as being rational and scientific. However, scientific knowledge through its goal of being objective, negates studies of power, ideologies and interests. Management models, methods and tools are used in a belief that they will deliver solutions.

The second normative/pragmatic myth is aligned with the right-hand side. This myth challenges parts of the rationality myth, typified by sayings such as 'action speaks louder than words' with a different emphasis than that of manager as rational decision maker. Instead, theoretical knowledge is regarded with suspicion and 'hands-on' experience privileged with an emphasis upon the unique nature of specific situations, 'trust me I was there' is a common argument (Berglund and Werr, 2000: 643). Whilst they acknowledge the centrality of these two myths, they did not regard them as opposite sides of a dichotomy (Barley and Kunda, 1992). Instead, they may be mixed and they are mixed. Managers utilise the latest theories (rationality myth) and pragmatically tailor them to their own unique challenges (normative/pragmatic myth). This is the position favoured in this textbook introducing theories, models and concepts, yet not forgetting the action oriented and pragmatic nature of organizational change.

In their editorial for a Special Issue of *Organization* themed around storytelling and change, Brown et al. (2009: 326) offer a provocative insight:

> ...no single perspective on organizing and processes of change has a monopoly on 'truth', and that the vivid insights that a storytelling approach may yield need always to be complemented by other ways of seeing and understanding.

We appear to live in an age of change leadership persuaded and even seduced by the agency of exceptional change leaders to make change happen. However, this might be at the expense of engaging with management and command and the very different problems leading, managing and command seeks to address. Grint (2005) has differentiated between three types of problem that leaders encounter by drawing on Rittell and Webber's (1973); wicked, tame and critical problems, as well as, Etzioni's (1964) three types of power; coercive, calculative and normative. He creatively highlights command, management or leadership being appropriate, for different types of problem. For example, if a problem is critical for the future of an organization, there may be a requirement for coercion. In this scenario there is a need to provide answers through command, rather than collaborative resolution of the problem. However, if the problem is tame, calculative power may be more appropriate with management organizing processes. Wicked problems, are those such as how to allocate limited car-parking spaces at university when both the students and staff need to park. It is this type of wicked problem which requires dialogue towards collaborative resolution through leadership.

What are the implications of myth-understandings for organizational change practice?

Myths are far more prevalent in organizational settings than often acknowledged.

> Myth can be friend or foe, and this is why it is important for present-day managers to recognize the myths present in their own worlds and in those of their organizations…The myths you believe in today become the reality you live in tomorrow. Can you afford to ignore them?
>
> (Hughes, 1995: 10)

Myths so far have largely been discussed in terms of enabling meaning making, but they can also be used to facilitate organizational transformation. Movva (2004) reports on a case study of the ice cream division of XYZ Company and the role myths played in facilitating an organizational transformation, bringing the abstract entity of the organization to life in mobilising energy for change. In a practitioner oriented article, McGeever (2009) sought to dispel the myths about cloud computing which he encountered at the time of writing.

McGeever (2009) was writing in the capacity of the Chief Financial Officer for a provider of on-demand, integrated business management software for growing and mid-sized businesses. In this practitioner setting, Table 1.2 highlights myths being debunked in order to sell software services. In this way, myths represent impediments the salesforce encountered, but by highlighting them a dialogue with potential customers is created. Academics may use myths in a similar manner in selling their theories, models and concepts (please see for example the mythical 70% change failure rate Beer and Nohria, 2000 promoted). Table 1.2 also highlights the dynamic nature of myths. McGeever (2009) highlighted misconceptions and misunderstandings he was encountering about cloud computing. However, with cloud computing today more effectively established these myths will have disappeared or dissipated considerably.

Gottschall (2016) offers a warning about the dark side to storytelling in his *Harvard Business Review* article, using the medical technology company *Theranos* as his case

Table 1.2 Cloud computing myths (McGeever, 2009)

Myth 1: My business can't afford to lose control of sensitive data by putting it in the hands of a third party.

Myth 2: Sales organizations benefit from cloud applications because their people are mobile. My financial staff stays put, so the cloud does nothing for me.

Myth 3: We can't afford the risk of being early adopters.

Myth 4: We don't chase the latest and greatest software functionality, so a constantly updated application isn't important.

Myth 5: Our business is too complicated and unique for a cookie-cutter online application.

example. The company founded by Elizabeth Holmes initially received very favourable coverage from business and technology journalists, until in October 2015 *The Wall Street Journal* reported that the company's flagship blood-testing technology was a complete failure. Whilst Gottschall's (2016) interest is with storytelling, he warns about a tendency to blur boundaries between truth and fiction in business and the inherent dangers in such an approach, a warning relevant to myth-understanding organizational change.

Myths are closely associated with organizational change practices as this chapter has highlighted. They may explicitly be challenged, such as Accenture (2016) or they may take on a mythical status such as Beer and Nohria's (2000) brutal fact that 70% of all organizational change initiatives fail. However, this chapter has hopefully conveyed that one person's myth may be another person's reality. The intention is that in introducing the major theories, models and concepts myths should be acknowledged and engaged with knowingly. They inform/misinform an applied field such as organizational change studies, although they should still be treated with caution.

What are the implications of myth-understandings for organizational change literature reviewing?

Rawlins (2014) warns that myths are often synonymous with misconceptions, falsehoods and deliberate deceptions in popular culture with these negative connotations tending to be carried over into academic literature, particularly management and leadership literature. However, in the field of organizational change discounting practitioner myths in favour of empirical realities may misrepresent how typically organizational change practices are understood.

> Organizational change is promoted and managed through strategic discourse by organizational leadership. Managers and change leaders use discourse to build support for changes; to respond to complaints, criticisms, and dissent; and to realign expectations following setbacks or failures.
>
> (Rawlins, 2014: 453)

For Rawlins (2014) engaging with myths allows greater complexity than storytelling and sensemaking, as myths play a vital role in managing organizational change within modern workplaces. The brutal fact that 70 per cent of all organizational change initiatives fail was promoted by two highly respected Harvard Business School professors (Beer and Nohria, 2000). It consequently features prominently in organizational change literature being frequently cited by academics. It appears to have a role in an academic literature review being evidence-based. However, Hughes (2011) highlighted how the failure assertion is not supported with any convincing academic evidence. The implication is that critical thinking must be applied to any literature reviewing, through seeking out research evidence and scholarship in support of any assertions made. Engaging with organizational change myth-understandings offers a bridge between theory and practice, see earlier Berglund and Werr's (2000) discussion. These myth-understandings orientate towards the applied nature of organizational change, even if subsequently you cite literature in support of a more research informed and evidence-based approach.

In the next section, engagement with organizational change myth-understandings is explained through their role in this textbook.

How are organizational change myth-understandings addressed in this textbook?

Bathurst and Monin (2010) encouraged a reawakening of interest in myth as stories deeply embedded within the rhetoric of dominant power brokers – managers. The centrality of myth embedded in practitioner accounts of change has been a theme of this chapter. However, organizational change myths are also embedded within academic rhetoric, particularly rhetoric emanating from powerful/influential business schools. This chapter has signposted ongoing interest in organizational change myths amongst academics and practitioners. There is unlikely to be a definitive listing of organizational change myths, given differences between individuals in terms of beliefs and values, the context-dependent nature of myths and the dynamic status of myths. However, Jarrett (2003) and Buchanan (2015) offered thoughtful/provocative listings (please see Table 1.3).

In Table 1.3, myths influencing theories and practices of organizational change are made explicit. In the two columns, we see similarities and differences in the myths each author chooses to highlight. Also, the fact that Jarrett (2003) was highlighting organizational change myths at the beginning of the last decade with Buchanan (2015) highlighting them more recently shows that they are not a passing fad/fashion.

ten Have et al. (2016) in their evidence-based approach to change management identify 18 assumptions they have encountered. Whilst they refer to these as 'assumptions' rather than 'myths', they fulfil a similar role to the myths featured in this chapter.

ten Have et al. (2016) use these popular change management assumptions as a starting point for their systematic review of the evidence informing/misinforming each assumption.

The myths in Table 1.5 are informed by my own studies of organizational change and working with changing organizations over three decades. The organizational change myths featured in Table 1.5 are slightly caricatured and paraphrased. You may agree with some of them and disagree with others. They help us to focus upon debates integral to organizational change theories and practices.

Table 1.3 Organizational change myths (Jarrett, 2003 and Buchanan, 2015)

The seven myths of change management (Jarrett, 2003)	I couldn't disagree more: eight things about organizational change that we know for sure but which are probably wrong (Buchanan, 2015)
1 Organizational change management creates value.	1 The pace is picking up.
2 Resistance can be overcome.	2 Leaders, not managers.
3 Change is constant.	3 We need transformational leaders.
4 Change can be managed.	4 Who is in charge of this project?
5 The change agent knows best.	5 Bureaucracy is dead.
6 Accepted wisdom is to follow the steps.	6 Simply best practice.
7 Big changes require big changes.	7 Avoid wheel reinvention.
	8 Change agents must be squeaky clean.

As already acknowledged, there are similarities and differences with those myths featured in Table 1.3 and the assumptions featured in Table 1.4, in essence, each listing of organizational change myths and assumptions reflects the unique beliefs, backgrounds and organizational change experiences of each author. In Table 1.5, some myths echo earlier myths informing studies of organizational change, others are new myths.

These myths are made explicit here in the belief that they offer an innovative means of introducing ongoing debates about theories and practices of organizational change. Probably the greatest organizational change myth today relates to differentiating management and leadership with leadership currently privileged over management, resulting in the popular prescription that we need change leaders rather than change managers. Whilst the separation of management and leadership is ill-advised, Part II and Part III deal with these concepts separately in order to aid exposition with Part IV encouraging their combination when challenging the mythical status of change leadership today. Each myth will feature in subsequent chapters of this textbook with the relevant chapters signposted in the second column of Table 1.5. The following discussion briefly introduces each myth featured in Table 1.5 and by association introduces debates featured in relevant chapters.

There is one best way to practice and study organizational change. This myth is concerned with reasonable expectations about organizational change best practices. However, because of the highly context-dependent nature of organizational change, what appears to work in one situation may not work in another situation. Whilst academics may prefer a particular school of thought or perspective, applying different approaches offers different insights when studying organizational change. *Change is the only constant,* for Peters (1988: 2) 'excellent firms don't believe in excellence – only in constant improvement and constant change'. This myth highlighted by Jarrett (2003) and Buchanan (2015) is very prevalent in organizations and amongst certain

Table 1.4 Eighteen popular change management assumptions (based on ten Have et al., 2016)

1	Seventy per cent of all change initiatives fail.
2	A clear vision is essential for successful change.
3	People will not change if there is no sense of urgency.
4	Trust in the leader is needed for successful change.
5	When managing change, a transformational leadership style is more effective than a transactional one.
6	Organizational change requires leaders with strong emotional intelligence.
7	Supervisory support is critical for the success of change.
8	To realise change in organizations, a powerful guiding coalition is needed.
9	Employees' capabilities to change determine the organization's capacity to change.
10	Participation is key to successful change.
11	Resistance to change is detrimental to the success of change.
12	A fair change process is important in achieving successful change.
13	Changing organizational culture is time-consuming and difficult.
14	Organizational culture is related to performance.
15	Goal setting combined with feedback is a powerful tool for change leaders.
16	Commitment to change is an essential component of a successful change initiative.
17	Financial incentives are effective ways to encourage change and improve performance.
18	Self-managing teams perform better in realising change than traditionally managed teams.

Table 1.5 Organizational change myths featured in this textbook and their respective chapters

Organizational change myth-understandings	The relevant chapter in this textbook
There is one best way to practise and study organizational change.	The what, why, when, how and where of organizational change (Chapter 2).
Change is the only constant.	The what, why, when, how and where of organizational change (Chapter 2).
Studies of organizational change are converging.	Studying organizational change (Chapter 3).
The more recent the school of thought the better.	Management studies (Chapter 4).
A fixed and objective history informs organizational change.	History, learning and organizational change (Chapter 5).
Managers/leaders can quickly change cultures.	Organizational cultural change (Chapter 6).
Employees experience an organizational change in a similar manner.	Individual differences, psychodynamics, identities and organizational change (Chapter 7).
There is an optimum teamworking approach for organizational change.	Groups, teamwork and organizational change (Chapter 8).
We are becoming more and more knowledgeable about leadership studies.	Leadership studies (Chapter 9).
We know how leaders influence organizational change.	Leading organizational change (Chapter 10).
Organizational change should be a power and politics free zone.	Power, politics and organizational change (Chapter 11).
We need to communicate like crazy at times of change.	Communicating organizational change (Chapter 12).
The goal is to overcome resistance to change.	Resistance and organizational change readiness (Chapter 13).
We need change leaders not change managers.	Managers, leaders and the agents of change (Chapter 14).
Change agency is located in individuals rather than being distributed.	Managers, leaders and the agents of change (Chapter 14).
Managing and leading change are primarily about using the right tools and techniques.	Management and leadership tools and techniques (Chapter 15).
The brutal fact is that about 70% of all organizational change initiatives fail.	Evaluating organizational change (Chapter 17).
Organizational change initiatives conclude at the point of successful implementation.	Sustaining organizational change (Chapter 18).

academics. On one level it is irrefutable. You will definitely have changed by the time you complete reading this chapter. However, the myth that has developed is that organizations need to constantly change, which merits further debate.

Studies of organizational change are converging. Knowledge of natural sciences such as physics was famously depicted as converging (Kuhn, 1962). The expectation was that management science would follow a similar trajectory, but instead a patchwork of fields of study developed with divergence, rather than convergence as the norm (Whitley, 1984). Organizational change as a field of study is diverging, rather than converging as we learn more about processes of organizational change. In terms of academic study, it seems reasonable to assume *the more recent the school of thought the better.* However, different schools of thought will feature in this textbook which, although historic, still have value today. For example, Trist and Bamforth

(1951) were early pioneers of socio-technical systems, but academics still undertake such work. Whilst it is tempting to privilege a 2016 reference over Trist and Bamforth (1951), this may be inappropriate. When we engage with myths, history seems fixed and objective suggesting that *a fixed and objective history informs organizational change*. However, in Chapter 5 it will be argued that multiple accounts of history exist, with certain accounts of history privileged over others. Kurt Lewin (1947) played an influential role in advancing our understanding of planned change, yet competing accounts of his historic contribution exist (see Burnes, 2004 for an appreciation of his contribution or Cummings et al., 2016 for a critique).

Cultural change was the major organizational change debate of the 1980s and 1990s both in terms of theories and practices. This debate subsided, but an interest in changing organizational cultures remains. The myth is the belief that *Managers/ leaders can quickly change cultures*. We now know that organizational cultures take time to change and that such cultural change cannot be mandated by a manager/ leader.

In terms of organizational change practices, a unitarist view is the norm working with an assumption that all employees pull in a common direction. The myth nested within this assumption is that *employees experience an organizational change in a similar manner*. We are still learning about gendered experiences of organizational change and more recently there has been interest in how psychodynamics and identities inform different experiences of organizational change. Groups and teams are integral to organizational change initiatives in large organizations, fuelling a belief that *there is an optimum teamworking approach for organizational change*. However, effective teamworking is likely to be highly context dependent negating a single optimum approach.

In studying leading change, we initially need to consider more generally leadership studies. The status of this field of study may be paraphrased as 'we are almost there'. However, the chapter will question the myth that, *we are becoming more and more knowledgeable about leadership studies*. This is not merely an academic exercise as knowledge about leading change is informed by what we know about leadership and what we know about organizational change. Theories and practices of leading organizational change are based upon a myth that *we know how leaders influence organizational change*. This is probably the most contentious myth in that most academics and practitioners appear to believe that we do know how leaders influence organizational change. However, convincing literature informing how leaders influence organizational change is more difficult to find (see Chapter 10).

The popular managerial caution that 'there is no place for politics in this organization', fuels a myth that *organizational change should be a power and politics free zone*. As well as practitioners explicitly steering clear of power and politics, mainstream organizational change literature tends to avoid power and politics. This myth is challenged in the belief that power and politics are endemic at times of organizational change and should be reflected in organizational change studies (please see Buchanan and Badham, 2008; Buchanan, 2015).

Clarke (1994) encouraged organizations to 'communicate like crazy' during organizational change initiatives which seemed sensible, captured in the myth *that we need to communicate like crazy at times of change*. Today we know far more about communicating change than when Clarke (1994) was writing and the last thing we need to do is communicate like crazy during times of organizational change. Another enduring myth is that *the goal is to overcome resistance to change*. The problem is presented as employees resisting change with the solution then for change managers/ leaders to overcome such resistance (please see Jarrett, 2003). One reason this myth appears to endure is that it celebrates managers/leaders and simultaneously disparages the majority of employees as resistors. This myth is closely related to the next myth that *we need change leaders not change managers* (please see Buchanan, 2015). In Western societies and organizations, heroic individuals are celebrated, although this might not be in the best interests of organizations and societies. Over the past two decades we have witnessed change leaders being favoured over change managers. However, there is very little empirical evidence to support this shift.

In managing and leading change, tools and techniques are often employed although a myth has developed that *managing and leading change is primarily about using the right tools and techniques*. An emphasis upon tools and techniques implies instrumental and linear actions resulting in a successful outcome if tools and techniques are used appropriately. However, this myth misrepresents and misunderstands processes of organizational change and why changes succeed and fail. Two Harvard Business School professors in the *Harvard Business Review* claimed that 'the brutal fact is that about 70% of all change initiatives fail' (Beer and Nohria, 2000: 133). Since they made their assertion, the myth that *the brutal fact is that about 70% of all organizational change initiatives fail* has become increasingly influential. However, the evidence base of this myth will be questioned. Finally, a myth grounded in notions of organizational change as an event, rather than as a process suggests that an organizational change initiative ends with successful implementation. However, this myth is increasingly being questioned as we learn more about the sustainability of organizational change outcomes (please see Buchanan et al., 2005).

Concluding commentary

Organizational change myth-understanding has been introduced in this chapter as the unifying theme for this textbook. It has been argued that myths inform organizational change practices, as well as, academic debates. Whilst it is tempting to separate organizational change myth-understandings from the empirical realities of organizational change, such separation might be artificial. One of the major debates in organizational change is focussed on a perceived need to overcome resistance to organizational change. The origins of the debate can be traced back to Coch and French's (1948) paper in *Human Relations*. Although their title referred to *overcoming resistance to change* the author's research encouraged a more participative approach towards organizational change. However, ever since, the emphasis of organizational change practice has been to overcome resistance to change. Whilst the chapter on resistance and change readiness will demonstrate how academic thinking has evolved in recent years, this myth-understanding of organizational change is still prevalent. As Gabriel (1991) warned in the sub-title of his account of organizational stories and myths, it is easier to slay a dragon than to kill a myth.

Discussion questions

What are the biggest myths in organizational change studies?
Why do organizational change theory and practice myths exist?
How do myths inform organizational change studies?
How do myths hamper organizational change studies?

References

Accenture. 2016. *Turning Change Upside Down: How New Insights Are Changing Old Assumptions*. Accenture Report, available at www.accenture.com/us-en/insight-turning-change-upside-down?c=str_ukwotffy16psgs&n=Turning_Change_Upside_Down_-_UK#block-myths-of-change

Armstrong, K. 2005. *A Short History of Myth*. Edinburgh: Canongate Books Ltd.

Barley, S.R., and G. Kunda. 1992. "Design and devotion: Surges of rational and normative ideologies of control in managerial discourse." *Administrative Science Quarterly*, 37(3): 363–399.

Bathurst, R.J., and N. Monin. 2010. "Finding Myth and Motive in Language: A Narrative of Organizational Change." *Journal of Management Inquiry* 19(3): 262–272.

Beer, M., and N. Nohria. 2000. "Cracking the Code of Change." *Harvard Business Review* 78(3): 133–141.

Berglund, J., and A. Werr. 2000. "The Invincible Character of Management Consulting Rhetoric: How One Blends Incommensurates While Keeping Them Apart." *Organization* 7(4): 633–655.

Brown, A.D., Y. Gabriel, and S. Gherardi. 2009. "Storytelling and Change: An Unfolding Story." *Organization* 16(3): 323–333.

Buchanan, D. 2015. "I Couldn't Disagree More: Eight Things About Organizational Change That We Know for Sure But Which are Probably Wrong." In *Perspectives on Change: What Academics, Consultants and Managers Really Think about Change* edited by B. Burnes, and J. Randall, 5–21. London: Routledge.

Buchanan, D., L. Fitzgerald, D. Ketley, R. Gollop, J.L. Jones, S.S. Lamont, A. Neath, and E. Whitby. 2005. "No Going Back: A Review of The Literature on Sustaining Organizational Change." *International Journal of Management Reviews* 7(3): 189–205.

Buchanan, D., and R. Badham. 2008. *Power, Politics and Organizational Change: Winning the Turf Game*. London: Sage Publications.

Burnes, B. 2004. "Kurt Lewin and the Planned Approach to Change: A Re-appraisal." *Journal of Management Studies* 41(6): 977–1002.

Burnes, B., and J. Randall (Eds). 2015. *Perspectives on Change: What Academics, Consultants and Managers Really Think About Change*. London: Routledge.

Clarke, L. 1994. *The Essence of Change*. Hemel Hempstead: Prentice Hall International.

Coch, L., and J.R.P. French (Jr). 1948. "Overcoming Resistance to Change." *Human Relations* 1(4): 512–532.

Cummings, S., T. Bridgman, and K.G. Brown. 2016. "Unfreezing Change as Three Steps: Rethinking Kurt Lewin's Legacy for Change Management." *Human Relations* 69(1): 33–60.

Etzioni, A. 1964. *Modern Organizations*. Englewood Cliffs, NJ: Prentice Hall.

Gabriel, Y. 1991. "On Organisational Stories and Myths: Why it is Easier to Slay a Dragon than to Kill a Myth." *International Sociology* 6(4): 427–442.

Gabriel, Y. 2008. *Organizing Words: A Critical Thesaurus for Social and Organization Studies*. Oxford: Oxford University Press.

Gottschall, J. 2016. "Theranos and the Dark Side of Storytelling." *Harvard Business Review* HBR.Org Online Article 18 October 2018.

Grint, K. 2005. "Problems, Problems, Problems: The Social Construction of 'Leadership'." *Human Relations* 58(11): 1467–1494.

Hughes, B. 1995. "Why do Managers Need Myths?" *Executive Development* 8(7): 8–10.

Hughes, M. 2011. "Do 70 Per Cent of All Organizational Change Initiatives Really Fail?" *Journal of Change Management*, 11(4): 451–464.

Jarrett, M. 2003. "The Seven Myths of Change Management." *Business Strategy Review* 14 (4): 22–29.

Kuhn, T.S. 1962. *The Structure of Scientific Revolutions*. Chicago: University of Chicago Press.

Lewin, K. 1947. "Frontiers in Group Dynamics." In *Field Theory in Social Science* edited by D. Cartwright, 301–336. London: Social Science Paperbacks.

Mann, T. 1947. *Essays of Three Decades*. London: Secker & Warburg.

McGeever, J. 2009. "Dispelling Myths that Limit Organizational Change." *Financial Executive* 25(9): 67–69.

Movva, R. 2004. "Myths as a Vehicle for Transforming Organizations." *Leadership and Organization Development Journal* 25 (1): 41–57.

Parry, K.W. 2011. "Leadership and organization theory." In *The SAGE Handbook of Leadership* edited by A. Bryman, D. Collinson, K. Grint, B. Jackson, and M. Uhl-Bien, 53–70. London: Sage Publications.

Peters, T. 1988. *Thriving on Chaos*. London: Macmillan.

Rawlins, J.D. 2014. "Mythologizing Change Examining Rhetorical Myth as a Strategic Change Management Discourse." *Business and Professional Communication Quarterly* 77(4): 453–472.

Rittel, H. and M. Webber. 1973. "Dilemmas in a General Theory of Planning." *Policy Sciences* 4 (2): 155–169.

Stephens, C. and Eisen, S. 1998. "Myth, Transformation and the Change Agent." In *Transforming Work* edited by J.D. Adams, 216–223. Alexandria, VA: Miles River.

ten Have, S., W. ten Have, A.B. Huijsmans, and M. Otto. 2016. *Reconsidering Change Management: Applying Evidence-Based Insights in Change Management Practice*. London: Routledge.

Trist, E.L., and K.W. Bamforth. 1951. "Some Social and Psychological Consequences of the Longwall Method of Coal-getting: An Examination of the Psychological Situation and Defences of a Work Group in Relation to the Social Structure and Technological Content of the Work System." *Human Relations*, 4(1): 3–38.

Whitley, R. 1984. "The Fragmented State of Management Studies: Reasons and Consequences." *Journal of Management Studies* 21(3): 331–348.

Chapter 2

The what, why, when, how and where of organizational change

Introduction and chapter questions

The first three chapters informing the introduction to this textbook are closely related. In the first chapter, the importance of evidence/research-based insights into organizational change was acknowledged. However, this was tempered with an acknowledgement that theories and practices of organizational change have to engage with a future that is uncertain and unknown. The mythical nature of organizational change is often understated in excessively assertive practitioner and academic rhetoric. Acknowledgement of uncertainties and ambiguities of processes of changing explains why studying organizational change is so interesting, but fuels the requirement to be clear on what is being studied which is the focus of this chapter. In the next chapter, the focus will be upon how organizational change has been studied and is being studied and how questioning organizational change studies advances understanding.

In this instance, the chapter content and questions closely mirror the chapter title in introducing and clarifying the focus of organizational change studies and practices. The chapter is organized around and provides answers to the following questions:

- What is the scope of organizational change?
- Why does organizational change occur?
- When does organizational change occur?
- How does organizational change occur?
- Where does organizational change occur?
- What questions need to be raised about organizational change classifications, typologies and change as a thing?

Whilst, the ambiguities and uncertainties of organizational change have been acknowledged, in studying organizational change we need to be as clear as possible about what we are studying? The first question relates to the breadth of what organizational change can involve. This can range from changes around the introduction of new technology through to implementing an employee engagement programme. In answering this question, it will quickly become apparent that organizational change can mean very different things to different people. The second question relates to 'so-called' imperatives for changing. These may vary in that a reason for changing might be espoused, such as improving customer service, whereas the latent rationale might be cutting costs. The third question relates to time and the many different ways we understand organizational change in terms of time. Is change a constant or do organizations experience periods of equilibrium? Does organizational change go through phases or is it more of a continuous process? The fourth question relates to making change happen, raising issues for managers and leaders as change agents, but also how organizational members are integral to making change happen. The fifth question relates to the importance of context in organizational change studies and practices. An organizational change in a charity will differ from an organizational change in a merchant bank. There will be differences even within an organization in terms of different functional areas such as marketing and finance and different levels of an organization. There are also likely to be regional and international differences in how change is experienced and managed/led. In the questioning section, previous classifications and typologies are revisited in order to demonstrate how a particular classification/typology will influence how we think about an organizational change, the common notion of organizational change as a thing is also questioned.

Understanding the scope of organizational change

The danger inherent in the label organizational change is that every aspect of organizational life might be regarded as an organizational change. In this way, a label covering everything conveys nothing. This section introduces the scope of organizational change studies in this textbook, as well as acknowledging what is outside the scope of this textbook. The scope of organizational change studies varies considerably with different authors offering different emphases. For example, Senior and Swailes (2016) in their account of organizational change draw particularly on psychology as informing and influencing the scope of their textbook, whereas, Dawson and Andriopoulos (2017) in their account of managing change, draw upon their interests in social theory, creativity, and innovation as informing their textbook.

Consequently, in studying organizational change, it is necessary to define what is meant by organizational change in the context of this textbook. It is informative to first think about defining an organization, before defining organizational change. Gabriel (2008) offers a synthesis of dominant elements in scholarly definitions of organization:

- long-term continuity,
- impersonality and formality,
- organizations purport to have goals,
- no-nonsense approach,
- division of labour and
- co-operation rather than coercion.

He regards these elements as defining organizations with impersonality and formality being essential elements. Gabriel (2008: 211) acknowledges changes in organizations being accompanied by '…new ways of looking at organizations, drawing attention to many irrational phenomena, the importance of language and discourse, their fragmented and episodic character and their diffuse or fuzzy boundaries'. The implication for studying organizational change is that how we understand organizations is changing. So, in subsequent chapters, particularly in the questioning sections irrational and discursive aspects of organizational change will be explored.

In defining an organizational change in this textbook, in combination with Gabriel's (2008) definition of an organization, Smith and Graetz's (2011: 1) description of a philosophy of organizational change is favoured.

>...the set of assumptions, tacit beliefs, conscious theories and implementation approaches that govern a change agent's way of looking at the organizational world and the best approach to introducing change.

The definition is more practically oriented than how Gabriel (2008) explains organization, although this is necessary, given the practical/prescriptive nature of some of the influential literature. For example, Kotter (1996/2012) has encouraged leading change through following eight steps. Whilst his approach will be critiqued in Chapter 10, we need a definition which includes such literature given the number of times it has been cited (please see Hughes, 2016). The change agency theme in the definition is welcomed, remembering that change agency may be located in a manager or a leader, or shared and dispersed throughout an organization. The change agency focus ensures that organizational change is not just an academic abstraction. The reference to 'best approach' initially appears to be problematic, but this is prefaced with reference to assumptions, tacit beliefs, conscious theories and implementation approaches. This negates notions of one best way, in favour of engaging with change agents and the informed choices that they make.

Whilst, this definition is favoured for this textbook it is worth acknowledging that no consensus definition of organizational change exists. The word change has been characterised as a container concept with the search for the underlying values of the word resulting in a whole range of meanings (De Caluwe and Vermaak, 2003). So many organizational change authors will be cited in the textbook and in an ideal world, they would share a common consensus definition. However, you will discover that organizational change is far more contested and contentious than that.

The three subsequent parts of this textbook signpost major themes of management, leadership and a combination of management and leadership. This treatment is unorthodox as there is a tendency towards demarcation between organizational behaviours (OB)/studies textbooks, leadership studies textbooks and management studies textbooks. This results in an OB textbook having a chapter on organizational change or a leadership studies textbook having a chapter on organizational change. Or in a managing change textbook, there will be a chapter on leading change. In this textbook, neither management nor leadership are privileged. Managing combined with leading is believed to be more beneficial than privileging one or the other. As Part III will highlight, in recent decades we have celebrated heroic leaders, potentially at the expense of more mundane and operational aspects of managing (as featured in Part II).

Three themes outside the scope of this textbook, which could have been included are organizational development (OD), project management and technological change. Each theme could potentially be included and each theme is the focus of textbooks in their own right. OD offers a tried and tested methodology for facilitating organizational change benefiting from a long history (please see the discussion of Burnes and Cooke, 2012 in Chapter 3). There will be references to OD in subsequent chapters, but it is not a major theme of this textbook. Also, in recent years there has been growing interest in how project management methodologies inform organizational change (please see discussion of Crawford and Nahmias, 2010 in Chapter 15). Again, there will be references to project management, but it is not a major theme of this textbook. Finally, it is difficult to envisage any organizational change in the current decade without a technological aspect. In two earlier textbooks (Hughes, 2006 and Hughes, 2010), chapters were deliberately included to acknowledge the increasing pervasiveness of technological change. However, the learning from these earlier text-books has been that when people study, teach and research organizational change, they tend to acknowledge technology, but leave it outside the scope of their teaching and research. In this instance, technological change as a major theme is not included, although as boundaries between organizational change and technological change increasingly blur, this exclusion will have to be revisited. Pragmatically focus, focus, focus must be the imperative when seriously studying organizational change.

Understanding why organizational change occurs

We often think and talk metaphorically about organizational change in terms of 'triggers', 'motors' and 'drivers'. Morgan and Sturdy (2000) acknowledge, that the identification of underlying, often hidden, logics of change or motors of change has a long history in ancient and modern philosophy. The focus here is to clarify different ways of understanding why organizational change occurs. Three overlapping themes are introduced here, change as a response to the environment, change as a response to fashion and change informed by research.

Environment

The most commonly quoted imperative for organizations changing relates to the environment in which an organization is located. UK higher education helps to illustrate such a position. Universities are increasingly regarded as being in competition with each other with league tables for student satisfaction, research quality and the impact of research. These rankings create the rationale for changing. If we introduce this change or that change, we potentially move up or down the league table. This position may be labelled as environmental determinism in that it is the environment that determines the change. The strategic role of managers and leaders is to scan the environment and respond to it.

Fashion

Another slightly cynical view of why organizations change is fashion. Just as the length of women's skirts or the breadth of men's trouser bottoms vary over time, so what organizations choose to do varies over time. This imperative to change is more subtle and pervasive than might first be imagined. One of the most popular approaches to organizational change of the past decade has been benchmarking. Benchmarking involves drawing comparisons between different parts of an organization or with another organization in order to inform change processes. In many ways, it is what we might call copying, but given its emphasis on looking to others, it is highly susceptible to fashion. The prevalence of management fashions is discussed further in Chapter 15.

Research

Ideally research plays a major role in informing why organizational change occurs. It certainly has a role to play, although probably not as significant as academics like to imagine. The focus of Chapter 8 is on groups and teams and the influential writings of Michael West (2012) will be featured. He is able to offer practical prescriptions based on his research, although this is an ideal rather than the norm. Often, organizational change suffers from allusions to research, rather than being research informed. Kotter (1996/2012) cited earlier initially appears to be a research-informed account of leading change, but as will be highlighted in Chapter 10 it does not stand up to close scrutiny. In fairness to Kotter and many others commentators on organizational change, he illustrates one of the ways social science differs from natural sciences. If a hospital prescribes us a drug, we know that its side-effects have been rigorously researched and evidence-based medicine reassures us. In management and organization studies, there has been increasing interest in evidence-based management (Rousseau et al., 2008). Evidence-based management has been applied to organizational change interventions by Barends et al. (2014) although they critically concluded that the body of evidence was low quality and growing lower.

Whilst research does have a role to play in organizational change studies, returning to why organizations change, it really may not be as important as academics like to assume or assert. Gouldner (1971: 29) drew attention to the centrality of background assumptions in the social sciences, yet we appear to have forgotten his insight that '...a social theory is more likely to be accepted or rejected because of the background assumptions embedded in them'. Gouldner (1971: 34) even questioned the perceived influence of social science in terms of what we know.

> The most basic changes in any science commonly derive not so much from the invention of new research techniques but rather from new ways of looking at data that may have long existed. Indeed, they may neither refer to nor be occasioned by 'data', old or new.

This position is unorthodox and does not sit well with what universities 'offer', yet when applied to why Kotter (1996/2012) is so frequently cited and why his prescriptions are so popular with practitioners, it is very informative. Do practitioners really look to the quantity and quality of the research evidence when managing and leading organizational change?

In concluding this section Sturdy's (2004) framework of reasons for the adoption of management ideas and practices remains a classic. Whilst he was interested in the more general adoption of management ideas and practices, it offers alternative answers to the focusing question of this section – why do organizations change?

Organizational change is likely to be informed by a variety of reasons (7 in Table 2.1) and echoed in the contingency maxim (it depends, 8 in Table 2.1). Sturdy (2004) offers an informative discussion of all eight reasons. The effective rationale (1 in Table 2.1) is by far the most pervasive in theories and practices of organizational change. Change as a response to anxiety and identity issues (2 in Table 2.1) will be explored further in Chapter 7 with regards to individuals experiencing organizational change. The influence of persuasive rhetoric (3 in Table 2.1) and other organizations (6 in Table 2.1) fits with the earlier discussion about fashion in this section. The influence of political interests (4 in Table 2.1) will be the focus of Chapter 11 and the influence of culture will be the focus of Chapter 6.

In Table 2.1, the emphasis has been on practical implications of different answers to the question, why do organizations change? Sturdy's (2004) approach also acknowledges how different theoretical perspectives inform understanding of the adoption of management ideas and practices and competing perspectives will be introduced in subsequent chapters.

Table 2.1 Why organizations change (based on an adaptation of Sturdy, 2004)

Why do organizations change?	What is the strength of this reasoning?	What is the weakness of this reasoning?
1 It is effective for the organization	Prescriptive	Idealistic
2 Due to change agent anxieties, identity issues	Emotion focussed	Essentialist (only one way)
3 Due to persuasive rhetoric	Integrative	Mono-directional
4 Due to political interests and effects	Critical	Functionalist
5 Culture as a bridge or barrier to the transfer of ideas	Contextual	Apolitical
6 Due to the influence of other organizations	Comparative and integrative	Deterministic
7 Variety of reasons	Inclusive	Non-integrative
8 It depends	Flexibility	Relativist (no absolute truths)

Understanding the relationship between time and organizational change

Time is integral to organizational change, yet until recently its coverage in the academic literature was surprisingly limited. At its simplest, we tend to think of an organizational change occurring as an outcome/event/thing arising out of a particular policy/practice. Lewin's (1947) three steps are perceived as being central to many accounts of organizational change; unfreeze, move and refreeze (please see Cummings et al. 2016, for a critical perspective on Lewin's 1947 work). In this section, three themes will be developed around phases, processes and becoming, in order to explain how thinking about the temporal nature of organizational change is gaining sophistication.

Prochaska and Di Clemente (1982) famously identified basic processes which could be applied to an individual's experience of change. Their findings evolved out of studying stages an individual went through in seeking to give up smoking:

   i   think about stopping smoking,
  ii   become determined to stop,
 iii   actively modify habits and
  iv   maintain the new habit of not smoking.

They found that there were fairly consistent stages that preceded and followed a change. They labelled the stage preceding a change as pre-contemplation, followed by contemplation, action and maintenance. This may seem tangential to organizational change but think how you have stopped doing something you were doing excessively...you didn't just stop invariably; there were precursors to stopping. Initially, you may have vaguely thought your actions were excessive with these vague thoughts metamorphosing in contemplation which informed your action (to stop) and hopefully maintenance. Whilst this is a model of an individual's experience of change, it potentially informs thought processes relating to an organizational change. An organization does not just change (an event). Change must involve processes which occur over time. Understanding the processual nature of changing is essential in understanding organizational change.

Burke (2014) presented a four-phase model for leading organizational change comprised of a pre-launch phase, a launch phase, a post-launch phase and a sustaining phase. At the pre-launch phase, leader self-examination is emphasised in terms of self-awareness and motives. The launch phase is what we traditionally think about as an organizational change such as merging two organizations. Burke (2014) emphasised the ongoing nature of an organizational change in his post-launch phase and highlighted the necessity of a sustaining phase. So, in terms of merging two organizations, the real challenges are at the post-launch and sustaining phases in bringing the two organizations together avoiding the merger being in name only. An important element of thinking about organizational change temporally relates to thinking about organizational change in terms of processes rather than things (see Van de Ven and Poole, 2005 and Tsoukas and Chia, 2002) and such process theories will be discussed further in the questioning section.

Understanding how organizational change occurs

The whole textbook relates to this question, so discussions here will be very much preliminary and introductory. In this section, four answers will be offered to the section question, how does organizational change occur? Each answer offers an explanation of how organizational change occurs, although they are not mutually exclusive. First, the discussion of why change occurs (please see Table 2.1) offers explanations of how change occurs. Second, Van de Ven and Poole's (1995) four ideal types of change offer four very different ways of thinking about how change occurs. Third, in recent decades, there has been significant interest in the agency of managers and leaders to make change happen and this theme will feature prominently in subsequent chapters. Fourth, and partially as an antidote to a potential overemphasis on manager/leader agency, the centrality of organizational members with regards to how organizational change occurs is highlighted.

Why informs how

If we revisit Table 2.1, Sturdy (2004) offers an explanation for the adoption of management ideas. By association, these rationales also help to explain how organizational change occurs. Change may be explained as occurring rationally/effectively through following the steps and prescriptions. Change may be explained in terms of addressing identity and anxiety issues of individuals, groups and teams. Change may be explained rhetorically through adopting favoured language, such as 'moving forwards'. If organizations and organizational change are regarded as a political process, change occurs through political activity. Organizational culture may be regarded as being integral to all organizations, with an implication that change occurs through managing culture. If the emphasis is placed upon comparing organizations, the implication is that change occurs through doing what successful organizations do and avoiding doing what unsuccessful organizations do. The implications of Table 2.1 are that organizational change occurs through a combination of these approaches.

Four ideal types

Van de Ven and Poole (1995) highlighted four ideal type explanations of processes of change in organizations: life cycle, teleology, evolution, and dialectics. These theories are particularly useful in explaining sequences of change events. Van de Ven and Poole (1995) explained life cycle theories as regarding change as being imminent with an underlying form, logic, program, or code regulating the process of change and moving the entity towards a subsequent end that is prefigured in the present state. If we think of our own birth, life and death, this underlying metaphor is very powerful in explaining change. Organizations are regarded as going through a natural process of change with an implication that managers/leaders may manage this process, but eventually, all organizations will reach a decline phase.

Teleological explanations explain the organizational change in terms of managers/leaders setting goals and planning. These approaches tend to be rational and functional. They favour the doctrine of a purpose or a goal guiding developments, such as a strategic plan or key performance indicators. This approach emphasises change occurring through the purposeful involvement of managers/leaders in processes of changing. This is reflected in a large body of prescriptive how to manage change literature. Evolutionary approaches emphasise the recurrent and cumulative, progression of variation and selection of organizational entities, in the belief that those organizations best able to adapt are the most likely to survive (see for example Hannan and Freeman, 1977). Van de Ven and Poole (1995) believed that which entities survive or fail could not be predicted.

Whilst the three previous accounts of how change occurs emphasise the functional and rational nature of how change occurs, the dialectical approach regards organizational change as far more contentious. Van de Ven and Poole (1995) suggest that dialectical theory explains the change as occurring through opposing values, forces or events in order to gain enough power to challenge the status quo. Braverman's (1974) explanation of organizational change occurring through deskilling and increasing management control illustrates a dialectical explanation, very different from a managerial explanation. Van de Ven and Poole (2005) subsequently explored alternative approaches to studying organizational change discussed further in the questioning section.

Manager and leader agency

We are living through an era in which there is a considerable belief in organizational change occurring as a consequence of the actions of managers and leaders. This is not a new phenomenon. We have been told for a long time wonderful stories about great leaders making history through initiating changes (Haslam et al., 2011). The agency of managers and leaders in making change happen will be explored further in subsequent chapters (particularly in Chapter 14). Popular notions of heroic managers and leaders are persuasive and even reassuring, but they do beg the question does change occur through the actions of a single person or small group of people or is it broader?

Shared, participative and collaborative

One of the earliest accounts of organizational change was Coch and French's (1948) "Overcoming Resistance to Change" (discussed further in Chapter 13). The debate subsequently focussed on the goal of the paper's title. However, if you read the paper, Coch and French's (1948) research findings revealed that participative/ collaborative approaches resulted in a more successful organizational change in contrast to non-participative/collaborative approaches. It is very telling that debate over subsequent decades focussed upon manager/leader agency in overcoming resistance despite the research encouraging a participative/collaborative approach to organizational change. Oreg (2006: 93) highlighted how the leadership of an organization could negatively impact organizational change, '…lack of faith in the organization's leadership was strongly related to increased reports of anger, frustration, and anxiety with respect to the change, to increased actions against it, and in particular to negative evaluations of the need for, and value of, the organizational change'. Over the past decade, there has been an appetite for strong leader/manager agency, yet Oreg's (2006) findings suggest unchecked leader agency may be part of the problem, rather than the solution in facilitating organizational change.

Understanding where organizational change occurs

The setting/context of an organizational change is crucial to understanding why and how an organizational change occurs. Understanding organizational change contextually offers an antidote to popular belief in one best way to manage/lead organizational changes. Many of the prescriptions in popular business books work with an assumption that the recipes and steps the author prescribes will be equally effective in all contexts. In a similar manner, Harvard Business School encouraged a popular myth that 70 per cent of all organizational change initiatives fail (please see Chapter 17 for further discussion). However, aggregate failure/success rates for all organizational changes are blind to the very diverse contexts in which organizational change occurs and the varied nature of organizational changes.

An important criticism of organizational change literature is that is has a distinct Anglo-American orientation (Brocklehurst et al., 2010). There are many countries with very different histories, national cultures and organizational cultures. Consequently, an Anglo-American oriented explanation and recommendation for managing change may not translate to a Japanese context. If we think more locally, there are considerable differences between public sector, private sector and third sector organizations. A research study into an organizational change in a private sector organization may not be applicable to a third sector organization. Organizational change was described as a container concept in that it can mean different things to different people and this is magnified when we consider the very different contexts in which organizational change occurs.

If we think about the context of organizational change more locally, private sector organizations will vary in terms of the sector in which they operate such as manufacturing or banking. Public services will vary in terms of an emergency service such as the fire brigade being very different from a council department dealing with waste collection. And the voluntary sector includes very different organizations, such as a drug addiction recovery organization working on a multi-agency basis in comparison to a local group protesting about the construction of a bypass. The container concept organizational change is likely to face different challenges in each of these unique contexts. In response to these challenges, academics have sought to recognise the context in their theories. The importance of context in studying organizational change is today taken for granted, but two pioneers who encouraged an appreciation of context in organizational change studies were Pettigrew and Dawson.

Pettigrew (1973, 1977, 1979, 1985, 1990) made a major contribution to understanding strategic change. His work highlighted the significance of power in shaping strategy (Pettigrew, 1973, 1977), the language of culture (Pettigrew, 1979), a large-scale study of change processes in ICI (Pettigrew, 1985) and combining the content, process and context of strategic change with longitudinal data (Pettigrew and Fenton, 2000). He has considerably encouraged an emphasis on studying both the processes and contexts of organizational change. He challenged notions of change as a single event, instead of understanding change as a process happening over time, typically with a major strategic change occurring over many years.

In studying change longitudinally and processually there is also a need to study the context in which changes take place. Pettigrew (1990: 269) defined contextualist analysis as drawing 'on phenomena at vertical and horizontal levels of analysis and the interconnections between those levels through time'. Four key points, crucial to a contextualist analysis of organizational change, were emphasised. The first was acknowledging embeddedness in terms of interconnected levels of analysis. Second, the importance of temporal interconnections in terms of the past, present and future was recognised. Third, there was a need to explore context and action and how context was a product of actions. Finally, there was an acknowledgement that the causation of change was neither linear nor singular, with the implication that a grand theory of change was unlikely to be fruitful. In contextualist analysis, rather than explaining organizational change in terms of a single dominant 'trigger' or 'driver', organizational change was explained in terms of different levels of analysis (embeddedness), the past, present and future (temporal), how actions shape the context and avoiding linear or singular explanations of change.

Dawson (2003) built on this contextualist analysis in suggesting that we need to think about both internal contexts and external contexts and that we need to think about them temporally. Political, Economic, Societal, Technological, Legal and Environmental (PESTLE) analyses are quite common as one way to understand the environment in which an organization operates. However, Dawson (2003) creatively encouraged thinking about context internally and externally and in terms of the past, present and future.

Past internal (inner) organizational environment
Past external (outer) organizational environment
Present internal (inner) organizational environment
Present external (outer) organizational environment
Future internal (inner) organizational environment
Future external (outer) organizational environment

Dawson (2003) encouraged a far more subtle consideration of the dynamic nature of context than is often the case with popular PESTLE style analyses. Instead of regarding change as being driven exclusively by the external environment, different aspects of the internal and external context were acknowledged and how these contexts change over time. So, following this reasoning, if you wanted to understand the organizational change in a high street supermarket, you need to understand the context externally in which the supermarket operates, but equally, you need to understand the inner context of the supermarket (employee demographics, culture, structure, etc.).

As well as understanding the inner and outer context in the present, you need to understand the inner and outer context of the supermarket in the past, and as far as possible engage with the context the supermarket is going to be operating in, in the future.

The cautionary note here is that the role of context, particularly the challenges of the environment may be overstated. Notions of rapidly changing environments may be partially explained in terms of American enthusiasm about the future (Pettigrew, 2003). There is a danger in engaging with a rapidly changing context that we begin to believe that we can control the future. However, '...our plans are based on a future that we know, with certainty, will not be realized' (March, 1981: 572). Dawson (2003), whilst favouring including the future in contextualising change, was philosophical about the outcome given the unforeseeable character of change meaning that the process cannot be predicted with outcomes often only understood in retrospect (please also see Dawson, 2014).

Questioning organizational change classifications, typologies and change as a thing

In this questioning section, two themes are developed first through revisiting three approaches to organizational change classification the different ways classification encourages us to think about organizational change are highlighted. Second, as a cautionary note, process theorists would question the focus on organizational change as a tangible 'thing' evident in this chapter.

Thinking differently about organizational change

In engaging with organizational change classifications, it quickly becomes apparent that there are alternative classifications which have respective strengths and weaknesses. Three different classifications of organizational change will be revisited not in an evaluative sense, but to demonstrate how classification encourages thinking differently about organizational change.

Many classifications are apparent in books and papers and three textbook classifications have been chosen here to illustrate the diversity of available classifications. The three classifications are the change classifications framework (Hughes, 2010), the change Kaleidoscope (Balogun et al, 2015) and the Time Scales, Resources, Objectives, Perceptions, Interest, Control and Source (TROPICS) Test (McCalman et al., 2015). Each approach to classifying organizational change has merits, whilst each encourages thinking very differently about organizational change (please see Table 2.2).

Through aligning three textbook treatments of classifying organizational change, Table 2.2 demonstrates how classifications influence how we think about and by association would manage/lead organizational change. In the first column, Hughes (2010) encourages a chronological approach to change classification. Questions are used to encourage engagement with the disparate elements in a process of changing. Questions seek to encourage engagement with history, time, communications, agency, power and politics and evaluation.

In the second column, Balogun et al.'s (2015) strategic approach emphasises the influence of context. They utilize the metaphor of a child's kaleidoscope to effectively convey the ever-changing nature of the context and the way that context should inform change implementation design choices. They offer a clever differentiation between the

Table 2.2 Classifying organizational change (Hughes, 2010; Balogun et al., 2015 and McCalman et al., 2015)

Change classifications framework (Hughes, 2010)	The change kaleidoscope (Balogun et al., 2015)	The TROPICS Test (McCalman et al., 2015)
What organizational change is taking place?	Outer organizational strategic context	Time scales
What has been the recent organizational history of change?	Middle strategic context (culture, competencies and current situation)	Resources
What rationale has been offered for this organizational change?	Design choices	Objectives
Who made the decision to change?	• Change path	Perceptions
What is the scale and scope of this organizational change?	• Change start point	Interest
What is the timescale for this organizational change?	• Change style	
How is this organizational change being communicated?	• Change target	Control and
Who is managing this change and how is it being managed?	• Change levers	Source
How will the success of this organizational change be evaluated?	• Change roles	
Who can influence the success of this organizational change?		

outer and middle context echoing Dawson's (2003) inner and outer context. The outer context encourages consideration of the external environment, whereas the middle context highlights the unique context within an organization. They regard the outer and middle contexts as dynamic and interrelated. This dynamism influences the design choices that a change agent can make.

McCalman et al. (2015) in the third column encourage change managers to undertake what they call a TROPICS test, in order to establish the uncertainties and the scope for control of a change project. The strength of a TROPICS test is the identification of intangibles initially not apparent which may derail a change project.

> The TROPICS test can be applied as an early warning device to access both the impact and magnitude of the impending change. It is capable of determining the most appropriate solution methodology for entering the change management process; this may be altered as the problem unfolds, by examining certain key factors associated with the transition process.
>
> (McCalman et al., 2015: 91)

When doing a TROPICS test for a specific change project for each factor, such as timescales, you rank if it is clearly defined or ill-defined. Each ranking factor may be joined up to graphically depict the clearly or ill-defined nature of the specific change project. This indicates if a hard or soft solution methodology is required: 'hard refers to a systems-based, mechanistic, solution methodology. Soft refers to an organization development, complex, solution methodology' (McCalman et al., 2015: 92).

So by way of contrast, Hughes (2010) highlights tangible elements in a change process which may be discussed as part of a process of changing. Balogun et al. (2015) highlight the importance of engaging with dynamic contexts in which change design choices are made. And McCalman et al. (2015) highlight intangible elements of an organizational change in identifying the most appropriate methodology. Each way of thinking is useful, but each classification encourages you to think differently about an organizational change. The learning is that just as there can never be one best way to make change happen, there cannot be one best way to classify/study organizational change.

Things or processes?

Process theory and theorists are introduced here as a counterpoint to earlier sections highlighting different ways of thinking about organizational change which tend to work with the assumption that a 'thing' referred to as organizational change exists. Tsoukas and Chia's (2002) paper was subtitled 'rethinking organizational change' and in many ways, they achieved their goal. Whilst, their application of process theory to organizational change was innovative, they acknowledged that the origins of this type of thinking could be traced back to James (1909) and Bergson (1946). Tsoukas and Chia (2002) regarded the bulk of research into an organizational change as adopting a synoptic view. By this they meant that change was viewed as an accomplished event, with key features variations, causal antecedents, and consequences. In this way, earlier accounts of organizational change featured in this chapter may be described as synoptic. They acknowledged that synoptic accounts had been useful, but that they did not go far enough. In particular, their concern was that synoptic accounts did not do justice to the open-ended micro-processes of organizational change. Synoptic accounts did not capture distinguishing features of organizational change in terms of fluidity, pervasiveness, open-mindedness and its indivisibility.

> Change must not be thought of as a property of organization. Rather, organization must be understood as an emergent property of change. Change is ontologically prior to organization – it is the condition of possibility for organization.
>
> (Tsoukas and Chia, 2002: 570)

They regarded change programmes as making things happen, but what happened when a change programme was initiated remained uncertain. They regarded change programmes as being made to work through local adaptations, improvisations and elaborations by human agents. They highlight that their view has particular implications for theories and practices of planned change which potentially did not recognise that the texture of organizations is always changing. Morgan (1986: 233) cited the Greek philosopher Heraclitus writing around the year 500 BC, 'You cannot step twice into the same river, for other waters are continually flowing on.'

Van de Ven and Poole (2005), in another influential paper visiting this debate, acknowledge that there was disagreement with regards the meaning of organizational change and how it was studied. They regarded Tsoukas and Chia's (2002) fundamental issue relating to the belief that organizations consisted of things or processes. They suggested that notions of process could be traced back to Heraclitus as identified by Rescher (1996: 10) that 'process is fundamental: The river is not an object but an ever-changing flow; the sun is not a thing, but a flaming fire. Everything in nature is a matter of process, of activity, of change'. Epistemologically, they differentiate variance methods (similar to earlier references to synoptic accounts) from process methods. Ontologically they differentiated organization as a noun (thing) from organizing as a verb conveying a process.

Bringing process studies more up to date, Langley et al. (2013) edited a special issue of the *Academy of Management Journal* themed around process studies of change in organization and management. In their editorial paper, they identified themes from the 13 contributions selected, and organized these around three major headings: the nature of process research, process research methods and substantive advances to process theories. Langley et al. (2013) emphasised the centrality of time and that different ontologies were evident within process and temporality studies featured in their special issue.

> Process questions take a researcher into a conceptual terrain of events, episodes, activity, temporal ordering, fluidity, and change. We see that process conceptualizations offer ways to understand emergence and change as well as stability, and they incorporate understandings of causality as constituted through chains of events rather than abstract correlations.
>
> (Langley et al., 2013: 10)

So whilst this chapter has offered a navigation for studying organizational change, we are left with a warning about change being concerned with fluidity and emergence as much as being tangible and amenable to classification.

Summary

The chapter may be succinctly summarised by answering the questions posed in the chapter's introduction with the original questions restated in italics.

What is the scope of organizational change? The scope of organizational change studies varies considerably with different authors offering different emphases. Smith and Graetz's (2011: 1) definition of organizational change favoured '...the set of assumptions, tacit beliefs, conscious theories and implementation approaches that govern a change agent's way of looking at the organizational world and the best approach to introducing change'. Themes outside the scope of this textbook, which could have been included are organizational development (OD), project management and technological change.

Why does organizational change occur? Organizational change was explained as occurring as a response to the environment, as a response to fashion and being informed by research.

When does organizational change occur? Time is integral to organizational change. At its simplest we tend to think of an organizational change as occurring as an outcome/event/thing arising out of a particular policy/practice. Prochaska and Di Clemente (1982) identified basic processes which could be applied to an individual's experience of change, pre-contemplation, contemplation, action, and maintenance. Burke (2014) presented a four-phase model for leading organizational change comprised of a pre-launch phase, a launch phase, a post-launch phase and a sustaining phase.

How does organizational change occur? Different explanations exist for how organizational change occurs. Why change occurs helps to explain how it occurs.

Van de Ven and Poole (1995) offered four ideal types of very different ways of thinking about how change occurs. In recent decades, there has been significant interest in the agency of managers and leaders to make change happen, partially as an antidote to potential overemphasis on manager/leader agency and the centrality of organizational members with regards to how organizational change occurs is another explanation.

Where does organizational change occur? The setting/context of an organizational change is crucial to understanding why and how an organizational change occurs. Understanding organizational change contextually offers an antidote to popular belief in one best way to manage/lead organizational changes.

What questions need to be raised about organizational change classifications, typologies and change as a thing? Revisiting three approaches to organizational change classification (Hughes, 2010; Balogun et al., 2015; McCalman et al., 2015) highlights the different ways classification encourages thinking differently about organizational change. Process theorists would question the focus on organizational change as a tangible 'thing' instead favouring thinking about change as a process.

Discussion questions

In understanding concepts, contrast can be very useful. The four 'understanding' questions are reversed here.

- Why is context often downplayed/ignored in popular organizational change prescriptions?
- What is outside the scope of studying organizational change?
- Why do multiple explanations exist for why organizational change occurs?
- How do organizational change classifications help/hinder studies of organizational change?

Navigating the organizational change classification literature

In reviewing the organizational change literature in a manner similar to the leadership studies literature, the volume of literature can be overwhelming as frequently acknowledged by respected academics.

> Anyone interested in organizational change cannot help but have noticed the phenomenal number of books and articles dealing with this subject that have been written over the years.
>
> (Demers, 2007: xi)

Over a decade later there is even more literature, with little consensus and many controversies. Pragmatically, Demers (2007) focussed on scholarly rather than practical literature. The nature of this chapter involved making choices about what to include and exclude and in a similar manner, you will need to make choices and make these choices explicit. In this way, processes of classifying change informing this chapter may inform navigating the literature. For example, in the questioning section, classification frameworks and typologies were revisited. These potentially would offer a framework for navigating the literature and organizing the literature.

Many themes introduced in this chapter are not stand-alone concepts. They re-appear in later chapters and you will often find further references in these chapters. Informing many of the debates in this chapter, are assumptions about knowledge (epistemology) and reality (ontology). There is no consensus around these debates, so you will need to adopt a position and use this to guide your literature reviewing, even if you encounter contradictory literature. The chapter used questions and you may find you are asking questions of the literature. Finally, other organizational change textbooks often have a chapter with a similar role to this one. It may be informative to look at the different ways authors deal with these contested issues. Each author will place different emphases, but different emphases can be informative.

References

Balogun, J., V. Hope Hailey, and S. Gustafsson. 2015. *Exploring Strategic Change*. Harlow: Pearson Education.

Barends, E., B. Janssen, W. ten Have, and S. ten Have. 2014. "Effects of Change Interventions: What Kind of Evidence do we Really Have?" *The Journal of Applied Behavioral Science* 50(1): 5–27.

Bergson, H. 1946. *The Creative Mind*. New York: Carol Publishing Group.

Braverman, H. 1974. *Labour and Monopoly Capital*. New York: Monthly Review Press.

Brocklehurst, M., C. Grey, and A. Sturdy. 2010. "Management: The Work that Dares not Speak its Name." *Management Learning* 41(1): 7–19.

Burke, W.W. 2014. *Organization Change: Theory and Practice*. Thousand Oaks, CA: Sage Publications.

Burnes, B., and B. Cooke. 2012. "Review Article: The Past, Present and Future of Organization Development: Taking the Long View." *Human Relations* 65(11): 1395–1429.

Coch, L., and J.R.P. French (Jr). 1948. "Overcoming Resistance to Change." *Human Relations* 1(4): 512–532.

Crawford, L., and A.H. Nahmias. 2010. "Competencies for Managing Change." *International Journal of Project Management* 28(4): 405–412

Cummings, S., T. Bridgman, and K.G. Brown. 2016. "Unfreezing Change as Three Steps: Rethinking Kurt Lewin's Legacy for Change Management." *Human Relations* 69(1): 33–60.

Dawson, P. 2003. *Understanding Organizational Change: The Contemporary Experience of People at Work*. London: Sage Publications.

Dawson, P. 2014. "Reflections: On Time, Temporality and Change in Organizations." *Journal of Change Management* 14(3): 285–308.

Dawson, P., and C. Andriopoulos. 2017. *Managing Change, Creativity and Innovation*. London: Sage Publications.

De Caluwe, L., and H. Vermaak. 2003. *Learning to Change: A Guide for Organisation Change Agents*. London: Sage Publications.

Demers, C. 2007. *Organizational Change Theories: A Synthesis*. Los Angeles, CA: Sage Publications.

Gabriel, Y. 2008. *Organizing Words*. Oxford: Oxford University Press.

Gouldner, A.W. 1971. *The Coming Crisis of Western Sociology*. London: Heinemann.

Hannan, M.T., and J. Freeman. 1977. "The Population Ecology of Organizations." *American Journal of Sociology* 82(5): 929–964.

Haslam, S.A., S.D. Reicher, and M.J. Platlow. 2011. *The New Psychology of Leadership: Identity Influence and Power*. Hove: Psychology Press.

Hughes, M. 2006. *Change Management: A Critical Perspective*. Wimbledon: CIPD Publishing.

Hughes, M. 2010. *Managing Change: A Critical Perspective*. Wimbledon: CIPD Publishing.

Hughes, M. 2016. *The Leadership of Organizational Change*. London: Routledge.

James, W. 1909. *A Pluralistic Universe.* Lincoln, NE: University of Nebraska Press.

Kotter, J.P. 1996/2012. *Leading Change.* Boston, MA: Harvard Business School Press.

Langley, A., C. Smallman, H. Tsoukas, and A.H. Van de Ven. 2013. "Process Studies of Change in Organization and Management: Unveiling Temporality, Activity and Flow." *Academy of Management Journal* 56(1): 1–13.

Lewin, K. 1947. "Frontiers in Group Dynamics." In *Field Theory in Social Science,* edited by D. Cartwright, 188–237. London: Social Science Paperbacks.

March, J.G. 1981. "Footnotes to Organizational Change." *Administrative Science Quarterly* 26(4): 563–577.

McCalman, J, R.A. Paton. and S. Siebert. 2015. *Change Management: A Guide to Effective Implementation.* London: Sage Publications.

Morgan, G. 1986. *Images of Organization.* Thousand Oaks, CA: Sage Publications.

Morgan, G., and A. Sturdy. 2000. *Beyond Organizational Change: Structure, Discourse and Power in UK Financial Services.* London: Macmillan.

Oreg, S. 2006. "Personality, Context, and Resistance to Organizational Change." *European Journal of Work and Organizational Psychology* 15(1): 73–101.

Pettigrew, A.M. 1973. *The Politics of Organizational Decision Making.* London: Tavistock Publications.

Pettigrew, A.M. 1975. "Towards a Political Theory of Organizational Intervention." *Human Relations* 28(3): 191–208.

Pettigrew, A.M. 1977. "Strategy Formulation as a Political Process." *International Studies of Management and Organization* 7(2): 78–87.

Pettigrew, A.M. 1979. "On Studying Organizational Cultures." *Administrative Science Quarterly* 24 (4): 570–581.

Pettigrew, A.M. 1985. *The Awakening Giant: Continuity and Change in ICI.* Oxford: Blackwell.

Pettigrew, A.M. 1990. "Longitudinal Field Research on Change Theory and Practice." *Organization Science* 1(3): 267–292.

Pettigrew, A.M. 2003. "Strategy as Process, Power and Change." In *Images of Strategy,* edited by S. Cummings and D. Wilson, 301–330. Oxford: Blackwell.

Pettigrew, A.M., and E.M. Fenton (Eds). 2000. *The Innovating Organization.* London: Sage.

Prochaska, J.O., and C.C. Di Clemente. 1982. "Transtheoretical Therapy: Toward a More Integrative Model of Change." *Psychotherapy: Theory, Research & Practice* 19(3): 276–288.

Rescher, N. 1996. *Process Metaphysics: An Introduction to Process Philosophy.* New York: SUNY Press.

Rousseau, D.M., J. Manning, and D. Denyer. 2008. "Evidence in Management and Organizational Science: Assembling the Field's Full Weight of Scientific Knowledge Through Syntheses." *Academy of Management Annals* 2(1): 475–515.

Senior, B., and S. Swailes. 2016. *Organizational Change.* Harlow: Pearson.

Sturdy, A. 2004. "The Adoption of Management Ideas and Practices: Theoretical Perspectives and Possibilities." *Management Learning* 35(2): 155–179.

Smith, A.C.T., and F.M. Graetz. 2011. *Philosophies of Organizational Change.* Cheltenham: Edward Elgar.

Tsoukas, H., and R. Chia. 2002. "On Organizational Becoming: Rethinking Organizational Change." *Organization Science* 13(5): 567–582.

Van de Ven, A.H., and M.S. Poole. 1995. "Explaining Development and Change in Organizations." *Academy of Management Review* 20(3): 510–540.

Van de Ven, A.H., and M.S. Poole. 2005. "Alternative Approaches for Studying Organizational Change." *Organization Studies* 26(9): 1377–1404.

West, M.A. 2012. *Effective Teamwork: Practical Lessons from Organizational Research.* Chichester: John Wiley & Sons.

Chapter 3

Studying organizational change

Introduction and chapter questions

Many decades ago Kahn (1974: 487) provocatively characterised organizational change as follows:

> A few theoretical propositions...repeated without additional data or development; a few bits of homey advice...reiterated without proof or disproof; and a few sturdy empirical observations quoted with reverence but without refinement or explication.

Unfortunately, studies of organizational change are still susceptible to such deficiencies. This textbook in general and this chapter, in particular, speak to Kahn's (1974) challenge. We know from our lived experience that organizational change is significant for societies and organizations. The level of our studies of organizational change needs to rise to such challenges, both through reviewing what we know about organizational change and questioning what we think we know about organizational change.

In the previous chapter, the focus was upon the specific scoping of organizational change in terms of the what, why, when, how and where questions. In this chapter, the focus is on the broader study of organizational change which will set the scene for more specific discussions of organizational change in Parts 2, 3 and 4. Whilst, organizational change is often envisaged as forward-looking and future focussed, it is necessary to recognise and acknowledge that studies of organizational change may be traced back to the middle of the last century. There isn't one best way to manage and lead organizational change. Equally there isn't one best way to study organizational change. This chapter is organized around and provides answers to the following questions:

  How does clarifying the influence of disciplines, fields and subfields inform studies of organizational change?
  How can different approaches to studying organizational change be differentiated?
  How has research informed organizational change studies?
  What would be the milestones in a critical chronology of organizational change?
  What perspective does critical management studies and critical leadership studies offer?

Understanding organizational change studies

The world appears differently to everyone, with no universal way to see organizations (Smith and Graetz, 2011). This diversity raises challenges for anyone studying organizational change. Consequently, two themes are developed in this section. First differences between disciplines, fields, and subfields are introduced as a means of highlighting how different approaches to knowledge territories inform our studies and explain differences. Second, Smith and Graetz's (2011) approach to differentiating approaches to organizational change is introduced as a means of explaining the different ways we understand organizational change theories and practices.

Academic disciplines, fields of study and subfields

In studying organizational change we need to clarify the type of subject area we are studying. Organizational change is best described as a field of academic study similar to other progressive fields: innovation studies (Fagerberg and Verspagen, 2009) and studies of projects (Soderlund, 2011) and leadership studies (Harvey and Riggio, 2011) with each field of study prone to debates, contradictions, and controversies. A field of study is very different from the academic disciplines which Kuhn (1962) famously studied. Academic disciplines such as sociology, economics and psychology potentially inform organizational change, but just to repeat organizational change is not an academic discipline and neither managing change nor leading change are academic disciplines.

When Kuhn (1962) mapped scientific revolutions he was concerned primarily with academic disciplines, not the fields of study featured here. Kuhn (1962) as a physicist favoured unified science aspirations of convergent natural sciences for academic disciplines. However, management and organization studies (MOS) followed a very different path. Whitley (1984, 2000) in his studies of the development of MOS highlighted a privileging of science, which he traced to the origins of the goal of an integrated, coherent and relevant 'science of management', informed by the convergent natural science aspirations of Kuhn (1962). MOS did not integrate around common theoretical goals and research skills but instead developed into multiple fields and subfields with differing goals, problems and research approaches (Whitley, 1984).

In studying organizational change and in all of the following chapters different disciplines, fields of study and subfields inform understanding. In reality, the differentiation will not be as clear as Table 3.1 depicts. However, these differentiations are more than semantic in that they underpin how organizational change is studied. Whilst organizational change is not a discipline, it is informed by many different disciplines, such as psychology and sociology. Each discipline encourages us to think differently about organizational change. For example, psychology encourages us to think about how individuals experience an organizational change, whereas sociology encourages us to think about how society shapes a change such as implementing a change in equality policies. There are many other disciplines such as history and geography which can influence organizational change and the implication is that each discipline will encourage you to think differently about organizational change. Some disciplines will engage you more than others. We are all different.

The real focus of this textbook is the middle level (please see Table 3.1), but the suggestion is that you cannot study organizational change as a field without acknowledging the influence of disciplines and subfields. Even studying fields such as

Table 3.1 The levels of disciplines, fields and subfields

Level	Definition	Example	Example
Discipline	Scientific Discipline, such as Physics	Psychology	Sociology
Field of Study	Subject/Branch of Knowledge	Organizational Change Studies	Leadership Studies
Subfield	Intersection/ Interrelationship Between Fields of Study	Organizational Change Leadership	

organizational change or leadership studies is not as bounded as might be imagined. In the next section, eight very different ways of thinking and practising organizational change will be introduced (based on Smith and Graetz, 2011). Finally, in studying organizational change, we need to be aware of the existence and influence of subfields. In Table 3.1, the example of a subfield is organizational change leadership which is particularly pertinent to the dual themes of managing and leading organizational change in this textbook. As Table 3.1 highlights, this subfield is informed in particular by two fields of study, organizational change studies and leadership studies, which are informed by disciplines such as psychology and sociology.

The implication of all of this is that the convergent consensus of one best way to study organizational change leadership is illusory. Instead, we tend to encounter competing and at times contradictory explanations. For example there is a strong emphasis on history in Chapter 5 and psychology in Chapter 8. This can initially feel challenging, yet once you embrace these diverse and multiple explanations it can be quite exhilarating. In subsequent chapters, competing explanations will feature as this is the favoured approach, yet this textbook could have favoured a single approach which would have given different emphases. In the next subsection, eight different approaches to explaining organizational change are introduced. This should help you to navigate later chapters and to understand controversies and contradictions you will encounter in your own organizational change literature reviewing.

Organizational change approaches

Over the past 35 years, many different frameworks for thinking about organizational change have been offered (please see Hughes, 2016a for a discussion of these). The framework presented here (please see Table 3.2) is based on Smith and Graetz's (2011) *Philosophies of organizational change* (please also see Graetz and Smith, 2010; Graetz et al., 2015).

The first strength of Smith and Graetz's (2011) approach is that many of the approaches featured in references in this textbook may be explained in terms of approaches featured in Table 3.2. An author may locate themselves in a single approach or a combination of approaches with their favoured approaches informing their research, teaching and scholarship. The second strength is that Table 3.2 helps to explain the different approaches adopted by practitioners towards managing and leading organizational change. There is another approach referred to by Smith and Graetz (2011: 183) as a dualities approach. They favour this approach in that '…managing

Table 3.2 Different approaches to change and its management (based on Smith and
           Graetz, 2011)

Approach	Nature of change	Management focus
Rational	Directed and planned	Strategy and planning
Biological	Ecological, organic and evolutionary	Environmental positioning and life cycles
Institutional	Determined by institutional pressure	Industrial standards and benchmarks
Resource	Determined by access to resources	Acquiring and discharging resources
Psychological	Embedded in the minds of those affected	Managing employee transitions
Systems	Interconnected with all aspects of organization	Change all constituents and components
Cultural	Determined by entrenched values	'Deep', rites, rituals and values
Critical	Conflict and values based, rejects universal rules	Acquiring power bases

change demands balancing and conciliating what often appear as conflicting dilemmas'. Organizational change is regarded as dynamic, complex and paradoxical. Ideally, this requires those studying and practising organizational change to understand all approaches and the insights that they provide. Dualities will be discussed further in Chapter 10 with regards to leading organizational change. In the meantime, it is informative to briefly clarify the implications for this textbook of each of the approaches in Table 3.2.

Rational based approaches reassuringly depict organizational change as being planned and directed, the role of managers and leaders is then to focus on their strategies and plans. This approach is by far the most common approach governing organizational change (Smith and Graetz, 2011). Rational based approaches are similar to what Burrell and Morgan (1979) referred to as a functionalist paradigm providing the dominant framework for academic sociology in the twentieth century and by far covering the largest proportion of theory and research in organization studies. It is telling that over 30 years later this orthodoxy is still dominant. Smith and Graetz (2011: 43) capture the mindset when discussing change management guru prescriptions '…that successful change lies firmly in the hands of leaders, all of whom can benefit by introducing the steps advocated. Conversely, unsuccessful change must be due to managerial or leadership inadequacy.' Subsequently, they write about this approach suggesting that there is a belief that 'change can be controlled because everything in an organization should be subservient to the will, vision and action of leaders' (Smith and Graetz, 2011: 45). A general weakness of the rational approach relates to assumptions about the nature of organizational change as certain and controllable '…no matter how logical, future action can rarely be clearly defined and calculated in advance' (Smith and Graetz, 2011: 45). Despite this flaw, the rational approach is particularly favoured by practitioners and echoed and endorsed frequently in business school teaching. This is because the approach presumes a sequential and planned pursuit of optimal solutions resulting in successful change. This is far more promising for practitioners and easier to teach than the other approaches.

Biological approaches depict the organizational change in ecological, organic and evolutionary terms. Managers and leaders focus on environmental positioning envisaging their organizations progressing through an evolutionary life cycle. The strength of this approach is its lifecycle explanations emphasising fitness and survival. The weakness is its overemphasis on environmental factors.

Institutional approaches depict organizational change as being determined by institutional (industry) pressure which results in managers and leaders placing emphasis upon industry standards and benchmarks. The strength of the approach is revealing the strong influence of environmental and institutional pressures to conform. The weakness is not encouraging a search for advantages over competitors/other providers.

Resource-based approaches depict organizational change as being determined by access to resources. Managers and leaders focus on acquiring and discharging resources and core competencies. The strength of this approach is the emphasis on acquiring resources in order to initiate and sustain change. The weakness is assuming that change cannot occur without internal resources.

Psychological based approaches depict organizational change as being embedded in the minds of those affected. These approaches encourage managing employee transitions and psychological adjustments informed by a belief that 'the impact of change is complex, powerful and potentially severe' (Smith and Graetz, 2011: 105). Psychological approaches encourage sharing knowledge and decision making, acknowledging all contributions within organizational change processes (please see discussion of individuals and groups in Chapters 7 and 8). Resistance to change is depicted as a psychological response to organizational change, which is believed to diminish when employees take ownership of change through bottom-up approaches to change (please see Chapter 13). Organizational development (OD) was identified as a particular psychological approach to addressing human responses to organizational change '…OD commits to the premise that change must emanate from a critical mass of engaged employees. Better performance comes with interested, valued and empowered employees' (Smith and Graetz, 2011: 113). The strength of this approach is emphasising the centrality of individuals within processes of organizational change and that individuals may have had a positive and/or negative experience of organizational change. The weakness of the approach is that through focussing on individuals more systemic aspects of organizational change, such as structure are overlooked.

System based approaches emphasise the interconnected nature of organizing. This results in managers and leaders initiating organizational change through considering all constituents and components of an organization. The strength of the approach is avoiding an assumption that change is contained within one organizational area. The weakness is the practicalities of keeping track of many different relationships between organizational variables.

Cultural based approaches depict organizational change as being determined by entrenched values, which encourages managers and leaders to attend to 'deep' rites, rituals and values (these approaches are the focus of Chapter 6). The strength of the approach is to show the importance of collective beliefs and norms. The weakness of the approach is the difficulty in directly addressing intangible organizational cultures.

Critical approaches place different emphases from other approaches on conflict, power and the rejection of universal rules. These approaches are not motivated by a desire to inform management and leadership practices, but instead draw attention to power and genuine empowerment and emancipatory practices. Smith and Graetz (2011) subtitled their critical philosophy chapter 'changing reality' depicting critical philosophy mainly as postmodernism. Postmodern approaches are less concerned with overarching, grand theories describing social behaviour. Instead, they are more interested in indeterminacy, ambiguity and contradiction of organizational life. Smith and Graetz (2011) do acknowledge Marx and Hegel, but radical structuralist explanations of organizational change are not featured. A strength of the critical approach is highlighting the centrality of power, ideology clashes and contradictions inherent in organizational change. The weakness is that all organizational change is explained through power or the favoured ideology of the critical scholar at the expense of other explanations.

How has research informed organizational change understanding?

Accounts of organizational change often appear prescriptive, even evangelical. Consequently, research plays an important role in academic studies of organizational change. Discussions in the previous subsection encourage diverse and at times contradictory research into organizational change. Reviews offer an overview of research in a subfield. The four published reviews of research featured here as well as being informative, illustrate how research-informed organizational change is still informed by choices and preferences of reviewers.

In the first review, Oreg et al. (2011) review research into recipients' reactions to change. In the second review, Burnes and Cooke (2012) re-evaluate Kurt Lewin's field theory. Evidence supporting/not supporting organizational change prescriptions is the focus of the third review (Barends et al., 2014). In the fourth and final review, Nelson-Brantley and Ford (2017) review research into leading change specifically within the context of nursing and healthcare systems.

Oreg et al. (2011) reviewed 60 years (1948–2007) of quantitative research into change recipients' reactions to change. They regarded how change recipients react to organizational change as being integral to organizational change theories and practices. Their review highlighted a model with three components:

a   explicit reactions to change, in which these reactions are conceptualised as tridimensional attitudes;
b   reaction antecedents that comprise pre-change antecedents (viz., change recipient characteristics and internal context) and change antecedents (viz., change process, perceived benefit/harm, and change content); and
c   change consequences, including work-related and personal consequences.

They acknowledge the different perspectives encountered when undertaking their review, which echoes debates featured in the previous two subsections. They (2011: 462) acknowledge jingle – jangle fallacies (Block, 1995) where '...different constructs are given the same label by different researchers (i.e., the jingle fallacy) and equivalent constructs are offered different labels (i.e., the jangle fallacy)'. Their review has theoretical and research implications in terms of the inconsistency of terms, distinctions between explicit reactions and change consequences as the majority of studies were based on self-report data. The practical implications include the importance of creating a supportive and trusting organizational culture and acknowledging recipients' concerns about the impact change will have on them.

Burnes and Cooke (2012) encouraged taking the 'long view' of organizational change, in that only by looking over the last 70 years is it possible to see the major developments and where gaps and inconsistencies lie. Burnes and Cooke (2013) also favoured the long view in their review and re-evaluation of Kurt Lewin's field theory. They highlight that although field theory was central to Kurt Lewin's work after his death, interest declined significantly until the 1990s when force field analysis came to be widely used. They compared force field analysis today with Lewin's original conception of field theory showing that it has significant weaknesses in terms of rigour, concluding that a return to Lewin's original conception of field theory would provide academics and practitioners with a valuable and much-needed approach to managing change (please also see, Burnes, 2004). The implication of these reviews is that we do need to revisit original sources and the contexts of those original sources (please also see Cummings et al., 2016 for further discussion).

Barends et al. (2014: 5) undertook a systematic review of organizational change research published in scholarly journals as they wanted to establish if popular organizational change management (OCM) prescriptions were based on 'solid and convergent evidence' (see also ten Have et al., 2016 featured in Chapter 1). They favoured an evidence-based management approach which has become popular over the past decade, '...there must be available a solid and convergent body of reliable and valid evidence from multiple studies of the same constructs and interventions' (Barends et al., 2014: 7). They found that the number of OCM studies had dramatically grown over the past 30 years, although with the field's methodological repertoire remaining limited. They (2014: 21) warned that '...practitioners should be sceptical about relying uncritically on research findings relevant to OCM as a basis for important decisions'. They do acknowledge that the dynamic nature of organizational change makes replication studies problematic and the ambiguous nature of terminology means that certain studies in database searches may have been missed.

Nelson-Brantley and Ford (2017) undertook a concept analysis of leading change in the context of nursing and healthcare systems. Concept analysis, a favoured methodology in nursing studies, is far less prominent in MOS. They adopted Walker and Avant's (2011) approach to concept analysis, identifying descriptions, antecedents, consequences and empirical referents of the concept. They identified five defining attributes of leading change: individual and collective leadership, operational support, fostering relationships, organizational learning, and balance. The antecedents they identified were external or internal driving forces and organizational readiness. The consequences of leading change they identified included improved organizational performance/outcomes and new organizational culture/values.

In summary, we see Oreg et al. (2011) reviewing quantitative studies to better understand change and recipients' reactions to change. We see Burnes and Cooke (2013) taking the 'long view' in their re-evaluation of Lewin's field theory. We see Barends et al. (2014) undertaking a systematic review of the evidence in support of organizational change prescriptions. And we see Nelson-Brantley and Ford (2017) undertaking a concept analysis of leading change in nursing and healthcare systems. All four reviews make a valuable contribution to studying organizational change. All four reviews appear similar in being reviews of research, but each is different in the informed choices the reviewers make in undertaking their reviews, that is the main learning from this subsection.

Questioning organizational change studies

Frahm's (2007) suggestion that there is much which needs questioning and challenging in organizational change studies still feels very relevant today. On a superficial level, there are many popular prescriptions about how to manage and lead organizational change, but they promise far more than they can ever deliver. Kotter's (1996/2012) prescription to take eight steps towards achieving a major corporate transformation appeals, but does a disservice to organizational change as a field of study (please see Chapter 10 for a further critique of Kotter, 1996/2012). The ambiguities and uncertainties of moving into an uncertain future make the subject fascinating, but they also encourage critique of organizational change studies (please see discussion of myth-understandings in Chapter 1). There have certainly been many critical accounts of organizational change studies and in this questioning section, two critical themes are developed. First, a chronology of critical accounts of organizational change studies is offered drawing on overviews in Hughes (2016a) and Hughes (2016b). Second, critical theorists feature prominently in critiques of organizational change and their approach and beliefs are introduced.

Organizational change – a critical chronology

The following critical chronology is highly selective given the volume of writing about organizational change. Selection criteria were contributions which had critically advanced organizational change studies over approximately the last 30 years. The selected writings vary considerably in their accessibility, with each contribution signposted with a year milestone. The perils of chronarchy are acknowledged (Burrell, 1992 and Cummings, 2002), but on balance it is worthwhile acknowledging such milestones.

1988 – Dunphy and Stace (1988) gave impetus to understanding differences in transformation and change and the dynamic nature of transformation and change. In their studies, they encountered four different forms of transformation and change; participative evolution, charismatic transformation, forced evolution and dictatorial transformation. Dunphy and Stace's (1988) differentiation has had considerable relevance to ongoing leadership debates about followership, distributed leadership and transformational leadership. Their contrasting of incremental and transformational accounts of organizational change offer an important antidote to current transformation and change rhetoric.

1995 – Van de Ven and Poole's (1995) typology has enabled theories explaining organizational change processes to be classified and differentiated. In particular, it surfaces underlying assumptions with regards to how change is explained as: a life cycle, as teleology, dialectic, or as evolution (please see Chapter 2 for explanation of each approach). In their literature review, they cross many traditional discipline boundaries, enabling them to explain processes of change in terms of social, biological, and physical sciences. Four ideal-type theories were used to distinguish characteristics of theories representing '...fundamentally different event sequences and generative mechanisms – we will call them motors – to explain how and why changes unfold' (Van de Ven and Poole, 1995: 511).

2001 – Pettigrew et al. (2001) highlight six interconnected analytical issues relating to where organizational change literature remained underdeveloped, critiquing the literature as acknowledged by leading scholars. The six analytical issues highlighted related to: multiple contexts/levels of analysis, time, history, process, and action, change processes and organizational performance outcomes, international comparisons on organizational change, receptivity and customisation, the engagement between scholars and practitioners. Introducing the Special Issue that they were editing they offered the following cautionary conclusion.

> ...there is the need to straddle the social and organizational sciences; to conceive of researchers and users as co-producers; to transcend current beliefs of scholars and users while also engaging with those beliefs, and to supplement disciplinary knowledge on change rather than attempt to supplant that knowledge. As ever in science as a human activity, the most fundamental challenges are to our own scholarly routines.
>
> (Pettigrew et al., 2001: 710)

2002 – Tsoukas and Chia (2002) (discussed in Chapter 2) believed that organizational change was being treated as exceptional rather than natural. They highlighted the pervasiveness of change in organizations through the notion of organizational becoming.

2003 – Grey (2003: 11) in his deliberately polemical critique of the fetish of change argued that change management initiatives were largely failures and that the usual explanations for such failures were inadequate, concluding '...that the whole business of change management should be given up on'.

2003 – Sturdy and Grey (2003) edited a Special Issue of *Organization* which took critical stock of organizational change management (OCM) highlighting a lack of acknowledgement of stability within organizations, the manageability of change being assumed and the existence of a pro-change bias.

2005 – By (2005), in his critical review of OCM, warned that what was currently available was a wide range of contradictory and confusing theories and approaches. They mostly lacked empirical evidence and were often based on unchallenged hypotheses with regards to the nature of contemporary OCM.

2005 – Van de Ven and Poole (2005) built on their 1995 paper (see earlier discussion) this time to differentiate accounts of organizational change in terms of scholars regarding organizations as consisting of things (variances) or as processes. This was the common thread they found running through the works that they reviewed. Scientific explanations were cast in terms of independent variables causing changes in a dependent variable, and explanations which told a narrative or story about how a sequence of events unfolded to produce a given outcome. Van de Ven and Poole (2005) emphasised time as the 'ether' of change, noting that we tend to judge occurrences of change against a background of time, but that time had largely been neglected within organizational scholarship.

2008 – Schwarz and Huber (2008) edited a Special Issue of the *British Journal of Management* which aimed to challenge the state of the field or the adequacy of current organizational change theories. What was telling was that they were only able to recommend two manuscripts for publication.

2013 – Langley et al. (2013) built on some of the earlier studies cited here, highlighting the influence of process studies in understanding organizational change, quantified in terms of more than 100 potential contributions to their special issue of the *Academy of Management Journal* themed around process studies of change in organization and management. In their editorial, they identified themes from the 13 contributions selected, organized around the major headings of: the nature of process research, process research methods and substantive advances to process theories. They emphasised the centrality of time differentiating process research from variance questions and co-variation between dependent and independent variables (compatible with Van de Ven and Poole, 2005). Different ontologies were evident within process and temporality studies and these differences were acknowledged.

> Process questions take a researcher into a conceptual terrain of events, episodes, activity, temporal ordering, fluidity, and change. We see that process conceptualisations offer ways to understand emergence and change as well as stability, and they incorporate understandings of causality as constituted through *chains of events rather than abstract correlations.*
>
> (Langley et al., 2013: 10)

2017 – Suddaby and Foster (2017) recently highlighted inadequacies in studying organizational change in that assumptions are not articulated, contextual conditions not clear, change not defined and the epistemological status is left unexamined. They identified four implicit models of history in the change literature: history-as-fact, history-as-power, history-as-sensemaking, and history-as-rhetoric.

In this short critical change chronology, the only consensus is a desire to challenge how organizational change was being studied at the time of writing. This chronology can initially appear depressing, but it reflects the advance of a field of study in questioning and challenging what is known about organizational change. The chronology highlights for scholars the different levels of interest and motivations for critiquing organizational change, which is mirrored in the rest of this textbook. Critical theorists have been prominent in their critiques of organizational change and their position is explained in the final subsection.

Critical management and leadership studies

One reason for critiquing organizational change is its role in privileging the interests of the few over the many. For example, in the UK, university undergraduates are asked to pay annual tuition fees of £9,000+. At the same time, university vice-chancellors (VC) are rewarded for managing and leading change with above inflation pay rises, performance bonuses, and enhanced and protected pensions. You may align yourself with the students or the VCs, but what is apparent is that managing and leading change is far from neutral. Dunphy (1996: 542) captured the ideological nature of organizational change as follows '...theories are necessarily infused with ideology. Our theories are value driven, often self-serving, grounded in social movements and driven by social forces.'

In this way, critical theory (CT) challenges greed and power believed to be inherent in capitalism, but equally, CT is itself ideologically infused. Gabriel (2008) in his critical thesaurus described CT as an influential intellectual tradition associated with the *Institute of Social Research* in Frankfurt, with the Frankfurt School drawing their inspiration from Marx and Freud in viewing Western civilisation as profoundly alienating.

In subsequent chapters, CT writings will be drawn upon particularly in the questioning sections. In particular, critical management studies (CMS) and critical leadership studies (CLS) have been influential. By way of introduction, CMS and CLS are introduced through highlighting two examples of such writing. Prichard (2009) acknowledged that CMS was a broad church, which seeks to show how conventional management knowledge is laced with relations of subordination, oppression and exploitation. CMS reflects experiences of organizations as exploitative, oppressive, intimidating and discriminatory. Prichard (2009) then explains how CMS might be taught in terms of three moves: first, distinguishing different forms of knowledge, second, locating organizational politics at the centre of work organization, third, using dramatic, empirically based scripts as a basis for engaging with organizational problems.

In *Is Critical Leadership Studies Critical?*, Learmonth and Morrell (2017) question the rebranding of 'manager' and 'worker' as 'leader' and 'follower'. They fear that managerialism (overemphasis on manager agency) as a critical target of CMS has been replaced with a form of leaderism (overemphasis on leader agency) which avoids bigger critical questions about the role of 'bosses' in our organizations and society. They fear that CLS is not critical enough about its own critical practices. The word 'manager' might have been changed for the word 'leader', but has anything substantially changed? Think back to Prichard's (2009) depiction of organizations as exploitative, oppressive, intimidating and discriminatory. Learmonth and Morrell (2017) warn that trying to be critical whilst simultaneously using leadership language strikes some odd notes. The paper offers a useful introduction to the contested nature of CLS and how it is similar or different from CMS (please also see Collinson's, 2017 eloquent response to criticisms of his work).

Summary

The chapter may be succinctly summarised through answering the questions posed in its introduction. The original questions are restated in italics.

How does clarifying the influence of disciplines, fields and subfields inform studies of organizational change? Organizational change is a field of study, rather than an academic discipline such as economics or sociology. Organizational change as a field of study features debates at the level of subfields, such as managing change and leading change.

How can different approaches to studying organizational change be differentiated? Many different frameworks for thinking about organizational change have been offered over the past 35 years. Smith and Graetz's (2011) *Philosophies of Organizational Change* (rational, biological, institutional, resource, psychological, systems, cultural, and critical approaches) illustrates different ways of thinking about theories and practices of organizational change.

How has research informed organizational change studies? Research plays an important role in academic studies of organizational change with literature reviews offering an overview of research in a subfield. The four published reviews of research were featured in order to illustrate how research informed organizational change is still informed by choices and preferences of reviewers.

What would be the milestones on a critical chronology of organizational change? A critical chronology of organizational change helps to demonstrate how studies of organizational change have gained greater sophistication. The featured authors were: Dunphy and Stace (1988), Van de Ven and Poole (1995), Pettigrew et al. (2001), Tsoukas and Chia (2002), Grey (2003), Sturdy and Grey (2003), By (2005), Van de Ven and Poole (2005), Schwarz and Huber (2008), Langley et al. (2013), Suddaby and Foster (2017).

What perspective does critical management studies and critical leadership studies offer? Critical theory informing critical management studies and critical leadership studies challenges greed and power believed to be inherent in capitalism, but equally Critical Theory itself is ideologically infused. Critical Theory as an influential intellectual tradition is associated with the Frankfurt School.

Discussion questions

- What are the advantages and disadvantages of thinking of organizational change studies in terms of convergence and in terms of divergence?
- Why is an emphasis placed on research in studying organizational change?
- Why are Smith and Graetz (2011) encouraging studying organizational change from a range of different approaches?
- Why has the study of organizational change attracted a large amount of critical interest?

Navigating the organizational change studies literature

A large amount has been written about organizational change and it can feel quite overwhelming particularly given the inevitable contradictions and inconsistencies which arise. This chapter has offered an informed navigation through the literature. However, you will have to make informed/pragmatic choices.

Overviews offer synthesis and classification of diverse literatures (please see Oreg et al., 2011; Burnes and Cooke, 2013; Barends et al., 2014 and Nelson-Brantley and Ford, 2017). In each of these instances, the authors present you with a focussed literature review and a commentary/classification about that literature. The references they cite then offer an opportunity to follow up references and delve deeper into a debate.

In terms of literature about the sociology of knowledge (disciplines, fields and subfields) in Hughes (2013), I review accounts of how knowledge about organizations is itself organized in terms of territories and territorial boundaries. More recently, I (Hughes, 2018) have written about organizational change leadership as a subfield which offers conceptualisations of the different ways to think about subfields in organizational change. In terms of approaches to organizational change *Philosophies of Organizational Change* (Smith and Graetz, 2011) is very readable (please also see Graetz and Smith, 2010; Graetz et al., 2015).

References

Barends, E., B. Janssen., W. ten Have, and S. ten Have. 2014. "Effects of Change Interventions: What Kind of Evidence do we Really Have?" *The Journal of Applied Behavioral Science* 50(1): 5–27.

Block, J. 1995. "A Contrarian view of the Five-Factor Approach to Personality Description." *Psychological Bulletin* 117(2): 187–215.

Burnes, B. 2004. "Kurt Lewin and the Planned Approach to Change: A Re-Appraisal." *Journal of Management Studies* 41(6): 977–1002.

Burnes, B., and B. Cooke. 2012. "The Past, Present and Future of Organization Development: Taking the Long View." *Human Relations* 65(11): 1395–1429.

Burnes, B., and B. Cooke. 2013. "Kurt Lewin's Field Theory: A Review and Re-evaluation." *International Journal of Management Reviews* 15(4): 408–425.

Burrell, G. 1992. "Back to the Future: Time and Organization." In *Rethinking Organization: New Directions in Organization Theory and Analysis*, edited by M. Reed., and M. Hughes, 165–183. London: Sage Publications.

Burrell, G.G., and G. Morgan. 1979. *Sociological Paradigms and Organisational Analysis. Elements of the Sociology of Corporate Life*. Aldershot: Gower.

By, R.T. 2005. "Organisational Change Management: A Critical Review." *Journal of Change Management* 5(4): 369–380.

Collinson, D. 2017. "Critical Leadership Studies: A Response to Learmonth and Morrell." *Leadership* 13(3): 272–284.

Cummings, S. 2002. *Recreating Strategy*. London: Sage Publications.

Cummings, S., T. Bridgman, and K.G. Brown. 2016. "Unfreezing Change as Three Steps: Rethinking Kurt Lewin's Legacy for Change Management." *Human Relations* 69(1): 33–60.

Dunphy, D. 1996. "Organizational Change in Corporate Settings." *Human Relations* 49(5): 541–552.

Dunphy, D., and D. Stace. 1988. "Transformational and Coercive Strategies for Planned Organizational Change: Beyond the O.D. Model." *Organization Studies* 9(3): 317–334.

Fagerberg, J., and B. Verspagen. 2009. "Innovation Studies – The Emerging Structure of a New Scientific Field." *Research Policy* 38(2): 218–233.

Frahm, J. 2007. "Organizational Change: Approaching the Frontier, Some Faster than Others (combined review of five books)." *Organization* 14(6): 945–955.

Gabriel, Y. 2008. *Organizing Words: A Critical Thesaurus for Social and Organization Studies*. Oxford: Oxford University Press.

Graetz, F., M. Rimmer, A. Lawrence, and A. Smith. 2015. *Managing Organisational Change*. Milton Queensland: John Wiley & Sons Australia.

Graetz, F., and A.C.T. Smith. 2010. "Managing Organizational Change: A Philosophies of Change Approach." *Journal of Change Management* 10(2): 135–154.

Grey, C. 2003. "The Fetish of Change." *TAMARA Journal of Critical Postmodern Organization Science* 2(2): 1–18.

Harvey, M., and R.E. Riggio (Eds). 2011. *Leadership Studies: The Dialogue of Disciplines*, Cheltenham: Edward Elgar.

Hughes, M. 2013. "Book Review Essay: The Territorial Nature of Organization Studies." *Culture and Organization* 19(3): 261–274.

Hughes, M. 2016a. *The Leadership of Organizational Change*. London: Routledge.

Hughes, M. 2016b. "Who Killed Change Management?" *Culture and Organization* 22(4): 330–347.

Hughes, M. 2018. "Reflections: Studying Organizational Change Leadership as a Subfield." *Journal of Change Management* 18(1): 10–22.

Kahn, R.L. 1974. "Organizational Development: Some Problems and Proposals." *Journal of Applied Behavioural Science* 10(4): 485–502.

Kotter, J.P. 1996/2012. *Leading Change*. Cambridge: Harvard Business Press.

Kuhn, T.S. 1962/2012. *The Structure of Scientific Revolutions*. Chicago, IL: University of Chicago Press.

Langley, A., C. Smallman, H. Tsoukas, and A.H. Van de Ven. 2013. "Process Studies of Change in Organization and Management: Unveiling Temporality, Activity and Flow." *Academy of Management Journal* 56(1): 1–13.

Learmonth, M., and K. Morrell. 2017. "Is Critical Leadership Studies 'Critical'?" *Leadership* 13(3): 257–271.

Nelson-Brantley, H.V., and D.J. Ford. 2017. "Leading Change: A Concept Analysis." *Journal of Advanced Nursing* 73(4): 834–846.

Oreg, S., M. Vakola., and A. Armenakis. 2011. "Change Recipients' Reactions to Organizational Change: A 60-year Review of Quantitative Studies." *The Journal of Applied Behavioral Science* 47(4): 461–524.

Pettigrew, A.M., R.W. Woodman, and K.S. Cameron. 2001. "Studying Organizational Change and Development: Challenges for Future Research." *Academy of Management Journal* 44(4): 697–713.

Prichard, C. 2009. "Three Moves for Engaging Students in Critical Management Studies." *Management Learning* 40(1): 51–68.

Schwarz, G.M., and G.P. Huber. 2008. "Challenging Organizational Change Research." *British Journal of Management* 19: S1–S6.

Soderlund, J. 2011. "Theoretical Foundations of Project Management: Suggestions for a Pluralistic Understanding." In *Oxford Handbook on the Management of Projects,* edited by P.W.G. Morris, J. Pinto, and J. Soderlund, 15–36. Oxford: Oxford University Press.

Smith, A.C.T., and F.M. Graetz. 2011. *Philosophies of Organizational Change.* Cheltenham: Edward Elgar.

Sturdy, A., and C. Grey. 2003. "Beneath and Beyond Organizational Change Management: Exploring Alternatives." *Organization* 10(4): 651–662.

Suddaby, R., and W.M. Foster. 2017. "History and Organizational Change." *Journal of Management* 43(1): 19–38.

ten Have, S., W. ten Have, A.B. Huijsmans, and M. Otto. 2016. *Reconsidering Change Management: Applying Evidence-Based Insights in Change Management Practice.* London: Routledge.

Tsoukas, H., and R. Chia. 2002. "On Organizational Becoming: Rethinking Organizational Change." *Organization Science* 13(5): 567–582.

Van De Ven, A.H., and M.S. Poole. 1995. "Explaining Development and Change in Organizations." *Academy of Management Review* 20(3): 510–540.

Van de Ven, A.H., and M.S. Poole. 2005. "Alternative Approaches for Studying Organizational Change." *Organization Studies* 26(9): 1377–1404.

Walker, L.O., and K.C. Avant. 2011. *Strategies for Theory Construction in Nursing.* Englewood Cliffs, NJ: Prentice Hall.

Whitley, R. 1984. "The Fragmented State of Management Studies: Reasons and Consequences." *Journal of Management Studies* 21(3): 331–348.

Whitley, R. 2000. *The Intellectual and Social Organization of the Sciences.* Oxford: Oxford University Press.

Part II

Managing change

Chapter 4

Management studies

Introduction and chapter questions

Many books and academic journals engage with management studies. The intention here is not to replicate those debates as it would be impossible in the context of a single textbook chapter. However, in engaging with managing change, it is possible to introduce broader debates about management which set the scene for the second part of this textbook with regards to managing change. In Chapter 9, leadership studies will be introduced similarly as a precursor to leading change discussions.

The management focus of this chapter requires clarification of the meaning of 'management'. Gabriel (2008: 169) explained the etymology of 'management' in terms of the French and Italian meaning to 'train a horse'. 'Management then originates in taming and domesticating a wild force of nature and turning it into a useful resource for humans.' He subsequently introduced major debates about managers, management and the nature of managerial work, which include:

- management – leadership relationships,
- moral and ethical aspects/responsibilities of managerial work,
- the nature of managerial knowledge, learning, acquisition and development and the limits of management, aspects of organizations which are unmanaged or unmanageable.

Whilst there has been considerable ongoing debate around concepts of managers and management, in many ways management has resisted 'taming'. Watson (1986) highlighted four very different conceptualisations of management (please see Table 4.1).

Each of Watson's (1986) different images of management highlighted different practitioner and academic mental models of management. What is useful about

Table 4.1 Management as art, science, magic and politics (based on Watson, 1986)

Management as science	Managers are successful because they have learned an appropriate body of knowledge, developing the ability to apply acquired skills/techniques.
Management as art	Managers are successful because they are born with appropriate intuition, intelligence and personality.
Management as magic	Managers are successful because they recognise nobody really knows what is going on, but they are able to engage in the expected rituals.
Management as politics	Managers are successful because they can work out the unwritten rules and play organizational games to win.

Table 4.1 is that it highlights the difference, rather than claiming that any one image is superior to other images. We are all likely to work with a particular favoured model of management. Management as science is typified by the Chartered Management Institute (CMI) featured in the next section and in this textbook and other textbooks, the emphasis is placed on learning appropriate knowledge. In many ways, management as science is the antithesis of management as art which may be paraphrased as 'either you have got it, or you haven't'. Management as magic is the most abstract of Watson's (1986) images. In the context of organizational change, the best way to understand it is in terms of cultural change with claims that through rituals and engaging with subjective experiences, managers can change cultures (please see Chapter 6 for further discussion). Finally, management as politics recognises manager involvement in power relations, which will be the focus of Chapter 11.

Watson's (1986) images of management help to differentiate how we conceptualise management. However, in introducing management for Part II, we still need to clarify management as a function, activity and group. Watson (2006) highlighted three related definitions of management favoured in this chapter (please see Table 4.2).

In defining management, Watson (2006) emphasised shaping, which as a label is able to embrace many different styles of management from very coercive through to very consultative/participative. He tempered his discussions of managing with caveats about managerialism (please see Chapter 3) and managism. Managism is a similar critical concept to managerialism, questioning discourses which celebrate the distinct expertise of managers enabling them to rationally drive organizations. Whilst Tables 4.1 and 4.2 seek to clarify what we mean by management, there will always be a subjective even ideological component to belief in management. Over the past decade, academic debates shifted away from managerialism towards leaderism with practitioners increasingly talking about leading rather than managing in delivering performance (Bresnen et al., 2015). Both the agency of managers (Part II) and leaders (Part III) in facilitating organizational change feature prominently in this textbook. However, in Part IV, it will be argued that the current emphasis on leaders and leadership may have gone too far. This chapter is organized around and provides answers to the following management studies questions:

-   Doing management, what are practitioners doing?
-   How do management idea families inform understanding about management?
-   What have been the most influential management idea families?
-   What do we know about the experience of being managed?
-   How could management good practices be informed by questioning traditional histories of management?

Table 4.2 Management as a function, activity and as a group

Management as a function	Shaping relationships, understandings and processes in work organizations in order to complete tasks so that the organization continues into the future
Management as an activity	Bringing about this shaping
Management as a group of people	Employees of an organization with official responsibilities for shaping relationships, understandings and processes

In the next section, the focus is on management practices in terms of a placement student attempting to solve the mystery of management and CMI's promotion of their Management Manifesto. Next, Huczynski's (2006) concept of management idea families is introduced as a means to establish the most influential management idea families and the six most influential are introduced. The focus then shifts towards those being managed, in order to offer a different perspective on management. The questioning section considers Cummings et al.'s (2017) recently published *A New History of Management* questioning traditional histories of management. Also, Cooke's (1999) critical historiography of change management is featured.

Doing management, what are practitioners doing?

In this section, a student's first experiences of being managed are revisited and at a far more institutional level, CMI's (2017) *Management Manifesto* is discussed. Organizations have changed considerably since Fineman and Gabriel's (1996) account of the first organizational experience of students doing placements as part of their degree studies. These accounts of early experiences of being managed offer poignant insights and, for many of these students, they were being managed for the first time (the tendency for undergraduates to work part-time was not the norm in this era).

Anna told her story of doing a six-month placement with a Greek publishing company in Athens. She was very candid in sharing her experiences and how working in an organization influenced her. Anna explained how as a student she had studied management, but that she wanted to understand first-hand the 'myth' of management. She boldly decided that she wanted to talk to her top manager in order to help her solve the 'mystery' of management.

> Finally one afternoon she was free and pleased to talk to me. I then realized for a moment that my request was difficult. I wanted to find out about everything. Was this feasible? I explained most of my thoughts to her, she understood all the worries that had been in my mind all this time.
>
> (Anna, cited in Fineman and Gabriel, 1996: 61)

The story goes on to explain what Anna learned which included the importance of management style and having a passion for what you do. The need to understand subordinates, to cooperate and be accessible to subordinates was also acknowledged.

In seeking an institutional perspective, the CMI's recently published *Management Manifesto* (CMI, 2017) offers insights into current issues for management as highlighted by a professional body. In the context of this textbook, the title of the manifesto – *Leadership for Change* is intriguing in emphasising leadership and change. In later chapters, manager/leader differentiations will be discussed, although rather than a manager vs leader dualism, a dualities aware approach will be favoured. In the management manifesto, five key areas where collaborative action is needed were identified:

1 Improving productivity through people
2 Building trust through better business cultures and governance
3 Inclusive leadership – harnessing diversity and challenging groupthink
4 Improving employability – better access and opportunities for young people
5 The age of apprenticeships – get in and go far in management

In their manifesto, they state the UK economy lost £84 billion a year resulting from poor people management. They suggest that trust matters and that the leader needs to build trust.

> The Edelman Trust Barometer reported its biggest-ever drop in trust in government, business, the media and NGOs in 2017. Many people are concerned by runaway executive pay and perceived 'rewards for failure'.
>
> (CMI, 2017: 8)

Whilst, the highlighting in a management manifesto of poor people management and the biggest ever drop in trust in the UK are troubling, they do serve as a potential catalyst for change. The manifesto highlights how increasing diversity in the workforce would help to challenge groupthink (groupthink is discussed in Chapter 8). They suggest that the UK needs 1.9 million new managers by 2024. In explaining how CMI is responding to this challenge, they regard the Chartered Manager Degree Apprenticeship as an important response to this challenge.

Management studies

In this section, Huczynski's (2006) overview of management idea families is featured as a means of succinctly introducing influential ideas and authors. However, in such overviews, there is a tendency to study management from the perspective of the manager rather than the managed. Consequently, in the second half of this section, the lived experience of being managed is featured as another way to study management from the perspective of the managed. This is particularly important as the majority of employees are managed rather than managers, and even managers are often managed by a more senior manager.

Management idea families

Huczynski's (2006) survey of popular management ideas of the twentieth century reviewed academic, as well as, practitioner writing. In his survey, he undertook a content analysis of professional journals, as well as, popular texts of selected readings and reprint series. More recent writers did not appear prominently in his content analysis, although this may partially be explained as a consequence of the length of time these publications have been published.

What was interesting from this content analysis was that beyond a small number of management writers, there was very little consensus around about who were the really influential contributors. The following most popular management writers of the twentieth century were identified:

1st = Henri Fayol, Douglas McGregor
3rd = Peter Drucker, Frederick Herzberg and Tom Peters
6th = Frederick Winslow Taylor, Rensis Likert and Chris Argyris

Although 129 management writers were identified, only six truly popular management idea families over the past 100 years were evident. Huczynski (2006: 30) defined a management idea as '...applied to all abstract thought units or systems of such units...where there can be said to be sufficient similarity between these ideas or systems of ideas, then the term family of management ideas will be used'.

He identified six management idea families: bureaucracy, scientific management, administrative management, human relations, neo-human relations and guru theory. Each management idea family is introduced with regards to key theorists informing the management idea highlighted.

Bureaucracy

Weber (1947) gave impetus to understanding organizations as bureaucracies and to structuralist explanations of organizational behaviour. Clegg et al. (2016: 450) in *Managing and Organizations* offer the following definition of bureaucracy as '...an organizational form consisting of a hierarchy of differentiated knowledge and expertise in which rules and disciplines are arranged not only hierarchically in regard to each other but also in parallel'. Structuralist analysis as encouraged by Weber (1947) suggested that the way organizations are structured was beyond choice. Instead, the structure was an outcome of modern, scientific and rational principles (Huczynski, 2006).

Weber's analysis (1947) focussed on economies and societies, rather than the organizational level of analysis of this textbook. However, his analysis has proved to be very influential in studying formal rationality and authority in organizations. He identified three major bases of authority; rational-legal, traditional and charismatic. Rational-legal authority focussed on following rules and general principles, whereas traditional authority focussed on following previous precedents. Charismatic authority drew attention to the 'magic' of the authority figure, offering an explanation of the authority of change managers and change leaders.

Scientific management

Scientific management as a management idea may be traced back to Taylor's (1911) influential book *The Principles of Scientific Management*. The focus of this management idea has been on shop-floor techniques to maximise the productivity of manual workers (Huczynski, 2006). Scientific management is sometimes referred to as Taylorism. Taylorism advocates increased managerial discretion over work through calculating and defining how work is undertaken. Belief in Taylorism has implications for how jobs and organizations are designed. Despite Taylor's (1911) writings being over a century old, they still infuse organizational change methodologies such as business process re-engineering and lean six sigma.

Administrative management

Administrative management is the third of the management idea families which Hucyznski (2006) identified. This management approach emphasised optimising efficiency through determining types of specialisation and hierarchy, through mechanistic forms of organizational design. Huczynski (2006) highlighted Fayol as the most popular writer in this management idea family. Fayol's (1949) *General and Industrial Management* was originally published in French in 1916 and was only translated into English in 1949. Fayol (1949) classified the activities of organizations as technical, commercial, financial, security, accounting and managerial. He also identified 14 general principles of management featured in Table 4.3.

Most of the terminology in Table 4.3 is self-explanatory. Esprit de corps requires clarification and may be explained in terms of its emphasis on harmony and cohesion

Table 4.3 Fourteen general principles of management (based on Fayol, 1949)

Division of work	Centralisation
Authority	Scalar chain (line of authority)
Discipline	Order
Unity of command	Equity
Unity of direction	Stability of tenure of personnel
Subordination of individual interest to the general interest	Initiative
Remuneration	Esprit de corps

amongst organizational members. Many of Fayol's (1949) 14 general principles of management are still evident in organizations today. Debates about managing and leading organizational change featured in subsequent chapters implicitly draw upon and build upon these general principles of management.

Human relations

Human relations as a management idea family, was informed by *The Human Problems of an Industrial Civilization* (Mayo, 1933). A major research project commenced at the Hawthorne plant of *American Telegraph and Telephone* in the mid-1920s. The findings from these studies highlighted the influence of workplace intervention, particularly interventions by psychologists and sociologists, informing subsequent management practice. Mayo's (1933) book is informed by the Hawthorne studies, although these studies were largely undertaken and witnessed by Mayo's colleagues, rather than by Mayo. The Hawthorne studies were regarded as a significant precursor to later studies of organizational change (Burke, 2014). These studies drew attention to psychological and human factors influencing productivity and morale. They signposted variables influencing worker satisfaction, encouraged more humanistic treatment of workers and informed later theoretical developments such as studies of group dynamics.

Neo-human relations

Neo-human relations was the fifth management idea family and described as the most popular management idea family. These management ideas can be traced back to the late 1950s and were unified around a common espoused belief in employee desires to grow and develop on the job. Four writers from this management idea family appeared in the ranking of the most popular management writers. Herzberg et al. (1959) studied Pittsburgh engineers and accountants. They identified factors believed to be strong determinants of job satisfaction: achievement, recognition, the work itself, responsibility and advancement (often referred to as motivators). Also, they identified reasons for job dissatisfaction: company policy and administration, supervision, salary, working conditions and interpersonal relations (often referred to as the hygiene factors). Herzberg's work gave impetus to the concept of job enrichment involving expanding the scope of jobs and increasing decision making by job holders.

   McGregor (1960) identified Theory X and Theory Y assumptions about motivation and human behaviour implicit in management literature, theory and practice. In Likert's (1967) System 4 theory, the importance of democracy in management was recognised. The Likert scale allowed organizations to be classified according to management approach:

System 1 – Autocratic management,
System 2 – Benevolent autocracy,
System 3 – Consultative management and
System 4 – Participative management

Likert (1967) favoured organizations adopting a system 4 participative management approach. Argyris (1973) highlighted six dimensions through which individuals progressed in developing healthy personalities within organizations. He remained sceptical that formal organizations were compatible with the goal of developing healthy personalities. In terms of organizational change, neo-human relations with its emphasis on managing human aspects of organizations was to inform organizational development.

Guru theory

Guru theory was the final management idea family Huczynski (2006) encountered. Guru theory aimed to help managers build strong businesses in successfully competing in chosen market segments. For Huczynski (2006) five beliefs underpinned guru theory.

i   Product and service innovations were dependent on many 'tries' by many employees.
ii Individual's action resulting in feelings was favoured over individual's feelings resulting in action.
iii The belief that organizations could coordinate through culture and value systems, rather than rules and commands.
iv The main source of innovation was regarded as being customers.
v   A strong customer orientation influenced management attitudes and behaviour towards staff.

Drucker made many contributions to the management literature introducing management by objectives (Drucker, 1954) and management by results (Drucker, 1964) into the management vocabulary. The writings of Tom Peters were prominent in the 1980s and 1990s. One of his most famous books was *In Search of Excellence* (Peters and Waterman, 1982) co-authored with Robert Waterman (discussed further in Chapter 6). Guru theory has been very influential in prescribing how organizational change is managed and led, and guru theory remains influential at the time of writing.

Being managed

Accounts of management are often written for and from the perspective of the manager, but for most of us we experience being managed rather than being the manager. Consequently, in studying management, we need to engage with the lived experience of being managed, starting with being managed well. Floor (2017) writing in the CIPD *People Management* magazine highlighted the hallmarks of great management.

Table 4.4 Hallmarks of great management (Floor, 2017)

1   They earn trust and give it
2   They coach and teach by example
3   They don't make it personal
4   They help us to shape our future
5   They don't feel threatened
6   They set clear goals and expectations
7   They praise
8   They have identified how you're motivated

The hallmarks of great management in Table 4.4 are self-explanatory. Floor (2017) acknowledges that it is not easy to recognise when our boss is trying to help us, but a reliable barometer is if we are happy in our job. These hallmarks may reflect an ideal rather than the lived experience of most people being managed. It is also informative to look at when being managed makes people unhappy in their job.

Carter (2016) poses the following question to his readers. Are you being bullied or performance managed? He suggests that the answer might be that you are being bullied, or the answer might be that you are being performance managed or the answer might be that you are not suited to your job. He highlights the existence of disciplinary procedures to penalise bullying to protect those experiencing bullying, although he warns that sometimes there is a fine line between experiencing performance management and bullying.

Fineman and Gabriel (1996) explored the placement experiences of their students in organizations. More recently Clarke and Scurry (2017) studied graduate experiences of public sector talent management programmes in the UK and Australia. They draw on psychological contract theory (unwritten expectations of the employment relationship) in order to explore how talent management programmes shape individual expectations and the influence of these expectations on participant experiences and evaluations. Clarke and Scurry (2017) were interested in exploring experiences of individuals on graduate talent management programmes in terms of three research questions:

1   How does participation in a talent management programme shape the psychological contract?
2   How do graduate expectations develop prior to, and during, the recruitment process?
3   How do met or unmet expectations influence how graduates evaluate the talent management experience?

The researchers shared verbatim accounts of being managed, although with the names of respondents anonymised to UKGrad or AusGrad. In terms of line manager support, Table 4.5 highlights two polarised views on the management support graduates experienced.

Clarke and Scurry (2017) drew three conclusions from their study: first, the value of psychological contracts for understanding how individuals experience and evaluate talent management programmes; second, the importance of managing and moderating for individuals on talent management programmes of the development of expectations; thirdly, that the success of public sector 'fast track' programmes is reliant on both talent management strategy and talent management implementation.

Table 4.5 Graduate experiences of support on public sector talent management programmes

(My manager) was brilliant in guiding me, and she understood the public service, and so, she taught me everything that she sort of knew and was very hands-on in that teaching, but also was quite happy to let me do my work and to give me that opportunity.	Initially, I spoke to my manager, didn't get any response from her, I then went to other members of my team, didn't get much of a response from them. Then went to other teams, didn't get much response from them, and then during a meeting, I just got really frustrated, I said, I literally have nothing to do and then this guy stepped up and said 'I'll be the supervisor' and he was great.
AusGrad 7, 2010, Male	AusGrad 2, 2011, Female

Questioning management studies

In one of the leading management journals, highly respected management academics Alvesson and Sandberg (2013) posed an awkward question – has management studies lost its way? Management and how it is studied is integral to organizations and societies across the world. We tend to work with a rarely stated assumption that what we know is cumulative. This may be paraphrased as – we are becoming more and more knowledgeable about management. If you are open to questioning management studies, one way to question it is through questioning the history informing/misinforming what we know today. Two themes will be developed here: first, the need for a new history of management (Cummings et al., 2017) will be explored and second, the traditional historiography of the management of change (Cooke, 1999) will be challenged.

A new history of management

Whereas Alvesson and Sandberg (2013) in answering their own question problematised unacknowledged assumptions in management and organization studies, Cummings et al. (2017: 2) argued that management studies had taken a narrow view on what in the past was relevant.

> Our thesis may be summed up in a sentence: if we think differently, truly innovatively, about management, we may have to look again at and rethink our historical assumptions about our field.

They illustrate their provocative account of management history by revisiting accounts of historic contributions as traditionally represented in management textbooks. This may be illustrated through how Adam Smith (1776) is often remembered in management textbooks for his account of a pin factory and the division of labour necessitating increased control of workers to be administered by managers. However, for Cummings et al. (2017: 314), this missed his real economic innovation '...that slavery and other forms of repressing a human's "sacred freedoms", such as being able to dispense with a person's labour as he or she sees fit, were misguided: ethically, fundamentally, but also economically'. In a similar manner Cummings et al. (2017) demonstrate the selective and ideological nature of remembering the contributions of Taylor (1911), Mayo (1933), Weber (1947) and Herzberg et al. (1959). Remember, these were some of the most influential contributors to management studies when gauged by Huczynski's (2006) content analysis. However, each contribution had been misrepresented in management textbooks, with the implication that management studies today is misinformed. They appear to be particularly annoyed with what they refer to as textbook distortions (oh dear), which they regard as originating in the 1970s and 1980s.

> ...comprehensive textbooks that supply all the materials necessary for a university course in management, divided into sub-field segments that could be matched to a particular lecture on a topic – e.g., managing change, human resource management and leadership – did not exist much before 1980.
>
> (Cummings et al., 2017: 231)

They are critical about change management in general and Lewin's (1947) three steps of unfreezing, move and refreeze which they regard as accreting throughout subsequent change theories (see also Cummings et al., 2016).

The historiography of the management of change

Historiography is the label for how history is written. In the previous subsection, Cummings et al. (2017) were questioning the historiography of management and, in this subsection, the historiography of the management of change is more specifically questioned.

> Change management's very construction has been a political process which has written the left out, and shaped an understanding of the field as technocratic and ideologically neutral.
>
> (Cooke, 1999: 81)

Organizational change textbooks often offer a history of how the field of organizational change developed. For example, Burke (2014) presents a chapter entitled "A Brief History of Organization Change" in his textbook (please see Table 4.6).

Table 4.6 is reassuring in suggesting that organizational change is based upon the firm foundations of earlier studies and echoes many concepts in Huczynski's (2006) management ideas families. Returning to Cooke (1999), Table 4.6 appears to be a neutral account of the history of organizational change, but it isn't the definitive

Table 4.6 Forerunners to the modern study of organizational change (based on Burke, 2014)

Scientific management
The Hawthorne studies
Industrial psychology
Survey feedback
Sensitivity training
Sociotechnical systems
Organizational development
The managerial grid
Coercion and confrontation
Management consulting

history of organizational change. It is 'a' history. Certain accounts of history are privileged over others. Some events are depicted as significant, whilst others by implication are not significant. Think back to what was selectively taken from Adam Smith (1776). Cummings (2002) sceptically warned about a general problem with traditional accounts of the history of modern thought, in that pioneering historians got the story 'down pat' so that no significant general history of management has been written subsequently. Accounts of organizational change history are quickly fixed and regarded as objective/neutral, which is ironic given the focus of our studies change. Cooke (1999) revisited key contributions in studying organizational change in order to demonstrate how these author's contributions had been misrepresented in managerialist accounts of their work. The following discussion features what is not acknowledged in the writings of Kurt Lewin and Edgar Schein.

Traditional representations of Kurt Lewin (1890–1947) tend to present him as the most important individual in the history of change management, inventing action research and originating group dynamics (Cooke, 1999). A workshop Lewin organized in New Britain in 1946 is regarded as making change management's potential apparent, however with two exceptions '...the point is never made that the workshop was about relationships between ethnic groups at a time of high levels of inter-ethnic conflict' (Cooke, 1999: 88). Cooke (1999: 92) highlights Lewin challenging laissez-faire leadership and US laissez-faire approaches to economic and social policy. He believed '...that it was right, proper and possible to intervene to effect social change on behalf of the disadvantaged'. The concern is these ideological elements tend to be missing from business school accounts of his contribution to change management. Burnes (2004: 979) subsequently encouraged reappraising the work of Lewin, 'For most of his life Lewin's main preoccupation was the resolution of social conflict and, in particular, the problems of minority or disadvantaged groups.'

Cooke (1999) explained how Schein (1990) regarded the concept of coercive persuasion as integral to theories and practices of organizational culture and leadership (coercive persuasion is discussed further in terms of the dark side of organizations in Chapter 16). His work was informed by his studies of the methods of the Chinese Communist Party (CCP) when he worked as a US army psychologist in the 1950s. However, what is telling in terms of change management historiographies is that coercive persuasion and the CCP which informed his writing are largely omitted.

Also, gender blindness/myopia in traditional historiographies of the management of change is evident (Cooke, 1999). French and Bell's (1984) classic organizational development textbook, failed to acknowledge the contribution of women such as Mouton, Schindler-Rainman, and Seashore in the history of how OD developed. However, in French and Bell's (1996) later edition, their contribution was acknowledged. Whilst, the omission of women from an authoritative history of OD is troubling, it effectively conveys themes of this section that management histories are never neutral and always selective. Nothing changed between the 1984 and 1996 editions in terms of events. However, the change was with regards to organizational scholarship critically perceived at this time as being a literature written by men for men and about men (Calas and Smircich, 1996). Cooke (1999) offers a final cautionary note about management historiography acknowledging that all understanding of management and organization studies is shaped by historiographical processes, with the implication that such processes are applicable to critical as well as acritical perspectives.

Summary

The chapter may be succinctly summarised by answering the questions posed in the chapter's introduction with the original questions restated in italics.

Doing management, what are practitioners doing? The first organizational experiences of students doing placements as part of their degree studies (Fineman and Gabriel, 1996) offer insights into managing. Anna as a placement student wanted to understand first-hand the 'myth' of management in order to solve the 'mystery' of management. CMI's (2017) management manifesto offered insights into current issues for management as reflected by one of their professional bodies.

How do management idea families inform understanding about management? Huczynski (2006) surveyed through content analysis popular management ideas of the twentieth century. Beyond a small number of management writers (Fayol, McGregor, Drucker, Herzberg, Peters, Taylor, Likert and Argyris), there was very little consensus around who were the really influential contributors.

What have been the most influential management idea families? There were only six truly popular management idea families over the past 100 years; bureaucracy, scientific management, administrative management, human relations, neo-human relations and guru theory.

What do we know about the experience of being managed? Floor (2017) highlighted the hallmarks of great management with a reliable barometer believed to be if you are happy in your job. Carter (2016) posed the following question to readers, 'Are you being bullied or performance managed?' And Clarke and Scurry (2017) studied graduate experiences of public sector talent management programmes in the UK and Australia.

How could management good practices be informed by questioning traditional histories of management? If management studies has lost its way (Alvesson and Sandberg, 2013) there may be a need for a new history of management (Cummings et al., 2017). Also, change management practices could be informed by critically exploring popular historiographies of the management of change (Cooke, 1999).

Discussion questions

- What do you like about the CMI's *Management Manifesto* and what would you like to see added?
- What was the problem with the 'old' history of management?
- How does thinking about management studies historically inform/misinform management today?
- How does engaging with the lived experience of being managed inform our understanding of management?

Navigating management studies literature

A large, diverse and at times contradictory body of management studies literature exists which is a starting point for considering managing organizational change. Any engagement with this literature will have to be selective and hopefully, this chapter offers you a roadmap, explaining how broader studies of management might inform managing change. The following suggestions range from the very practical to the very critical so that you can match them to your own particular purposes.

Professional bodies such as the Chartered Management Institute and the Chartered Institute of Personnel and Development work with today's managers and seek to develop tomorrow's managers. In studying management, it is informative to look at how they synthesise and communicate a body of knowledge about management. In a similar manner, textbooks often offer short histories of management which are persuasive and reassuring, but, as the questioning section highlighted, they may misrepresent the complexities of studying management and the ideological way it is presented.

Journals offer more research informed/evidence-based accounts of management studies. *Management Decision* has been popular with MBA students for many years, engaging with both critical and management aspects. Amongst academic journals, the *Journal of Management Studies* and *Human Relations* are highly respected for their scholarly coverage of management studies. Professional groupings of management academics, such as the *British Academy of Management* (BAM) produce informative journals such as the *British Journal of Management* and the *International Journal of Management Reviews*. The latter, as its title suggests, is particularly informative, organized around focussed reviews of management literature. In a similar manner to BAM, the *European Academy of Management* and the American *Academy of Management* produce informative journals. Finally, in terms of journals, there are journals which primarily seek to inform management development and education, such as *Management Learning* and *Academy of Management Learning and Education*.

References

Alvesson, M., and J. Sandberg. 2013. "Has Management Studies Lost Its Way? Ideas For more Imaginative and Innovative Research." *Journal of Management Studies* 50(1): 128–152.

Argyris, C. 1973. "Personality and Organization Theory Revisited." *Administrative Science Quarterly* 18(2): 141–167.

Bresnen, M., P. Hyde, D. Hodgson, S. Bailey, and J. Hassard. 2015. "Leadership Talk: From Managerialism to Leaderism in Health Care After the Crash." *Leadership* 11(4): 451–470.

Burke, W.W. 2014. *Organization Change: Theory and Practice*. Thousand Oaks, CA: Sage Publications.

Burnes, B. 2004. "Kurt Lewin and the Planned Approach to Change: A Re-appraisal." *Journal of Management Studies* 41(6): 977–1002.

Calas, M.B., and L. Smircich. 1996. "From the 'Woman's' Point of View: Feminist Approaches to Organization Studies." In *Handbook on Organizations*, edited by S. Clegg and C. Hardy, 212–252. London: Sage Publications.

Carter, P. 2016. You Can't Handle the Truth: Are You Being Bullied or Performance Managed? HR Zone. Available at www.hrzone.com/perform/people/you-cant-handle-the-truth-are-you-being-bullied-or-performance-managed

Chartered Management Institute. 2017. *Leadership for Change: CMI's Management Manifesto*. London: Chartered Management Institute.

Clarke, M., and T. Scurry. 2017. "The Role of the Psychological Contract in Shaping Graduate Experiences: A Study of Public Sector Talent Management Programmes in the UK and
Australia." *The International Journal of Human Resource Management* (2017) (forthcoming).

Clegg, S., M. Kornberger, and T. Pitsis. 2016. *Managing and Organizations: An Introduction
to Theory and Practice.* London: Sage Publications.

Cooke, B. 1999. "Writing the Left out of Management Theory: The Historiography of the
Management of Change." *Organization* 6(1): 81–105.

Cummings, S. 2002. *Recreating Strategy.* London: Sage Publications.

Cummings, S., T. Bridgman, and K.G. Brown. 2016. "Unfreezing Change as Three Steps: Rethinking Kurt Lewin's Legacy for Change Management." *Human Relations* 69(1): 33–60.

Cummings, S., T. Bridgman., J. Hassard, and M. Rowlinson. 2017. *A New History of Management.* Cambridge: Cambridge University Press.

Drucker, P.F. 1954. *The Practice of Management.* New York: Harper & Row.

Drucker, P.F. 1964. *Managing for Results.* New York: Harper & Row.

Fayol, H. 1949. *General and Industrial Management.* Translated by P. Straws. London: Pitman.

Fineman, S., and Y. Gabriel. 1996. *Experiencing Organizations.* London: Sage Publications.

Floor, H. 2017. "Opinion: Eight Signs You're Being Managed Well." *People Management.*
Available at www2.cipd.co.uk/pm/peoplemanagement/b/weblog/archive/2017/11/01/opinion-
eight-signs-you-re-being-managed-well.aspx

French, W.L., and C.H. Bell. 1984/1996. *Organisation Development: Behavioural Science
Interventions for Organisational Improvement.* Englewood Cliffs, NJ: Prentice Hall.

Gabriel, Y. 2008. *Organizing Words: A Critical Thesaurus for Social and Organization Studies.* Oxford: Oxford University Press.

Herzberg, F., B. Mausner, and B. Snyderman. 1959. *The Motivation to Work.* New York: Wiley.

Huczynski, A. 2006. *Management Gurus,* Revised Edition, London: Routledge.

Lewin, K. 1947. "Frontiers in Group Dynamics: Concept, Method and Reality in Social
Science; Social Equilibria and Social Change." *Human Relations* 1(1): 5–41.

Likert, R. 1967. *The Human Organization: Its Management and Values.* New York: McGraw
Hill.

Mayo, E. 1933. *The Human Problems of an Industrial Civilization.* New York: Macmillan.

McGregor, D. 1960. *The Human Side of Enterprise.* New York: McGraw Hill.

Peters, T.J., and R.H. Waterman. 1982. *In Search of Excellence.* New York: Harper and Row.

Schein, E.H. 1990. *Organizational Culture and Leadership.* San Francisco: Jossey Bass.

Smith, A. 1776. *An Inquiry into the Nature and Causes of the Wealth of Nations.* Editor
Edward Canaan (1937). New York: Random House.

Taylor, F.W. 1911. *The Principles of Scientific Management.* New York: Harper and Row.

Watson, T. 1986. *Management, Organisation and Employment Strategy: New Directions in
Theory and Practice.* London: Routledge.

Watson, T. 2006. *Organising and Managing Work.* Harlow: FT Prentice Hall.

Weber, M. 1947. *The Theory of Social and Economic Organization.* Glencoe, IL: Free Press.

Chapter 5

History, learning and organizational change

Introduction and chapter questions

Organizational change theories and practices often look forward to successful futures. However, the past in terms of history and learning potentially has a significant role to play in these theories and practices. In this chapter, the focus shifts to history and learning with specific reference to organizational change, with the caveat that a textbook could be devoted to either organizational history or organizational learning. The chapter builds on the previous chapter which introduced the concept of historiography with particular reference to management studies. Suddaby and Foster (2017: 20) recently reminded us about the centrality of history to theories and practices of organizational change, 'Our explicit theories of change and our ability to change, thus, vary by our implicit models of history.' And in terms of organizational learning, learning has been described as a dynamic transformational process which is continuously extended and redefined in response to the context in which it takes place (Antonacopoulou and Gabriel, 2001).

Whilst such views are favoured in this chapter, they are not the orthodoxy. In *Leading Change*, Kotter (1996: 142) wrote 'cleaning up historical artifacts does create an even longer change agenda, which an exhausted organization will not like. But purging of unnecessary interconnections can ultimately make a transformation much easier.' Kotter in problematizing history and by association learning from the past may be missing a significant element of managing and leading organizational change. Stadler and Hinterhuber (2005) studied historically how strategic change had been led in Shell, Siemens and Daimler Chrysler. They found that negative aspects of change could have been avoided if leaders had taken into account the histories of the organizations they were leading and in particular recognised and acknowledged the company's core values. Whereas what they often encountered were charismatic and overambitious leaders failing to learn from past experiences of their respective organizations.

Engaging with history and learning is complicated by definitional issues relating to history and learning. The concept of historiography suggests that multiple competing accounts of history exist. So although Stadler and Hinterhuber (2005) studied documents informing them about the recent histories of Shell, Siemens, and Daimler Chrysler, they were inevitably selective. They had to work with an assumption that their historical accounts of Shell, Siemens, and Daimler Chrysler were the authoritative accounts of these organizational histories, but different authors would probably have offered different accounts of the histories of these companies. Consequently, in this chapter, there is a focus on organizational history with the caveat that multiple accounts of such histories will always exist, rather than a singular authoritative account of organizational history.

One of the challenges of studying organizational learning is that a consensus definition of organizational learning does not exist. So, for this chapter, the following definition of organizational learning is favoured.

> ...a learning process within organizations that involves the interaction of individual and collective (group, organizational, and inter-organizational) levels of analysis and leads to achieving organizations' goals.
>
> (Popova-Nowak and Cseh, 2015: 299)

What is particularly useful about this definition is that it draws attention to learning at the level of individuals, groups and whole organizations. Popova-Nowak and Cseh (2015) acknowledge organizational learning and learning organization being used interchangeably and the learning organization will be discussed subsequently with particular reference to the writings of Senge (1990/2006). Again Popova-Nowak and Cseh's (2015: 300) definition of the learning organization is useful in introducing the debate '...a type of organization with several characteristics that facilitate learning processes within it: continuous learning, inquiry and dialogue, collaborative team learning, empowerment, leadership, systems that capture and share learning, global thinking, and strategic leadership.' However, by way of a cautionary note, when Popova-Nowak and Cseh (2015) searched for meaning in the organizational learning literature, they encountered multiple tentative answers to novel questions, with a lack of consistency in theoretical frameworks.

This chapter is organized around and provides answers to the following questions about the role of history and learning in organizations with specific reference to processes of organizational change.

- How do organizations learn from past experiences?
- How does the concept of organizational history potentially relate to organizational change?
- What is organizational learning and what do we know about it?
- What are learning organizations and what do we know about them?
- What assumptions inform history and organizational change?
- What are the critiques of organization learning and learning organizations?
- What do we know about organizational unlearning and forgetting?

In the next section, firsthand insights into how organizational members learn from the past and why they should learn from the past are offered. The concept of organizational history is introduced and applied to organizational change. This is followed by a similar introduction and application of the closely related concepts of organizational learning and the learning organization. In the questioning section, three more critical themes are developed. First, assumptions informing history and organizational change are highlighted. Second, critiques of organizational learning and the learning organization are presented. Third, critical notions of organizational unlearning and organizational forgetting are introduced.

What are practitioners doing? How do organizations learn from past experiences?

Business historians Seaman and Smith (2012: 46) in the *Harvard Business Review* practitioner magazine made the case for leaders using their company histories as a tool to shape the future, 'In its most familiar form, as a narrative about the past, history is a rich explanatory tool with which executives can make a case for change and motivate people to overcome challenges.' They offer a series of practical tips (please see Table 5.1) on how to use organizational history.

Instead of cleaning up historical artifacts (Kotter, 1996), Table 5.1 highlights how historical artifacts become a resource for leaders to utilise when leading change.

> Because a shared history is central to group identity, past experiences can be summoned up in times of great challenge and change to inspire people's energy and commitment.
>
> (Seaman and Smith, 2012: 47)

The implication is that in looking to the future, organizations should not forget their past. Another way to look to the future, yet to also learn is through the development of a learning and development (L&D) strategy. The Chartered Institute of Personnel and Development (CIPD) publicised best practice advice on how an L&D strategy might be developed (please see Table 5.2).

Table 5.1 Seven tips for getting history on your side

Tip	Description
No.1	Visit your corporate archives or begin compiling them.
No.2	Interview departing executives and long-tenured employees in order to enrich the archives.
No.3	Establish what is known and understood about the history and values of the company.
No.4	Use today's media to engage audiences inside and outside the organization in an ongoing dialogue about the meaning of the past to the company.
No.5	Conduct post-mortems on projects and major initiatives, recognising that you can learn from failure, as well as, success.
No.6	Seek a historical perspective before making major decisions.
No.7	Talk about history at every opportunity in terms of what it says about the company you are today or want to become.

Table 5.2 Introducing a learning and development strategy (based on CIPD, 2017 fact sheet)

What is a learning and development strategy?	CIPD (2017) offers the following definition: 'a learning and development (L&D) strategy is an organizational strategy that articulates the workforce capabilities, skills or competencies required, and how these can be developed, to ensure a sustainable, successful organization.'
What are the influences on an L&D strategy?	The following are influences on an L&D strategy: business strategy, operational and cultural factors. They encourage valuing talent and keeping the strategy updated.
How do you align stakeholders with an L&D strategy?	CIPD (2017) encourages a RAM approach. Ensuring the strategies' *relevance* to business challenges. Ensuring *alignment* with other strategies in the business. And *measuring* through effective and consistent evaluation.
How do you turn the L&D strategy into action?	An L&D strategy is a statement of intent. More specific factors which need to be addressed include; setting L&D priorities, performance management and appraisal and the provision of budgets and resources.

Source: CIPD (2017) Learning and development strategy: An introduction. www.cipd.co.uk/knowledge/strategy/development/factsheet. Accessed 17 November 2017.

Table 5.2 recognises that organizations are interested in learning and the development of strategies to encourage learning and development. Processes of organizational learning will be discussed subsequently.

Theories and practices of organizational change go in and out of fashion as different ideas capture the imagination of scholars and practitioners. *Reflections* was a journal which bought together organizational learning researchers, consultants and practising managers (launched in 1998). In 2015, the Society for Organizational Learning (SoL) North America Council made the difficult decision to discontinue publication of *Reflections* (see Molloy and Wallace, 2015 for further discussion). Only time will tell if this development was indicative of practitioner interest moving away from organizational learning.

Understanding organizational history and organizational learning

> ...organizational learning is the process through which the past affects the present and the future.
>
> (Argote, 2011: 439)

In this section, three overlapping themes of organizational history, organizational learning, and the learning organization are introduced, major contributions to these debates acknowledged with each theme related to organizational change.

Organizational history

In 2006, a new journal was launched in which the founding editors offered a ten-point agenda for management and organizational history (please see Table 5.3).

Table 5.3 Ten-point agenda for management and organizational history

	Agenda point	Description
1	The 'historic turn in organization theory'	A more historical orientation in management and organization theory.
2	Historical methods and styles of writing	Alternative methods and diverse styles of writing appropriate for studying organizations historically.
3	The philosophy and historical theorists	The relevance for management and organization theory of philosophers of history.
4	Corporate culture and social memory	The historical dimension of culture and memory in organizations.
5	Organizational history	The emergence of a distinctive field of research.
6	Business history and theory	The engagement between business history and organization theory.
7	Business ethics in history	The meaning and ethics of past business behaviour.
8	Metanarratives of corporate capitalism	Historiographical debate concerning the rise of capitalism and the modern corporation.
9	Management history and management education	The link between the history of management thought and the teaching of management and organization theory.
10	Public history	The relation between business schools and increasing public interest in history.

The launch of a new journal with its ten-point agenda (please see Table 5.3) highlighted growing interest in and engagement with organizational history (see Mills et al., 2016 revisiting the ten-point agenda). In the following discussion, Table, 5.3 is selectively drawn upon. Numbered points related to organizational change are signposted in brackets. Increasingly we acknowledge the historic turn in organization theory (1) hence its discussion in this organizational change textbook. The historic turn acts as a counterpoint to universalism viewing organizational theory as applying to all societies at all times. It also acts as a counterpoint to presentism, viewing research as being reported as if it occurred in a decontextualised and extended present.

> ...the present is often assumed to be a period of unprecedented change, heralding the dawning of a new age. But this is usually done without proper consideration of possible historical precedents.
>
> (Booth and Rowlinson, 2006: 6)

In this quotation, we see a recurrent shortcoming in much of the prescriptive organizational change literature. This is the idea that we are living through times of unprecedented change. Chapter 6 focuses on corporate culture and its manageability. Interest in corporate culture amongst practitioners and academics in the 1980s gave impetus to studying organizational history in terms of its influence on corporate culture and social memory (4). History also gives us a longitudinal perspective in studying organizational cultural change.

There is a need for current interest in ethics and corporate social responsibility to be grounded in history (7). For example, Booth and Rowlinson (2006) cite private company involvement with the Third Reich. In terms of organizational change, Kotter's (1996) analysis was based on observations of companies he was working with as a Harvard Business School (HBS) professor, although he anonymised the names of these companies. What we do now know is that HBS had a very close relationship with Enron at the time Kotter was writing.

> Harvard Business School produced five glowing case studies on Enron, the last of which was published in August 2001, only a few months prior to Enron's collapse. Harvard professors co-authored books with Enron officers and reaped generous financial rewards for their services for Enron.
>
> (Eun-jung, 2015: 30)

Dark side activities of Enron will feature in Chapter 16. HBS producing glowing case studies based on Enron is informative with regard to the choice of best practice case studies, given that management history and management education are closely aligned (9).

There is a need for caution with regards to the historiography of management studies as discussed in the previous chapter. Booth and Rowlinson (2006) highlight a textbook tendency to separate management and organization history from the specific theme of the textbook. Instead, they favour the integration of history into management and organization studies. Acknowledging the relevance of history encourages an appreciation of organizational learning, the focus of the next subsection.

Organizational learning

Easterby-Smith and Lyles (2011a) in their introductory chapter to their organizational learning and knowledge management handbook, suggest that it was a conference two decades earlier which gave impetus to organizational learning. Presentations at the conference were subsequently published in a special issue of *Organization Science* in 1991. Since then, they suggest that there has been a rapid expansion of interest in organizational learning. In terms of differentiating organizational learning from the learning organization, Tsang (1997) regarded organization learning as referring to the academic study of learning processes of/and within organizations (please see also, Argyris, 1999). He (1997) differentiated the learning organization as an ideal type with the capacity to learn effectively and prosper, where the focus was more on practical impact and the improvement agenda.

The earliest accounts of organizational learning have been attributed to Cyert and March (1963) and Cangelosi and Dill (1965). Easterby-Smith and Lyles (2011b) regarded Cyert and March's (1963) book as a key breakthrough with the authors introducing the idea that an organization could learn and that knowledge could be stored over time. They emphasised the role of rules, procedures and routines in response to external shocks in explaining how an organization adapts to its environment. Cangelosi and Dill (1965) highlighted tensions between individual and organizational learning. This was to be a theme developed further particularly by Argyris and Schon (1978). They differed from Cyert and March (1963) in that they highlighted human behaviour not following the lines of economic rationality.

Argote's (2011) overview of the past, present, and future of organizational learning research, is particularly informative in differentiating different streams of thought which inform the concept of organizational learning. In terms of the past, Argote (2011) highlights three streams, the contributions of Cyert and March (1963) and Argyris and Schon (1978) have already been acknowledged and she adds a third stream referred to as the 'learning curve' tradition citing Dutton and Thomas (1984) as illustrative of this stream. Subsequently, a co-mingling of these streams has occurred as well as new currents developing. One current related to the role of experience in organizational learning processes and outcomes, focusses on how organizational learning occurs as organizations acquire experience, another current relates to the importance of the context in which learning occurred. Context moderates the relationship between learning processes, outcomes, and experiences. So, learning in a small church will be profoundly different from learning in a large international merchant bank. Another current of organizational learning processes relates to creating, retaining and transferring knowledge, with an acknowledgement that more work had been done on knowledge retention and transfer than on knowledge creation.

Argote (2011) encouraged further work on the current themes but also highlighted opportunities for organizational learning research. These related to more attention to how knowledge is created and greater understanding of how dynamic capabilities in strategic management develop through organizational learning. The use of multiple methods for organizational learning research was encouraged using qualitative interpretive methods. New forms of organizing, such as virtual organizations, were regarded as making it harder for organizations to interpret experience, but also provided opportunities to learn from new sources of experience. In a similar manner, developments in technology raised challenges and opportunities for organizational learning researchers.

Learning organization

It was the publication of Peter Senge's (1990) book *The Fifth Discipline* which gave real impetus to theories and practices of the learning organization (Mintzberg et al., 2009). However, notions of the learning organization were evident in earlier writings of Argyris and Schon (1978), Peters and Waterman (1982) and Deming (1986). Subsequently, Pedler et al.'s (1991) 'learning company', 'the living company' of De Geus (1997) and Nonaka's (2008) 'knowledge-creating company' may be regarded as variations on the notion of a learning organization.

The learning organization as envisaged by Senge (1990) was comprised of five component technologies/disciplines: systems thinking, personal mastery, mental models, building a shared vision and team learning. Systems thinking was to become an important element within the concept of the learning organization making connections with academics and practitioners who were interested in systems and complexity. Personal mastery spoke to the tacit knowledge that we often possess, which is often unacknowledged. In particular, Senge (1990) was interested in the existence and acknowledgement of high levels of proficiency within organizations. It is through mental models that we make sense of the world. So for example, a mental model might relate to working hard and being successful in the belief of being promoted if the hard work and success are recognised and valued. The mental model does not mean this will be the case, but it does offer a means of organizing thinking. Senge (1990) was interested in understanding mental models at work and subsequently the language of 'mental models' has been adopted in the workplace (please see Marshak, 2006 for further discussion about mental models with regards to organizational change). In a similar manner 'building a shared vision' has become common language in many workplaces. However, for Senge (1990), this shared vision was to be developed by people working together. Finally, there was an emphasis on team learning recognising that the intelligence of the team exceeded that of its individual members (please see Chapter 8, for further discussion about groups and teams). Senge (2006) published a second edition of *The Fifth Discipline* and despite many significant developments between 1990 and 2006, the book remained largely the same.

Senge et al. (2014: 1) reflected upon the twenty-fifth anniversary of *The Fifth Discipline,* with Peter Senge stating 'a lot has changed in the world in 25 years, but to me it always seems like we're doing more or less the same thing...in many ways, the main thing that has changed is the context of work'. Senge explained how initially *The Fifth Discipline* captured the imagination of businesses, but subsequently, it engaged civil society and government and this development appeared to be important to him.

Questioning organizational history and organizational learning

In this questioning section, assumptions informing the historic turn in organizational change studies are highlighted, as well as, major criticisms of organizational learning and the learning organization. In recent years, there has been increasing interest in understanding the closely related concepts of unlearning and forgetting in organizations and these concepts are introduced.

History and organizational change

Suddaby and Foster's (2017) recent guest editorial on the theme of 'history and organizational change' is the focus of this subsection. Normally, the questioning section critically questions theories offered in earlier sections. However, in this instance both authors co-authored Mills et al.'s (2016) revisiting of the ten-point management and organizational history agenda as advanced by Booth and Rowlinson (2006). Suddaby and Foster (2017) identify four implicit models of history in the change literature: History-as-Fact, History-as-Power, History-as-Sensemaking, and History-as-Rhetoric, relevant to debates featured in this chapter, but also to debates featured throughout this textbook.

Theories and practices of organizational change are underpinned by different assumptions about history featured in each of the four models. Assumptions have implications for our ability to effect change (agency), define change and the perceived difficulty of changing. Suddaby and Foster (2017) major on introducing and explaining each assumption about history and organizational change. Each assumption is briefly introduced with particular emphasis on variations.

History-as-Fact: This assumption highlights shock as a trigger for organizational change, with a focus on structure as the unit of change and change as occurring incrementally. This assumption depicts history as objective, 'these assumptions suggest that because time and history reduce agency, change is very difficult to accomplish because any change effort must face the herculean task of overcoming the past' (Suddaby and Foster, 2017: 21).

History-as-Power: This assumption highlights conflict as a trigger for change, with a focus on power relations as the unit of change and change occurring episodically. This assumption highlights history as objective. The focal point here is power structures of the various coalitions or entities within an organization.

History-as-Sensemaking: This assumption highlights reflexivity as a trigger for change, with a focus on meaning as the unit of change and change as being understood retrospectively. This assumption highlights history as subjective. The emphasis here is on reality consisting of experiences, objects and events in human consciousness, rather than in reality of experiences, objects, and events typified by history-as-fact assumptions.

History-as-Rhetoric: This assumption highlights plurality as the trigger for change, with the focus on narratives as the unit of change and change occurring instrumentally. This assumption highlights history as subjective 'participants in processes of organizational change are assumed to have high degrees of agency in creating narratives of the past designed to facilitate strategic change in organizations' (Suddaby and Foster, 2017: 30).

Critiques of organizational learning/learning organization

There are academics and practitioners of organizational learning/learning organizations who favour such approaches to organizational change. However, even amongst proponents, there will be critiques of competing theories, models and concepts. This was what Popova-Nowak and Cseh (2015) were alluding to when they encountered a lack of consistency in theoretical frameworks.

Argyris (1999), a key contributor to debates about organizational learning, high-lighted challenges that it was contradictory, that it was a meaningful notion, but not always beneficial and he asked do organizations really learn? Theories of learning in general and organizational learning in particular – begin from a starting point of individual learning. Argyris (1999) believed that prescriptions such as Senge's offered useful guides with regards to enabling productive organizational learning. However, he did have concerns with regards to analytical difficulties being ignored, no real at-tention paid to processes threatening the validity and utility of organizational learn-ing, and a lack of attention to implementation difficulties. Critiques of the learning organization have been offered by Jackson (2001), Coopey (2004), Friedman et al. (2005) and Ortenblad (2007). Mintzberg et al. (2009: 237) were very pragmatic about organizational learning writing: 'the learning organization is all the rage right now, and mostly for good reason. But it is no panacea for anything. People have to learn, but they also have to get on with doing the regular work efficiently (Horses wear blinders for good reason).'

Caldwell's (2012) critique of Senge's (1990) learning organization published in the *Journal of Change Management* is particularly relevant given his emphasis on organ-izational change aspects of the learning organization. Caldwell (2012) avoids the uni-versalism Booth and Rowlinson (2006) warned about at the beginning of the chapter recognising the promise Senge's (1990) learning organization offered at the time it was proposed. The book offered readers a moral vision of re-humanising American workplaces through challenging notions of bureaucratic corporations and top-down change leadership. Instead, broader systemic and ecological virtues of community shared learning and personal development were encouraged. Caldwell's (2012) cri-tique had two major respects. First, Senge's (1990/2006) systems/structural model was theoretically flawed. Second, the model was substantively flawed as a model for increasing the dispersal of human agency, power, knowledge, and autonomy in work-places. Caldwell's (2012: 17) critical review concludes '...Senge's learning organiza-tion never really matched up to these theoretical and practical challenges, and we must now countenance its final abandonment as a vision of organizational change and human agency.'

Organizational unlearning and forgetting

Starbuck (2017) was recently invited to reflect on his contributions to debates about organizational learning and unlearning over many decades. A major insight was that organizational and academic interest in organizational learning may have been at the expense of understanding organizational unlearning, which he be-lieved was particularly evident at times of crisis. Although learning often produces undesirable outcomes, people might be able to discard or ignore what they have learned.

Starbuck et al. (1978) encountered behaviours which they decided to call 'unlearn-ing' during their studies of companies that were facing very serious crises. What they discovered through their case study research was that the companies that they were studying were dependent on their previous methods of working. They struggled to unlearn because they were unable to discover what was wrong with their previous learning. Half of their case study companies closed with 'weathering the storm' consuming large amounts of financial and human resources. However, half of their case study companies became profitable again, although this invariably involved the replacement of all senior managers who were unable to unlearn what had served them well in the past.

> Learning changes more than just the knowledge in people's brains; it also alters behaviors and physical objects.
>
> (Starbuck, 2017: 32)

When organizations faced severe crises which challenged the existence of the organization, senior managers invariably did not have relevant experience of such crises, yet they were unable to unlearn their old behaviours.

Organizational forgetting

De Holan and Phillips' (2011) contribution to the *Handbook of Organizational Learning and Knowledge Management,* draws upon their earlier writings about organizational forgetting. The concept offers a critical counterpoint to preoccupations with organizational learning and learning organizations, as well as, knowledge management. The concept also relates to notions of organizational history and organizational memory, perhaps we underestimate organizational forgetting. They acknowledge that we know far less about organizational forgetting than knowledge creation and transfer, but that understanding organizational forgetting is important. De Holan and Phillips (2011) highlight empirical and theoretical work underpinning organizational forgetting. Just as organizations can acquire new knowledge, they can lose knowledge either purposely or voluntarily. Knowledge may be lost through unlearning as discussed in the previous subsection. However, a parallel stream of thinking has developed around the negative consequences of forgetting.

In Table 5.4, De Holan and Phillips (2011) offer a useful differentiation between forgetting and unlearning. They highlight the unintentional way established knowledge is lost, whereas unlearning established knowledge is regarded as more purposeful. In their conclusions, they are candid that understanding organizational forgetting is still a work in progress. They encourage further research in three areas which helps to synthesise their insights. First, some knowledge loss is involuntary referred to as forgetting. They encourage further research into causes of forgetting, types of errors and mishaps that increase forgetting error rates. Second, some knowledge loss is voluntary, what has been referred to as unlearning. They regard such unlearning as an organizational capability, particularly with regard to its impact on the success of organizational change (please see the previous subsection). Third, they raise an issue about why some new knowledge is successfully integrated into the memory system when other new knowledge isn't. In particular, they suggest an interesting research agenda around where knowledge is embedded into an organization, in terms of

Table 5.4 Modes of organizational forgetting (based on De Holan and Phillips, 2011)

	New knowledge	Established knowledge
Unintentional	Failed innovation	Forgetting
Purposeful	Aborted learning	Unlearning

routines, structures, understandings, and assets. Mena et al. (2016) have conceptualised how corporate irresponsibility may be forgotten. They regard such collective forgetting as potentially having positive and negative consequences.

Summary

The chapter may be succinctly summarised through answering the questions posed in the chapter's introduction. The original questions are restated in italics.

How are organizations learning from the past? Leaders potentially use their company histories as a narrative about the past, providing a rich explanatory tool with which executives make a case for change motivating people to overcome challenges (Seaman and Smith, 2012). Organizations may develop a learning and development strategy, following CIPD (2017) best practice advice.

How does the concept of organizational history potentially relate to organizational change? Increasingly we are acknowledging the historic turn in organization theory as a counterpoint to universalism and presentism. Engaging with culture and cultural change requires the study of organizational history in terms of its influence on culture and social memory. Current interest in ethics and corporate social responsibility needs to be grounded in history as management history and management education are closely aligned.

What is organizational learning and what do we know about it? Organization learning refers to the academic study of learning processes of/and within organizations (Tsang, 1997). Argote's (2011) overview of the past, present, and future of organizational learning research, differentiates different streams of thought which inform the concept of organizational learning.

What are learning organizations and what do we know about them? The learning organization is an entity/ideal type with the capacity to learn effectively and prosper, where the focus is more on practical impact and the improvement agenda (Tsang, 1997). The publication of Senge's (1990) book *The Fifth Discipline* gave real impetus to theories and practices of the learning organization and was comprised of five component technologies/disciplines; systems thinking, personal mastery, mental models, building a shared vision and team learning.

What assumptions inform history and organizational change? Suddaby and Foster (2017) identify four implicit models of history in the change literature: History-as-Fact, History-as-Power, History-as-Sensemaking, and History-as-Rhetoric.

What are the critiques of organization learning and learning organizations? Argyris (1999) highlighted accounts of organizational learning being contradictory and, although it was a meaningful notion, it was not always beneficial and awkwardly did organizations really learn? Subsequently, Popova-Nowak and Cseh (2015) reviewed the literature encountering a lack of consistency in theoretical frameworks. Caldwell (2012) critiqued Senge's (1990/2006) learning organization as a systems/structural model which was theoretically flawed and substantively flawed as a model for increasing the dispersal of human agency, power, knowledge, and autonomy in workplaces.

What do we know about organizational unlearning and forgetting? Organizational and academic interest in organizational learning may have been at the expense of understanding organizational unlearning. Although learning often produces undesirable outcomes, people might be able to discard or ignore what they have learned (Starbuck, 2017). This unlearning potentially could be purposeful, whereas De Holan and Phillips (2011) highlighted the prevalence of organizational forgetting which is unintentional.

Research case study showcase: Facit's inability to change

The Facit case study reported by Starbuck (2017) in *The Learning Organization* is showcased here. For the full case and further analysis, please visit the original source.

Case study source

Starbuck, W.H. 2017. "Organizational Learning and Unlearning." *The Learning Organization* 24(1): 30–38.

The case study

Facit was a Swedish company in the 1970s making and selling office equipment, which included typewriters. However, their core products were the best mechanical calculators in the world. They hired the best mechanical engineers in order to design calculators which were faster and smaller than those made by their competitors. Over time, engineering knowledge was embedded into the calculators as well as knowledge about the needs and abilities of people using their mechanical calculators. The company borrowed large amounts of money to build modern factories enabling Facit to make large numbers of calculators at low unit costs.

Facit's success was informed by their 50 years of experience in that they had learned where to locate factories and work procedures with regards to factory layout and smooth work flows. They utilised specialist machinery which sped up production and production of products of the highest quality. Their considerable experience informed how they selected and trained employees, the inventory they kept on hand and knowing the dependable suppliers. Sales personnel knew customers' buying preferences and their frequency of purchases. Facit's management were very knowledgeable about mechanical engineering, technologies and Facit customers enabling them to profitably run the company. Accumulated learning allowed them to operate very effectively despite personnel changes and changes in product features and economic conditions. These changes created only minor disturbances in their way of operating.

The downside to their way of operating was that, whilst efficient, they ignored some features in their environment. Equally, although their personnel selection, training and promotion meant that people were good at doing what they had learned to do, they lacked other capabilities. Their mechanical engineers were very up to date with the latest mechanical technologies, but this was at the expense of paying attention to developments in electronics happening at this time. Their senior managers who understood mechanical engineering did not want to venture into different technologies which would make their knowledge and experience obsolete.

The standardisation and routinisation meant skills and plant layouts which worked so well for making mechanical calculators, would require substantial changes for electronic calculators. Facit in regarding its competitive environment as making and selling mechanical calculators did very little scanning of the development of electronic devices and the companies making them.

Subsequently, senior management at Facit were surprised by the arrival of small hand-held calculators manufactured by competitors. They reassured themselves that electronic calculators might take some of their business, but that this loss would be a small fraction of their income. When their sales personnel interviewed their customers about whether the customers would switch, they reported that their customers said they would continue to buy mechanical calculators. However, Facit profits turned negative for three consecutive years and sales and employment dropped. In response, the company attempted re-organizations, replacing the general manager several times. Each new general manager predicted a turnaround, but the turnaround never happened.

The companies' office equipment and typewriter plants were sold to generate cash, in order to enable selling mechanical calculators at a loss. Finally, senior management conceded that electronic calculators constituted a technological revolution that they were unable to embrace. Facit did subsequently experience a resurrection, but as a computer company instead of an electronic calculator company.

Case study questions

1   Why was Facit's learning around successfully manufacturing mechanical calculators an impediment to manufacturing electronic calculators?
2   How might embracing the concepts of forgetting and unlearning have enabled Facit to act differently?

Discussion questions

1   What are the challenges of relating organizational history to organizational change?
2   Why did organization learning capture the imagination of senior managers?
3   Why is organizational learning often missed?
4   Why do you think that organization unlearning has largely been overlooked?

Navigating organizational history and organizational learning literature

In engaging with organizational history and organizational learning literature, a common dilemma for this textbook is raised. Each of these subfields is informed by its own body of literature and the literature from the disciplines of history and education respectively. The subfield of knowledge management has also been touched upon. The implication is that there will not be a neatly bounded history, learning and organizational change body of literature. Instead, any literature will have to draw from different sources. One way to begin to address this challenge is through identifying academic journals which focus on these different subfields. Whilst these issues could feature in most general management and organization studies journals, the following may help in giving an overview of the debates.

In terms of organizational history, *Management and Organizational History* is very relevant to the issues featured in this chapter and benefits from its critical perspective. Also, *Business History* is relevant with a strong emphasis on empirical historical studies. In terms of organizational learning, *Management Learning* is another critical journal with papers often focussing on organizational learning. There is also *The Learning Organization*, which is an applied journal and *Academy of Management, Learning and Education* is also worth checking out. The *Journal of Knowledge Management* commenced in 1997 with six issues now published every year. *Reflections* has featured in this chapter and was published between 1998 and 2015. It is very relevant to this chapter given its focus on knowledge, learning and change. Papers published in the journal, typically had an applied orientation. In looking to journals with a specific focus, even if the papers published are not particularly relevant, the end-of-paper references offer an overview of the literature as identified by the author of the paper. In *Organizational Learning* (Harvard Business Review, 2001) classic articles published in *Harvard Business Review* are gathered together. Whilst, the articles are inevitably dated, they do feature some of the major contributors to debates around organizational learning.

References

Antonacopoulou, E.P., and Y. Gabriel. 2001. "Emotion, Learning and Organizational Change: Towards an Integration of Psychoanalytic and Other Perspectives." *Journal of Organizational Change Management* 14(5): 435–451.

Argote, L. 2011. "Organizational Learning Research: Past, Present and Future." *Management Learning* 42(4): 439–446.

Argyris C. 1999. *On Organizational Learning*, Oxford: Blackwell.

Argyris, C., and D. Schon. 1978. *Organizational Learning: A Theory of Action Approach*. Reading, MA: Addision Wesley.

Booth, C., and M. Rowlinson. 2006. "Management and Organizational History: Prospects." *Management & Organizational History* 1(1): 5–30.

Caldwell, R. 2012. "Systems Thinking, Organizational Change and Agency: A Practice Theory Critique of Senge's Learning Organization." *Journal of Change Management* 12(2): 145–164.

Cangelosi, V., and W. Dill. 1965. "Organizational Learning: Observations Toward a Theory." *Administrative Science Quarterly* 10(2): 175–203.

CIPD. 2017. Learning and Development Strategy: An Introduction. Available at https://www.cipd.co.uk/knowledge/strategy/development/factsheet.

Coopey, J. 2004. "Crucial Gaps in the 'Learning Organization': Power, Politics and Ideology." In *How Organizations Learn: Managing the Search for Knowledge*, edited by K. Starkey, S. Tempest, and A. McKinlay, 525–542. London: Thomson Learning.

Cyert, R.M., and J.G. March. 1963. *A Behavioral Theory of the Firm*. Englewood Cliffs, NJ: Wiley.

De Geus, A. 1997. *The Living Company: Habits for Survival in a Turbulent Environment*. London: Nicholas Brealey.

De Holan, P.M., and N. Phillips. 2011. "Organizational Forgetting." In *Handbook of Organizational Learning and Knowledge Management* edited by M. Easterby-Smith, and M.A. Lyles, 433–452. Chichester: John Wiley.

Deming, W.E. 1986. *Out of the Crisis*. Cambridge: Cambridge University Press.

Dutton, J.M., and A. Thomas. 1984. "Treating Progress Functions as a Managerial Opportunity." *Academy of Management Review* 9(2): 235–247.

Easterby-Smith, M., and M.A. Lyles (Eds). 2011a. *Handbook of Organizational Learning and Knowledge Management*. Chichester: John Wiley & Sons.

Easterby-Smith, M., and M.A. Lyles. 2011b. "The Evolving Field of Organizational Learning and Knowledge Management." In *Handbook of Organizational Learning and Knowledge Management* edited by M. Easterby-Smith and M.A. Lyles, 1–22. Chichester: John Wiley & Sons.

Eun-jung, S. 2015. *Verita$: Harvard's Hidden History*. Oakland, CA: PM Press.

Friedman, V., R. Lipshitz, and M. Popper. 2005. "The Mystification of Organizational Learning." *Journal of Management Inquiry* 14(1): 19–30.

Harvard Business Review. 2001. *Harvard Business Review on Organizational Learning*. Boston, MA: Harvard Business School Press.

Jackson, B. 2001. *Management Gurus and Management Fashions*. Routledge: London.

Kotter, J. 1996. *Leading Change*. Boston, MA: Harvard Business School Press.

Marshak, R.J. 2006. *Covert Processes at Work: Managing the Five Hidden Dimensions of Organizational Change*. San Francisco, CA: Berrett-Koehler Publishers.

Mena, S., J. Rintamäki, P. Fleming, and A. Spicer. 2016. "On the Forgetting of Corporate Irresponsibility." *Academy of Management Review* 41(4): 720–738.

Mills, A.J., R. Suddaby, W.M. Foster, and G. Durepos. 2016. "Re-visiting the Historic Turn 10 Years Later: Current Debates in Management and Organizational History – An Introduction." *Management and Organizational History* 11(2): 67–76.

Mintzberg, H., B. Ahlstrand, and J. Lampel. 2009. *Strategy Safari: The Complete Guide Through the Wilds of Strategic Management*. London: FT Prentice Hall.

Molloy, J., and D. Wallace. 2015. "From the Editors, Publisher's Note 14.4." *Reflections*, 14(4): ii–ii.

Nonaka, I. 2008. *The Knowledge-Creating Company*. Boston, MA: Harvard Business School Press.

Ortenblad, A. 2007. "Senge's Many Faces: Problem or Opportunity?" *The Learning Organization*, 14(2): 108–122.

Pedler, M., J. Burgoyne, and T. Boydell. 1991 and 1997. *The Learning Company: A Strategy for Sustainable Development*. London: McGraw Hill.

Peters T.J., and R.H. Waterman. 1982. *In Search of Excellence: Lessons from America's Best Run Companies*. New York: Harper & Row.

Popova-Nowak, I.V., and M. Cseh. 2015. "The Meaning of Organizational Learning: A Meta-Paradigm Perspective." *Human Resource Development Review* 14(3): 299–331.

Seaman, J.T., and G.D. Smith. 2012. "Your Company's History as a Leadership Tool." *Harvard Business Review* 90(12): 44–52.

Senge, P. 1990 and 2006. *The Fifth Discipline: The Art and Practice of the Learning Organisation*. London: Random House Business Books.

Senge, P., with F. Schneider, and D. Wallace. 2014. "Peter Senge on the 25th Anniversary of The Fifth Discipline." *Reflections* 14(3): 1–12.

Stadler, C., and H.H. Hinterhuber. 2005. "Shell, Siemens and Daimler Chrysler: Leading Change in Companies with Strong Values." *Long Range Planning* 38(5): 467–484.

Starbuck, W.H. 2017. "Organizational Learning and Unlearning." *The Learning Organization* 24(1): 30–38.

Starbuck, W.H., A. Greve, and B.L.T. Hedberg. 1978. "Responding to Crises." *Journal of Business Administration* 9(2): 111–137.

Suddaby, R., and W.M. Foster. 2017. "History and Organizational Change." *Journal of Management* 43(1): 19–38.

Tsang, E.W. 1997. "Organizational Learning and the Learning Organization: A Dichotomy Between Descriptive and Prescriptive Research." *Human Relations* 50(1): 73–89.

Chapter 6

Organizational cultural change

Introduction and chapter questions

> Organizational culture is one of the major issues in academic research and education, in organization theory as well as in management practice. There are good reasons for this: the cultural dimension is central in all aspects of organizational life.
>
> (Alvesson, 2013: 1)

Alvesson's (2013) opening quotation highlights the all-pervasive nature of organizational culture. Organizational culture touches upon all aspects of organizational life ranging from introducing new technology through to employee engagement. In this sense, this chapter connects with many other chapters in this textbook. For example, there are overlaps with organizational identity discussed in Chapter 7 and Groupthink discussed in Chapter 8. A change initiative may not be labelled as a cultural change, yet all significant change initiatives require and assume that a change in organizational culture will take place. There is a danger in managers emphasising change agendas which ignore the cultural dimension of change work (McCalman and Potter, 2015). Organizational culture is closely related to national culture with each form of culture potentially informing the other. Hofstede (1984, 1991) famously undertook extensive survey work of employees working for IBM (a global technology and innovation company) and its subsidiaries in different countries highlighting how national culture influenced work in IBM in different parts of the world in different ways (see also Project GLOBE, House et al., 1999). However, the focus here is upon organizational cultures rather than national cultures.

Organization culture and cultural change have captured the imagination of academics and practitioners for many decades. Possibly it is because cultural philosophy seeks to understand organizational behaviour that it has proven to be so popular with change managers, and few can argue against the wisdom of better organizational diagnosis (Smith and Graetz, 2011). Many varied and different definitions of culture exist. In this chapter, Schein's (2010: 18) definition is favoured given his centrality to organization culture debates.

> The culture of a group can now be defined as a pattern of shared basic assumptions learned by a group as it solved its problems of external adaptation and internal integration, which has worked well enough to be considered valid and, therefore, to be taught to new members as the correct way to perceive, think, and feel in relation to those problems.

Explorations of organizational culture are closely associated with organizational climate. It is consequently necessary to differentiate culture and climate. Schneider et al. (2013) differentiate climate as the meaning that organizational members attach to workplace experiences, whereas culture represents the underlying assumptions and values which drive those tangible experiences. Climate may be regarded as more current, whereas culture is deeper and more enduring. In discussions about culture, reference is sometimes made to 'strong' and 'weak' cultures. Scaffold (1988) and Flynn and Chatman (2001) highlighted how the word 'strong' had been used as a synonym for 'positive' and as a synonym for 'shared' with the implication that strong cultures would result in improved performance (see also Deal and Kennedy, 1982 for their discussion about strong and weak cultures).

This chapter is organized around and provides answers to the following questions about understanding organizational culture, considering how organizational culture might change and the challenges of changing organization culture.

> How do practitioners experience organizational cultural change?
> What do we know about organization culture?
> How do organization cultures change?
> What critical questions need to be addressed in terms of organizational cultural change theories and practices?

In the next section, experiences of organizational cultural change are highlighted as an orientation towards the applied nature of these debates. In seeking to understand organizational cultural change, it is necessary to understand organizational culture. Major milestones informing our understanding are revisited. The focus then shifts to theorising and undertaking cultural change. The enthusiasm for cultural change, at its height in the 1980s and 1990s needs to be critically tempered with critical questions raised about the manageability of cultural change. Finally, the chapter is summarised, discussion questions raised and guidance offered with regards to navigating organization culture and cultural change literature.

What are practitioners doing? Experiencing organizational cultural change

Sarah Smith (2016) offers a fascinating insider account of culture within the global investment management group Aberdeen Asset Management PLC. She is well placed to discuss this particular culture having joined as a graduate recruit who now works as the graduate recruitment and programme manager. She reflects upon how factors such as recruitment and selection, the graduate recruitment programme, feedback and appraisal all inform and transmit the culture of Aberdeen Asset Management. She humorously highlights the challenges of joining a new organization and embracing their culture.

> Having graduated with a sense of purpose and a drive to make a difference in the business world, I was confused about why my SWOT analysis of reorganizing the stationery cupboard or applying Porter's Five Forces to the file reconciliation were not more appreciated.
>
> (Smith, 2016: 241)

What unfolds is an account of how Sarah had to learn about the Aberdeen Asset Management and its culture and how she now helps new recruits to learn about and embrace this company's unique culture.

Alvesson and Sveningsson (2016) in *Changing Organizational Culture* present a research-informed case study of cultural change in a global high technology company called Global Tech and the creation of a separate legal entity called Technocom. Through their insider research, they offer insights into ongoing processes of organizational cultural change highlighting the cultural change programme from various participant points of view. They demonstrate how the experience of cultural change is very contingent upon who you ask, acknowledging that their reconstructions of participant views are slightly ironic.

Strategic architects engage in careful planning informed by qualified knowledge input and then human resource (HR) people and middle managers implement these plans. 'Strategic architects do not interfere with details and process. They plan, decide, give instructions and set the ball rolling. The strategic architect sets the wave' (Alvesson and Sveningsson, 2016: 166).

The consultant is tasked by the strategic architect with assisting in developing the new culture with the objective of primarily satisfying their client. Seminars are conducted and many proposals gathered. However, the strategic architect is the client and their views are always the most influential. If they are not contracted to assist with subsequent stages, they are disinclined to assist HR and middle managers in implementing the cultural change.

The facilitators often drawn from HR create the change through ensuring that the intentions and objectives of senior management are carried out by middle management.

> Instructions from top management and the imperatives of the large sum of money already invested in the design make compliance reasonable. As delivery persons – operating the post office – they should not interfere too much with the senders and receivers of messages.
>
> (Alvesson and Sveningsson, 2016: 166)

The compliant implementers in the roles of middle managers and their subordinates engage in cultural change as a strategic idea of senior management which has the feel of an HR project. Implementers view themselves as information gatherers, gathering information for senior management but not engaging with this information. It is up to the senior managers what they choose to do with this information.

The non-implementers regard cultural change initiatives as just another idea of the people at the top of the organization working in conjunction with the consultants and HR. For non-implementers, what is important is doing real work and delivering.

> The change programme will divert attention from more urgent tasks. The non-implementers find working with culture and organization soft and fluffy. This is another 'HR thing' nothing important.
>
> (Alvesson and Sveningsson, 2016: 167)

Alvesson and Sveningsson (2016) use the metaphor of passing a baton to explain how the cultural change project is passed from person to person in the belief that the change will materialise through the next person in line doing what is expected.

In parallel with this metaphor, cultural change is likened to a postal system in which information is delivered but the post women/men never tamper with the post.

In this chapter, many of the publications cited use qualitative methods to understand organizational culture and cultural change frequently offering first-hand practitioner accounts in the reports of their research (see, for example, Johnson, 1990; Morgan and Sturdy, 2000; Schein, 2010; Gover et al., 2015).

Understanding organizational culture

The concept of organizational culture has been described by Pettigrew (1990) (after Winston Churchill) as a riddle, which is wrapped in a mystery, which is wrapped in an enigma. For Schein (2010) whilst culture is an abstraction, the forces it creates in social and organizational situations are powerful. Both of these scholars, whilst encouraging engagement with culture, warn us about the slipperiness of this concept. Schein (2010) highlights how culture is informed by many observable events and underlying forces (please see Table 6.1).

These events and forces (please see Table 6.1) inform understanding about culture. They also complicate understanding, drawing upon very different literature potentially informing understanding about culture. In beginning to focus upon culture, Schein (2010) encourages analysing culture at three different levels. In Table 6.2, level means the degree to which the cultural phenomenon is visible to observers.

In Table 6.2, the range of levels from very tangible overt manifestations (Level 1) through to deeply embedded, unconscious, basic assumptions (Level 3) are highlighted. Schein (2010) emphasised that it is important to initially understand the basic underlying assumptions as this understanding informs understanding at the other two levels. Unfortunately, organizational culture is frequently misunderstood through only looking at artefacts, rather than at the deeper levels.

Table 6.1 Observable events and underlying forces informing culture (Schein, 2010)

Observed behavioural regularities when people interact	Embedded skills
Group norms	Habits of thinking, mental models, and/or linguistic paradigms
Espoused values	Shared meanings
Formal philosophy	Root metaphors or integrating symbols
Rules of the game	Formal rituals and celebrations
Climate	

Table 6.2 The three levels of culture (Schein, 2010)

1 Artefacts level
   • Visible and feelable structures and processes
   • Observed behaviour (difficult to decipher)
2 Espoused beliefs and values level
   • Ideals, goals, values, and aspirations
   • Ideologies
   • Rationalisations (may or may not be congruent with behaviour and other artefacts)
3 Basic underlying assumptions level
   • Unconscious, taken-for-granted beliefs and values (determine behaviour, perception, thought and feeling)

When we think about organizational culture, we often have a metaphor in mind. Alvesson (2013) highlighted six metaphors which have been applied to organizational culture.

1   *Exchange regulator* – control mechanism aided by a common value and reference system.
2   *Compass* – giving a sense of direction and guidelines for priorities.
3   *Social glue* – common ideas, symbols and values are sources of identification with the group.
4   *Sacred cow* – basic assumptions and values which point to a core of the organization.
5   *Affect regulator* – guidelines and scripts for emotions and affections.
6   *Mental prison* – creating a fixed world within which people adjust.

These metaphors are likely to be implicit rather than explicit, yet they may have a considerable influence on thinking inside organizations and academic writing. For example, in reading Schein's (2010) *Organizational Culture and Leadership* the compass, social glue and sacred cow metaphors were apparent although not explicitly stated.

Mintzberg et al. (2009) highlighted the Scandinavian Institutes for Administrative Research, formed in 1965 undertaking early pioneering academic work into culture. McCalman and Potter (2015) and Parker (2000) highlight the importance of early management and organization studies writers in understanding organization culture. However, organization culture appears to have really captured the organizational and academic imagination in the 1980s and 1990s. For Smith and Graetz (2011), the concept of organizational culture emerged in response to an absence of explanations of how certain values and beliefs gain prominence. For Brewis (2017), interest in organizational culture emerged in the late 1970s as a result of challenges facing Western management practitioners and theorists at that time, these included:

> a general decline in religious belief,
> the expansion of highly technical work and the growth of service industries,
> the limitations of mechanical 'theory x' type approaches to managing people,
> innovative production methods,
> the emergence of the 'Japanese miracle'.

In the 1970s, 1980s and 1990s, four accounts of organizational culture (Handy, 1978; Peters and Waterman, 1982; Deal and Kennedy, 1982; and Kotter and Heskett, 1992) proved particularly influential in encouraging interest in organizational culture amongst both practitioners and academics. Handy (1978) drew upon Harrison's (1972) ideas in his description of four cultures using simple symbols and references to Greek mythology. The power culture emphasised a single power source. The role culture emphasised rules, procedures and job descriptions. The task culture emphasised expertise, rather than position or charisma and the person culture emphasised the individual as part of the collective.

In *In Search of Excellence,* Peters and Waterman (1982) highlighted the potential benefits of successfully managing cultural change. They highlighted relationships between organizational culture and performance, based on their studies of (at the time) successful companies which included IBM, Boeing, Walt Disney and McDonald's. The book, billed as 'lessons from America's best-run companies', identified eight attributes of excellent companies: a bias for action, close to the customer, autonomy and entrepreneurship, productivity through people, hands-on, value driven, stick to the knitting, simple form – lean staff and simultaneous loose-tight properties.

Through examining hundreds of companies, Deal and Kennedy (1982) identified four general corporate culture types based upon the degree of risk and speed of feedback, illustrated with examples from particular organizations. The tough-guy macho culture was typified by management consultants. The work-hard/play-hard culture was typified by computer companies. The bet-your-company culture was typified by oil companies and the process culture by insurance companies.

Kotter and Heskett (1992) in *Corporate Culture and Performance* emphasised the link between organizational culture and performance which appeared to be integral to the debates from previous decades. They suggested that their work provided empirical evidence that the culture of a corporation influences economic performance drawing their evidence from the likes of Hewlett-Packard, Xerox, ICI, Nissan and First Chicago.

It is important to acknowledge that these four accounts of culture were exceptionally influential at the time of writing. Over the last two decades, there has been continued interest in organization culture, though nothing like the levels of interest in the 1980s and 1990s. However, subsequent concerns have been expressed about these pioneering studies. Wilson (2001) argued that Handy (1978) ignored covert agendas within organizations and perpetuated gendered roles and inequalities. The most striking flaw of *In Search of Excellence* was the subsequent demise of companies forming the basis of the research study (please see Guest, 1992 and Collins, 2000 for critiques). Collins (2007) offered a more balanced evaluation of Tom Peters acknowledging his considerable contribution to management and organization studies.

Deal and Kennedy (1999), reappraised their own contribution to corporate cultural change with the benefit of almost two decades' hindsight, acknowledging 'there must be a million consultants promising to help "change the cultures" of companies. Many of these consultants are even making a reasonable living from the practice. What a lot of bollocks' (Deal and Kennedy, 1999: 35). Whilst, Kotter and Heskett (1992) claimed an empirical link between culture and performance, there is a need for caution in making such an association (Rosenzweig, 2007: O'Reilly et al., 2014).

As Smith and Graetz (2011) highlighted, few can argue against the wisdom of better organizational diagnosis. Handy (1978), Peters and Waterman (1982), Deal and Kennedy (1982) and Kotter and Heskett (1992) have been discussed here as a means of diagnosing an organizational culture. Such diagnosis could form the basis of an attempt to change a culture with Morgan and Sturdy (2000) highlighting, though not prescribing the traditional ingredients of a cultural change programme: identify the current shared values and norms, state what the culture should be, identify the gap between the two and develop a plan to close the gap.

Understanding organizational cultural change

> Cultural change is not a passing fad: it has always been a significant challenge for managers because it is not an organizational variable; culture is the organization. Culture is a social construction. People make it and it is only through determined, intellectual, cooperative action of people that culture can be changed.
>
> (McCalman and Potter, 2015: 4)

Any attempt to change an existing culture must be informed by an understanding of the existing culture with the previous section offering different means to diagnose an organizational culture. In this section, four approaches to organizational cultural change are highlighted. First, Jung et al. (2009) highlights the many instruments available for exploring organizational culture. Second, Schein (2010) highlights the merit of matching the stage of organizational growth to particular change mechanisms. Third, the cultural web (Johnson et al., 2013) offers an approach to cultural change which proved popular with practitioners. Fourth, Meyerson and Martin (1987) highlight the existence of three different views of culture and cultural change with implications for how it is managed. These discussions will be critically tempered in the questioning section as it is important to acknowledge that such change interventions seek to change deep values and beliefs (Smith and Graetz, 2011).

Jung et al. (2009) innovatively identified 70 instruments for exploring culture. Whilst, their interest was in improving public administration, these instruments appear to have wider applicability. They are highlighted here as an extension to discussions in the previous section about diagnosis being closely related to changing culture.

> Practitioners are interested in the management of organizational culture, and they are looking for answers and solutions: how can an organization's culture be changed and adjusted to meet organizational needs?
>
> (Jung et al., 2009: 1087)

Their listing of instruments for exploring organizational culture includes the competing values framework (Likert scale), culture gap survey and the organizational culture profile (Ashkanasy). What is apparent is the breadth of organizational culture instruments which are available and the need to match the instrument to a particular situation. The characteristics of the identified instruments vary from dimensional to typological, from quantitative to qualitative and a combination of these. Dimensional approaches focus on specific cultural variables such as job satisfaction or values, whereas dimensions are much broader in scope. In terms of methodological approaches, self-report questionnaires were the most prominent. They warn that cultural assessment can be a starting point for solving organizational problems, but may also create problematic solutions.

Another means of changing an organizational culture is through acknowledging that organizations go through processes of growth and decline over time with such processes having implications for cultural change. Schein (2010) championed thinking about cultural change in these terms (please see Table 6.3).

Table 6.3 Culture change mechanisms (based on Schein, 2010)

Organizational stage	Change mechanism
Founding and early growth	1 Incremental change through general and specific evolution
	2 Insight
	3 Promotion of hybrids within the culture
Midlife	4 Systematic promotion from selected subcultures
	5 Technological seduction
	6 Infusion of outsiders
Maturity and decline	7 Scandal and explosion of myths
	8 Turnarounds
	9 Mergers and acquisitions
	10 Destruction and rebirth

Table 6.3 depicts a natural process of culture evolving and changing as an organization grows and ages. At the founding and early growth stage, the founders, and their assumptions have a considerable influence on the culture, which often endures over time. The culture of these young and successfully growing companies is likely to be closely adhered to. Any changes are likely to be incremental reflecting self-guided evolution. Evolutionary change will be characterised by hybrids of existing cultures and practices. At the midlife organizational stage, problems of succession become apparent. Founders relinquish control with new general managers appointed or promoted. Through systematic promotion from selected subcultures, cultures are changed. The diffusion and introduction of new technology will influence the culture at this stage as well as the introduction of outsiders. Continued success raises two problems at the organizational maturity and decline stages in that basic assumptions become more strongly held and organizations and espoused values and ideals may be out of sync with actual assumptions. Against this backdrop, scandals, myths, turnarounds, mergers and acquisitions, destruction and rebirth all may have an influence on an organization's culture.

The cultural web was popularised through the best-selling strategy textbook *Exploring Strategy* (Johnson et al., 2013). However, the cultural web's origins can be traced back to Gerry Johnson's earlier writings. The paradigm at the centre of the cultural web was introduced in *Strategic Change and the Management Process* (Johnson, 1987). It was his paper *Rethinking Incrementalism* (Johnson, 1988) which introduced the concept of the cultural web. In "Managing Strategic Change: Strategy, Culture and Action" (Johnson, 1992) the concept was fully introduced and its applicability to strategic change highlighted. Johnson (1990, 1992), through his development and dissemination of the cultural web, encouraged interest in symbolism with regard to strategic change. This was in the belief that social, political, cultural and cognitive dimensions of managerial activities give rise to the sort of incremental strategic change typifying organizations which can be employed to galvanise more fundamental strategic change. In Table 6.4, the cultural artefacts which Johnson encouraged identifying are introduced. Examples and additional questions which may help to identify such cultural artefacts are offered.

It is only through exploring all of the artefacts in Table 6.4 that the paradigm can be identified. Cultural web terminology evokes the idea of a spider's web. At the centre of this web, Johnson (1992: 29/30) placed the paradigm defined as '...a cognitive structure or mechanism: however, this set of taken-for-granted assumptions and beliefs, which is more or less collectively owned, is likely to be hedged about and protected by a web of cultural artefacts'. The paradigm is very different from an organization's mission statement. A paradigm generated through a cultural web process may even be negative.

Cultural webs have been used to inform cultural change initiatives, being used to diagnose the existing culture and the desired culture. Completing a culture web for an existing culture may help to answer the following questions:

1 To what extent does the existing culture support or hinder the desired changes that need to be made?
2 To what extent does the existing culture need to be changed if the desired changes are to be implemented?
3 To what extent does the existing culture underpin existing organizational competencies that need to be retained?

These creative questions may inform a change agenda with a cultural web subsequently drawn of the desired culture.

Table 6.4 Questions for identifying cultural artefacts and the paradigm (based on Johnson, 1992)

Symbols
Examples: Organizational logos, office layouts, and car parking spaces
    Question: What language and jargon are used?
    Question: What status symbols exist?
    Question: Which symbols denoting the purpose of the organization exist?

Power structures
Examples: Managerial groupings and the most powerful functional areas
    Question: How is power distributed in the organization?
    Question: What are the main blockages to change?
    Question: How is the organization led?

Organizational structures
Examples: Organizational hierarchy (chart) and informal structures
    Question: Is the organization hierarchical?
    Question: Do structures encourage collaboration or cooperation?
    Question: Top down/bottom up decision making?

Control systems
Examples: Performance measurement and reward systems
    Question: How closely monitored are employees?
    Question: Are there too many/not enough controls?
    Question: How are good behaviours rewarded?

Rituals and routines
Examples: The Christmas party and meetings around the water cooler
    Question: Which regular routines are valued?
    Question: What are the key rituals?
    Question: What behaviours do the routines encourage?

Stories and myths
Examples: Stories about mavericks and myths about promotion opportunities
    Question: What core beliefs do the stories reflect?
    Question: Who are the heroes and villains?
    Question: What norms do the mavericks deviate from?

The paradigm
Example: Client satisfaction at all costs
    Question: What are the taken-for-granted assumptions and beliefs?
    Question: What paradigm do the cultural artefacts suggest?
    Question: What is the dominant culture?

Meyerson and Martin (1987) in their classic paper highlighted three different views of cultural change. Whilst written almost three decades ago the different ways of understanding cultural change and by association, its management remains very relevant.

> ...what we notice and experience as cultural change depends directly on how we conceptualize culture.
>
> (Meyerson and Martin, 1987: 623)

All the earlier discussions of culture and cultural change have worked with different conceptualisations of culture and Meyerson and Martin's (1987) account of cultural change helps us better understand differences between these conceptualisations and the implications of different conceptualisations. The three views of cultural change depicted as paradigms offer alternative points of view that organizational members/ researchers bring to their experience of culture.

Paradigm one – integration: Culture is regarded as an integrating mechanism, the glue holding together a potentially diverse group of organizational members. This view of culture emphasises consistency, consensus and the leader as a primary source of cultural content.

Paradigm two – differentiation: Instead of regarding culture as an integrating mechanism, culture is characterised in terms of differentiation and diversity. Culture is regarded as being composed of a collection of values and manifestations, some of which may be contradictory. Paradigm two emphasises fluctuations in subcultures and changes in connections between subcultures and the dominant culture. Environmental (or external) catalysts for change that have localised impacts on organizational functioning are emphasised. Paradigm two draws attention to localised, incremental changes, towards deviances, adaptations and experiments among and within subunits.

Paradigm three – ambiguity: Whereas paradigms one and two minimise the experience of ambiguity, paradigm three accepts and even embraces the presence of ambiguity. Complexity and lack of clarity are legitimated and made the focus of attention.

> Consensus, dissensus, and confusion coexist, making it difficult to draw cultural and subcultural boundaries.
>
> (Meyerson and Martin, 1987: 637)

Any change amongst and between individuals involves a cultural change at the organizational and sub-organizational level. In paradigm three, it is difficult to notice the change because of the ambiguity and continual change characterising this perspective.

Meyerson and Martin (1987) regard it as crucially important to view organizational culture from all three paradigms. However, they concede that for organizational members/researchers it is far easier to view culture from only one paradigmatic perspective, which is normally the first paradigm.

Gover et al. (2015) offered research-informed recommendations for managers tasked with planned cultural change agendas. First, consider how they measure the success of their cultural change initiatives. Second, consider what the drivers for cultural change are in their organization, and how individuals view these drivers. Third, be cautious not to presume that employees will respond to culture change in a particular way, based on certain demographic variables.

Questioning explanations of organizational cultural change

Levels of interest in organizational cultural change of the 1980s and 1990s declined. However, culture remains a central aspect of organizational life (Alvesson, 2013). Cultural change is not a passing fad (McCalman and Potter, 2015) and the aim of this questioning section is to temper the unrealistic expectations often placed upon cultural change, whilst not negating the fact that organizational cultures do change. The questioning in this section is organized around three themes; the search for evidence, hyperculture and culture as a critical variable versus culture as a root metaphor and the implications for cultural thinking.

In search of evidence

Peters and Waterman (1982) in their book *In Search of Excellence* gave impetus to managing culture. Over 30 years later, the expectation would be that we have a large body of evidence confirming that particular cultures do deliver heightened business performance (excellence). However, in reviewing this literature the best that currently could be said is that we are still searching for the evidence. Many of the authors (Parker, 2000; Brewis 2017; Alvesson, 2013; McCalman and Potter, 2015; Alvesson and Sveningsson, 2016) previously cited are sceptical about the research evidence in support of cultural change. O'Reilly et al. (2014) in considering the promise and problems of organizational culture revisited the evidence that culture is an important determinant of firm performance. One of the problems encountered was that whilst research on culture had become methodologically more sophisticated, researchers in using diverse measures of culture and performance stalled paradigm development (Sackmann, 2011). O'Reilly et al. (2014) highlighted how a lack of clarity impeded attempts to link organizational culture and performance. Firstly, designing studies and obtaining data allowing an assessment of culture across organizations is a daunting task. Second, there have been disagreements about the definition and measurement of both culture and performance. Third, there has been an evolution in understanding about firm performance over the decades with a greater emphasis placed upon strategy and environmental conditions. O'Reilly et al. (2014) were unable to find consistent evidence that culture contributes to financial performance.

Hyperculture

Alvesson and Sveningsson (2016) critically used the label 'hyperculture' to refer to a set of positive statements about values, often decoupled from everyday life thinking and practices.

> Employing the term 'hyperculture', we address the formulated culture and the activities to express, reinforce and/or change it in terms of its highly packaged and therefore very tangible nature and ceremonial talk and as a somewhat surreal fantasy, with a remote connection to everyday practices, meanings, and experiences.
> (Alvesson and Sveningsson, 2016: 132)

Cultural change programmes are written down and packaged in particular ways. HR assembles the parts of the cultural toolbox so that it resembles an effectively co-ordinated and tightly knit package. Culture as a parcel with a toolbox, manual and labels was very different to how culture was envisaged by scholars of organizational culture (Alvesson and Sveningsson, 2016). Another aspect of hyperculture is how culture is manufactured through the HR function, rather than the consultants presenting the cultural values. The paradox is that the consultant invariably invents the culture, but HR has the role of presenting the culture to employees. The people holding up or promoting the new values become disconnected from the consultants who developed them. The concern is that organizations rely upon consultants and HR who may not have the deep organizational understanding and consequently produce something that is easy and accessible but may misrepresent and misunderstand what an organization is really all about. Hyperculture highlights how culture is only explicitly talked about on a few occasions with these occasions akin to ceremony and ritual.

Many people remembered that there had been culture meetings and a programme in circulation in the company but, at the same time, they were scarcely aware of its particular content nor did they have any particular knowledge about whether it may have mattered in any respect.

(Alvesson and Sveningsson, 2016: 136)

Alvesson and Sveningsson (2016) acknowledged that ceremonies can be positive, inspirational and pride enhancing. Finally, hyperculture highlights how culture can take on the role of grandiose fantasies about the future which can be heightened by mixing normative and descriptive elements. The danger here is that senior management claims about new cultural values are believed to be real, rather than merely being espoused.

Culture as a critical variable versus culture as a root metaphor

Alvesson (2013) draws an important distinction between literature which treats culture as a critical variable which an organization has and literature which treats culture as something which an organization is. This distinction was originally highlighted by Smircich (1983). In this textbook chapter, much of the literature cited has engaged with culture as a critical variable. However, in the context of this questioning section, it is worthwhile highlighting a different way of thinking about culture.

The notion of culture as a critical variable is drawn from traditionalist, objectivist and functionalist views of social reality. Earlier discussions about strong/weak cultures and culture informing performance are compatible with such notions. These notions place emphasis upon managing organizational culture as a critical variable.

> ...getting the right culture in place is expected to have recognizable effects on important outputs such as loyalty, productivity and perceived quality of service.
>
> (Alvesson, 2013: 21)

Alternatively regarding culture as a root metaphor stresses that an organization is culture rather than it having a malleable culture which can be managed. Every aspect of organizational life is culture. Consequently, there is interest in subjective experiences and socially shared experiences. This way of thinking about culture doubts and discourages notions of culture as something which can be managed.

Thinking about culture as a critical variable suffers from the following cultural thinking traps (Alvesson, 2013). The first trap is *reifying culture* as a thing or as thing-like. This reification is very apparent in senior management pronouncements that they are going to 'change the culture around here', but equally, earlier academic discussions inevitably fall into this trap. Both in terms of practice and theory, reifying culture can misrepresent and misunderstand the subtleties and complexities of organizational culture. The second trap is *essentializing culture*, describing a culture in terms of a few essential traits with an essential integrated trait used to describe the whole, such as performance oriented, service-minded or socially responsible. Again this trap depicts culture superficially avoiding inevitable conflicts and contradictions. The third trap is *unifying culture* through referring to groups or collectives. The danger is equating formal or legal boundaries with cultural boundaries. In any organization, there will be multiple cultural groups and orientations. The fourth trap is *idealizing culture*. The concern here is with a focus on ideas and meanings, not necessarily the ideals of an organization. Ideas and meanings are considered without any context, instead of being generated within an organization with reference to context. Cultural meanings are developed and reshaped in context, rather than being merely delivered (see earlier postal analogy). The fifth trap is *consensualizing culture* based upon an assumption that an acknowledgement of culture equates to unity and shared values. However, shared meanings do not necessarily imply consensus and harmony. Alvesson (2013) suggests that the sixth trap *totalizing culture* has two meanings; using a very wide view embracing almost everything and the other is restricting oneself to values, ideas and meanings. Finally, *otherizing culture* refers to using contrast, for example, putting good against bad. Again, these black and white juxtapositions misunderstand and misrepresent culture.

These cultural thinking traps are a negative way to conclude the chapter, but they do highlight the challenges of understanding organizational culture and cultural change and act as a counterpoint to early unrealistic expectations that organizational culture could easily be 'managed'. The cultural thinking traps also highlight an increasing sophistication in thinking about organizational culture as we appreciate and acknowledge the challenges involved.

Summary

The chapter may be succinctly summarised through answering the questions posed in the chapter's introduction, the original questions are restated in italics.

How do practitioners experience organizational cultural change? Practitioners' lived experience of culture and cultural change will vary considerably giving very different answers to this question. Sarah Smith's (2016) experience of absorbing the culture in Aberdeen Asset Management PLC and how she now introduces this culture to new graduates was offered as an illustration of practitioner experience of culture. Also, Alvesson and Sveningsson's (2016) account of cultural change in a global high technology company helped to highlight the different experiences of cultural change of those in the roles of strategic architects, consultants, facilitators, compliant implementers, and non-implementers.

What do we know about organization culture? Pettigrew's (1990) notion of organizational culture as a riddle, wrapped in a mystery, wrapped in an enigma is an important cautionary note when answering this question. Schein (2010) encouraged analysis of culture at different levels: the artefacts level, the espoused beliefs and values level and the basic underlying assumptions level. Another way of thinking about organizational culture was in terms of metaphors with Alvesson (2013) highlighting the following metaphors: exchange regulator, compass, social glue, sacred cow, affect regulator and mental prison. Handy (1978), Peters and Waterman (1982), Deal and Kennedy (1982) and Kotter and Heskett (1992) offered four influential accounts of organizational culture which were discussed.

How do organization cultures change? Jung et al. (2009) highlighted many instruments available for exploring organizational culture and these instruments might be utilised in order to change an organizational culture. Another way of thinking about how organization cultures change is in terms of different change mechanisms at different stages of organization growth (Schein, 2010). Also changing an organizational culture may be thought about in terms of drawing a cultural web (Johnson et al., 2013) of the current culture and the preferred culture. Finally, how cultures change may be contingent upon your view of culture and culture change (Meyerson and Martin, 1987).

What critical questions need to be addressed in terms of organizational cultural change theories and practices? O'Reilly et al. (2014) revisited the evidence that culture is an important determinant of firm performance but was unable to find consistent evidence. 'Hyperculture' was highlighted which emphasised positive statements about values, often decoupled from everyday life thinking and practices (Alvesson and Sveningsson, 2016). The chapter concludes on a cautionary note acknowledging that much of the literature depicts culture as a critical variable rather than culture as a root metaphor. The implication that an organization has a culture, rather than is a culture is problematic resulting in a series of cultural thinking traps.

Research case study showcase: the perpetuation of organization culture at Spartans Football Club

Ogbonna and Harris' (2014) case study of the perpetuation of culture at Spartans Football Club published in the *British Journal of Management* is showcased here. For the full case study and further analysis please visit the original source.

Case study source

Spartans Football Club (SFC) is a pseudonym for an English Premier League football club. The English Premier League formed in February 1992 is the most lucrative and most watched in the world. The league was formed in order to exploit lucrative revenue opportunities arising out of the globalisation of football. SFC was run in a manner similar to a small family concern by a benevolent authoritarian for over 30 years. This coincided with the most successful period in the club's history in terms of on-field activities. Ogbonna and Harris (2014) were granted extensive access to SFC which informed their case study. They were able to use multiple data-gathering techniques including archival research, focus group discussions, non-participant observation and face-to-face interviews. Ogbonna and Harris (2014: 668) defined culture '…as the set of values, beliefs, norms and assumptions that are shared by a group and that guide their interpretations of and responses to their environments'. They (2014: 668) defined cultural perpetuation '…as the continuation of core cultural values, beliefs, norms and assumptions such that they become enduring in a way that new generations of organizational members are conditioned to adopt them in responding to various organizational contingencies'.

Ogbonna, E., and L.C. Harris. 2014. "Organizational Cultural Perpetuation: A Case Study of an English Premier League Football Club." *British Journal of Management* 25(4): 667–686.

Case study

Whereas this chapter has largely been concerned with cultural change, Ogbonna and Harris (2014) were interested in how the perpetuation of culture might act as an impediment to organizational change. SFC wanted to transform the culture of their organization through organizational change

(Continued)

initiatives, but the perpetuation of the past culture appeared to act as an impediment to change. Ogbonna and Harris (2014) through their research identified intra-cultural factors (historical legacy, symbolic expressions, sub-cultural dynamics and employment practices) and extra-cultural factors (the role and influence of supporters as key external stakeholders) as perpetuating the existing culture.

How did the historical legacy of SFC perpetuate the existing culture?

Informants regarded the rich history of SFC as providing a focal point which guided everyday activities at SFC. It was SFC's past successes which were particularly important in their attachment to their organization's history.

> Ironically, despite evidence of a lack of comparable present-day success, the strength of culture arising from the strong historical legacy of success hampered a variety of strategic initiatives that the current leaders believed were necessary.
>
> *(Ogbonna and Harris, 2014: 677)*

Many informants strongly believed that sticking to the values and behaviours associated with the successful past would return SFC to success. The rich history of success was a strong frame of reference perpetuating cultural beliefs and practices.

How was culture perpetuated through symbolic expressions?

The interviews and observations revealed that particular sentiments which related to specific symbols were recurring activities in SFC. Symbolic expressions provided a bridge between 'the past' (the historical legacy) and 'the present'. A good illustration of this was SFC employing ex-players who frequently promoted the virtue of maintaining traditional SFC values. Another symbolic expression of the past was the onsite SFC museum which the researchers found to be littered with symbolic meaning and nuance. The irony was that the museum in celebrating the successful past of SFC reinforced the existing culture of SFC, simultaneously making change in SFC difficult.

How did subcultural dynamics perpetuate the culture?

The success or failure of the SFC first team in football matches was integral to SFC. SFC executives wanted to shift this reliance on the team. However, given the centrality of the team subculture to SFC, this subculture had achieved a very powerful position which even enabled it to influence the direction of the organization.

> Such is the power of the team subculture that executives and other staff at SFC are discouraged from visiting the first team building as the team subculture has a 'traditional' preference for isolation.
>
> *(Ogbonna and Harris, 2014: 678)*

Given the dominance of the team subculture at SFC its acceptance of changes that executives were proposing was crucial to successful implementation of change. However, it was within the team subculture that belief that success would return to SFC, if the team (and the organization) maintained the values and norms, which had served SFC, thrived.

How do employment practices perpetuate the culture?

The research revealed two aspects of employment practices significant to promoting cultural endurance, as well as, undermining cultural change efforts, the longevity of employment and recruitment and promotion policies. The Personnel Manager explained instances in which departmental heads would insist on the inclusion of candidates through informal word-of-mouth recommendations onto interview short-lists. These candidates were favoured in selection processes, rather than following newly espoused organizational values encouraging transparent and fair human resource policies and practices.

How did key external stakeholders influence the perpetuation of culture?

Whereas the previous perpetuating factors were internal to SFC, there was another perpetuating factor which despite being external to SFC was very influential. Research revealed a strong relationship between SFC and its most important external stakeholders: the supporters (or fans). Whilst, research revealed fans as outside the formal organization they did influence organizational members' perceptions and actions. In this way, they perpetuated the existing culture and made the implementation of change difficult. It was die-hard fans who had the most influence on organizational members, directly and indirectly resisting espoused changes.

> Die-hard fanatics commonly have an encyclopaedic knowledge of the history of SFC which they celebrate through a variety of rituals and activities, including pre-match or half-time events, meetings, and taking the lead in singing specially rehearsed songs in adoration of their club and their favourite players during matches.
>
> *(Ogbonna and Harris, 2014: 680)*

Ogbonna and Harris (2014) acknowledge that SFC is an unusual organizational research setting. However, it helps us to appreciate the implications of the ebb and flow of cultural perpetuation for organizational culture theories and practices, an appreciation which they believe has been largely missing from organizational culture theories and research.

Case study questions

1 How can the perpetuation of culture at SFC be explained in terms of (Schein, 2010) three levels of culture?
2 What are the positive aspects of the perpetuation of culture at SFC?

Discussion questions

1   Why is more attention paid to artefacts, rather than basic underlying assumptions (Schein, 2010)?
2   Why does managing organizational culture appeal to managers and leaders?
3   What are the research challenges in establishing how culture influences performance?
4   Does the acknowledgement of cultural thinking traps (Alvesson, 2013) help or hinder the development of convincing organizational culture theories?

Navigating the organizational cultural change literature

Any attempt to understand cultural change requires an understanding of organizational culture and this line of reasoning has informed this chapter. Organizational culture is a central concept in management and organization studies. One of the most comprehensive accounts of organizational culture was Brown (1998). It is dated now, but good for the backstory of how and why interest in organizational culture developed. Alvesson's (2013) *Understanding Organizational Culture* now in its second edition, has become the key text in this field of study. Mintzberg et al.'s (2009) *Strategy Safari* and Smith and Graetz's (2011) *Philosophies of Organizational Change* feature chapters on organizational culture. Both of these accounts are recommended, highlighting how you can understand strategy from a cultural perspective and organizational change from a cultural perspective, but that these schools of thought/philosophies are in competition with other schools/philosophies in explaining strategy and organizational change. In terms of understanding organizational culture, most generic management and organization studies textbooks devote a chapter to this topic.

A theme of this chapter has been that any attempt to manage cultural change must be grounded in an understanding of organizational culture. Schein's (2010) *Organizational Culture and Leadership,* now in its fourth edition offers a bridge between understanding culture and understanding how cultures change. McCalman and Potter (2015) in *Leading Cultural Change: The Theory and Practice of Successful Organizational Transformation* offers a comprehensive overview of three large and related bodies of literature: leadership, culture, and change. Their book benefits from the application of the theories reviewed to cultural change within Glasgow City Council. Parker (2000) offers an informative and provocative historic overview of writing about organization culture, which is a good starting point for anyone who wants to go back to the origins of contemporary debates about culture and cultural change.

References

Alvesson, M. 2013. *Understanding Organizational Culture*. London: Sage Publications.
Alvesson, M., and S. Sveningsson. 2016. *Changing Organizational Culture: Cultural Change Work in Progress*. London: Routledge.
Brewis, J. 2017. "Culture." In *Introducing Organizational Behaviour and Management*, edited by D. Knights and H. Willmott, 344–374. Andover: Cengage Learning EMEA.
Brown, A. 1998. *Organisational Culture*. London: FT Pitman Publishing.
Collins, D. 2000. *Management Fads and Buzzwords: Critical-Practical Perspectives*. London: Routledge.
Collins, D. 2007. *Narrating the Management Guru: In Search of Tom Peters*. London: Routledge.
Deal, T.E., and A.A. Kennedy. 1982. *Corporate Cultures: The Rites and Rituals of Corporate Life*. Reading, MA: Addison-Wesley.

Deal, T.E., and A.A. Kennedy. 1999. *The New Corporate Cultures: Revitalizing the Workplace after Downsizing, Mergers and Reengineering.* London: Orion Business.

Flynn, F.J., and J.A. Chatman. 2001. "Strong Cultures and Innovation: Oxymoron or Opportunity." In *International Handbook of Organizational Culture and Climate*, edited by C. Cooper, S. Cartwright, and P.C. Earley, 263–287. Chichester: John Wiley and Sons.

Gover, L., M. Halinski., and L. Duxbury. 2015. "Is it Just Me? Exploring Perceptions of Organizational Culture Change." *British Journal of Management* 27(3): 567–582.

Guest, D. 1992. "Right enough to be dangerously wrong: An analysis of the in search of excellence phenomenon." In *Human Resource Strategies*, edited by G. Salaman, 5–19. London and Milton Keynes: Sage and the Open University Press.

Handy, C.B. 1978. *The Gods of Management.* Harmondsworth: Penguin.

Harrison, R. 1972. "Understanding Your Organization's Character." *Harvard Business Review* 50(3): 119–128.

Hofstede, G. 1984. *Culture's Consequences: International Differences in Work Related Values.* Beverley Hills, CA: Sage Publications Inc.

Hofstede G. 1991. *Cultures and Organizations, Software of the Mind.* Maidenhead: McGraw-Hill.

House, R.J., P.J. Hanges, S.A. Ruiz-Quintanilla, P.W. Dorfman, M. Javidan, M. Dickson, and V. Gupta. 1999. "Cultural Influences on Leadership and Organizations: Project GLOBE." *Advances in Global Leadership* 1(2): 171–233.

Johnson, G. 1987. *Strategic Change and the Management Process.* Oxford: Blackwell.

Johnson, G. 1988. "Rethinking Incrementalism." *Strategic Management Journal* 9(1): 75–91.

Johnson, G. 1990. "Managing Strategic Change: The Role of Symbolic Action." *British Journal of Management* 1(4): 183–200.

Johnson, G. 1992. "Managing Strategic Change – Strategy, Culture and Action." *Long Range Planning* 25(1): 28–36.

Johnson, G., R. Whittington, K. Scholes, D. Angwin, and P. Regner. 2013. *Exploring Strategy Text and Cases.* Harlow: Pearson Higher Education.

Jung, T., T. Scott, H.T. Davies, P. Bower, D. Whalley, R. McNally, and R. Mannion. 2009. "Instruments for Exploring Organizational Culture: A Review of the Literature." *Public Administration Review* 69(6): 1087–1096.

Kotter, J.P., and J.L. Heskett. 1992. *Corporate Culture and Performance.* New York: The Free Press.

McCalman, J., and D. Potter. 2015. *Leading Cultural Change: The Theory and Practice of Successful Organizational Transformation.* London: Kogan Page Publishers.

Meyerson, D., and J. Martin. 1987. "Cultural Change: An Integration of Three Different Views." *Journal of Management Studies* 24(6): 623–647.

Mintzberg, H., B. Ahlstrand, and J. Lampel. 2009. *Strategy Safari: Your Complete Guide Through the Wilds of Strategic Management.* Upper Saddle River, NJ: Pearson Education Limited.

Morgan, G., and A. Sturdy. 2000. *Beyond Organizational Change: Structure, Discourse and Power in UK Financial Services.* London: Macmillan.

Ogbonna, E., and L.C. Harris. 2014. "Organizational Cultural Perpetuation: A Case Study of an English Premier League Football Club." *British Journal of Management* 25(4): 667–686.

O'Reilly, C.A., D.F. Caldwell, J.A. Chatman, and B. Doerr. 2014. "The Promise and Problems of Organizational Culture CEO Personality, Culture, and Firm Performance." *Group and Organization Management* 39(6): 595–625.

Parker, M. 2000. *Organizational Culture and Identity: Unity and Division at Work.* London: Sage Publications.

Peters, T., and R. Waterman. 1982. *In Search of Excellence.* New York: Harper and Row.

Pettigrew, A.M. 1990. "Organizational Climate and Culture: Two Constructs in Search of a Role." In *Organizational Climate and Culture*, edited by B. Schneider, 413–434. San Francisco, CA: Jossey Bass.

Rosenzweig, P. 2007. *The Halo Effect: How Managers let Themselves be Deceived*. London: Pocket Books.

Sackmann, S.A. 2011. "Culture and Performance." In *The Handbook of Organizational Culture and Climate*, edited by N.M. Ashkanasy, C.P. Wilderom, and M.F. Peterson, 188–224. Thousand Oaks, CA: Sage Publications.

Saffold, G.S. 1988. "Culture Traits, Strength, and Organizational Performance: Moving Beyond 'Strong' Culture." *Academy of Management Review* 13(4): 546–558.

Schein, E.H. 2010. *Organizational Culture and Leadership*. San Francisco, CA: John Wiley & Sons.

Schneider, B., M.G. Ehrhart, and W.H. Macey. 2013. "Organizational Climate and Culture." *Annual Review of Psychology* 64: 361–388.

Smircich, L. 1983. "Concepts of Culture and Organizational Analysis." *Administrative Science Quarterly* 28(3): 339–358.

Smith, A., and F.M. Graetz. 2011. *Philosophies of Organizational Change*. Cheltenham: Edward Elgar Publishing.

Smith, S. 2016. "Developing a Culture: The Balance Between Change and Consistency." In *Perspectives on Change: What Academics, Consultants and Managers Really Think About Change* edited by B. Burnes and J. Randall, 234–245. New York: Routledge.

Wilson, E. 2001. "Organizational Culture." In *Organizational Behaviour Reassessed: The Impact of Gender*, edited by E.M. Wilson. London: Sage Publications.

Chapter 7

Individual differences, psychodynamics, identities and organizational change

Introduction and chapter questions

Textbook definitions of an organization highlight the centrality of individuals to all organizations. For example, Mullins with Christy (2016) in defining an organization, regard an organization as structures of people, which exist to achieve specific purposes, common aims and objectives through planned and co-ordinated activities. The focus of this chapter is understanding those 'people' referred to here as individuals who work within an organization and particularly in the context of organizational change. Often individuals work in groups and teams which are the focus of the next chapter (Chapter 8). The goal here is to understand individuals in the context of organizational change. they may be initiating an organizational change or they may be responding to an organizational change.

In an early paper encouraging the application of psychodynamic thinking to organizational transformation and change, it was suggested that 'trying to change something is often like moving a cemetery' (Kets de Vries and Balazs, 1998: 612). These authors succinctly and eloquently capture the debates this chapter engages with. Why do we sometimes act illogically and dysfunctionally? Why do we often cling to the status quo? What conscious and unconscious obstacles to change might exist? It is helpful to think about our own processes of changing rather than some abstract other person, we might be leading or managing a change, or we might be the target of a change initiative or we may simply be observing a process of organizational change.

Three strands of thinking unify this chapter, with each strand independent yet related to the other strands. First, we can seek to understand individuals and their differences, the classic way organizational behaviour textbooks deal with individuals. Second, we can delve into the psychodynamics of individual experiences of organizational change in particular drawing attention to the unconscious aspects of organization life. Third, we can focus on identity work and how people subjectively construe themselves through their identities, 'I am a bank manager at the Bank of Plentiful Money, but I am also a mother.'

Each strand of thinking is pertinent to understanding how people experience organizational change. By volume literature relating individuals and their differences to organizations in general and organizational change, in particular, is by far the largest literature. Identity literature appears to have gained prominence in terms of academic interest in recent years, although psychodynamic explanations of organizational change remain influential.

This chapter is organized around and provides answers to the following questions about the role of understanding individuals, psychodynamics, and identities in processes of organizational change.

What is it like to experience organizational change?

What do we know about individual differences, psychodynamics, and identities when applied to organizational life?

How do studies of individual differences, psychodynamics, and identities inform our understanding of organizational change?

What critical questions need to be addressed when studying individual differences, psychodynamics, and identities?

In the next section, first-hand insights into people's experiences of organizational change are offered. Approaches to understanding individuals, psychodynamics and identities in organizations are introduced generically, before being applied specifically to organizational change. In engaging with individuals, psychodynamics and identities it is necessary to engage with and understand the limitations of these approaches. Finally, the chapter is summarised, discussion questions raised and guidance offered with regard to navigating the individual, psychodynamic and identity literature.

What are practitioners doing? Individual experiences of organizational change

In focussing upon individuals, psychodynamics and identity, first, it is informative to look at stories of people's first-hand experiences of organizational change. Whilst, rather dated now Stuart (1995) offered a fascinating account of manager's experiences of organizational change. More recently, Driver (2009) examined stories of change to establish what they tell us about how people experience organizational change and the conscious and unconscious meanings they attach to it. In particular, she examined stories of change as failed fantasies about work, self and organization. The stories were gathered by students doing her *Managing Change* graduate course. Eighteen of the stories were classified as gripes, ten as traumas, one as tragedy and 11 as epics. The following extract is taken from Harry's story about someone who felt betrayed after losing through a reassignment, a hospital job which he loved.

> The hardest thing to understand about the whole situation is how an organization …can transfer one so easily without any explanation as to why. I had worked hard to get to that position and had worked even harder to be successful at it and had it taken away from me so easily…When you invest that much of your life into something, you want it to be a good experience.
>
> (Driver, 2009: 362)

Bonnie, a children's programme coordinator in a not-for-profit organization, experienced restructuring after administration changes.

> I worked there for three more years, but it went from something that I took seriously and something that I loved to something where I just showed up every day and brought movies and candy. It was really easy for the pay; I just got to sit there and watch movies all day. It really turned into a joke.
>
> (Driver, 2009: 364)

Driver (2009) suggests that the stories convey what is often fundamentally lacking in lived experiences of work and self during times of change. Gover et al. (2016) in their study of organizational cultural change in a Canadian hospital setting offered rich qualitative insights into experiences of organizational change. The following quotations relate to why the culture in the hospital has changed.

In Table 7.1, the quotations based on real life experiences of organizational change offer insights into the different ways individuals experience organizational change, and the unconscious and emotional aspects of an organizational change.

Bordia et al.'s (2006) "Management Are Aliens! Rumors and Stress During Organizational Change" offers another innovative window on the experience of organizational change through researching rumours within a large Australian public hospital undergoing change. Of the returned completed surveys, 776 respondents answered questions about rumours allowing them to code rumours (please see Table 7.2).

Table 7.1 Why culture has changed (based on Gover et al., 2016)

Why culture changed	Quotations
Sheer amount of change	'I think people are happier, number one, because I think they were a little bit worried before. So many things were changing and some people were freaking and they were not doing very well with the change. Now they realize the change is not so bad and they can embrace it.'
People leaving the organization	'Staff that were completely disengaged, and had been here being disengaged forever, and dragging everyone down with them. And we've gotten rid of a lot of them. And I don't mean fired, I mean it's just through attrition, through retirements, and moving on, and things like that, which is good.'

Table 7.2 Example of organizational change rumour types and categories (based upon Bordia et al., 2006)

Organizational change rumour category	Examples
Job loss	Rumours of downsizing, job losses, technology regarded as replacing staff
Negative work practice changes	Increased workload for less pay
Negative impact on career	Lack of career advancement, negative changes to terms of employment
Loss of job facilities	'Staff car park to go'
Improved work environment	'There will be lots of lifts and the toilets will be self-flushing'
No staff reductions	No job losses, increased number of jobs
Positive work practice changes	'Voice recognition for X-ray reporting'
Changes to the structure and nature of the organization	'The new hospital will be a private hospital'
Poor change management	Statements criticising change planning and management practices
Negative changes to service delivery	'There will be no oxygen available in bathrooms, only portable oxygen'
Positive changes to service delivery	Positive statements about advances in patient care
Gossip and innuendo about individuals	Statements alleging staff turnover and nefarious activities
Not a rumour or unclassifiable	Preponderance of rumours or respondent stating that they do not listen to rumours

Table 7.2 highlights interrelated aspects of organizational change, such as resistance, communications and leadership (discussed in subsequent chapters). However, for the purposes of this chapter, it highlights the different ways individuals will experience the same organizational change informed by rumours. By implication, the experience of one individual may inform the experience of others through the rumours about organizational change they share.

Understanding individual differences, psychodynamics and identities

In this section, an introduction and overview of how we understand individuals, psychodynamics and identity in organizations is presented, which informs subsequent discussion about individuals, psychodynamics, and identity with regards to organizational change.

Individual differences

Oswick and Marshak (2012) highlighted the prevalence of journeying metaphors in explaining organizational change. A change manager might be heard to say 'Are you on the bus?' The assumption is that everyone in an organization is having a shared/universal experience of an organizational change, travelling in the same direction, at the same pace towards a common destination. Whilst, such assumptions make leading/managing an organizational change easier, they are unrealistic in terms of what we know about individuals and individual differences. The type of questions differential psychologists ask relate to the ways people differ from each other and why (Revelle et al., 2011). There are many ways in which individuals experiencing the same organizational change differ, but for illustrative purposes personality, individual transitions and gender will be featured in this subsection. These individual differences are subsequently related to organizational change in the next section.

Gabriel (2008: 220) defines personality as '...a term that indicates those qualities that make a person different from others, unique'. Gabriel (2008) acknowledges that there have been many attempts to systematically analyse personality, with these attempts broadly following two approaches – nomothetic and idiographic. Nomothetic approaches look for law-like generalizations in identifying personality types, with psychological/personality tests favoured by employers being indicative of such an approach. Idiographic approaches focus upon unique, ad hoc and accidental factors believed to shape personality. Psychodynamics featured in the next subsection is indicative of an idiographic approach, so here the focus is upon nomothetic accounts of personality. Wilson (2018) describes a psychometric test as a means of assessing a person's ability or personality in a structured way. She identifies three main types of test: ability, personality and interest. In Table 7.3, the three best known psychometric tests are highlighted.

Wilson (2018) highlights that 95 per cent of the FTSE 100 companies, the police, and the civil service use personality tests to select staff.

Another way of thinking about individual differences is in terms of the different ways we deal with transitions as individuals. Holmes and Rahe (1967) famously rated the significance of social adjustments we have to make when confronted by a life event such as the death of a spouse (ranked 100), pregnancy (ranked 40) and holidays (ranked 13). This type of ranking helps us to appreciate that regardless of organizational change

Table 7.3 Best-known psychometric tests (Wilson, 2018)

1   The 16PF test is based upon 16 factors such as 'unassertive/dominant' and 'objective/
    sensitive'.
2   Eysenck's personality test is based upon a small number of basic dimensions of
    people such as 'stable/unstable' and 'introvert/extrovert'.
3   The Myers-Briggs Type Indicator (MBTI) test examines four bipolar personality
    dimensions 'extraversion/introversion', 'sensing/intuition', 'thinking/feeling' and
    'judging/perceiving'.

all of our lives are characterised by a series of individual transitions which we have to navigate, some significant, others less significant. What such rankings highlight is that whilst a hierarchy is specified, we may experience an event such as a holiday very differently from other individuals.

One life event we all have to adjust to at some point is the death of a spouse (ranked 100) and/or a close family member (ranked 63). Kübler-Ross's (1969) model featured in *On Death and Dying* has been influential in beginning to explain the experience of such a life changing event. Kübler-Ross (1969) identified five stages individuals go through when facing up to death. First, there was denial and isolation during which the dying patient questioned the truth of their diagnosis. Second, there was anger with the dying patient experiencing feelings such as anger, rage, envy and resentment. Third, there was bargaining with the dying patient attempting to reach an agreement which would postpone the inevitable. Fourth, there was depression with the dying patient's anger replaced with numbness and growing stoicism. Fifth, there was acceptance when the dying patient reached a certain degree of quiet acceptance. Decades later, the stages individuals experience still feel applicable to making sense of major life events we have to navigate. However, Kübler-Ross (1969) has been the subject of significant controversy in recent decades. Larson's (2014) book review of *Beyond Kübler-Ross: New Perspectives on Death, Dying and Grief* (Doka and Tucci, 2011) offers an overview of how this field of study has moved forwards and the limitations of seeing dying in terms of a series of linear progressive stages. More than 40 years later, we experience death differently in terms of medicine and hospices and we grieve differently in terms of developments in counselling and therapies. However, for Larson (2014: 351), Kübler-Ross should not be remembered for her stage model, which was never empirically supported, 'her contribution lies instead in her call to action, her insistence that we listen to dying persons and stop avoiding the conversations that are essential to enhancing quality of life at the end of life'.

Another significant difference which can be lost in the enthusiasm to lead or manage change relates to gender. In the context of the *Wiley-Blackwell Handbook of Individual Differences*, Revelle et al. (2011) pose the question whether men and women are different. They answer yes, although they acknowledge that how and why continues to be an important question for differential psychologists. Alvesson and Billing's (2009) *Understanding Gender and Organizations*, introduces major debates relating gender and organizations (see also Gatrell and Swan, 2008). Alvesson and Billing (2009: 5) acknowledge that gender patterns are complex and often contradictory 'the gender-in-organizations perspective focuses on women and men as fairly robust categories and investigates how these are treated, behave and/or experience work and life'. They highlight an increasing interest in gender and organizations in recent decades. However, there is still an assumption of knowledge and knowledge production as gender neutral, with attempts to address this assumption sometimes regarded as tick-box exercises. Alvesson and Billing (2009: 11) acknowledge that social science does not only study gender but contributes actively to the construction of gender, 'Gender studies is a political project, where knowledge production is oriented towards change.' Alvesson and Billing (2009) present three major positions in gender studies:

1   Notions of gender as central/relevant to understanding social relations, institutions and processes
2   Gender relations as constituting a problem characterised by domination/subordination, inequalities, oppression, and oppositions
3   Gender relations as social constructions

Focussing more specifically upon gender and management/leadership, Alvesson and Billing (2009) doubt that there are any definitive answers instead favouring the development of sensitivity towards different ways of framing and reasoning about women and management/leadership. They highlight four different positions which could be taken. First, the equal opportunities position highlights fundamental inequalities and injustices in society with women regarded as being a discriminated group denied the same opportunities as men. The rationale for this position is often moral and political. The second position is meritocratic with irrational social forces seen as preventing the full utilisation of qualified human resources (women). The concern here is less with fairness and more about achieving maximum efficiency for social institutions. The third position consciously draws attention to differences between men and women through highlighting the special contribution of women.

> Women are believed to prefer a people-oriented and democratic leadership style, to make the social structure less hierarchical, and to change the workplace climate so that empathy and intuition become more significant.
>
> (Alvesson and Billing, 2009: 171)

The fourth position, the alternative values position is the most radical. The assumption here is that women and men do not share interests, priorities and basic attitudes. Alternative values proponents are anti-management, being more interested in developing alternative social institutions, rather than the idea of integrating women into existing institutions (see also, Gipson et al., 2017).

Psychodynamics

Another way to think about the experiences of individuals inside organizations is in terms of psychodynamics. Kets de Vries and Miller (1984 and 1986) gave impetus to psychoanalytic accounts of organizing through their accounts of the neurotic organization. Halton (1994) highlighted psychoanalysis as an approach to contributing to what goes on in institutions. He (1994: 11) suggested that the approach involved '… understanding ideas developed in the context of individual therapy, as well as, looking at institutions in terms of unconscious emotional processes'. He regarded institutions in a manner similar to individuals as developing defences against emotions which were felt to be too threatening or painful to acknowledge. He acknowledged the contribution of Melanie Klein through her psychoanalytic work in the 1920s, which enabled us to conceptualise the unconscious inner world within everyone.

Whilst the approach involves the application of psychoanalysis to organizational life, the term psychodynamics is often preferred as being less treatment oriented (Carr and Gabriel, 2001).

Gabriel (1999) gave impetus to studying psychodynamic aspects of organizations. Traditionally students are taught organizational behaviour (OB) which applies social psychology theories to organizations. Psychodynamics does not supplant OB but instead seeks to complement OB explanations of organizational life. Instead of focussing upon individual behaviours and differences, the focus turns to meanings behind and motivations for such behaviour. This focus leads to an interest in images, symbols, myths and emotions. More recently, there has been an increasing interest in understanding the dark side of organizations (Tourish, 2013; Linstead et al., 2014) and in these critical accounts the psychodynamic aspects of the behaviours of individuals are again apparent. For Linstead et al. (2014: 170) 'accepting that the dark side may be deeply rooted in an inner darkness of the individual psyche can open up a different perspective at the individual level' (please see Chapter 16 for further discussion about the dark side of organizations).

Identities

Whilst, identity may be engaged with at the level of individuals, groups and organizations, here the focus is at the individual level and identity work in particular.

> When we join an organization, we surrender some of our individuality (we wear uniforms, conform to various behaviours and link our identity to work ('I am a nurse', I am a 'doctor'))
>
> (Walsh et al., 2011: 208)

> Identities, people's subjectively construed understandings of who they were, are and desire to become, are implicated in, and thus key to understanding and explaining, almost everything that happens in and around organizations.
>
> (Brown, 2015: 20)

Alvesson and Willmott (2002) in their classic paper gave impetus to studying identity in the context of work and organization. Through exploring links between organizational control and identity regulation, they developed an analysis of identity work addressing the interplay between self-identity, identity work and the regulation of identity. They consciously encouraged a research and scholarship agenda offering a way into what at times can be a discursive body of literature. Alvesson and Willmott (2002) highlighted how discourses of quality management, service management, innovation, and knowledge work (organizational change could be added to this list) promote interest in passion, soul, and charisma. This has resulted in an increased managerial interest in regulating employees 'insides', self-images, feelings, and identifications with these developments requiring greater understanding about the employee as an identity worker. They believe that, as cultural mechanisms are introduced or refined to gain/sustain employee commitment managing identity work becomes more salient and critical to employment relationships.

Table 7.4 Identity influenced, regulated and changed in work organizations (Alvesson and Willmott, 2002)

1 Defining the person directly – for example, a 'male middle manager'.
2 Defining the person by defining others – referencing one person by the characteristics of others.
3 Providing a specific vocabulary of motives – what is important and natural for a person to do is established.
4 Explicating morals and values – moral stories and espoused values orient identity.
5 Knowledge and skills – construction of knowledge and skills as key resources in regulating identity.
6 Group categorisation and affiliation – regulating identity through ascribing social categories to individuals.
7 Hierarchical location – status distinctions can be central for the regulation of identities.
8 Establishing and classifying a distinct set of rules of the game – establishing the 'natural' way of doing things.
9 Defining the context – explicating the scene as a precondition for people acting in it.

In Table 7.4, nine modes of identity regulation identified by Alvesson and Willmott (2002) are highlighted and numbered. They regard 1 and 2 as relating directly to the employee, 3, 4 and 5 as referring to action orientations, 6 and 7 referring to social relations and 8 and 9 as referring to the scene – the wider social, organizational and economic terrain.

In bringing identity work up to date, Brown's (2015) recently published literature review is very informative. He acknowledges that studies of identity have a long heritage going back to the 1950s, but that the last three decades have witnessed identity moving to the centre of intellectual debates. Brown's (2015: 21) interest in identity work was concerned with studies of individual agency and their limitations. The term identity refers to '...the meanings that individuals attach reflexively to their selves as they seek to answer questions such as: "how shall I relate to others?"' One reason Brown (2015) regards theorising identity work as important is through bridging levels of analysis in organization studies. For example, studies investigating relationships between individuals, dyads, groups, organizations, professions and communities are regarded as being potentially fruitful.

Individual differences, psychodynamics, identities and organizational change

In the previous section, individual differences, psychodynamics and identities were generically introduced and explained. In this section, these concepts are applied to understanding organizational change. Whilst organizations are comprised of individuals, groups and teams believed to be working towards some common purpose, experiences of organizational change will differ considerably. Smith and Graetz (2011) in their overview of organizational change philosophies acknowledged that change management philosophies often ignore the different ways individuals experience organizational change. However, within what they refer to as the 'psychological philosophy of organizational change' there is an opportunity to treat the impact of change as complex, powerful and potentially severe. In the following discussion, considerations of individual differences, psychodynamics and identities are used to navigate the literature. However, in considering both theories and practices of organizational change, these boundaries are artificial.

Individual differences and organizational change

In focussing upon the ways individuals differ, personality, individual transitions and gender featured in the previous section and these approaches may be applied to explaining the different ways that an individual experiences organizational change. Garrety et al. (2003) studied employees at Sprogwheels a male-dominated industrial plant in Australia, in particular, focussing upon an organizational change programme being facilitated by external consultants using a Myers-Briggs Type Indicator (MBTI) of personality types. They focussed upon how employees interpreted and deployed the MBTI discourse, highlighting how from the subject's point of view some identities at Sprogwheels were desirable and others objectionable.

> The MBTI can be interpreted as a discursive tool that purports to define what sorts of people exist in the world. Its dichotomies and lists of weaknesses lay out ready-made directions for self-improvement.
>
> (Garrety et al., 2003: 223)

They found that in contrast to 'tough' and 'weak' identities which characterised the old Sprogwheels. They found that MBTI furnished a richer set of possibilities and that employees themselves reproduced, resisted or reconfigured power relationships during organizational change.

Kumar and Kamalanabhan (2005) conducted research into a large public sector undertaking in India. They were interested in the influence of personality on employees' ability to cope with organizational change. They found that the personality factors of perceived control, optimism and change self-efficacy had a significant relationship on coping with organizational change. Caldwell and Liu (2011) investigated the influence of personality in response to organizational change drawing their data from 532 employees in 26 organizations in the south-eastern US, finding that:

> …influences of personality on individual reactions to change are complex. While the positive influences of an individual's openness to experience on job satisfaction tend to occur only when fairness associated with change implementation is high, positive influences of conscientiousness are the highest when both procedural fairness is high and the extent of impact on the individual's job is low.
>
> (Caldwell and Liu, 2011: 74)

Herrmann and Nadkarni (2014) focussed upon the personalities of chief executive officers (CEO) managing strategic change. Their data drawn from 120 medium-sized enterprises in Ecuador revealed a dual role for these CEOs requiring personality traits to initiate strategic changes and traits to improve the performance effects of strategic change.

In terms of individual transitions, Elrod and Tippett's (2002) informative review of how individuals respond to change and transition drew together many of the models which have been used to explain human involvement in organizational change processes. They drew two main conclusions from their review. First, that most models followed Lewin's (1947) Three-Step model of change and second that models tended to describe a degradation of capabilities at the intermediate stages of a change process, with an implication that things often got worse before they got better. They refer to Kübler-Ross (1969) discussed earlier and whilst she never depicted human transitions graphically as a curve, her pioneering work appears to have given impetus to later organizational transition curves (see, for example, Schneider and Goldwasser, 1998 and Conner, 1998). A third way of thinking about individual differences in the context of organizational change is in terms of gender.

Ely and Meyerson (2000) in developing their framework for gender and organizational change reviewed three traditional frameworks. These were labelled 'fix the women', 'value the feminine' and 'create equal opportunities'. They highlight how each framework offered a different definition of gender, different definitions of the problem, different visions of gender equity and approaches towards organizational change. However, they perceived weaknesses in each of these traditional frameworks and instead they favoured a fourth framework labelled 'assess and revise work culture'. They regarded gender as defining a system of oppressive relations reproduced in and by social practices. The problem was that these social practices were designed for and by a white heterosexual class of privileged men. Their vision of gender equity was concerned with identifying and revising these oppressive social practices (similar to Alvesson and Billing's, 2009 alternative values position). Their favoured approach towards change was emergent involving localised processes of incremental change. The benefits of the framework were in exposing the lack of neutrality in organizational change practices.

Linstead et al. (2005) mirrored Ely and Meyerson's (2000) concerns in their critical review of approaches to gender and change management encouraging organizational change to be read from a more gendered perspective. They acknowledged that we know far more about the gendered nature of organizational change than we knew a decade ago, but that we have barely scratched the surface. Again, there are parallels with Ely and Meyerson (2000) when Linstead et al. (2005) encourage thinking about change and gender in terms of the way gender affects how managers think and act.

> ...Management is inescapably embodied and therefore, also a gendered experience, an experience which is different for men and women whether they are the managers or the managed...This gender in management approach argues that, because men and women are socialized differently, they manage differently.
>
> (Linstead et al., 2005: 546)

Linstead et al. (2005) revisited unfreeze, change, refreeze models inspired by Lewin's (1947) writing regarding these models with their emphasis upon steps as masculinist models of change. Their counterpoint is that feminine values would provide an alternative to the dominance of masculine identities in workplaces. This leads into the next two subsections which focus upon psychodynamics and identities.

Psychodynamics and organizational change

Ket de Vries and Balazs's (1998) paper 'Beyond the Quick Fix', persuasively makes the case for the application of psychodynamic principles to organizational transformation and change. They argue that through observing different stages of individual change, parallels may be drawn between individual and organizational change processes. They highlight how we often have anxieties with regards to engaging in something new or once again being exposed to old dangers.

They highlight that there are prerequisites for us to embark upon personal change; negative emotions, a focal event and a public declaration of intent. Negative emotions are straightforward. For the focal event, they suggest thinking metaphorically of the 'last straw' and they suggest that the public declaration is literally when some-body publicly declares their intent to change. These three prerequisites are believed to lead into the inner journey which contributes to the internalisation of the change. They see these stages of personal change as being equally applicable at an organizational level.

In introducing a special issue of the *Journal of Organizational Change Management*, Carr and Gabriel (2001) took the opportunity to offer their own overview of the psychodynamics of organizational change management. They acknowledge that psychoanalysis has gone beyond its patient-analyst origins developing theories of group behaviour, work relations, leadership, religion, art, and culture. The commonality in all these developments is the view that unconscious forces stimulate or stifle creativity, cooperation, achievement and learning. They acknowledge that psychoanalysis draws attention to the psychological work required to keep organizations going and enable them to change, as well as, the precarious nature of many human relationships. They acknowledge that at the time of writing they did not find an appreciation of psychodynamic processes in the management of change literature. However, they believed that psychoanalysis was very relevant in understanding the unconscious and emotional responses organizational change creates.

> Some of these forces can be seen as inhibiting change, resisting it or denying it, others can be seen as propelling change, fuelling it with energy and hope, yet others can be seen as maintaining change by ensuring that necessary psychological and emotional adjustments are made.
>
> (Carr and Gabriel, 2001: 418/419)

Since the encouragement of Kets de Vries and Balazs (1998) and Carr and Gabriel (2001) to apply psychodynamics to organizational change management, there has been far greater engagement, although what quickly becomes apparent is that authors inevitably focus upon an aspect of the larger psychoanalysis/psychodynamics literature in demonstrating its applicability to organizational change. Vince's (2002) psychodynamic understanding of organizational change is illustrated through application to Hyder PLC, the largest private company in Wales.

> A key insight provided by psychodynamic studies is that people in organizations desire and encourage change whilst also avoiding and resisting it. The act of organizing involves attempts to make change happen at the same time as creating ways to contain or control it.
>
> (Vince, 2002: 1194)

The unifying concept which he carefully introduces is labelled the politics of imagined stability. He revisits Gabriel's (1999) writings cited earlier, noting that emotion creates, perpetuates and holds together individuals and organizations.

> Individually and collectively, organizational members act as if an organization is a coherent entity that can be described in terms of mission, assumptions and underlying values (or even primary task). In other words, people tend to relate more to organizations as fixed and coherent than we do to the idea of organizations as diverse, living enterprises.
>
> (Vince, 2002: 1192)

Vince's (2002) concern is that organizations might be taken in by their own fantasies (Gabriel, 1999) imagining stability. The politics element is both social and strategic with social politics referring to, for example, gendered social relations. Strategic politics is concerned with 'the way we do things around here'. The politics of imagined stability offers a different perspective on the management of change which characterises and informs the limits and possibilities of organizational change in specific contexts. In *Covert Processes at Work: Managing the Five Hidden Dimensions of Organizational Change*, Marshak (2006) identified six dimensions of organizational change: reasons, politics, inspirations, emotions, mindsets, and psychodynamics with reason regarded as overt whereas the other dimensions were viewed as covert.

Walsh et al. (2011) drew upon psychodynamic literature and their own experiences in understanding organizational change in an Australian health service setting, noting that health settings are highly emotional environments. They highlight three critical paradoxes: behaviour and interaction are influenced by interpersonal mechanisms, mechanisms which are critically important in the evolution of workplace cultures and these mechanisms markedly influence organizational functioning. Their concern is that technical structural-functionalist approaches to organizational change do not fit with the reality of change in organizations, in that people do not respond to a technical orientation in a passive or rational/predictable way. They believe that once unconscious mechanisms at play in health services are recognised, it is possible to discuss anxieties directly and in mutually supportive ways. Addressing anxieties undermines the need for defences and breaks down assumptions behind 'us' and 'them' thinking.

Identities and organizational change

In focussing upon identities, artificial boundaries between individuals, their personalities and their identity increasingly blur. Garrety et al. (2003), for example, were interested in personality, but equally identity and emotions. In seeking to understand identity work and organizational change in the context of this textbook, Sturdy et al.'s (2006) account of managers' reflections on studying management ideas in the context of an MBA are intriguing. Those managers studied found the management ideas they were taught were inappropriate for application in organizations or were impeded by their organizations. However, they regarded the acquisition of management ideas as giving them a sense of 'self-confidence' which was reinforced through management education discourses. These managers and part-time students largely dismissed the specific managerial tools and techniques they were taught (discussed further in Chapter 15). Instead '...the strategic perspective and the acquisition of a specific managerial discourse was seen as useful both in terms of decision making and career progression' (Sturdy et al., 2006: 851). The MBA primarily legitimised their adoption and enactment of the identity of manager. In the context of organizational change, those 'managing change' may be involved in similar identity construction. Watson (2009) regards identity as having enormous potential as a bridge between individual agency, choice, and creation of self, in contrast with history, culture and the social shaping of identity.

Beech et al. (2011) were interested in apparent contradictions between accounts of self as change-oriented and subsequent inaction, regarding the issue of self-identity (their own notion of who they are) was central to explaining this contradiction.

> The delineation of people into pro- and anti-change identities is problematic as it does not allow for the possibility that some people may simultaneously hold

positive and negative views about a particular change initiative. Questioning individual, psychodynamic and identity-based explanations.

(Beech et al., 2011: 291)

Instead of regarding people as having a unique and bounded identity, they favoured a
view of identity as not fully formed. They highlighted an interplay between an individual's 'self-identity' and their 'social identity' (the notion of that person in external
discourses, institutions, and culture). During organizational change, identities may be
expressed and influences can be internalised in different ways simultaneously (Beech
et al., 2011).

Questioning individual difference, psychodynamic and identity-based explanations

Studying individual differences, psychodynamics and identity work offers different
perspectives and explanations for how individuals experience organizational change.
In this way, they deepen our understanding of the subtleties and complexities of organizational change, particularly those overt and unconscious aspects often overlooked
in more traditional analyses. Each approach has strengths, but also weaknesses.
Weaknesses do not necessarily negate adopting an explanation, but explanations do
need to be used knowingly.

Individual-based approaches

In many ways, interest in psychodynamics and identities appears to have been fuelled
by shortcomings in individual-based accounts of organizational life and it is consequently necessary to acknowledge these limitations. O'Doherty (2017) highlights
the concept of the individual as a recent and Western social invention as there was
a time, when we thought of ourselves not so much as individuals, but as role holders. In looking at individuals in isolation from other factors there are real dangers,
that if an organizational change is successful it is attributed to heroic individuals
and if unsuccessful, individuals are blamed for their shortcomings and for 'resisting
change' (see Chapter 13). There are real dangers in attempting to explain organizational change at the level of individuals in that wider external economic, political, social and technological factors are ignored, as well as, cultural and structural
explanations.

Personality, individual transitions and gender affect us differently in how we experience organizational change. Today, personality testing is very prevalent in organizations as a methodology for recruiting and promoting employees. The potential danger
of such reliance is that it encourages us to think in terms of the traits of individuals
and potentially to discriminate, with individual traits perceived either positively or
negatively. Psychological testing reflects a nomothetic approach which whilst presenting itself as an objective science may have biases built into assumptions about what
makes a 'good' or 'bad' employee. Hurtz and Donovan (2000) revisited the 'big 5'
personality dimensions used to gauge job performance. The big five personality dimensions as identified by Barrick and Mount (1991) were openness to experience,
conscientiousness, extraversion, agreeableness and neuroticism. Hurtz and Donovan
(2000) were interested in the validity of explicit 'big 5' measures for predicting job
performance and contextual performance. Analyses with contextual performance

showed more complex relations among the 'big 5' and performance, requiring a more critical interpretation of the big 5-performance relationship.

In terms of individual transition models, the contribution of Kübler-Ross's (1969) bereavement work was acknowledged as a metaphor for how individuals might experience organizational change. However, there is something slightly crass in comparing an individual's experience of death with an individual's experience of, for example, business process re-engineering. The other caution is that whilst Kübler-Ross (1969) was a pioneer, her work has been the subject of considerable critique in the death and bereavement studies fields as discussed earlier. Gouldner (1971) famously highlighted the influence of background assumptions in formulating social theories. The stages of bereavement may have been favoured in modelling organizational change transitions, as much because of their background assumptions as any empirical evidence. Whilst, Elrod and Tippett (2002) gathered empirical studies together supporting the utility of these individual transition models, there is a need to question any transitional model which purportedly explains the diverse experiences of individuals during times of organizational change. The concern is that organizational change is depicted as a rational and linear process which these transition curves imply, with implications for managing, leading and experiencing organizational change.

Gender was highlighted as a significant difference in understanding experiences of organizational change. Linstead et al. (2005) acknowledged that we know far more about the gendered nature of change than we knew a decade ago, but that we have barely scratched the surface and this still seems to be applicable today. There is a need for caution when offering gendered explanations of organizational change given the evidence base. Also, when we look to studies of organizations and gender, Alvesson and Billing (2009) acknowledge that there are no definitive answers instead favouring developing a sensitivity for different ways to frame and reason women and management/leadership. The implication is that academics favouring an equal opportunities position will offer a very different explanation from those favouring an alternative values position.

Psychodynamic based approaches

The special issue of the *Journal of Organizational Change Management* devoted to psychodynamics and organizational change (Carr and Gabriel, 2001) cited earlier included a contribution, which whilst supportive of the contribution of psychoanalysis to understanding organizational change, also highlighted limitations. Kirsten (2001) focussed her concerns upon Kets de Vries and Miller's (1984 and 1986) accounts of the neurotic organization, which she regarded as more concerned with individual imbalances and their consequences, rather than problems of domination and control highlighted in the critical tradition. There was a tendency to individualise problems of structural inequality and control (this critique appears to be applicable to the earlier discussion of individual differences). Four problems in individual-based accounts of organizational neurosis were identified. First, in the relationship between organizational neurosis, the leader and organizational structure is unclear. Second, there are problems with individual and organizational identity with regards to power and control. Focussing upon individuals and in particular company executives encourages others to see power and control as residing within individuals. Third, the solution to the neurotic organization is perceived in terms of curing top executives through therapy, removing top executives or creating change through a dramatic failure in an organization. The concern here is that there is no acknowledgement of the agency of organizational members. Fourth, there is a danger in personalising an organization as neurotic in that the organization is separated from the internal and external power structures that control it.

Identity-based approaches

Whilst the study of identity work has gathered momentum in recent years, Brown (2015) acknowledged that how identities should be theorised and researched has been the subject of significant debate. He summarises these debates in terms of the extent to which identities are:

i   chosen by or ascribed to individuals;
ii generally stable, evolutionarily adaptive or fluid;
iii unified and coherent or fragmented and possibly contradictory;
iv motivated (or not) motivated by a need for positive meaning; and
v   framed (or not framed) by a desire for authenticity.

Brown (2015) acknowledged that the concept of identity work is not neutral as a metaphor. It creates patterns and is not merely a reflection of relationships and understandings. In reflecting upon his review of the identity work literature, Brown (2015) identified two of the most significant academic objections that have been made in studying identity work. First, it has been suggested that identity work is too limited in scope to account for the people aspects of organizations, and second, that there are moral dangers attached to its use and that further research might focus on the ethics of identity work.

Summary

The chapter may be succinctly summarised through answering the questions posed in the chapter's introduction. The original questions are restated in italics.

What is it like to experience organizational change? The unifying theme of this chapter has been that we all experience organizational change in unique ways? These experiences have been explained in terms of individual differences, psychodynamics and identities.

What do we know about individual differences, psychodynamics, and identities when applied to organizational life? In terms of individual differences, for illustrative purposes personality, individual transitions and gender were featured. Gabriel (2008) highlighted that broadly there were two approaches – nomothetic and idiographic with the 16PF test, Eysenck's personality test and Myers-Briggs Type Indicators commonly used in organizations (Wilson, 2018). Another way of thinking about individual differences was in terms of the different ways we deal with transitions as individuals. The influence of Kübler-Ross's (1969) model of bereavement in understanding individual differences was acknowledged. Another significant individual difference highlighted was gender with Alvesson and Billing (2009) highlighting different positions: equal opportunities, meritocratic, special contribution and alternative values. Another way of thinking about the experiences of individuals inside organizations was in terms of psychodynamics.

How do studies of individual differences, psychodynamics, and identities inform our understanding of organizational change? Personality, individual transitions, and gender may be applied to explaining the different ways that an individual experiences organizational change. Garrety et al. (2003) researched the experience of Myers-Briggs Type Indicator (MBTI) of personality types. Kumar and Kamalanabhan (2005) researched the influence of personality on employees' ability to cope with organizational change and Caldwell and Liu (2011) investigated the influence of personality in response to organizational change. Herrmann and Nadkarni (2014) focussed upon the personality traits required by CEOs initiating change. In terms of individual transitions, Elrod and Tippett's (2002) informative review of how individuals respond to change and transition was highlighted. In terms of gender Ely and Meyerson (2000) developed a framework for gender and organizational change as a critique of three traditional frameworks, labelled 'fix the women', 'value the feminine' and 'create equal opportunities'.

Vince (2002) applied a psychodynamic understanding of organizational change to Hyder PLC, introducing the concept of the politics of imagined stability. Vince's (2002) concern was that organizations might be taken in by their own fantasies. Marshak (2006) and Walsh et al.'s (2011) psychodynamic contributions were also featured. Beech et al. (2011) highlighted apparent contradictions between accounts of self as change-oriented and subsequent inaction, regarding the issue of self-identity (their own notion of who they are) was central to explaining this contradiction.

What critical questions need to be addressed when studying individual differences, psychodynamics, and identities? Interest in psychodynamics and identities appears to have been fuelled by perceived shortcomings in individual-based accounts of organizational life. The concept of the individual is a recent and Western social invention (O'Doherty, 2017). There are real dangers in attempting to explain organizational change at the level of individuals in that wider external economic, political, social and technological factors are ignored, as well as, cultural and structural explanations. Personality testing is very prevalent in organizations as a methodology for recruiting and promoting employees. However, such tests potentially discriminate and stereotype, with individual traits perceived either positively or negatively.

In terms of individual transition models, whilst, Elrod and Tippett (2002) gathered empirical studies together supporting the utility of these individual transition models, there is a need to question any transitional model which purportedly explains the diverse experiences of individuals during times of organizational change. Gender was highlighted as a significant difference in understanding experiences of organizational change. However, there is a need for caution when offering gendered explanations of organizational change given the evidence base. In terms of psychodynamic approaches to organizational change, Kirsten (2001) focussed her concerns upon Kets de Vries and Miller's (1984 and 1986) accounts of the neurotic organization, which she regarded as more concerned with individual imbalances and their consequences, rather than problems of domination and control highlighted by the critical tradition with a tendency to individualise problems of structural inequality and control. Brown (2015) acknowledged that the concept of identity work was not neutral as a metaphor. It created patterns and is not merely a reflection of relationships and understandings.

Research case study showcase: on being a leader in the US Coast Guard

Eriksen's (2008) self-reflexive case of being a leader in the US Coast Guard reported in the *Journal of Organizational Change Management* is showcased here. For the full case and further analysis please visit the original source.

Case study source

Eriksen (2008) undertook autoethnography in which his own experience of leading change in the US Coast Guard became the topic of investigation. He writes in the first person employing self-questioning in order to confront things less than flattering about himself. Unlike a large amount of management and organization studies research, he was not attempting to convey universal truths about leading or changing, but instead to offer a self-narrative of an organizational change experience which the reader might relate to, providing a lens through which a reader might obtain personal insights into leading organizational change. This approach is informed by a belief that organizational members need to internalise change in order for it to change their attitudes, values and behaviours.

Eriksen., M. 2008. "Leading Adaptive Organizational Change: Self-reflexivity and Self-Transformation." *Journal of Organizational Change Management* 21(5): 622–640.

Case study

When the Coast Guard Academy was founded in 1876, it only admitted men. It was regarded as a US institution where boys went to become men. The first women were admitted to the US Coast Guard 100 years later, in 1976. Advances had been made in gender equality. However, the Coast Guard remained a male-dominated, male-identified and male-centred culture, equality in Coast Guard policy did not necessarily equate to women experiencing equality in their day-to-day lives. When female cadets graduated into the operational Coast Guard as officers, their level of representation dropped dramatically.

Erikson's (2008) directed studies formed the basis of a change initiative within the Coast Guard. The intention was that through the cadets' and his interactions and influence, the Coast Guard Academy could move towards becoming a place of greater gender equality. Erikson (2008) realised that the most effective way to facilitate change at an academic institution was with the students.

> We operated from the assumption that the female cadets and I would be changed through our community of inquiry and practice of self-reflexivity.
> *(Erikson, 2008: 626)*

Three critical incidents (the towel incident, 'men' talking about directed study participants and paternalism) made it painfully clear to Erikson (2008) that he was not embodying the organizational change he was seeking, forcing him to face his own sexism and paternalism.

(Continued)

The towel incident

The weights room at the academy was a room few women entered. Erikson (2008) went to get a towel to dry himself off after a shower, grabbing two extra towels for two male officers who were still lifting weights, he held out two towels for them, exclaiming 'Here you go ladies.'

> As the words came out of my mouth, I recognized their inappropriateness and my hypocrisy. My comment was meant to be 'jokingly' derogatory and was based on the premise that women are physically weak and any 'Man, especially one who lifts free weights, would be insulted by such a comment.' It would be calling them the exact opposite of who they were trying to be. Then my thoughts immediately went to my interactions and work with the female cadets, and a sick feeling entered my stomach.
>
> *(Erikson, 2008: 627)*

He reflects that given the normalcy of the comment it passed without comment. He acknowledges his self-embarrassment, but that the moment allowed him to see himself.

'Men' talking about a directed study participants

Over time word spread about the directed study and working with women cadet participants. However, discussions with male military colleagues tended to focus on the attractiveness of the female cadets, rather than the purpose of the directed study. After the towel incident, Erikson (2008) watched himself more closely. Although his reflex would be to join such conversations, he realised he could no longer engage in this banter. This meant giving up the opportunity of male bonding through connecting with male military colleagues. He began to realise that through years of this type of conversation about women, he was reducing them to sexual objects.

> Regardless of the nature of our relationship, the conversation would invariably include a discussion of them as sexual objects; basically, the conversation would be a discussion about whether or not we would want to have sex with this woman and why so or why not.
>
> *(Erikson, 2008: 628)*

Paternalism

During his last year at the academy, a female officer confided to him how she had been sexually harassed. Subsequently, he mentioned these incidents to a commander that was working at headquarters in Washington DC. He believed his motivation was to help the commander understand that a sexist culture and climate still existed at the academy. The goal was to persuade a senior figure at headquarters to take such issues seriously, encouraging taking actions to improve lives of females at the academy. The commander reported these incidents to the Coast Guard investigative committee into sexual assault charges and other sexual harassment issues at the academy. The female officer was subsequently contacted by the Coast Guard investigative committee.

> The female officer called me a few days after that and asked me if I had reported the incident. I said yes and explained to her how it had all unfolded. She was and still is very upset with me. I had violated her trust. I had taken away her agency.
>
> *(Erikson, 2008: 628)*

Erikson (2008) initially attempted to rationalise that although he had violated her trust, it had been for the best of intentions in that actions would be taken to improve the sexist culture and climate of the academy. Despite these attempts at rationalisations, he still felt horrible about himself. It was only after further reflection and discussion with a retired female Army officer, the Director of Diversity at the Academy, and his wife, he understood and accepted that he had taken away the female officers' agency. He understood and accepted that she would inevitably suffer negative experiences having to report the incidents and that the Coast Guard would not be able to protect her from suffering retribution.

> While organizational policies can change, it is only through a fundamental change in who organizational members are in relation to one another that an organization has meaningfully changed. Meaningful organizational transformation does not occur without a corresponding self-transformation, most importantly of the individual leading the change.
>
> *(Erikson, 2008: 634)*

Case study questions

1   How does acknowledging/appreciating individual differences inform understanding this US Coast Guard leadership case?
2   How does acknowledging/appreciating psychodynamics inform understanding this US Coast Guard case?
3   How does acknowledging/appreciating identity inform understanding this US Coast Guard leadership case?

Discussion questions

1   What has driven interest in psychodynamics and identities in studying organizations in recent decades?
2   How do we reconcile our uniqueness as individuals with attempts to understand and engage with the different ways individuals experience organizational change?
3   What is the interface between attempts to manage/lead organizational change and identity work?
4   What are the advantages and disadvantages of differentiating the organizational change experiences of men and women?

Navigating individual difference, psychodynamic and identity focussed organizational change literature

Three strands of thinking relating to individual differences, psychodynamics and identities have unified this chapter. The end of chapter references offers a good starting point to engage with these very different literatures. There is a need for caution when doing further literature reviewing as large bodies of literature inform the three strands which largely exists outside the management and organization studies scope of this textbook. So psychology and social psychology have been very influential in informing our understanding of individuals in organizations. Psychology, psychiatry, counselling, health and sociology literature has informed understanding of psychodynamics and identities in organizational settings. In engaging with individual differences, psychodynamics and identities, these topics are contested within their respective disciplines and fields of study. Another caveat worth acknowledging is the artificiality of the demarcation between individuals, psychodynamics and identity adopted here. This demarcation aids exposition in the context of a chapter. However, on a particular organizational change initiative, individual differences, psychodynamics and identity work are likely to be simultaneously present. This is mirrored in the literature which does not compartmentalise the literature as presented here. The following notes potentially offer help in navigating these different kinds of literature.

An acknowledgement of individual differences has become a staple of organizational behaviour (OB) textbooks. Best-selling OB textbooks (Mullins with Christy, 2016 and Buchanan and Huczynski, 2016) are a good starting point in beginning to engage with individual differences. O'Doherty's (2017) chapter on *Individual Differences, Personality, and Self,* cited earlier is worth a look as it is very different from the normal OB textbook treatments. In seeking to understand individual differences, the challenge is that it is impossible to address every individual difference. Hence it is necessary to focus on those individual differences most pertinent to your interests. In looking to personality, these debates are often very prominent in social psychology textbooks. In terms of individual transitions in the context of organizational change, the Elrod and Tippett (2002) paper was informed by a comprehensive chronological review of the literature. In terms of gender, Wilson's (2018) OB textbook makes many informative connections between gender and organizations and Alvesson and Billing's (2009) book is very informative and importantly very readable.

In engaging with the psychodynamics literature, books such as *Organizations in Depth: The Psychoanalysis of Organizations* (Gabriel, 1999) gave impetus to relating psychoanalysis to organization studies. These books are important in orienting you towards the specific principles and beliefs. Before attempting to apply psychodynamics/psychoanalysis to organizational change, the latter builds upon the former. In terms of applications to organizational change, the writings of Alan Carr were initially very influential with the writings of Russ Vince subsequently becoming more influential. Identity literature may be engaged with at the level of individuals, groups and organizations. This raises choices about focussing potentially upon individual identity rather than organizational identity literature. Brown's (2015) paper cited earlier was very informative, published in the *International Journal of Management Reviews* and reported a very knowledgeable review of diverse identity literature unified through the theme of identity work.

References

Alvesson, M., and Y.D. Billing. 2009. *Understanding Gender and Organizations.* London: Sage Publications.

Alvesson, M., and H. Willmott. 2002. "Identity Regulation as Organizational Control: Producing the Appropriate Individual." *Journal of Management Studies* 39(5): 619–644.

Barrick, M.R. and M.K. Mount. 1991. "The Big Five Personality Dimensions and Job Performance: A Meta-Analysis." *Personnel Psychology* 44(1): 1–26.

Beech, N., I. Kajzer-Mitchell, C. Oswick, and M. Saren. 2011. "Barriers to Change and Identity Work in the Swampy Lowland." *Journal of Change Management* 11(3): 289–304.

Bordia, P., E. Jones, C. Gallois, V.J. Callan, and N. DiFonzo. 2006. "Management are Aliens! Rumors and Stress During Organizational Change." *Group & Organization Management* 31(5): 601–621.

Brown, A.D. 2015. "Identities and Identity Work in Organizations." *International Journal of Management Reviews* 17(1): 20–40.

Buchanan, D.A., and A.A. Huczynski. 2016. *Organizational Behaviour.* Harlow: Pearson Education.

Caldwell, S.D., and Y. Liu 2011. "Further Investigating the Influence of Personality in Employee Response to Organisational Change: The Moderating Role of Change-Related Factors." *Human Resource Management Journal* 21(1): 74–89.

Carr, A., and Y. Gabriel. 2001. "The Psychodynamics of Organizational Change Management: An Overview." *Journal of Organizational Change Management* 14(5): 415–421.

Conner D.R. 1998. *Managing at the Speed of Change.* Chichester: John Wiley and Sons.

Doka, K.J., and A.S. Tucci (Eds). 2011. *Beyond Kübler-Ross: New Perspectives on Death, Dying and Grief.* Washington, DC: Hospice Foundation of America.

Driver, M. 2009. "From Loss to Lack: Stories of Organizational Change as Encounters with Failed Fantasies of Self, Work and Organization." *Organization* 16(3): 353–369.

Elrod II, P.D., and D.D. Tippett. 2002. "The 'Death Valley' of Change." *Journal of Organizational Change Management* 15(3): 273–291.

Ely, R.J. and D.E. Meyerson. 2000. "Theories of Gender in Organizations: A New Approach to Organizational Analysis and Change." *Research in Organizational Behavior* 22: 103–151.

Eriksen., M. 2008. "Leading Adaptive Organizational Change: Self-reflexivity and Self-Transformation." *Journal of Organizational Change Management* 21(5): 622–640.

Gabriel, Y. 1999. *Organizations in Depth: The Psychoanalysis of Organizations.* London: Sage Publications.

Gabriel, Y. 2008. *Organizing Words: A Critical Thesaurus for Social and Organization Studies.* Oxford: Oxford University Press.

Garrety, K., R. Badham, V. Morrigan, W. Rifkin, and M. Zanko. 2003. "The Use of Personality Typing in Organizational Change: Discourse, Emotions and the Reflexive Subject." *Human Relations* 56(2): 211–235.

Gatrell, C., and E. Swan. 2008. *Gender and Diversity in Management: A Concise Introduction.* London: Sage Publications.

Gipson, A.N., D.L. Pfaff, D.B. Mendelsohn, L.T. Catenacci, and W.W. Burke. 2017. "Women and Leadership: Selection, Development, Leadership Style, and Performance." *The Journal of Applied Behavioral Science* 53(1): 32–65.

Gouldner, A. 1971. *The Coming Crisis in Modern Sociology.* New York: Avon.

Gover, L., M. Halinski, and L. Duxbury. 2016. "Is it Just Me? Exploring Perceptions of Organizational Culture Change." *British Journal of Management* 27(3): 567–582.

Halton, W. 1994. "Some Unconscious Aspects of Organizational Life: Contributions from Psychoanalysis." In *The Unconscious at Work: Individual and Organizational Stress in the Human Services,* edited by A. Obholzer, and V.Z. Roberts, 11–18. London: Routledge.

Herrmann, P., and S. Nadkarni. 2014. "Managing Strategic Change: The Duality of CEO Personality." *Strategic Management Journal* 35(9): 1318–1342.

Holmes, T.H., and R.H. Rahe. 1967. "The Social Readjustment Rating Scale." *Journal of Psychosomatic Research* 11(2): 213–218.

Hurtz, G.M., and J.J. Donovan. 2000. "Personality and Job Performance: The Big Five Revisited." *Journal of Applied Psychology* 85(6): 869–879.

Kirsten, A. 2001. "Organizing for Powerlessness. A Critical Perspective on Psychodynamics and Dysfunctionality." *Journal of Organizational Change Management* 14(5): 452–467.

Kets de Vries, M.F., and K. Balazs. 1998. "Beyond the Quick Fix: The Psychodynamics of Organizational Transformation and Change." *European Management Journal* 16(5): 611–622.

Kets de Vries, M.F., and D. Miller. 1984. *The Neurotic Organization: Diagnosing and Changing Counterproductive Styles of Management*. San Francisco, CA: Jossey-Bass.

Kets de Vries, M.F., and D. Miller. 1986. "Personality, Culture, and Organization." *Academy of Management Review* 11(2): 266–279.

Kumar, R., and T.J. Kamalanabhan. 2005. "The Role of Personality Factors in Coping with Organizational Change." *International Journal of Organizational Analysis* 13(2): 175–192.

Kübler-Ross, E. 1969. *On Death and Dying*. New York: Touchstone.

Larson, D.G. 2014. "Taking Stock: Past Contributions and Current Thinking on Death, Dying, and Grief: A Review of Beyond Kübler-Ross: New Perspectives on Death, Dying and Grief edited by Kenneth J. Doka and Amy S. Tucci." *Death Studies* 38(5): 349–352.

Lewin, K. 1947. "Frontiers in Group Dynamics II. Channels of Group Life; Social Planning and Action Research." *Human Relations* 1(2): 143–153.

Linstead, S., J. Brewis, and A. Linstead. 2005. "Gender in Change: Gendering Change." *Journal of Organizational Change Management*, 18(6): 542–560.

Linstead, S., G. Maréchal, and R.W. Griffin. 2014. "Theorizing and Researching the Dark Side of Organization." *Organization Studies* 35(2): 165–188.

Marshak, R.J. 2006. *Covert Processes at Work: Managing the Five Hidden Dimensions of Organizational Change*. Oakland, CA: Berrett-Koehler Publishers.

Mullins, L.J., with G. Christy. 2016. *Management and Organisational Behaviour*. Harlow: Pearson Education Limited.

O'Doherty, D. 2017. "Individual Differences, Personality and Self." In *Introducing Organizational Behaviour and Management* edited by D. Knights, and H. Willmott, 74–117. London: Thomson Learning.

Oswick, C., and R.J. Marshak. 2012. "Images of Organization Development." *The Routledge Companion to Organizational Change*. London: Routledge.

Revelle, W., J. Wilt, and D.M. Condon. 2011. "Individual Differences and Differential Psychology." In *The Wiley-Blackwell Handbook of Individual Differences*, edited by T. Chamorro-Premuzic, S. von Stumm, and A. Furnham, 1–38. London: Wiley-Blackwell.

Schneider, D.M., and G. Goldwasser. 1998. "Be a Model Leader of Change." *Management Review* 87(3): 41–45.

Smith, A., and F.M. Graetz. 2011. *Philosophies of Organizational Change*. Cheltenham: Edward Elgar.

Stuart, R. 1995. "Experiencing Organizational Change: Triggers, Processes and Outcomes of Change Journeys." *Personnel Review* 24(2): 3–88.

Sturdy, A., M. Brocklehurst, D. Winstanley, and M. Littlejohns. 2006. "Management as a (Self) Confidence Trick: Management Ideas, Education and Identity Work." *Organization* 13(6): 841–860.

Tourish, D. 2013. *The Dark Side of Transformational Leadership: A Critical Perspective*. London: Routledge.

Vince, R. 2002. "The Politics of Imagined Stability: A Psychodynamic Understanding of Change at Hyder PLC." *Human Relations* 55(10): 1189–1208.

Walsh, K.D., J. Crisp, and C. Moss. 2011. "Psychodynamic Perspectives on Organizational Change and Their Relevance to Transformational Practice Development." *International Journal of Nursing Practice* 17(2): 205–212.

Watson, T.J. 2009. "Narrative, Life Story and Manager Identity: A Case Study in Autobiographical Identity Work." *Human Relations* 62(3): 425–452.

Wilson, F.M. 2018. *Organizational Behaviour and Work: A Critical Introduction*. Oxford: Oxford University Press.

Chapter 8

Groups, teamwork and organizational change

Introduction and chapter questions

The previous chapter focussed upon individuals and their experiences of organizational change. However, it is more likely that leaders/managers will deal with groups/ teams in times of organizational change with individuals finding themselves organized into groups and teams. Many discussions in the previous chapter inform this chapter, in that there will be individual differences even within groups and teams and concepts of psychodynamics and identity equally inform understanding about activities in groups and teams. Most major decisions in organizations are made by groups of people, rather than individuals as work tasks are often too complex for a single individual to deal with (Arnold et al., 2016).

In engaging with groups and teams, one of the main challenges is semantic. Group and team terminology overlaps and both labels (group/team) will be used in this chapter unless an author specifies a group or a team. Belbin (2000) in distinguishing groups from teams acknowledged that 'team' came into fashion displacing earlier references exclusively to 'groups'. He acknowledged that despite this shift, group psychology as a field still existed in its own right and he regarded the term 'team' as being borrowed from sport, Table 8.1 highlights differences between teams and groups.

The distinctions in Table 8.1 are helpful in beginning to differentiate teams from groups, although they appear to be infused with Belbin's (2010) beliefs in teamwork, which will be discussed later. However, given the centrality of these labels, it is important to clarify what is meant by a group and by a team.

> A group is a small assembly of people who find themselves together for a period of time, and who generally have a sense of sharing a quality or predicament. Many groups are set up for the purpose of accomplishing a joint task or meeting a challenge.
>
> (Gabriel, 2008: 124)

Table 8.1 Six differences between a team and group (based on Belbin, 2000)

	Team	Group
Size	Limited (typically up to four)	Medium or large
Selection	Crucial	Immaterial
Leadership	Shared or rotating	Solo
Perception	Mutual knowledge Understanding	Focus on leader
Style	Role spread co-ordination	Convergence conformism
Spirit	Dynamic interaction	Togetherness and persecution of opponents

Teams are particular types of group in which the successful completion of a task depends as much on the interaction between the team members as on how well they each perform their individual tasks.

(Gabriel, 2008: 299)

The notion of a team as a particular type of group is useful and favoured in this chapter with the chapter generically explaining how groups work in organizations as a precursor to understanding teamworking in organizations. In reviewing the literature organizations and managers appear to prefer the applied term 'team', whereas a lot of the research featured in the chapter, particularly psychological studies focuses upon 'groups'. Cartwright and Zander (1960) highlighted basic assumptions held by practitioners and academics about groups and group dynamics, which still appear relevant today and orientate us towards studying groups:

i   Groups are inevitable and ubiquitous
ii   Groups mobilise powerful forces which produce effects of utmost importance to individuals
iii Groups may produce both good and bad consequences
iv   A correct understanding of group dynamics – obtainable from research – permits the possibility that desirable consequences from groups can deliberately be enhanced.

This chapter is organized around and provides answers to the following questions about groups, teamwork, and organizational change.

•   What are the practicalities of working in teams?
•   What do we understand about group and teamwork in organizations?
•   How do studies of group and teamwork inform our understanding of organizational change?
•   What critical questions need to be addressed when studying groups and teamwork?

In the next section, practitioner guidance on building successful collaborative teams is highlighted. This is followed by an overview of generic studies of groups and teams in organizations. This is the prerequisite for understanding groups and teams and organizational change. In engaging with studies of groups and teams, it is necessary to engage with and understand the limitations of these approaches. Finally, the chapter is summarised, discussion questions raised and guidance offered with regard to navigating the groups' and teams' literature.

What are practitioners doing? The practicalities of group and teamwork

In the practitioner magazine *Harvard Business Review*, Gratton and Erickson (2007) highlighted eight factors that lead to success in building collaborative teams. Their practical prescription, based upon research into team behaviour in 15 multinational companies revealed four collaboration conundrums for teams. Four traits which were crucial to teams, also undermined them: large size, virtual participation, diversity and high education levels. They identified eight factors that led to success (please see Table 8.2).

Table 8.2 Eight factors that lead to collaborative team success (Gratton and Erickson, 2007)

1 Investing in signature relationship practices (facilities such as open floor plans to encourage communication).
2 Modelling collaborative behaviour (senior executives demonstrating highly collaborative behaviour themselves).
3 Creating a 'gift culture' (mentoring and coaching).
4 Ensuring the requisite skills (HR departments teaching collaboration).
5 Supporting a strong sense of community (makes people more likely to share knowledge).
6 Assigning team leaders that are both task and relationship-oriented (rather than either/or).
7 Building in heritage relationships (include at least a few people who know each other).
8 Understanding role clarity and task ambiguity (sharply defined team roles with latitude how tasks are achieved).

In Table 8.2, best practice prescriptions Gratton and Erickson (2007) identified through their research are highlighted. They note that not all collaborative tasks are complex and highlight a series of questions which may be asked of a project in order to establish its complexity. Again in *Harvard Business Review*, Haas and Mortensen (2016) drew upon Hackman (2002) in sharing the secrets of great teamwork.

> Though teams face an increasingly complicated set of challenges, a relatively small number of factors have an outsized impact on their success. Managers can achieve big returns if they understand what those factors are and focus on getting them right.
> (Haas and Mortensen, 2016: 72)

They highlight what they refer to as 4D teams (diverse, dispersed, digital and dynamic) and the enabling conditions required for these teams. The enabling conditions are first a compelling direction with challenging and consequential goals, second, a strong structure comprised of the right mix and number of members, third, a supportive context including the reward, information, education and training systems. Fourth, a shared mindset is required in order to avoid an 'us' and 'them' mentality.

Understanding groups and teamwork in organizations

In this section, the focus is on studies of groups and teams in organizational settings. In terms of groups, milestone research studies are considered chronologically and in terms of teamwork, the writings of Meredith Belbin and Michael West are featured.

Group work in organizations

There has been over a century of research into small groups with the field blossoming in the North American social psychology of the 1940s, 1950s, and 1960s. Studies addressed groups and leadership, communication, social influence, conflict, norms and other aspects of groups. In the late 1960s and 1970s, research into groups declined, although in the 1980s and 1990s there had been a resurgence in group related topics in social psychology (McGrath et al., 2000).

Table 8.3 A selective chronology of small group studies

Year	Academics	Focus
1936	Sherif	Pivotal and peripheral norms
1955	Asch	Study of conformity
1957	Osborn	Brainstorming
1965	Tuckman	Stages of group development
1972/1982	Janis	Groupthink

As acknowledged earlier, the psychological study of groups is a field of study in its own right. In Table 8.3, significant studies of groups are highlighted, which are particularly pertinent to organizational change. The following discussion introduces each study in chronological order.

Sherif (1936) was able to identify how group norms emerge through his pioneering experiments in which volunteers were asked to judge the movement of a light spot in a darkened room. The light spot didn't actually move. When the movement of the light spot was judged by a three-person group their responses converged and remained the same that the light had moved and this continued as much as a year after the trial. In a similar manner, Asch (1955) although attempting to disprove Sherif (1936), confirmed his findings. The study involved judging the lengths of three lines, whilst the individual subject could judge effectively, when other people acting in collusion with Asch gave erroneous judgments. This invariably influenced the research subject. Gabriel (2008: 204) has defined a norm as '…generally accepted standards of behaviour that exercise a powerful influence over the ways we act, we think, and we feel'. The studies of Sherif (1936) and Asch (1955) help us to appreciate these influences in a group setting. The notion of a group storming ideas, referred to as brainstorming has passed over into everyday language. However, the basis of this approach may be traced back to Osborn's (1953) studies in which group members were encouraged to offer novel ideas through a climate without criticism.

Tuckman (1965) and Tuckman and Jensen (1977) were influential in conceptualising the different stages of small group development. Bonebright (2010) in her historical review offered a 40-year account of the development of Tuckman's model of small group development. Tuckman's (1965) influential contribution to the *Psychological Bulletin* was literature review based and focussed upon interpersonal relationships and task activity. Bonebright (2010) highlighted Tuckman (1965) hypothesising a four-stage model, requiring each stage to be navigated in order to reach effective group functioning, but only in the summary did he coin the famous phrases: forming, storming, norming and performing (please see Table 8.4).

Tuckman and Jensen (1977) updated the model highlighted in Table 8.4. They revisited the original model and reviewed subsequent literature, proposing a fifth stage of 'adjourning', reflecting the full life cycle of the group.

Groupthink occurs when groups become more concerned with reaching consensus than with reaching consensus in a way that ensures its validity. Groupthink can be avoided by safeguarding consideration of alternatives, independence of views, and private acceptance.

(Smith et al., 2015: 337)

Table 8.4 Tuckman's (1965) four stages of group development (based on Bonebright, 2010)

Stage of group development	Description
Forming	This stage is concerned with testing and dependence; relationships are established.
Storming	A time of intergroup conflict, reflecting a lack of unity and polarisation around interpersonal issues.
Norming	Cohesion in the group develops with acceptance of others' idiosyncrasies.
Performing	The functional role relatedness of the group develops supportive of task performance.

Janis (1972, 1982) analysed foreign policy disasters of different governments at different times. These disasters included the 'Bay of Pigs' which featured 1,400 Cuban exiles invading Cuba only to be surrounded by 20,000 Cuban soldiers, resulting in high human and financial costs for the United States. In these instances, Janis (1972, 1982) encountered very capable groups making very poor policy choices and he labelled this phenomenon 'groupthink'. These groups were believed to overestimate their power and morality, to be closed to warning signs and towards other groups and they pressurised group members into uniformity.

Teamwork in organizations

Van Hootegem et al. (2005) in their review of the development of teamworking cite Beyerlein (2000) acknowledging that it has been a focal point of interest for practitioners and academics for more than half a century. The following discussion introduces the contributions of Meredith Belbin and Michael West.

Belbin (2010) in the third edition of his book (first written in 1981) on team roles suggested that the book was a journey into the language that he developed to express how individuals should contribute to work teams. He acknowledged, that having spent half his life in recruitment, he was intrigued by the selection of individuals for team roles. At Henley Management College, there was an emphasis upon syndicate groups undertaking management games/executive management exercises in educating and developing managers. Belbin (2010: 3), who was involved in these games/exercises, noted that 'the innovation we introduced in these experiments was to link the output of teams with the input; in other words, we chose the teams'.

Team roles featured in Table 8.5 have been influential in organizations and Belbin (2010) acknowledged the influence of his team role typology on organizations and studies of organizations, but he was keen to address misconceptions which had arisen. The first misconception is that team roles measure personality, whereas team roles are functions of different demands made on team members. Second, since people cannot change their team roles, some degree of learning and adjustment is possible. Third, those team roles vary with culture, whereas basic types of team roles have been identified in all cultures. Fourth, people in some types of society cannot adapt to team roles. Structures of authority can make it difficult for team roles to flourish, but once

Table 8.5 Team role descriptions (based on Belbin, 2010)

Team role	Description
Co-ordinator (originally referred to as the chairman)	Controlling the way the team moves towards group objectives.
Implementer (originally referred to as the company worker)	Specifies turning concepts and plans into practical working procedures.
Monitor evaluator	Specifies analysing problems and evaluating ideas and suggestions.
Plant	Specifies advancing new ideas and strategies with special attention to major issues.
Resource investigator	Specifies exploring and reporting on ideas and developments and resources outside the group.
Shaper	Specifies shaping the way in which team effort is applied, directing attention to setting of objectives and priorities.
Specialist	Someone supplying rare knowledge and skills, preferring to contribute on that limited front.
Team worker	Specifies supporting members in their strengths and underpinning members in their shortcomings.
Completer-finisher	Specifies ensuring that the team is protected as far as possible from mistakes of omission and commission.

tyranny is removed, new personality growth opportunities arise. The final misconception is that people should be encouraged to overcome weaknesses to enable them to perform in each of the team roles. It is more important to perform certain roles well than to cover a range of roles (please see Aritzeta et al., 2007 for an assessment of the construct validity of Belbin's (1981) team roles).

West (2012) regarded the landscape of teamworking as changing fundamentally over the last 200 years and in his book *Effective Teamwork: Practical Lessons from Organizational Research*, he sought to map effective teamworking, noting that the large collectives referred to as organizations are a fairly recent phenomenon. West (2012) identified the basic conditions of effective teamwork which included:

* having a real team whose membership is clear,
* which is of the right size,
* relatively stable on membership,
* working on a task that requires teamwork,
* the team must have an overall purpose that adds value, translated into clear, challenging team objectives,
* the team needs the right people as team members with the required skills in the right roles,
* team members must be enablers, not derailers.

Whereas Belbin (2010) had focussed on team roles, West (2012) highlighted the components of an effective team: task effectiveness, team member well-being, team viability (likelihood of continuing to work together), team innovation and inter-team cooperation (working with other teams). This allowed him to identify four extreme types of team functioning: the resilient team (high task effectiveness), the driven team (high task effectiveness), the dysfunctional team (poor task effectiveness) and the

Table 8.6 Why work in teams (based upon West, 2012)

Teams offer an effective means of enacting organizational strategy
Teams enable organizations to speedily develop and deliver products and services
Teams enable organizational learning and retaining learning
Cross-functional teams can promote quality management improvements
Cross-functional design teams are able to undertake radical change
Innovation is promoted through the cross-fertilisation of ideas
Organizations can be co-ordinated more effectively if the unit is the team, not the individual

complacent team (poor task effectiveness). In Table 8.6, rationales for teamworking are highlighted with West (2012) supporting these with references to research evidence.

However, in engaging with teamwork it is important to acknowledge barriers to effective teamwork which potentially include: loss of effort, poor problem solving and decision making and low creativity (West, 2012) with research evidence in support of these barriers.

Groups, teamwork and organizational change

In taking stock of what is known about groups/teamwork and organizational change, this section is divided into four subsections. First, we look at the pioneering contributions of Lewin (1947) and Bion (1961) which underpin many group-based accounts of organizational change and then look at socio-technical systems and teamwork approaches to organizational change. It is also worth acknowledging that group work theories (please see Table 8.3) discussed earlier may be specifically applied to organizational change.

So the pivotal and peripheral norms Sherif (1936) highlighted and the tendency to conform in groups which Asch (1955) identified are highly applicable to groups engaged in organizational change. Brainstorming (Osborn, 1953) offers a creative approach to problem solving which could be applied to problems arising out of a change initiative. Tuckman's (1965) identification of the stages of group development offers a diagnostic which could be applied to a group tasked with making change happen or a group experiencing change. Finally, groupthink (Janis 1972/1982) offers a cautionary note for senior managers leading/managing an organizational change initiative.

Lewin, group dynamics and organizational change

Burnes (2004) offered an important and influential reappraisal of Kurt Lewin's writings, explaining and emphasising the importance of the four elements contributing to theories and practices of organizational change. These elements were field theory, group dynamics, action research and the three-step model, Lewin saw these as a unified whole with each element supporting and reinforcing the whole. In this subsection, the focus is upon group dynamics with other elements featured in other chapters. Burnes (2004) acknowledged that Lewin was the first psychologist to write about group dynamics and how groups shape the behaviour of their members. Burnes (2004: 982) cited Kippenberger (1998) highlighting that Lewin was addressing two questions:

1   What is it about the nature and characteristics of a particular group which causes it to respond (behave) as it does to the forces which impinge on it, and
2   how can these forces be changed in order to elicit a more desirable form of behaviour?

The study of group dynamics is a response to these two questions. The subject of group dynamics stems largely from Lewin's (1947) work (Fontana, 2000). The implication of Lewin's work on group dynamics for organizational change was that the focus should not be upon individuals in isolation, as these individuals are under group pressure to conform (please see earlier discussion of Sherif, 1936 and Asch, 1955). Instead, organizational change initiatives should focus on the group level, concentrating on such factors as group norms, roles, interactions and socialisation processes. Burnes (2012) notes that Lewin's (1947) work can appear to have little relevance today, but cautions against this given the prevalence of group decision making and self-management being referred to today as empowerment. His work challenged stereotypes and age discrimination, today more commonly referred to as managing diversity.

Bion, groups and organizational change

In the context of organizational change, the writings of Wilfred Bion are less frequently cited than Kurt Lewin but offer an interesting psychoanalytic perspective on groups and organizational change. Rioch (1970) offers an informative introduction to Bion's (1961) writings which highlights how they might be applied to organizational change. Rioch (1970) identifies Bion's (1961) central thought that within every group two groups are present, the 'work group' and the 'basic assumption' group. Although this is metaphorical rather than literal, groups behave as two groups engaging in an unconscious fantasy. The 'work group' is concerned with the task of the group and the structure of the group is to further the attainment of the task.

> The work group constantly tests its conclusions in a scientific spirit. It seeks for knowledge, learns from experience, and constantly questions how it may best achieve its goal. It is clearly conscious of the passage of time and the processes of learning and development.
>
> (Rioch, 1970: 468)

Bion (1961) identified and labelled three different kinds of basic assumption groups: dependency, fight-flight and pairing groups deduced from three distinct emotional states. The basic assumptions relate to assumptions basic to behaviours, one presents as if something was the case. The basic assumption of the dependency group is attaining security through members being protected by one individual. A church is used to illustrate this assumption. The basic assumption of the fight-flight group is that preservation can only be achieved through fighting someone/something or running away from someone/something. An army is used as an illustration. The basic assumption of pairing is that the group has met for the purpose of reproduction, bringing forth a Messiah/Saviour. The aristocracy is used to illustrate this assumption (see French and Simpson, 2010 for further exploration and development of Bion's theory of groups).

Socio-technical systems approach

Trist and Bamforth (1951) are regarded as the earliest proponents/pioneers of this approach. Trist was a social psychologist and Bamforth, an ex-miner. Their studies focussed upon the advent of mechanisation in the mining industry. They developed the concept of the working group, which they regarded as an interdependent socio-technical system. The longwall method of coal mining was being facilitated through mechanisation, which included pneumatic drills and conveyor belts. Under the new systems of working, miners were far more closely supervised than previously when they used picks to extract coal and they organized themselves. Despite the mechanisation of coal mining, the anticipated benefits were not being realised. Consequently, Trist's (1981) own overview of the evolution of socio-technical systems is particularly pertinent. Trist (1981) regarded socio-technical analysis as being undertaken at three levels: the primary work system, the whole organization, and macrosocial phenomena with relations between levels influencing the feasibility of the type and scope of projects.

The socio-technical concept was regarded as arising in conjunction with field projects undertaken by the Tavistock Institute and the British coal mining industry in the late 1940s and early 1950s. Whereas engineers had always designed the technology required, the paradigm shift was in beginning to appreciate the human costs, the social aspects of technological change.

> The idea of separate approaches to the social and the technical systems of an organization could no longer suffice for one such as myself who had experienced the profound consequences of a change in socio-technical relations...
>
> (Trist, 1981: 10)

In terms of responding to this paradigm shift, Trist (1981) regarded the small self-regulating group as offering a way forward. Van Hootegem et al. (2005) locate team-working within socio-technical organization design.

> ...the socio-technical view stresses that the organization structure must be designed so that (a) interdependent operations are grouped together into organizational units and (b) these units are assigned as much decision latitude as possible (cf. Karasek, 1979). Interdependency is thus the obverse of the team model, with autonomy being the reverse. They are inextricably intertwined.
>
> (Van Hootegem et al., 2005: 169)

Two instances of these insights are discussed: business process reengineering (BPR) and empowerment. They suggest that BPR focussed on work processes, yet lacked a view of how different processes should fit into an organization. Whilst not novel, some applications of BPR have resulted in socio-technical insights being applied on an unprecedented scale. Semi-autonomous work groups, also referred to as teamworking and self-managing teams may be regarded as empowerment and they have also advanced socio-technical thinking. Watson (2006: 336) described a socio-technical system as 'an approach to work design in which the technical and the social/psychological aspects of the overall workplace are given equal weight and are designed at the same time to take each other into account'.

Teamwork and organizational change

West (2012: 3) starts his account of effective teamwork, featured in the previous section, with a quotation from Margaret Mead 'never doubt that a small group of thoughtful, committed citizens can change the world. Indeed, it is the only thing that ever has.' In "Twelve Steps to Heaven: Successfully Managing Change Through Developing Innovative Teams", West et al. (2004) offered an input-process-output model for identifying elements necessary for developing team innovation, which was informed by relevant theory and research (please see Table 8.7).

Table 8.7 An input-process-output model for team innovation (based upon West et al., 2004)

Inputs	Processes	Outputs
The task 1 Intrinsically motivating 2 High level of extrinsic demand	8 Norms for innovation 9 Reflexivity 10 Leadership supportive for innovation 11 Conflict and dissent 12 Bridging across teams	**Innovation** • Radicalness • Novelty • Magnitude
Group composition 3 Selection of innovative people 4 Diversity in skills and demography		
The organizational context 5 Rewards for innovation 6 A learning and development climate 7 A climate for innovation		

The model featured in Table 8.7 highlights the aspects of the team task, team composition, organizational context and team processes in developing innovative teams to successfully manage change. More recently, West (2012: 20) acknowledged that '… teams appear to be an enabling factor in change processes, perhaps because teams can take responsibility for implementing agreed changes and can do so more effectively than individuals working alone'.

Francis (2003) researched specifically teamworking and change and the contradictions which can arise. The research adopted a social-constructionist approach towards the introduction of team-based working in a manufacturing organization. The case organization RubCo was undertaking a major change programme which emphasised teamworking and a shift in management style through cultural change. She found that the change agents drew upon different and competing discourses (please see Chapter 12 for further discussion of discourse) in managing change. These were control-centred and people-centred discourses with the control-centred approaches aligned with a planned and rational approach towards change and the people-centred approaches acknowledging change as more complex and uncertain.

> Engineers were more likely to draw on the control-centred discourse while talking about 'One Team', illustrated in the language used by the team leader of one manufacturing area in describing his role in organizational change.
>
> (Francis, 2003: 79)

Research interviewees from the HR department described their expectations of teamwork through terms such as, 'employee involvement' and 'development' (people-centred discourse). However, as the change unfolded, Francis (2003) detected a constant struggle between the different groups and their different discourses.

Questioning group and teamwork theories

As this chapter has highlighted, group theories are a field of study in their own right with the potential to inform organizational change theories and practices. Equally, teamwork has become increasingly popular within organizations again potentially informing organizational change theories and practices. Any application of group and teamwork theories needs to be undertaken knowingly with an acknowledgement of weaknesses and limitations of theories being used. In the next subsection, limitations of the group and teamwork theories are discussed. This is followed by a subsection highlighting the dark side of groups and teams.

Group and teamwork theory limitations

Smith et al. (2015) acknowledge that, when Sherif (1936) and Asch's (1955) studies have been replicated, they produce the same results that people are influenced by and often adopt the opinions of other group members. The cautionary note here would be that the research is based on artificial experimental settings, although in mitigation it would be difficult to meaningfully replicate the research in real-life settings. In her historical review of Tuckman's (1965) model of the stages of group development, Bonebright (2010) discusses the limitations of the model. She acknowledges that Tuckman (1965) acknowledged limitations himself. The original literature review did not reflect a range of different small group development settings, with therapy settings significantly over-represented. The model has been generalised to different settings far beyond its origins. Tuckman (1965) acknowledged that there was a lack of research rigour to his observations. Subsequently, Rickards and Moger (2000) highlighted the inability to explain how groups change over time. They felt that the model failed to address the effects of team development on creativity in problem solving and that the model failed to discuss neither failure to achieve success in task performance nor the ability to show outstanding task performance.

Esser (1998) undertook a review of Janis's (1972/1982) groupthink research 25 years later, concluding that groupthink research has had and continues to have considerable heuristic value. He shows how other research studies have come to similar conclusions. Although his review is largely appreciative, he does draw cautionary conclusions about the quantity and quality of groupthink research leaving something to be desired. The research is based on historical cases of poor decision making involving analysing and reanalysing the same set of five cases, in searching for the antecedents and symptoms as described by Janis.

Burnes (2004) acknowledged that from the 1980s onwards there had been increasing levels of criticism of Lewin's (1947) contribution. Burnes (2004) highlights four major criticisms and provides responses to them. In this limitations subsection, the criticisms are summarised. First, Lewin's planned approach to organizational change is too simplistic and mechanistic given that organizational change is perceived as a continuous and open-ended process. Second, Lewin's work is not able to incorporate radical and transformational change, only being relevant to incremental and isolated change projects. Third, Lewin has been criticised for ignoring power and politics and the conflictual nature of organizational life. Fourth, Lewin has been depicted as encouraging a top-down and managerial approach to organizational change, when situations require bottom-up change.

There has been an undercurrent of psychoanalysis/psychodynamics seeking to inform understanding of groups throughout this chapter. In this chapter, Bion's (1961) notion of the presence of two groups the 'work group' and the 'basic assumption' group is featured. The cautionary note here would not be the critique of Bion's (1961) contribution, as much as, the danger of applying the works of a psychoanalyst in isolation. Fotaki et al. (2012) in their paper introducing a Special Issue of *Organization Studies* highlight the advances that have been made and the interplay between different approaches, academic disciplines and perspectives. The caution is that Bion's (1961) contribution is part of a larger body of work. Du Gay and Vikkelsø (2012) apply Bion's (1961) work knowingly to organization change management highlighting provocatively that each of the basic assumptions of dependency, fight-flight and pairing are apparent within studies of organizational change. Their critical counterpoint has implications for this chapter and this textbook.

The socio-technical systems approach (Trist and Bamforth, 1951) challenged the dominant paradigm in the middle of the last century and the approach has maintained an enduring appeal for many academics. However, Knights and McCabe (2003) questioned the historiography of socio-technical systems approaches highlighting how the autonomous self-regulated teamworking of miners could be viewed as their exercise of power drawing upon their knowledge of the work. Teamworking helped to make the work safer and more socially collaborative and although teamworking is presented neutrally as a practical solution for workplace problems, it may be regarded as a dominant ideology shaping beliefs about managing and organizing. Knights and McCabe (2003) through their critical analysis illustrated how the existence of a dominant teamworking ideology obscured explanations of teamworking in terms of power, knowledge and subjectivity.

The dark side of groups and teams

In reflecting upon and seeking to theorise groups, teams and organizational change, there is an implicit assumption that groups and teams in organizations are invariably beneficial for members and organizations. However, there is a potential dark side of groups and teams which merits acknowledgement. The experience of the two world wars shaped psychological research and theories about groups. Bion (1961) was a tank commander in World War I and for Altman (2016) the trauma of that experience and subsequently treating soldiers in hospital wards drove his studies of groups. War provided both an impetus for researching group processes and a focus for group research (Rose, 1989).

> The concept of the group was to become the organizing principle of psychological and psychiatric thought concerning the conduct of the individual...The invention of the 'group', the conception of 'social' or 'human' relations as key determinants of individual conduct, were the most consistent lessons of the psychological and psychiatric experience of war.
>
> (Rose, 1989: 48)

Management and organizational studies were at a crossroads at the time of the world wars, with the group, becoming the unit of analysis rather than the individual. Rose (1989: 52) was concerned that group and team research became preoccupied with performance 'the problems of economic reconstruction would insert these issues of the group into the heart of the economic debate, managerial practice and psychological innovation'. Sinclair (1992) challenged team working ideology which has subsequently prevailed amongst management consultants, experts, trainers and educators. Teams have been presented as solutions to organizational problems.

Stein and Pinto (2011) drew attention to the dark side of groups. They drew upon psychodynamic literature in order to develop two constructs: the gang at work and intra-organizational ganging illustrated through a case study of Enron. They believe that group-level aspects played a key role in Enron's demise, relating this back to Bion's (1961) distinction between groups and gangs.

> External gangs also differ markedly from workgroups in terms of both individual-level aspects (e.g., personality, identity, cognition) and group-level aspects (e.g., composition, atmosphere, interpersonal concern, function, and leadership)...
>
> (Stein and Pinto, 2011: 697)

They regard a gang at work as a cohesive group of employees, led by a tyrannical leader seeking to maintain dominance in the organization through engaging in and encouraging 'dark side' behaviours and simultaneously denigrating ordinary organizationally healthy behaviours. In the organizations that Stein and Pinto (2011) studied, at least two or three gang-at-work dark side behaviours (immoral, illegal and illegitimate) co-occurred. Stein and Pinto's (2011) work is featured in the Research case study showcase for this chapter.

Summary

The chapter may be succinctly summarised through answering the questions posed in the chapter's introduction. The original questions are restated in italics.

What are the practicalities of working in teams? Gratton and Erickson (2007) highlighted eight factors that led to success in building collaborative teams with their practical prescription, based on their research into team behaviour in 15 multinational companies. They suggested that the four traits crucial to teams, also undermined them: large size, virtual participation, diversity and high education levels. Haas and Mortensen (2016) drawing upon Hackman (2002) highlighted what they referred to as 4D teams (diverse, dispersed, digital and dynamic) and the enabling conditions required for these teams.

What do we understand about group and teamwork in organizations? There has been over a century of research into small groups with the field blossoming in the North American social psychology of the 1940s, 1950s, and 1960s (McGrath et al., 2000). Group studies particularly pertinent to organizational change themes featured here include Sherif (1936), Asch (1955), Osborne (1953), Tuckman (1965) and Janis (1972/1982). Belbin (2010) through management games/executive management exercises identified the roles required in effective teams: co-ordinator, implementer, monitor evaluator, plant, resource investigator, shaper, specialist, team worker and completer-finisher. West (2012) in discussing effective teamworking identified the basic conditions of effective teamwork as well as rationales for teamworking.

How do studies of group and teamwork inform our understanding of organizational change? This question may be answered in four ways in terms of the pioneering contributions of Lewin (1947), Bion (1961), the contribution of socio-technical systems and teamwork approaches to organizational change. The implication of Lewin's (1947) group dynamics work was that the focus should not be upon individuals in isolation, as these individuals are under group pressure to conform. Instead organizational change initiatives should focus upon groups. Bion's (1961) central thought was that within every group, the 'work group' and the 'basic assumption' group were present with the basic assumption groups (dependency, fight-flight and pairing groups) having three distinct emotional states. Trist (1981) regarded socio-technical analysis as being undertaken at three levels: the primary work system, the whole organization, and macrosocial phenomena with relations between levels influencing the feasibility of the type and scope of projects. The socio-technical concept was regarded as arising in conjunction with field projects undertaken by the Tavistock Institute and the British coal mining industry in the late 1940s and early 1950s. West et al. (2004) offered an input-process-output model for identifying elements necessary for developing team innovation, which was informed by relevant theory and research and Francis (2003) found change agents drawing upon different and competing discourses in implementing teamworking.

What critical questions need to be addressed when studying groups and teamwork? Any application of group and teamwork theories needs to be undertaken knowingly with an acknowledgement of weaknesses and limitations of theories in use. Burnes (2004) acknowledged that, from the 1980s onwards, there had been increasing levels of criticism of Lewin's (1947) contribution. There is a danger in applying Bion's (1961) contribution, in isolation from the larger body of psychoanalytic work. Knights and McCabe (2003) questioned the historiography of the socio-technical systems approaches, highlighting how autonomous self-regulated teamworking of miners could be viewed as their exercise of power drawing upon their knowledge of the work. Stein and Pinto (2011) drew attention to the dark side of groups. They believed that group-level aspects played a key role in Enron's demise, relating this back to Bion's (1961) distinction between groups and gangs.

Research case study showcase: a 'gang at work' in Enron

Stein and Pinto's (2011) research case study of a 'gang at work' in Enron reported in *Group and Organization Management* is showcased here. For the full case and further analysis, please visit the original source. The focus here is on groups, but the case study also offers rich insights into psychodynamics and the dark side of organizational life.

Case study source

Enron was created in 1986 through the merger of Houston Natural Gas and InterNorth (a natural gas pipeline company). Ken Lay was the chairman and CEO. Through the influence of Jeffrey Skilling, Enron moved into trading and finance with record profits and soaring revenues. However, in 2001 Enron filed for bankruptcy. Jeffrey Skilling (Chief Executive Officer) and Andrew Fastow (Chief Financial Officer) were jailed for fraud and other offences for 24 and 6 years, respectively. A large literature now exists attempting to make sense of what happened at Enron. It is these texts and the human narratives contained within them which inform this case study. They acknowledge that with the exception of O'Connor's (2002) account of groupthink in the Enron boardroom, group-level factors have been neglected.

Stein, M., and J. Pinto, J. 2011. "The Dark Side of Groups: A 'Gang at Work' in Enron." *Group and Organization Management* 36(6): 692–721.

Case study

Stein and Pinto (2011) highlight five dynamics (1–5) which help to illustrate features of a gang at work in Enron. They acknowledge that other factors do contribute towards explaining what happened at Enron, but they seek to address the neglect of group-level factors in earlier analyses.

1. The lack of a clear and coherent organizational identity

This dynamic manifested in two ways. Eccentricity and illegitimate behaviour was actively encouraged, with being ordinary regarded as the kiss of death. Jeffrey Skilling who became the Chief Executive Officer cultivated the image of the Star Wars villain, Darth Vader dressing up as him at company functions.

> Indeed, Enron was full of Star Wars imagery, with a key deal being named JEDI, a partnership being called Chewco, and business entities being named Kenobe Inc and Obi-1 Holdings.
>
> *(Stein and Pinto, 2011: 703)*

The second way this dynamic manifested was through organizational hypocrisy. The Enron 'Vision and Values' statement encouraged four principles; respect, integrity, communication and excellence. However, immoral, illegitimate, and illegal activities in Enron appeared to be tolerated, even encouraged.

2. The engendering of a masculine, macho culture which disowned weakness, uncertainty, and vulnerability

The culture in Enron was extremely masculine and macho. Enron's performance review system is discussed further in Chapter 16, but in essence it involved all managers being reviewed on a six-monthly basis with the poorest performers being removed from Enron. One consequence of these reviews was that the Performance Review Committee had considerable power. Dissent against the masculine and macho culture would potentially be reflected in a poor performance review.

The atmosphere of a 'boys club' developed amongst senior managers in which sexual misconduct was not only accepted, but became widespread throughout Enron. Macho activities were organized by Enron which were hosted by Jeffrey Skilling, such as bungee jumping, rock climbing and jeep races through the desert. Other aspects of the macho culture Enron cultivated included 'Hottie Boards' and the 'Women of Enron Calendar'. Strip clubs were used as venues for lunches and dinners and charged to Enron as expenses.

3. The emergence of the 'gang at work' and its leader

The key driver of Enron's dark side practices was not Ken Lay (the founder of Enron), but instead Jeffrey Skilling. It was under Skilling's leadership that a 'gang at work' formed with this small but influential group of senior staff kept together through the carrot of substantial rewards and the stick of brutal

(Continued)

punishment. Beenen and Pinto (2009: 279) were cited 'if you were going to ask a bunch of questions, he would intimidate you and make you feel you were not smart enough to get it. You are either in our smart guy club or not. That is how he suckered people in. "Ah! You are smart like me".' The gang bonds were strengthened through gang member adulation of Skilling which became almost cult-like.

4. The projection of the wanted aspects onto the 'asset-light' business and the unwanted aspects onto the 'asset-heavy' business

Enron was originally an asset-heavy utility, working with physical infrastructure such as gas pipelines. Enron's core competencies were in these asset-heavy utilities. In 1990, when Jeffrey Skilling arrived, he created the asset-light Gas Bank. This was regarded as a financial innovation in creating a new market mechanism between gas producers and consumers. However, it also offered a vision of how Enron could be reinvented as a financial services company with a significant shift away from asset-heavy business to asset-light business. This new approach was embraced by Enron, but instead of diminishing the asset-heavy approach, a highly competitive rivalry was engendered between the two ways of doing business. Unconscious splitting took place encouraged by Skilling's innovations and the excitement generated by the new way of trading. Increasingly the wanted aspects of the organization were regarded as being associated with the asset-light business and the unwanted aspects associated with the asset-heavy business.

   The asset-heavy utilities business in which Enron's core competencies existed increasingly came to be viewed with disdain and as problematic. This splitting was further encouraged through Skilling's language favourably differentiating the asset-light business from the asset-heavy business.

5. The fracturing of the organization into 'asset-heavy' and 'asset-light'

Competition between the two ways of doing business was further fuelled through highly personal conflict between the respective leaders. Jeffrey Skilling (asset-light business) and Rebecca Mark (asset-heavy business) were the same age. Both had graduated from Harvard Business School and their ambitions were focussed on the top job at Enron. Skilling attacked Mark, showing contempt towards her and referring to her work as a 'mess'. In parallel he disparaged the asset-heavy focus of other utilities companies. By implication, this disparagement was directed at Rebecca Mark and the asset-heavy business she led. Skilling was promoted to CEO in 1999 and Mark resigned in 2000.

> Although it is true that Mark's projects had yielded losses, the implication that his asset-light option was better was entirely illusory, buoyed up by mark-to-market accounting and a variety of dishonest and illegal practices.

Yet Skilling believed that asset-light trading could not go wrong, and, consequently, no limits or constraints should be placed on it.

(Stein and Pinto, 2011: 709)

The concept of a 'gang at work' in Enron adds to our understanding of what happened at Enron. The lack of a clear and coherent organizational identity (1) enabled the development of a gang. The encouragement of a masculine and macho culture (2) reinforced the development of a gang. The emergence of the gang was facilitated through its leader Jeffrey Skilling (3). The asset-light business reflected the wanted gang and the asset-heavy business reflected the unwanted gang (4). The fracturing of the organization occurred when the asset-light gang won (5).

Case study questions

1   How could Asch's (1955) findings on conformity and Janis's (1972/1982) groupthink be applied to this case?
2   How might Bion's (1961) differentiation between a 'work group' and a 'basic assumption' group be applied to this case?

Discussion questions

1   What are the advantages and disadvantages of group/teamwork for individuals in a group or team?
2   What is the appeal of group work and teamwork for organizations?
3   What has fuelled the application of psychoanalysis/psychodynamics to understanding groups?
4   What are the strengths and weaknesses of emphasising team roles in engaging with teamworking?

Navigating the groups and group/teamwork literature

This chapter has adopted an approach of first understanding how people behave in groups and group dynamics and then using this understanding to inform more applied debates about group/teamwork and their application to organizational change. The implication is that in literature reviewing, reviewing groups and teams literature generically first will inform subsequent literature reviewing. An academic specialising in group studies is not primarily interested in organizational change and similarly, an academic specialising in organizational change is not primarily interested in groups. The art of literature reviewing is appreciating overlaps between two fields of study. In this chapter, as well as, management and organization studies literature, sociology, psychology and psychotherapy literature has featured. An innocent question, may be posed: what role do groups play in organizational change? However, the different kinds of literature offer very different answers with very different emphases.

Many generic management and organization studies journals such as the *British Journal of Management, Human Relations* and *Management Learning* feature coverage of groups and teams. Specific journals such as *Group and Organization Management* and *Small Group Research* are also worth checking out.

References

Altman, N. 2016. "Wilfred Bion: From World War I to Contemporary Psychoanalysis." *International Journal of Applied Psychoanalytic Studies* 13(2): 163–178.

Aritzeta, A., S. Swailes, and B. Senior. 2007. "Belbin's Team Role Model: Development, Validity and Applications for Team Building." *Journal of Management Studies* 44(1): 96–118.

Arnold, J., and R. Randall with F. Patterson, J. Silvester, I. Robertson, C. Cooper, B. Burnes, D. Harris, C. Axtell. 2016. *Work Psychology: Understanding Human Behaviour in the Workplace*. Harlow: Pearson Education Limited.

Asch, S.E. 1955. "Studies of Independence and Conformity: A Minority of One Against a Unanimous Majority." *Psychology Monographs* 70: 1–70.

Beenen, G., and J. Pinto. 2009. "Resisting Organizational-Level Corruption: An Interview with Sherron Watkins." *Academy of Management Learning and Education* 8(2): 275–289.

Belbin, R.M. 1981 and 2010. *Management Teams: Why They Succeed or Fail?* Oxford: Butterworth-Heinemann.

Belbin, R.M. 2000. *Beyond the Team*. London: Routledge.

Beyerlein, M.M. (Ed.). 2000. *Work Teams: Past, Present and Future*. Boston, MA: Kluwer Academic.

Bion, W.R. 1961. *Experiences in Groups, and Other Papers*. London: Tavistock.

Bonebright, D.A. 2010. "40 Years of Storming: A Historical Review of Tuckman's Model of Small Group Development." *Human Resource Development International* 13(1): 111–120.

Burnes, B. 2004. "Kurt Lewin and the Planned Approach to Change: A Re-Appraisal." *Journal of Management Studies* 41(6): 977–1002.

Burnes, B. 2012. "Kurt Lewin and the origins of OD." In *The Routledge Companion to Organizational Change*, edited by D. Boje, B. Burnes, and J. Hassard, 15–30. New York: Routledge

Cartwright, D.E., and A.E. Zander. 1960. *Group Dynamics Research and Theory*. London: Tavistock Publications.

Du Gay, P., and S. Vikkelsø. 2012. "Reflections: On the Lost Specification of 'Change'." *Journal of Change Management* 12(2): 121–143.

Esser, J.K. 1998. "Alive and Well After 25 Years: A Review of Groupthink Research." *Organizational Behavior and Human Decision Processes* 73(2): 116–141.

Fontana, D. 2000. *Personality in the Workplace*. Basingstoke: Palgrave Macmillan.

Fotaki, M., S. Long, and H.S. Schwartz. 2012. "What can Psychoanalysis Offer Organization Studies Today? Taking Stock of Current Developments and Thinking about Future Directions." *Organization Studies* 33(9): 1105–1120.

Francis, H. 2003. "Teamworking and Change: Managing the Contradictions." *Human Resource Management Journal* 13(3): 71–90.

French, R.B., and P. Simpson. 2010. "The 'Work Group': Redressing the Balance in Bion's Experiences in Groups." *Human Relations* 63(12): 1859–1878.

Gabriel, Y. 2008. *Organizing Words: A Critical Thesaurus for Social and Organization Studies*. Oxford: Oxford University Press.

Gratton, L., and T.J. Erickson. 2007. "Eight Ways to Build Collaborative Teams." *Harvard Business Review* 85(11): 1–11.

Haas, M., and M. Mortensen. 2016. "The Secrets of Great Teamwork." *Harvard Business Review* 94(6): 70–76.

Hackman, J.R. 2002. *Leading Teams: Setting the Stage for Great Performances*. Boston, MA: Harvard Business Press.

Janis, I.L. 1972. *Victims of Groupthink*. Boston, MA: Houghton Mifflin.

Janis, I.L. 1982. *Groupthink*. Boston, MA: Houghton Mifflin.

Karasek, R.A. 1979. "Job Demands, Job Decision Latitude, and Mental Strain: Implications for Job Redesign." *Administrative Science Quarterly* 24(2): 285–309.

Kippenberger, T. 1998. "Planned Change: Kurt Lewin's Legacy." *The Antidote* 14: 10–12.

Knights, D., and D. McCabe. 2003. *Organization and Innovation: Guru Schemes and American Dreams*. Maidenhead: Open University Press.

Lewin, K. 1947. "Frontiers in Group Dynamics II. Channels of Group Life; Social Planning and Action Research." *Human Relations* 1(2): 143–153.

McGrath, J.E., H. Arrow, and J.L. Berdahl. 2000. "The Study of Groups: Past, Present, and Future." *Personality and Social Psychology Review* 4(1): 95–105.

O'Connor, M. 2002. "The Enron Board: The Perils of Group." *University of Cincinnati Law Review* 71: 1233.

Osborn, A.F. 1953. *Applied Imagination: Principles and Procedures of Creative Thinking.* New York: Charles Scribner's Sons.

Rickards, T., and S. Moger. 2000. "Creative Leadership Processes in Project Team Development: An Alternative to Tuckman's Stage Model." *British Journal of Management* 11(4): 273–283.

Rioch, M.J. 1970. "The Work of Wilfred Bion on Groups." In *Organization Change: A Comprehensive Reader,* edited by W.W. Burke, D.G. Lake, and J.W. Paine, 2008, 466–480. Chichester: John Wiley & Sons.

Rose, N. 1989. *Governing the Soul: The Shaping of Private Self.* London: Routledge.

Sherif, M. 1936. *The Psychology of Social Norms.* New York: Harper Row.

Sinclair, A. 1992. "The Tyranny of a Team Ideology." *Organization Studies* 13(4): 611–626.

Smith, E.R., D.M. Mackie, and H.M. Claypool. 2015. *Social Psychology.* London: Psychology Press.

Stein, M., and J. Pinto. 2011. "The Dark Side of Groups: A 'Gang at Work' in Enron." *Group and Organization Management* 36(6): 692–721.

Trist, E. 1981. "The Evolution of Socio-Technical Systems: A Conceptual Framework and an Action Research Program." *Occasional Paper 2*. Toronto: Ontario Quality of Working Life Centre.

Trist, E.L., and K.W. Bamforth. 1951. "Some Social and Psychological Consequences of the Longwall Method." *Human Relations* 4(3): 3–38.

Tuckman, B.W. 1965. "Development Sequence in Small Groups." *Psychological Bulletin* 63: 384–399.

Tuckman, B.W., and M.A.C. Jensen. 1977. "Stages of Small-Group Development Revisited." *Group and Organization Management* 2(4): 419–427.

Van Hootegem, G., J. Benders, A. Delarue, and S. Procter. 2005. "Teamworking: Looking Back and Looking Forward." *The International Journal of Human Resource Management* 16(2): 167–173.

Watson, T.J. 2006. *Organising and Managing Work.* Harlow: FT Prentice Hall.

West, M.A. 2012. *Effective Teamwork: Practical Lessons from Organizational Research.* Chichester: John Wiley & Sons.

West M.A., G. Hirst, A. Richter, and H. Shipton. 2004. "Twelve Steps to Heaven: Successfully Managing Change Through Developing Innovative Teams." *European Journal of Work and Organizational Psychology* 13(2): 269–299.

Part III

Leading change

Chapter 9

Leadership studies

Introduction and chapter questions

As leadership studies is a field of study in its own right, any study of leadership and organizational change requires an understanding of leadership as a pre-requisite. This chapter offers an overview of leadership studies informing the leading change theme of Part III. However, Grint (2000: 1) a respected leadership scholar has warned that '...before I first began to study leadership in a serious manner, my knowledge of it was complete'. In studying leadership, Grint was overwhelmed by the volume of leadership literature he encountered acknowledging perversely the more knowledge that he acquired, the less he really understood leadership. Consequently, the goal of this chapter is not to attempt to comprehensively cover everything written about leadership but to offer a navigation towards understanding leadership, particularly with regard to understanding leadership and organizational change.

In one sense, terms such as 'leader' and 'leadership' through their everyday usage potentially negate defining them. However, vagueness and ambiguity impede academic studies of leadership. Leadership has been recognised as a perniciously vague concept with Spicker (2012) acknowledging that although there were too many definitions to state, he was able to summarise general classes of definition.

> *Motivation and influence* – leaders defined as motivating and influencing other people.
> *Leadership as a set of personal attributes or traits* – leaders defined in terms of what the leader does.
> *Leadership as management* – leadership understood as management by a different name.
> *Leadership as a system of authority* – leaders defined as running things, being in charge or carrying responsibility for collective function.
> *Leadership as a relationship with subordinates* – leaders defined in terms of their relations with others.
> *Leadership as a set of roles* – leader defined as a pioneer acting as a role model for others.

You are likely to favour a particular definition of leadership and those writing about leadership will favour particular definitions. Definitions do not merely define a leader, but also influence how leadership is understood. A universal definition of a leader and leadership will not be offered here, but Grint (2005: 1) identified four ways of understanding leadership which are favoured in this chapter.

Person: Is it WHO 'leaders' are that makes them leaders?
Result: Is it WHAT 'leaders' achieve that makes them leaders?
Position: Is it WHERE 'leaders' operate that makes them leaders?
Process: Is it HOW 'leaders' get things done that make them leaders?

This fourfold typology offers a way forward in beginning to understand the subtleties of leadership in very different situations whilst also speaking to different leadership practices. In studying change leadership, person, result, position and process offer four different ways to understand a change leader, with all four potentially applicable to a single leader. We can study change leaders in terms of their traits, personalities and physical attributes (person). Are the most successful change leaders charismatic extroverts? We can study the achievements of change leaders (result) such as turning around a failing hospital or merging two large pharmaceutical companies. We can study where change leaders are most visible and equally where their influence is least visible (position). Did that supermarket Chief Executive turnaround the failing supermarket through frequently being seen on the shop floor? Finally, we can study the processes the change leader utilises (process). Did the change benefit from the change leader closely following Kotter's (1996/2012) eight leading change steps?

   This chapter is organized around and provides answers to the following leadership studies questions:

   What definitional issues do leaders and leadership raise?
   How do practitioners undertake leadership?
   How does a historic perspective inform leadership studies?
   How do competing paradigms, philosophies and perspectives influence leadership studies?
   How does acknowledgement of followers inform leadership studies?
   How do history and orthodoxy impede the development of leadership studies?
   What critical insights does the treatment of gender and followers offer with regards to leadership studies?
   How might we rethink leadership studies?

The first question has already been addressed. The second section draws upon two practitioner oriented studies which offer insights into leadership practices. This is followed by an overview of leadership theories which looks at leadership in different ways. First, looking at leadership theory from a historical perspective, secondly, from the perspective of paradigms and philosophies and thirdly, in terms of interactions with followers. In the questioning section, the ways in which leadership studies orthodoxy impedes leadership studies is explored. First, the influence of history is critically considered. Second, the influence of leadership orthodoxy is considered as an impediment to changes in leadership studies. This slightly abstract notion is illustrated through a discussion about how understanding gender and followers have been impeded within orthodox leadership studies. The chapter concludes with a summary which answers questions posed in this section, asks discussion questions and offers guidance on navigating the leadership studies literature.

Leadership: what are practitioners doing?

Before exploring leadership theories, practitioner oriented accounts of leadership offer an informative introduction to leadership practices. However, there is a need for caution when working with practitioner oriented leadership literature as Spicker

(2012) warns leadership as an idea is highly prescriptive, offering instructions on how things can be done. Consequently, the practitioner oriented accounts of leadership featured here have been chosen because of their base in research, rather than merely being authoritative opinions.

Chambers et al.'s (2010) "The Future of Leadership: A Practitioner View" was written by three practitioners and spoke to leadership practitioners. Writing after the global financial crisis, they explored the perceived crisis of leadership and questions asked subsequently of banking leaders.

> To what extent did leaders contribute to the global financial crisis?
> To what extent should these leaders have had greater foresight and been attuned to the real risks within their own businesses?

These questions pertinent to banking leaders are equally pertinent to all organizational leaders regardless of the sector in which they operate. In their survey of the leaders of 16 global companies, they found that the work of Deborah Ancona (2005) and her colleagues was particularly useful. They welcomed the focus upon what leaders actually did with assumptions made that leadership was: distributed, personal and developmental, a process for creating change and developed over time. In drawing their conclusions, they acknowledged the tensions for leaders arising out of increasing levels of ambiguity and complexity. Speaking of the crisis of leadership, they suggested that 'the important feature here, we believe, is a transparent link between the leader's values and what they say and do in practice' (Chambers et al., 2010: 268). This raises the question what are organizations looking for when they select a leader?

Carnes et al. (2015) addressed this question through focussing upon the role of personality and implicit leadership theories. They noted that there had been a paucity of studies that attempted to understand formal leader selection processes. In their research, they simulated a formal leadership selection process to investigate personality differences and the rater's implicit leadership theories on applicant interview scores. Their research findings suggested that organizations might not be using the most effective tools to select future leaders. In terms of practical implications, they suggested that '...a combination of structured interviews with other assessment methods could prove to be more reliable and valid than using structured interviews alone' (Carnes et al., 2015: 374).

Leadership theories

The breadth and depth of leadership theories can be intimidating for both students and academics '...there appear to be as many theories of leadership as there are leaders!' (Gill, 2011: 63). In this sense, classifications and typologies bring order to theorising leadership. In this discussion, three typologies are employed as a means of focussing upon the breadth of leadership literature. First, leadership studies may be understood historically through tracing the historical evolution of leadership theorising. Second, through highlighting competing philosophies, paradigms and perspectives informing leadership studies, background assumptions may be highlighted. Third, leadership may be understood in terms of those following the leader. The irony here is that most of the leadership studies literature is focussed upon the minority group, the leaders, rather than the majority group, followers/collaborators. Three focuses have been chosen because they are particularly relevant to the leading change theme of Part III.

Thinking historically about leadership studies

History may be used as a framework for explaining and differentiating popular leadership theories. In this way, the historical pedigree and evolution of leadership studies is regarded as one of its strengths. House and Aditya (1997: 464) capture this cumulative strength as follows 'the social scientific study of leadership began in the early 1930s...The development of a body of informed and empirically supported leadership literature has been truly cumulative'. The notion of leadership studies as cumulative is important and closely relates to notions of progress within Western societies and organizations. Textbook accounts of leadership are often organized chronologically which again reinforces notions of a truly cumulative development of leadership studies. The coverage of leadership theories on the leadership-central website illustrates such a historical perspective (please see Table 9.1).

If we look to Antonakis and Day (2017) in *The Nature of Leadership*, they offer a brief history of leadership, dividing leadership into nine major schools: trait, behavioural, contingency, contextual, sceptics, relational, new leadership, information-processing and biological/evolutionary. They locate trait theories as commencing in the 1900s and biological/evolutionary theories as commencing in the 2010s. Importantly, however, they highlight how interest in trait theories was very active between the 1920s and the 1950s. Interest then declined only for interest to become very active again in the 1990s. The implication here is that rather than the linear development of theories, interest in particular leadership theories may oscillate over time. The other dilemma is that whilst there are commonalities in these histories, for example, trait approaches appear in both of the above histories, other approaches such as Great Man Theory or sceptics are unique to particular historical eras.

Glynn and DeJordy's (2010) overview 'leadership through an organization behavior lens' of 50 years of leadership research aligns with the organizational change theme of this textbook. They note that organizational behaviour leadership theories over the 50 years tended to cluster around three main themes: leadership traits, leadership behaviours and leadership contingencies.

Early leadership study emphasised a search for the traits that distinguish leaders from the rest of us. Leaders possessed special, unique or extraordinary personality attributes, abilities, skills or physical characteristics that others did not have (Stogdill, 1948). Trait theories echo great man theories referred to earlier, in that leadership was originally envisaged as the province of males, with such leaders having a heroic/mythical sense of destiny. Trait theories were followed by the emergence of behavioural theories of leadership which focussed upon the leader's style of action. These styles were typically categorised in terms of task orientation emphasising work goals or objectives and people orientation emphasising interpersonal relationships. They suggest

Table 9.1 Leadership theories as depicted on www.leadership-central.com

Great man theory (the 1840s)
Trait theory (the 1930s–1940s)
Behavioural theories (1940s–1950s)
Contingency theories (the 1960s)
Transactional leadership theories (the 1970s)
Transformational leadership theories (the 1970s)

Source: www.leadership-central.com/leadership-theories.html#axzz3wYYXQfoj.
Accessed 7 January 2016.

that this approach can be traced back to Lewin, Lippitt and White (1939) identifying three leadership styles: autocratic, democratic and laissez-faire. Subsequently, Katz and Khan (1960) at Michigan identified two leadership styles: production-oriented and employee-oriented. Stodgill et al. (1962) in the Ohio State Studies identified differentiated leadership styles in terms of consideration and initiating structure. Consideration referred to the degree a leader acted in a friendly and supportive manner towards subordinates and initiating structure referred to the degree to which a leader defines and structures his/her role and the roles of subordinates towards achieving group goals. Glynn and DeJordy (2010) acknowledge that despite the early promise and large body of behavioural research, it was impossible to identify a universally effective style.

The shortcomings of trait and behavioural approaches fuelled interest in contingency approaches. Contingency theories worked with an assumption that leadership could vary across situations and that there may not be a universally effective way to lead with different contexts requiring different kinds of leadership. Fiedler (1964) focussed upon the favourableness of the environment for the leader. Subsequently, path-goal theory delineated four basic leadership styles, directive, supportive, participative or achievement oriented, with each deployed as they fitted the work environment and the followers' needs (House, 1971). Vroom and Yetton (1973) focussed upon the relative complexity of the task and the expertise of followers. In their normative model, the leaders' type of participation (autocratic, democratic or consultative) in decision making should fit the situation.

In many ways, these three themes are only half the story as, leading change (Kotter, 1996/2012) and transformational leadership (Bass and Riggio, 2006) were to prove influential and these approaches will be explained in the next chapter. As Glynn and DeJordy (2010: 122) suggest '…we find a general progression from leadership traits to behavioural styles, and finally, leadership contingencies as well as the dynamics of transformation and change, and networks'. In parallel to the historical development of leadership studies, in recent decades, leadership scholars have been involved in a quest to establish a general theory of leadership (Goethals and Sorenson, 2006) which transcends the historical categorisations featured here, although to date this quest has not been fruitful.

Thinking philosophically about leadership studies

Leadership studies in a manner similar to management studies as featured in Part II is informed by competing paradigms, philosophies and perspectives as introduced in Part II. In shifting the focus to leadership studies, a good place to start is Harvey and Riggio's (2011) edited reader *Leadership Studies: The Dialogue of Disciplines*. As the title suggests, these respected leadership writers were interested in the different ways leadership study was informed by different academic disciplines. Featured disciplines included the classics, philosophy, history, sociology, psychology, management, political science, education and literature. In each chapter, authors explained how leadership is understood from the perspective of their own discipline. Each discipline will be informed by competing philosophies and paradigms resulting in different perspectives even within the boundaries of a single discipline. Riggio (2011) regarded leadership studies as an 'emerging discipline' on the verge of being recognised as a discipline in the next few years. Riggio (2011: 13) believed that disciplinary status would be achieved through convergence and consensus of leadership studies 'in my opinion, it is this low level of consensus that has been the stumbling block for leadership studies reaching disciplinary status'. He acknowledged that this was a controversial view and this consensus view of leadership orthodoxy is challenged in the questioning leadership section.

Mabey's (2013) overview of the leadership literature is more pluralistic in recognising competing discourses. Through reviewing the leadership development literature, he was able to highlight four leadership discourses each reflecting different assumptions underlying leadership studies. By far, the most prevalent leadership discourse evident within leadership theories was the functionalist discourse with functionalist discourses emphasising organizational performance and the centrality of leaders in delivering this performance. These theories emphasised leadership capabilities and competencies, through which leadership will maximise the productivity of an organization. The other three leadership discourses are far less prevalent, but worth sharing as they reveal assumptions underpinning leadership theories. Interpretive discourses emphasise leadership as being socially and culturally constructed.

> ...the interpretive discourse sees leadership as socially constructed, co-created and evolving with an emphasis upon systemic context and inter-subjective appreciation.
>
> (Mabey, 2013: 365)

Socially constructed notions of leadership will be discussed further in the questioning section. The two remaining leadership discourses which Mabey (2013) identified were dialogic and critical discourses. Dialogic discourses depict leaders and leadership as partial and ill-defined. The leader persona or identity is ongoing and negotiated. Critical discourses are evident in those leadership theories which question the privileging of economic efficiency and productivity over consideration of justice and ethics.

A third way to think about leadership studies is through using Smith and Graetz's (2011) *Philosophies of Organizational Change*, introduced in Chapter 3. The philosophies of organizational change they highlighted were; rational, biological, institutional, resource, psychological, systems, cultural, critical, and dualities. These social science oriented philosophies are equally applicable to leadership studies.

Each of the philosophies highlighted in Table 9.2 offers a different way to think about leadership studies, encouraging particular methodologies and particular emphases. A leadership scholar may locate their work within one of these philosophies or a combination of philosophies. Hughes (2016) illustrated how each of these philosophies was evident in papers published in a single academic journal *The Leadership Quarterly*. The implication is that when reading a leadership paper, it is likely to be the favoured philosophy of the author which either appeals or doesn't appeal, even though the author is unlikely to use the explicit terminology of Table 9.2.

Thinking about leadership studies in terms of followers

In *Leadership: A Very Short Introduction,* Grint (2010) ironically asked, what about the followers? The question was grounded in his own experiences of studying, researching and teaching leadership. The paradox was that a huge quantity of leadership studies literature has been generated and by association we now have a surplus of leadership theories, but despite all this industry when studying leadership, we have far fewer insights into the subject of leadership, the followers. Unfortunately, this imbalance in understanding leaders/followers is not a new phenomenon.

Table 9.2 Understanding leadership studies in terms of different philosophies (Smith and Graetz, 2011)

Philosophy (Smith and Graetz 2011)	Philosophy summarised
Rational	Planned and directed change with strategy and planning emphasised
Biological	Ecological, organic and evolutionary change, emphasis on life cycles
Institutional	Emphasis on industry influence gauged through standards and benchmarks
Resource	Emphasis upon resource access determining change
Psychological	Change embedded within the minds of those affected
Systems	Emphasis upon interconnected nature of organizations
Cultural	Emphasis upon entrenched values and beliefs
Critical	Emphasis upon power, genuine empowerment and emancipation
Dualities	Dynamic/complex

Going back to Burns' (1978) famous study of leadership, the need for leadership theories and practices to engage with followers was apparent. Rost (1993) a student of Burns, undertook an extensive survey of the leadership literature and found the leadership literature to be lacking in coverage of followers. However, for Rost it wasn't just that followers were not featuring within the leadership literature, he found them being actively disparaged. Followers were depicted as part of the sweaty masses, separated from the elites. They were presented as not being able to act intelligently without the guidance and control of others, letting other people (elites) take control of their lives, and being depicted as unproductive unless directed by others. Abrahamson (2004: 210) appears to echo this view in the following quotation.

> Leaders purportedly climb to the top of the mountain, gaze to the horizon, see the future, and come back down and share their vision with the troops who cannot see past the foothills.

Whilst, followers have been underrepresented within leadership literature and research (Baker, 2007; Kellerman, 2013), there has been an increasing acknowledgement that leadership cannot really be understood without understanding followers and their relations with leaders. As an alternative to the usual textbook treatment of leadership studies, Hoyt et al. (2006) offer four different perspectives for thinking about leader-follower relations: as an exchange, in terms of procedural justice, in terms of charisma and identification with the leader and in terms of the transforming/transformational effects of leadership. The exchange perspective regards leader-follower relations as a psychological exchange. Leaders offer followers vision, direction, protection and security. Whilst, followers offer leaders commitment, focus, loyalty and cooperation. Hoyt et al. (2006) acknowledge that this perspective has been challenged, with other perspectives responding to perceived weaknesses. The second perspective is procedural justice arguing that leaders making decisions fairly gain more voluntary compliance than leaders who simply distribute rewards fairly.

> If people are given a chance to make their case, if they are treated with dignity and respect, and if the leader is honest and unbiased in making decisions, followers will feel that they have been treated fairly, that they have had procedural justice.
>
> (Hoyt et al., 2006: 115)

A procedural justice perspective acknowledges the crucial needs of self-validation and self-worth and the role they play both in terms of leading and following. The third perspective emphasises charisma and identification with the leader within leader–follower relations. Charismatic leaders inspire followers through a strong vision and a compelling commitment to the vision. As part of this process, it is necessary for these followers to identify with the leader. The fourth perspective relates to the trans-forming/transformational leadership which Burns (1978) gave impetus to. This trans-formational theme will be developed further in the next chapter, but more generally highlights the centrality of leader–follower relations in times of transformation and change.

Questioning leadership studies

Calas and Smircich (1991) famously described leadership as a seduction, and leader-ship still has a capacity to seduce. One critical challenge relates to earlier discussions about the ambiguity of leadership.

> The fervour of the cult of leadership makes it difficult to analyse the concept critically. It is hard to falsify propositions, because empirical evidence about one concept or understanding of leadership is not necessarily germane or relevant to other parts.
>
> (Spicker, 2012: 37)

As was mentioned in the introduction, leadership has different meanings for different people, complicating critique of a concept which is so ambiguous and variable. In this questioning section, four critical themes are developed. First, we highlight the way history impedes change in leadership studies and reinforces the incremental progres-sion of orthodoxy. Second, the way leadership studies orthodoxy acts as an impedi-ment to further studies. Third, we look at how orthodoxy has hampered engagement with women/gender in leadership studies and fourth, how depictions of followers limit their agency. The questioning section concludes more positively with ways to rethink leadership studies.

Questioning the influence of history

History has a tendency to reassure us through feeling fixed and unequivocal, whilst the future is acknowledged as uncertain, by association the past is far more certain. In this critical discussion, the tone is far less reassuring in suggesting that a particular version of leadership history has been favoured, whilst simultaneously competing ac-counts of leadership history have been marginalised. Leadership has been described as '…an ageless topic…' contrasted with management as '…largely the product of the last 100 years…' (Kotter, 1990: 3). The danger with this notion of leadership as an 'ageless topic' is that it privileges leadership over the newcomer – 'management' (see Part IV for further discussion about leader/manager differences). There are fur-ther limitations within depictions of leadership as an ageless topic as Grint (2005: 8) highlights when he writes 'indeed, the metaphorical straight line that connects the problems of the past to the solutions of the future resonates with the popularity of the quest for an "answer" to the leadership "question"'.

Rost (1993: 8) explained the apparent success of orthodox accounts of leadership as generating '...a mythological story of leadership that has been told over and over again and that almost everyone believes'. He drew upon Edelman's (1971) symbolic theory of rewards in developing his notion of a mythological narrative of leadership. First, research into leadership has been working. Second, leadership scholars have done what they are supposed to do – increase understanding of leadership. Third, progress has been made, and as a result, both scholars and practitioners have an increasingly sophisticated understanding of leadership. Fourth, a better understanding of leadership will help make organizations more productive. The concern with the mythological leadership narrative is that it limits alternative conceptualisations of leadership, keeping leadership studies within its existing orthodoxy (see also Gemmil and Oakley, 1992). Kelly (2014: 915) more recently wrote about leadership as '...arguably an empty signifier par excellence in that it has evaded attempts to confront its emptiness for hundreds of years'.

Questioning the influence of orthodoxy

In the earlier leadership theories section, multiple paradigms informing leadership studies were introduced. The rational/functionalist paradigm was by far the most influential and this influence can be related back to the previous history subsection. The potential danger with the rational/functionalist paradigm is that it maintains orthodoxy and status quo, for example, not directly challenging inequalities, such as, gender and leadership. There have been recurrent references to the flawed nature of leadership studies, but they seem to go unheeded (please see Table 9.3).

What is troubling about the quotations in Table 9.3 is not just that such criticisms can be traced back over the last 35 years, but that all of these critical commentaries come from respected professors of leadership, who have no vested interest in critically questioning their own field of study. The implication here particularly for Part III is there is a need for caution when engaging with leadership theories. The rhetoric makes them very persuasive, but paraphrasing Kellerman (2012), rhetoric equates to neither rigour nor replicability. This subsection has highlighted how an enduring orthodoxy of leadership studies and practices impedes any real development in leadership studies and practices. As such critiques may appear remote from the lived experience of leadership, the next two subsections highlight how leadership orthodoxy marginalises women and followers within leadership theories and practices.

Table 9.3 Critically questioning leadership studies

The fundamental crisis underlying mediocrity is intellectual. If we know all too much about our leaders, we know far too little about leadership (Burns, 1978: 1).

Although leadership research seems to be increasing exponentially we have yet to establish what it is, never mind whether we can teach it or predict its importance (Grint, 2005: 1).

...leadership studies as a field has never been and is not now entirely respectable, at least not among traditional academics, who consider it more art than science, neither rigorous nor replicable, not a suitable subject for serious study (Kellerman, 2012: 160).

(Editorial of the journal *Leadership*) ...yet another problem in the field – its unrelenting triviality (Tourish, 2015: 138).

Orthodoxy, leadership and gender

Prugl (2012) posed the beautifully subversive question, what if Lehman Brothers had been Lehman Sisters? Her paper which analyses the aftermath of the 2008 global financial recession highlighted how the English language press presented the financial crisis as a product of macho/masculine financial sector leaders. However, even in constructing a myth of women as financially responsible, the media was still guilty of stereotyping on grounds of gender. In going back to the origins of the leadership and gender story, Bolden et al. (2011) suggest that you could begin with great man theories as featured in the earlier leadership theory section. They note that academic practices can be slow to catch up with changing working practices, acknowledging that this was certainly the case in terms of studying gender, management and leadership. Studies really only began in the late 1970s under the label 'women in management'. But again, just as Prugl (2012) highlighted stereotyping at work, so with the benefit of hindsight 'women in management' today appears stereotyped. The unfortunate implication was that women should adapt to enter the male world of management. Bolden et al. (2011) acknowledged progress being made with more serious academic engagement with leadership and gender, rather than notions of getting women into management. Although even with greater theoretical sophistication they acknowledged the dilemma in differentiating men and women, potentially taking us back to Prugl's (2012) stereotypes.

Alvesson and Billing (2009) in their engaging account of understanding gender and organizations offer a way forward. They warn against trying to find definitive answers to questions about gender and management/leadership, instead favouring greater sensitivity to different ways of framing and reasoning about women and managerial or leadership jobs. They highlight four positions (introduced in Chapter 7) which are regarded as tactical, rather than being as basic as a paradigm. The equal opportunities position highlights fundamental injustices and inequalities in society and working life. This position is moral and political in seeking greater fairness in society and working life.

> The equal opportunities argument for paying attention to the problem of female leaders and their low numbers is basically of a political and moral nature. In modern society there is a strong conviction that everyone should have a fair chance, irrespective of gender, race and so on.
>
> (Alvesson and Billing, 2009: 167)

The meritocratic position rather than adopting an ethical-political point of view seeks to combat irrational social forces, which impede full utilisation of human resources. Meritocrats are concerned with gaining maximum efficiency from social institutions, rather than primarily seeking workplace fairness. The third position referred to as the special contribution position does not focus primarily on fairness or equality but instead draws attention to the dissimilarities between the genders and their potential special contributions. The fourth position may be regarded as a more radical version of the previous position.

> The key assumption is that in general women do not share the interests, priorities and basic attitudes to life that are common among men – or perhaps rather dominating groups of men.
>
> (Alvesson and Billing, 2009: 175)

The implication of this is anti-management, so rather than integrating women into management developing alternative social institutions would be the best way to progress leadership.

Orthodoxy, leaders and their followers

In the earlier leadership theories section, the neglect of followers within leadership theories and practices was highlighted. In this critical discussion, even the concept of followers following the leader may have insufficient agency. Rost (1997: 11) wrote 'I tried to redeem the word followers in my book by reconstructing it with new meaning. But it didn't work. Everywhere I went to give seminars or speeches, the people attending them told me that following was essentially a passive concept and the word followers was not redeemable.' Whilst Burns (1978) and Rost (1993) did much to encourage greater engagement with followers, Rost (1997) subsequently favoured the term 'collaborator'. This shift is more than semantic, particularly when leadership and organizational change are combined. In the context of organizational change the term collaborator speaks to issues of participation and engagement. The term collaborator suggests that rather than responsibility for successful organizational change residing solely with a heroic individual leader, responsibility is far more shared and collaborative. Instead of the weary dualism of leaders leading change and subordinates resisting change, both leaders and collaborators potentially achieve change. In a manner similar to how inappropriate labels such as 'resistance to change' misrepresent the responses of individuals, groups and teams to organizational change (please see Chapter 13), well-intentioned references to followers and followership may do more harm than good. Haslam et al.'s (2011: 2) account of the old psychology of leadership looks back without the usual nostalgia, simultaneously critiquing earlier accounts and offering ways forward. They '...argue for a new psychology that sees leadership as the product of an individual's "we-ness", rather than his or her "I-ness"'.

Rethinking leadership studies

Bolden et al. (2011) in *Exploring Leadership* are keen to differentiate their book from other leadership books. They emphasise four perspectives which resonate with themes in this chapter. They encourage critical, interdisciplinary, multilevel and balanced perspectives on leadership. In terms of a critical perspective, they highlight how we talk and think about leadership potentially influences leadership practices. This was illustrated in this chapter through the favoured leadership studies label of 'follower', which doesn't just describe what most of us do, but prescribes what we should do. Encouragement towards interdisciplinary leadership studies chimes with discussions around philosophies, paradigms and perspectives earlier in the chapter. Each academic discipline is informed by a competing and varying mix of philosophies, paradigms and perspectives. There is certainly no one best/universal way to think about leadership. So once this interdisciplinarity is acknowledged, you have a more complex yet richer way to think about leadership. Imagine how when you look into a child's kaleidoscope through twisting it you may see very different things.

In rethinking leadership, a multilevel perspective is also important. It is too simplistic to think about leaders as those adopting the hierarchically superior positions. A distributed approach to leadership may be favoured which would place far less emphasis upon hierarchical superiority. Finally, encouraging a balanced perspective involves weighing up the pros and cons of competing for leadership approaches and this has been mirrored through introducing influential theories, as well as questioning orthodoxy in this section.

Haslam et al. (2011: 22) offer a way forward for leadership studies and practice again resonating with earlier discussions in this chapter. They emphasise '...the importance of context, the role played by followers, the function of power, and the dynamics of transformation'. We tend to work with universal stereotypes of leaders, but the context in which leadership happens will have a significant influence. Any rethinking of understanding leaders and leadership must place a greater emphasis upon followers. Power is often implicit, rather than explicit within leadership studies and practices, but any rethinking requires a far greater emphasis upon power and politics (please see Chapter 11, for coverage of power and politics). Finally, understanding the dynamics of transformation must be part of rethinking leadership studies and practices, which provides the rationale for the combination of chapters in Part III.

Summary

The chapter may be succinctly summarised through answering questions posed in the chapter's introduction. The original questions are restated in italics.

What definitional issues do leaders and leadership raise? We often work with an assumption that we have a common understanding of leaders and leadership when really we are working with different understandings. For example, Spicker (2012) acknowledged different classes of definition explaining leadership in terms of: motivation and influence, personal attributes or traits, as management, as a system of authority, as a relationship with subordinates and as a set of roles. Grint (2005) highlighted four ways of understanding leadership in terms of; person, result, position and process.

How do practitioners undertake leadership? "The Future of Leadership: A Practitioner View" (Chambers et al., 2010) was written by three practitioners and spoke to leadership practitioners. They explored the perceived crisis of leadership and questions asked subsequently of banking leaders. In terms of what do organizations look for when selecting a leader, Carnes et al. (2015) felt organizations might not be using the most effective tools to select future leaders. They suggested a combination of structured interviews and other assessment methods could prove more reliable and valid than using structured interviews alone.

How does a historic perspective inform leadership studies? The historical development of leadership has been described as truly cumulative (House and Aditya, 1997). In Glynn and DeJordy's (2010) review of the past 50 years of leadership theory, they highlighted three main themes: leadership traits, leadership behaviours and leadership contingencies. They found a general progression from leadership traits to behavioural styles, and finally, leadership contingencies as well as the dynamics of transformation and change, and networks.

How do competing paradigms, philosophies and perspectives influence leadership studies? Leadership studies are informed by different academic disciplines, including the classics, philosophy, history, sociology, psychology, management, political science, education and literature with Riggio (2011) describing leadership studies as an 'emerging discipline'. Mabey's (2013) overview of the leadership literature identified different assumptions underlying leadership studies in terms of four leadership discourses: functionalist, interpretive, dialogic and critical. Smith and Graetz (2011) highlighted the philosophies of organizational change: rational, biological, institutional, resource, psychological, systems, cultural, critical, and dualities which are equally applicable to leadership studies.

How does acknowledgement of followers inform leadership studies? There is a huge quantity of leadership studies literature, but, despite all this industry when studying leadership, we have far fewer insights into the subject of leadership, the followers. Hoyt et al. (2006) offered four different perspectives for thinking about leader–follower relations: as an exchange, in terms of procedural justice, in terms of charisma and identification with the leader and in terms of the transforming/transformational effects of leadership.

How do history and orthodoxy impede the development of leadership studies? History has a tendency to reassure us through feeling fixed and unequivocal, whilst the future is acknowledged as uncertain, by association the past is far more certain. For Rost (1993) the apparent success of orthodox accounts of leadership has generated a mythological story of leadership that has been told over and over again and that almost everyone believes. The concern with the mythological leadership narrative is that it limits alternative conceptualisations of leadership, keeping leadership studies within its existing orthodoxy (please also see Gemmil and Oakley, 1992 and Kelly, 2014).

What critical insights does the treatment of gender and followers offer with regards to leadership studies? Bolden et al. (2011) acknowledged progress being made with more serious academic engagement with leadership and gender, rather than notions of getting women into management. Alvesson and Billing (2009) in their engaging account of understanding gender and organizations offered a way forward warning against trying to find definitive answers to questions about gender and management/leadership. They highlighted four positions: equal opportunities, meritocratic, special contribution and radical (see also Gipson et al., 2017). The neglect of followers within leadership theories and practices has been acknowledged, but even the concept of 'followers' following the leader is believed to have insufficient agency.

How might we rethink leadership studies? Bolden et al. (2011) emphasised four perspectives which resonate with themes in this chapter. They encouraged critical, interdisciplinary, multilevel and balanced perspectives on leadership. Haslam et al. (2011) offered a way forward for leadership studies and practice again resonating with earlier discussions in this chapter, emphasising the importance of context, the role played by followers, the function of power, and the dynamics of transformation.

Research case study showcase: what do leadership scholars think/feel about the relevance of leadership studies?

Butler et al.'s (2015) research case study into the views of leadership studies scholars on the relevance debate reported in the *British Journal of Management* is showcased here. For full details and further analysis please visit the original source.

Case study source

Butler et al. (2015) innovatively explored the motivations of leadership scholars in pursuit of relevance in leadership studies. The authors acknowledge the slipperiness of the concept of relevance given that it is not a neutral term. Their research speaks to the different meanings of relevance for different scholars.

(Continued)

In particular the researchers focus on scholars working with organizations (often labelled consultancy), rather than their campus-based work. The researchers conducted interviews with 72 leadership scholars based in North America, the UK, Europe and Australasia with 68 of these respondents involved in some form of practitioner engagement. In the following case study, the focus is on a grouping of leadership scholars, rather than a single organization. First name references refer to first names cited in the paper (Butler et al., 2015), quotation marks and page numbers are offered for verbatim quotations.

Butler, N., H. Delaney, and S. Spoelstra. 2015. "Problematizing 'Relevance' in the Business School: The Case of Leadership Studies." *British Journal of Management* 26(4): 731–744.

Case study

The majority of Butler et al.'s (2015) leadership scholars framed relevance of leadership studies in terms of its potential usefulness for practitioners.

> Unsurprisingly, consulting activities, executive education, leadership coaching and other types of practitioner engagements feature prominently in the narratives of relevance among our respondents. For Emily, 'the direct, the obvious impact I have is through consulting', while Colin 'does a hell of a lot of consulting' in order to pass on 'what we know from science to firms'.
> *(Butler et al., 2015: 735–736)*

The research revealed four motivations for leadership scholars engaging with practitioners. First, there was believed to be a positive impact on leaders and organizations of such practitioner engagement, although respondents had very differing views on this impact. Second, many leadership scholars framed practitioner engagement as a win-win.

> The interesting questions…come from talking to practitioners, giving keynotes, just thinking about how can I possibly translate this material to a practitioner audience and how do I respond to some of the difficult questions that they have? That's where the interesting research questions come from.
> *(Peter cited in Butler et al., 2015: 736)*

A third motivation for leadership scholars engaging with practitioners was material rewards. Again, this varied considerably amongst the respondents. Some did not accept personal payments, but others regarded it as supplementing their academic salary. Tensions with institutional research and teaching obligations were acknowledged. Butler et al. (2015) highlighted honest reflections of their respondents challenging noble or normative narratives of practitioner engagement for purely altruistic reasons. A fourth motivation for leadership scholar engagement with practitioners, related to improved feelings of self-worth amongst scholars.

> As Tessa says: 'I often feel proud when I go and work with an industry-related group', since leadership 'matters to them' in a way that other academic theories do not.
> *(Butler et al., 2015: 738)*

The necessity of leadership scholarship being relevant for leadership practition-ers is often emphasised institutionally and by policy makers. Whilst, Butler et al. (2015) responded to this call to bridge a perceived rigour/relevance gap, their research also highlighted potential tensions and risks when leadership scholars engage with practitioners.

> Many of our respondents acknowledged that they are confronted with situations in outside organizations that put their scholarly values to the test, leading them – in some cases – to compromise the norms of academic research.
>
> *(Butler et al., 2015: 738)*

Lisbeth was cited acknowledging pressure to adopt certain approaches which she felt were sub-standard, which effectively silenced her scientific opinion in order to be relevant. Robert acknowledged feeling 'like a merchant', as he was paid to be 'the nice face' of his university in front of corporations.

> The whole field of leadership studies is 'tainted' because 'leadership schol-ars are being paid an enormous amount of money in order to tell or make leaders feel good about themselves'.
>
> *(Emily cited in Butler et al., 2015: 739)*

A particularly interesting insight of Butler et al.'s (2015) research was that few of their leadership scholars could determine the impact on practitioners and their organizations of their external activities. In lieu of explicit impact measures, income received and personal pride were sometimes used as common proxies.

Case study questions

1   If leadership is a perniciously vague concept (Spicker, 2012), what are the implications for discussions in this case study?
2   What are the advantages and disadvantages for campus-based leadership education of leadership scholars engaging with leadership practitioners?

Discussion questions

1   Why is defining leadership such a slippery concept?
2   Why are historical accounts of leadership so persuasive?
3   Why might leadership studies orthodoxy exist?
4   Why has so little attention been focussed upon followers and what are the impli-cations for leadership theory and practice?

Navigating the leadership literature

The greatest challenge of the leadership literature is the amount of literature and the variable and contradictory nature of this literature. Many academic accounts start by acknowledging this and then add to this literature mountain. *Leadership: A Very Short Introduction* (Grint, 2010) is a good place for anyone new to this literature to start. Whilst the title sounds a bit Mickey Mouse, Grint is a very knowledgeable leadership author and there is an art to meaningfully synthesising this discursive literature. At the opposite end of the continuum are academic handbooks, a relatively new phenomenon with *The SAGE Handbook of Leadership Studies* (2011) being a good place to start. Gill's (2011) textbook treatment is also particularly relevant to this chapter – *Theory and Practice of Leadership,* in which he offers an accessible chronological account of the development of leadership theories. A general theory of leadership has proved elusive and may continue to be elusive, but if you want to read discussions from influential leadership scholars focussed upon this quest Goethals and Sorenson's (2006) edited reader is informative. If you are interested in exploring leadership critically and challenging leadership orthodoxy as introduced in the questioning section, Western's (2013) *Leadership: A Critical Text* is recommended. The textbook adopts a critical theory approach which will not be for everyone, but given the acritical nature of so much of the leadership literature, it is a welcome contribution.

References

Abrahamson, E. 2004. *Change Without Pain: How Managers Overcome Initiative Overload, Organizational Chaos, and Employee Burnout.* Boston, MA: Harvard Business School Press.

Alvesson, M., and Y.D. Billing. 2009. *Understanding Gender and Organizations.* London: Sage Publications.

Ancona, D. 2005. *Leadership in an Age of Uncertainty.* Research Brief. Cambridge, MA: MIT Leadership Center.

Antonakis, J. and D.V. Day. 2017. *The Nature of Leadership.* Los Angeles: Sage Publications.

Baker, S.D. 2007. "Followership: The Theoretical Foundation of a Contemporary Construct." In *Discovering Leadership,* edited by J. Billsberry. Houndmills: Palgrave Macmillan in association with OU.

Bass, B.M., and R.E. Riggio. 2006. *Transformational Leadership.* Mahwah, NJ: Lawrence Erlbaum Associates Inc/Psychology Press.

Bolden, R., B. Hawkins, G. Gosling, and S. Taylor. 2011. *Exploring Leadership: Individual, Organizational and Societal Perspectives.* Oxford: Oxford University Press.

Burns, J.M. 1978. *Leadership.* New York: Harper Row Publishers.

Butler, N., H. Delaney, and S. Spoelstra. 2015. "Problematizing 'Relevance' in the Business School: The Case of Leadership Studies." *British Journal of Management* 26(4): 731–744.

Calas, M.B., and L. Smircich. 1991. "Voicing Seduction to Silence Leadership." *Organization Studies* 12(4): 567–602.

Carnes, A., J.D. Houghton, and C.N. Ellison. 2015. "What Matters Most in Leader Selection? The Role of Personality and Implicit Leadership Theories." *Leadership and Organization Development Journal* 36(4): 360–379.

Chambers, L., J. Drysdale, and J. Hughes. 2010. "The Future of Leadership: A Practitioner View." *European Management Journal* 28(4): 260–268.

Edelman, M. 1971. *Politics are Symbolic Actions.* Chicago, IL: Markham.

Fiedler, F.E. 1964. *A Theory of Leader Effectiveness.* New York: McGraw-Hill.

Gemmil, G., and G. Oakley. 1992. "Leadership: An Alienating Social Myth." *Human Relations* 45(2): 113–129.

Gill, R. 2011. *Theory and Practice of Leadership.* London: Sage Publications.

Gipson, A.N., D.L. Pfaff, D.B. Mendelsohn, L.T. Catenacci, and W.W. Burke. 2017. "Women and Leadership: Selection, Development, Leadership Style, and Performance." *The Journal of Applied Behavioral Science* 53(1): 32–65.

Glynn, M.A., and R. DeJordy. 2010. "Leadership Through an Organization Behaviour Lens: A Look at the Last Half-Century of Research." In *Handbook of Leadership Theory and Practice: A Harvard Business School Centennial Colloquium,* edited by N. Nohria and R. Khurana, 119–157. Cambridge, MA: Harvard Business Press.

Goethals, G.R., and G.L.J. Sorenson (Eds). 2006. *The Quest for a General Theory of Leadership*. Cheltenham: Edward Elgar.

Grint, K. 2000. *The Arts of Leadership*. Oxford: Oxford University Press.

Grint, K. 2005. *Leadership: Limits and Possibilities*. Houndmills: Palgrave Macmillan.

Grint, K. 2010. *Leadership: A Very Short Introduction*. Oxford: Oxford University Press.

Harvey, M., and R.E. Riggio (Eds). 2011. *Leadership Studies: The Dialogue of Disciplines*. Cheltenham: Edward Elgar.

Haslam, S.A., S.D. Reicher, and M.J. Platlow. 2011. *The New Psychology of Leadership: Identity Influence and Power*. Hove: Psychology Press.

House, R.J. 1971. "A Path-Goal Theory of Leader Effectiveness." *Administrative Science Quarterly* 16(3): 321–338.

House, R.J., and R.N. Aditya. 1997. "The Social Scientific Study of Leadership: Quo Vadis?" *Journal of Management* 23(3): 409–473.

Hoyt, C.L., G.R. Goethals, and R.E. Riggio. 2006. "Leader-Follower Relations: Group Dynamics and the Role of Leadership." In *The Quest for a General Theory of Leadership* edited by G.R. Goethals and G.L.J. Sorenson, 96–122. Cheltenham: Edward Elgar.

Hughes, M. 2016. *The Leadership of Organizational Change*. London: Routledge.

Katz, D., and R.L. Kahn. 1960. "Leadership Practices in Relation to Productivity and Morale." In *Group Dynamics* edited by D. Cartwright and Z. Zander, 554–570. Evanston, IL: Harper and Row.

Kellerman, B. 2012. *The End of Leadership*. New York: HarperCollins Publishers.

Kellerman, B. 2013. "Leading Questions: The End of Leadership – Redux." *Leadership* 9(1): 135–139.

Kelly, S. 2014. "Towards a Negative Ontology of Leadership." *Human Relations* 67(8): 905–922.

Kotter, J.P. 1990. *A Force for Change: How Leadership Differs from Management*. New York: Free Press.

Kotter, J.P. 1996/2012. *Leading Change*. Boston, MA: Harvard Business School Press.

Lewin, K., R. Lippitt, and R.K. White. 1939. "Patterns of Aggressive Behavior in Experimentally Created Social Climates." *Journal of Social Psychology* 10(2): 269–299.

Mabey, C. 2013. "Leadership Development in Organizations: Multiple Discourses and Diverse Practice." *International Journal of Management Reviews* 15(4): 359–380.

Prugl, E. 2012. "If Lehman Brothers had been Lehman Sisters...Gender and Myth in the Aftermath of the Financial Crisis." *International Political Sociology* 6(1): 21–35.

Riggio, R.E. 2011. "Is Leadership Studies a Discipline?" In *Leadership Studies: The Dialogue of Disciplines*, edited by M. Harvey and R.E. Riggio, 119–128. Cheltenham: Edward Elgar.

Rost, J.C. 1993. *Leadership for the Twenty-First Century*. Westport, CT: Praeger.

Rost, J.C. 1997. "Moving from Individual to Relationship: A Post-Industrial Paradigm of Leadership." *The Journal of Leadership Studies* 4(4): 3–16.

Smith, A.C.T., and F.M. Graetz. 2011. *Philosophies of Organizational Change*. Cheltenham: Edward Elgar Publishing.

Spicker, P. 2012. "Leadership: A Perniciously Vague Concept." *International Journal of Public Sector Management* 25(1): 34–47.

Stogdill, R.M. 1948. "Personal Factors Associated with Leadership: A Survey of the Literature." *Journal of Psychology* 25(1): 35–71.

Stodgill, R.M., O.S. Goode, and D.R. Day. 1962. "New Leader Behavior Description Subscales." *Journal of Psychology* 54(2): 259–269.

Tourish, D. 2015. "Some Announcements, Reaffirming the Critical Ethos of Leadership, and What we Look for in Submissions." *Leadership* 11(2): 135–141.

Vroom, V.H., and P.W. Yetton. 1973. *Leadership and Decision Making*. Pittsburgh, PA: University of Pittsburgh Press.

Western, S. 2013. *Leadership: A Critical Text*. London: Sage Publications.

Chapter 10

Leading organizational change

Introduction and chapter questions

> Virtually every sector and all levels of staff appear to be represented and engaged in the search for leadership. Everyone, it seems, is being invited to join in.
>
> (Storey, 2011: 3)

This chapter joins Storey's (2011) search for leadership with particular reference to the leadership of organizational change. For Storey, interest in the 1980s in change management was one of the catalysts for increasing interest in leadership. Organizations required change management and leadership offered a response which had wide appeal. Haslam et al. (2011) acknowledged wonderful stories about the role that great leaders have played in making history and initiating changes. In this way, the leadership of organizational change offers another wonderful story. In the context of this chapter we need to understand how through leadership the success/failure of organizational change is influenced, the major theories, models and concepts informing this understanding, as well their limitations.

Whilst themes of leadership and organizational change are very prevalent in organizations and societies, we do not have a consensus on the meaning of these words. The ambiguities of both organizational change (Chapter 2) and leadership studies (Chapter 9) have been introduced and the variability of terms in use which impedes both theory and practice. In this chapter, transformational leadership will be included given its popularity. It does appear to speak to the organizational change theme of this textbook, but it is a concept which speaks primarily to the transformation of subordinates. Ford and Ford (2012: 31) in their review of empirically informed leadership and organizational change literature highlighted 'a vocabulary that adds confusion and vagueness to both the research and its conclusions'.

In this chapter, universal definitions of leadership and organizational change cannot be imposed given the breadth of definitions already in use, but there is a need for caution. Another cautionary note relates to the apparent differentiation between management and leadership. Riggio (2011: 120), a leadership academic, highlighted a time 'when the field of management began to make the shift from viewing those in positions of power and control as mere "managers" to viewing them as taking on higher-level "leadership" activities...'. Riggio's view is not shared. In this part of the textbook, leadership is the focus as an important aspect of organizational change, but management is equally important and this view will be developed in the final part of this textbook. In the interim, the cautionary note is that it is not as easy as some authors imply to detect where managing change ends and leading change begins.

This chapter is organized around and provides answers to the following leading organizational change questions:

How do practitioners lead organizational change?
What challenges impede theorising leading organizational change?
How might organizational change leadership bricolage inform understanding?
How does a mythical change leadership narrative impede our understanding?
What are the criticisms of Kotter's (1996/2012) *Leading Change*?
What are the criticisms of transformational leadership?
How does the concept of the dark side inform our understanding of the leadership of organizational change?

In the next section, leading change (Kotter, 1996/2012) and transformational leadership (Bass, 1985) as two of the most influential approaches favoured by practitioners are featured. This is followed by an acknowledgement of the challenges of theorising leading organizational change and the notion of bricolage is presented as a way forward. The notion of a mythical leading organizational change narrative is introduced and the limitations of Kotter's (1996/2012) leading change and transformational leadership are acknowledged, as well as, a potential dark side of leading organizational change.

Leading organizational change: what are practitioners doing?

Buchanan and Macaulay (2014) in their practitioner oriented article, 'How to be a Successful Change Leader', offer prescriptions for practitioners which are grounded in research and scholarship. They highlight four challenges change leaders increasingly face: first, maintaining control over an increasingly overwhelming change agenda, second, the need to maintain the pace and momentum of a change agenda, third, the need to avoid initiative decay and fourth, avoiding over-focussing upon individual leaders. They highlight how change leaders need to lead through three key themes: multi-loading, hunting in packs and playing the political game. Multi-loading involves what they refer to as 'sweating the small stuff' and relentless targeted and ongoing communications with feedback. Hunting in packs is about being one of several change champions and distributing responsibility (playing the politics game is discussed further in Chapter 11).

Parry (2011: 57) in his contribution to *The Sage Handbook of Leadership* took critical stock of the state of scholarship in this area.

Leadership and organizational change are inextricably intertwined. However, 'organizational change' has become an interest for organizational consultants more so than for empirical researchers. There are many more books and articles on practitioner or conceptual scholarship than on theoretical or empirical scholarship. Much of the practitioner work is case study-based and anecdotal and not rigorous in its conduct.

(Parry, 2011: 57)

In terms of theory and practice, two approaches have proved to be particularly influential when gauged by citations. Kotter's (1996/2012) *Leading Change* and transformational leadership (Bass and Riggio, 2006) have been by far the most influential approaches (Hughes, 2016). They both use the language of transformation and may equally have given impetus to the increasing use of transformation terminology in organizations and societies. Also, both Bass (1985) and Kotter (1990) acknowledged the differentiation between transformational and transactional leadership made by Burns (1978) in leadership, although neither author appeared to take on board the moral form of transforming leadership emphasising followers which Burns (1978) was primarily encouraging. In the following discussion, leading change and transformational leadership are positively introduced as practitioner oriented prescriptions. In the subsequent 'Questioning leading organizational change' section, criticisms are highlighted.

Leading change

Kotter's (1996/2012) *Leading Change* is by far the most cited book in the whole field of organizational change studies (Hughes, 2016). However, it has also proved to be influential with practitioners, being included in TIME's (2016) 25 most influential business management books. The impetus for interest in change leadership, since the early 1980s can be attributed to the severe challenges in managing innovation and culture change faced by the large American corporations (Caldwell, 2003). There was a belief that special kinds of leadership were critical during times of strategic organizational change (Nadler and Tushman, 2004). Kotter (1996: 26), a great advocate of leadership, asserted that 'successful transformation is 70 to 90 percent leadership and only 10 to 30 percent management'. Kotter warned that focussing on managing change neglected leading change. There is support for such a view in terms of the disproportionate amount of managing change research and scholarship in comparison to change leadership research and scholarship.

"Leading Change: Why Transformation Efforts Fail" (Kotter, 1995) was published in *Harvard Business Review* and drew upon Kotter's experience of working with over 100 companies seeking to make fundamental changes. A strength of his contribution was that he built upon his earlier work (Kotter, 1990; Kotter and Heskett, 1992). Kotter conceded (1995: 59) 'a few of these corporate change efforts have been very successful. A few have been utter failures. Most fall somewhere in between, with a distinct tilt toward the lower end of the scale'. As well as giving impetus to interest in the theory and practice of leading change, the paper encouraged interest amongst practitioners and academics in evaluating the effectiveness of change initiatives (discussed further in Chapter 17). Kotter himself acknowledged that in the space of a short paper, everything may sound too simplistic and in 1996 he addressed this concern by using the eight steps as the structure for his book *Leading Change* featured in Table 10.1.

The book which received many testimonials from senior managers had the strap line 'an action plan from the world's foremost expert on business leadership'. Kotter (1996) challenged the view that companies were unable to change, which high change failure rates suggested, instead choosing to identify patterns evident in the successful companies that he had studied. He argued that change was associated with a multistep process which could never be effective without high-quality leadership. Subsequently, Kotter was invited to follow up *Leading Change* by Deloitte Consulting with a project which involved the Deloitte team headed by Dan Cohen interviewing over 200 people in more than 90 US, European, Australian and South African organizations in

Table 10.1 Eight errors (Kotter, 1995) and the eight-stage process for creating major change (Kotter, 1996)

Eight errors resulting in transformation failure (Kotter, 1995)	Eight leadership steps towards transformation success (Kotter, 1996/2012)
Error 1: Not establishing a great enough sense of urgency	1 Establishing a sense of urgency
Error 2: Not creating a powerful enough guiding coalition	2 Forming a powerful guiding coalition
Error 3: Lacking a vision	3 Creating a vision
Error 4: Under-communicating the vision by a factor of ten	4 Communicating the vision
Error 5: Not removing obstacles to the new vision	5 Empowering others to act on the vision
Error 6: Not systematically planning for, and creating short-term wins	6 Planning for and creating short-term wins
Error 7: Declaring victory too soon	7 Consolidating improvements and producing still more change
Error 8: Not anchoring changes in the corporation's culture	8 Institutionalising new approaches

order to collect stories that could help people more deeply understand the eight-step formula. In the preface of *The Heart of Change* (Kotter and Cohen, 2002), Kotter offered a helpful clarification of what he meant by transformation:

> By transform I mean the adoption of new technologies, major strategic shifts, process reengineering, mergers and acquisitions, restructuring into different sorts of business units, attempts to significantly improve innovation, and cultural change.

In 2012, a revised edition of *Leading Change* was published. It was substantially the same book, but with refreshed penguin imagery and a new preface.

Transformational leadership

Downton (1973) first coined the phrase transformational leadership although it was Burns' (1978) study of leadership and followership which gave impetus to transformational leadership. Diaz-Saenz (2011) described transformational leadership as the single most studied and debated idea within the field of leadership studies over the past 30 years. Two key publication milestones in the development of transformational leadership were *Leadership and Performance Beyond Expectations* (Bass, 1985) and *Transformational Leadership* (Bass and Riggio, 2006). Bass (1985: xv) himself referred to *Leadership and Performance Beyond Expectations* as an 'initial statement' and 'preliminary scaffolding'. However, many of the components of transformational leadership were evident in this early exposition (please see Table 10.2).

In promoting transformational leadership, Bass (1985: 4) wrote as follows:

> More quantity is no longer enough; quality must improve dramatically. Leaders may help in bringing about a radical shift in attention. For instance, groups oriented toward traditional beliefs will be shifted so that they come to value modern approaches. The contextual framework may be changed by leaders.

Table 10.2 Key components of Bass's (1985) transformational leadership

Transformational or transactional leadership dependent upon antecedents of:
- External environment
- Organizational environment

Transformational leadership factors
- Charismatic leadership
- Individualised consideration
- Intellectual stimulation

Transactional leadership factors
- Contingent reward
- Management by exception

Bass and Riggio (2006) suggested that transformational leaders went beyond exchanges or agreements, achieving superior results through employing one or more of four components; idealised influence, inspirational motivation, intellectual stimulation and individualised consideration. The focus of transformational leadership was upon leaders transforming followers/subordinates with Bass and Riggio (2006) conceding that little research had examined how transformational leadership affected organizational change.

In terms of understanding, what are practitioners doing? Haslam et al. (2011: 41) warned, '...would-be-leaders often resort to a literal interpretation of the term "transformational" and seek to demonstrate their leadership credentials by restructuring their organization at the first available opportunity'. This is not a criticism of transformational leadership but instead seeks to highlight a negative legacy of this common misunderstanding of transformational leadership (Haslam et al., 2011).

Leading organizational change theories

As Parry (2011) warned, there were many more practitioner/conceptual books and articles than theoretical/empirical scholarship. The concern was that the practitioner work was case study-based anecdotal and not rigorous in conduct. The findings from "The Leadership of Organization Change: A View from Recent Empirical Evidence" (Ford and Ford, 2012), which focussed exclusively on literature published in peer-reviewed journals between 1990 and 2010, was even more troubling. They reviewed all academic peer-reviewed papers identifying 27 papers between 1990 and 2010. Subsequently, they excluded certain papers resulting in a final tally of 14 papers.

> There is simply too little empirical research that specifically addresses the leadership of change to warrant a prescription for what works...we find, the available research equivocal and incomplete regarding both what constitutes effective leadership and the impact of change leaders' approaches, behaviors, and activities on change outcomes of any type.
>
> (Ford and Ford, 2012: 22)

It is perverse given the interest within organizations and wider societies in both leadership and in organizational change that so little is empirically known about the leadership of organizational change. The first sub-section seeks to explain the challenges researching and theorising leading organizational change raises and the second sub-section looks positively and proactively to creatively drawing upon existing research informed theories. This section draws upon learning from a literature review covering 35 years of leadership and organizational change studies (please see Hughes, 2016 for the full review).

Leading organizational change theoretical challenges

As was suggested in the previous section, transformational leadership (Bass and Riggio, 2006) and leading change (Kotter, 1996) have been the most influential approaches if gauged by citations. Whilst, these approaches will be critically questioned in the next section, their prevalence may have acted as an impediment to developing alternative theories of leading organizational change. Merton's (1968, 1988) work on the diffusion of ideas through scientific communities highlighted how the distribution of citations tended to be skewed towards a small number of scholars. With these scholars accounting for the majority of citations, he labelled this phenomenon the 'Matthew Effect'. This is believed to have been the case with regards to leading organizational change with leading change and transformational leadership explanations overshadowing other explanations. Further challenges relate to the existence of competing and contradictory definitions of leadership and definitions of organizational change. It is difficult to develop theory when the subject of theorising is so variable.

Researching leadership and organizational change raise significant research design challenges particularly in terms of ambiguity, contexts, dynamism and evaluation. There is considerable ambiguity around independent components of leadership and organizational change even without combining them. Leadership and organizational change speak to unknown futures implying certainties which only the passage of time can confirm (please see March, 1981; Dawson, 2014). Empirical findings from research into leadership and organizational change will be particular to a sector and/ or national cultural context, raising the challenge of the contextual nature of findings (please see Pettigrew et al., 2001). Leadership and organizational change are processes, rather than things (Van de Ven and Poole, 2005) requiring research designs to address the processual and emergent nature of leadership. The dynamism of both leadership and organizational change is challenging but in combination particularly challenging. Grint (2005) highlighted claims of leadership as critical to all organizational success (and failure) being as commonplace as claims to have discovered the recipe for success. Success is often taken for granted or masked within organizational histories written by leaders celebrating how they successfully transformed their organizations (please see Collins, 2000 and Huczynski, 2006 for further discussion). Researching the influence of a leader upon change, requires an evaluation of organizational change, which is not as straightforward as might be imagined (please see Pettigrew et al., 2001).

Leading organizational change bricolage

The challenges highlighted in the previous sub-section do not negate the need for research/theory, but rather they are explanations for the paucity of theory. We do have theoretical insights, but they do not match the practitioner interest in leading organizational change. In Hughes (2016), many disparate theories were drawn together and a bricolage approach was encouraged. Here the bricolage approach is explained and potentially fruitful theories are highlighted.

Weick's (1993) writings about improvisation offer an alternative perspective which embraces uncertainty. Weick (1993) favoured more fluid recipes as opposed to static blueprints, attention rather than intention and bricolage with its acknowledgement of the flexible use of repertoires and resources. So instead of leaning heavily upon leading change and transformational leadership theories, the spirit of bricolage offers a way forward for leadership and organizational change theories and practices. Change leadership bricolage also respects the uniqueness of every leader, collaborator, organization and organizational change with an implication that there is no singular/universal approach to lead change, but reflexive leaders aware of their own unique context improvise approaches to lead change, which may still be informed by empirical evidence, but drawn upon more flexibly and creatively, rather than prescriptively.

Five research informed accounts of leading organizational change are highlighted here. They are not necessarily the best nor the most applicable, but they do illustrate how potentially we can draw upon earlier work. This particular assemblage of theories is contingent on issues such as, the particular change being led, the context in which a change is being led, the capabilities and competencies of the leader, etc. The implication is that there is no one best way either to lead organizational change or to theorise such practice, but instead, it is necessary to assemble the most appropriate theories to guide practice or to offer an explanation of practice.

Each of the theories featured in Table 10.3 benefits from being research informed and engaging with relevant literature, yet also has the potential to guide practices of leading organizational change. Each paper is briefly described below, but the best way to understand what is being suggested is to go back to the original source.

How can leaders achieve deliberate strategic change in organizations where strategic leadership roles are shared, objectives are divergent and power is diffuse? This was the practice-oriented research question which Denis et al. (2001) addressed. Their process theory of strategic change was developed in healthcare settings. Their research informed the development of an emerging process theory of leadership and strategic change in pluralistic settings.

Paglis and Green (2002) studied manager motivation for attempting the leadership of change drawing upon Bandura's (1986) social cognitive theory they developed their construct of leadership self-efficacy (LSE). They concluded that first, although mastery experiences are traditionally viewed as one of the most important influences on self-efficacy, this was not supported by their findings. Second, there was a lack of influence of superiors' behaviour on managers' LSE. And manager crisis perceptions did not moderate the relationship between LSE and proposed leadership attempts.

Table 10.3 Five leading organizational change theories

Author/s	Year	Title
Denis et al.	2001	The dynamics of collective leadership and strategic change in pluralistic organizations
Paglis and Green	2002	Leadership self-efficacy and managers' motivation for leading change
Higgs and Rowland	2005	All changes great and small: exploring approaches to change and its leadership
Tyler and De Cremer	2005	Process-based leadership: fair procedures and reactions to organizational change
Battilana et al.	2010	Leadership competencies for implementing planned organizational change

In terms of how you lead organizational change, Higgs and Rowland (2005) in "All Changes Great and Small: Exploring Approaches to Change and its Leadership" offered readers guidance in terms of competing approaches and relating approaches to leader behaviours. Their paper informed by literature reviewing and case studies of 70 change stories, drew upon 40 informants in seven organizations. Through their research, they were able to answer three research questions:

1   What approach to change management is likely to be most effective in today's business environment? Approaches based upon acknowledgement of complexity and emergence were found to be most successful.
2   What leadership behaviours tend to be associated with effective change management? They identified three leadership behaviours associated with change management; shaping behaviour, framing change and creating capacity.
3   Are leadership behaviours related to an underlying assumption within different approaches to change? They identified four approaches to change: directive (simple), master (sophisticated), self-assembly (DIY) and emergence. The dominance of behaviours varied within each approach.

"Process-based Leadership: Fair Procedures and Reactions to Organizational Change" (Tyler and De Cremer, 2005) is included as a reminder of the importance of fair leadership procedures. They (2005: 529) hypothesised '…that those who are more strongly identified with their company will be more influenced by procedural justice information'. Their research focussed upon the actions of leaders leading a company through examining employee acceptance of a merger.

In "Leadership Competencies for Implementing Planned Organizational Change", Battilana et al. (2010) focussed on clinical managers in the UK National Health Service implementing change projects between 2003 and 2004. Two of their findings speak specifically to how you lead organizational change.

1   Those leaders more effective at task-oriented behaviours were more likely to focus on mobilising and evaluating activities.
2   Those leaders more effective at person-oriented behaviours were more likely to focus on communicating activities.

Research studies featured here highlight that leading organizational change has an impact on both the leaders and the led and that the nature and extent of that impact depend on the form of leadership, as well as the way approaches to change, leader behaviours, and change activities are measured.

The studies cited here as change leadership bricolage are far less reassuring than Kotter (1996/2012) and Bass and Riggio's (2006) approaches. Change leadership bricolage is more discursive, complicated and even at times contradictory. It offers an alternative to the dependency of addictive quick fixes certain consultants and business schools may offer.

Questioning leading organizational change theories

Calas and Smircich (1991) famously described leadership studies as a seduction, not in terms of what it says, but in terms what it does not say or the undecidability of what it might be saying. When leadership is combined with organizational change, this seduction is magnified and reinforced through our cultural predisposition towards leadership (Haslam et al., 2011; Storey, 2011 and Tourish, 2013). The following discussion takes critical stock of what we know about leading organizational change. In attempting to see beyond the seduction, the intent remains to critically inform practices in organizations. Four themes are developed, first, highlighting the mythical leading organizational change narrative. Second, Kotter's (1996/2012) influential account of leading change is critiqued. Third, transformational leadership is critiqued and fourth, a dark side of leading organizational change is highlighted.

The mythical leading organizational change narrative

Rost (1993: 8) depicted leadership as a mythical narrative (please see Chapter 9), in order to explain the apparent success of orthodox accounts of leadership 'it has generated a mythological story of leadership that has been told over and over again and that almost everyone believes'. If you look to textbook accounts of leadership, they often depict a historic evolution of leadership theorising implying that we are becoming increasingly knowledgeable about leadership. Rost (1993) did not favour this mythological narrative but highlighted it as limiting alternative conceptualisations of leadership and keeping leadership studies in its outdated paradigm (see also Gemmill and Oakley, 1992). More recently, Kelly (2014) highlighted the negative ontology of leadership, tantalisingly offering the possibility of a better definition, research design, methodology and theoretical framework, whilst simultaneously stopping any significant shift in the dominant leadership studies paradigm.

Whilst, Rost, Gemmill and Oakley and Kelly were writing about leadership in general, their writings appear to be highly applicable to leading organizational change. The critical writings of Parry (2011) and Ford and Ford (2012) cited earlier do not appear to be the norm. The norm appears to be that leading organizational change has been sufficiently researched and theorised and we are just at the 'fine tuning' stage of what we know. However, Haslam et al. (2011: 2) question the arrogance of such accounts of leadership:

> ...the proof of leadership is not the emergence of a big new idea or the development of a vision for sweeping change. Rather, it is the capacity to convince others to contribute to processes that turn ideas and visions into reality that help to bring about change.

In terms of leading organizational change, the quotation suggests that the focus should not be upon heroic leaders, but the many 'others' involved in processes of changing. There are echoes here of the concerns expressed by Burns (1978: 1) about leadership studies 35 years earlier, 'if we know all too much about our leaders, we know far too little about leadership'.

Critique of leading change

The main challenge in evaluating Kotter's (1996/2012) vision of leading change in an academic context is, where is the evidence? Tantalising anecdotes are frequently offered in support of the many assertions made in the book. These anecdotes helped the book to its bestseller status, superficially offering the legitimacy of a book based on case studies, but there is so little detail provided that it is difficult to draw conclusions from any of the cases cited. For example:

> When one of the most visionary, charismatic executives I've known was appointed president of a $1.7 billion division of a large US company, the level of excitement at that business rose dramatically.
>
> (Kotter, 1996: 117)

Kotter uses this anecdote in support of one of his steps. However, the sectoral context of the 'large US company' is not disclosed, making it impossible for anyone to undertake a thorough longitudinal analysis of the subsequent success or failure of this US company. Did the 'visionary, charismatic executive' lead the company to a lengthy period of success or subsequently into rapid decline? Was the large US company Enron? The book does not contain a list of supporting references and, in the body of the book, there are only cursory references to Kotter's earlier publications. The essence of the whole book, specifically the eight steps, is supported exclusively with a reference to Kotter's (1995) own paper. However, reading this paper in search of empirical case study evidence reveals very little. The omission of references to theory could be explained in terms of its practitioner focus. However, Kotter's work has influenced academic writing (see, for example, the number of critical change commentators who cite Kotter's 1995 anecdotal reference to change failure rates).

In Hughes (2016), seven weaknesses were highlighted in Kotter's (1996/2012) *Leading Change* (please see Table 10.4). Failings in Kotter's (1996/2012) transformation explanations are summarised in Table 10.4. The following discussion briefly explains each of these failings.

Resistance to change: In *Leading Change* Kotter (1996/2012) worked with an assumption that resistance to change was the problem and strong leadership was the solution. However, the utility of overcoming resistance to change and crudely categorising people as being either for or against a leader's particular change (Piderit, 2000) has been questioned (please see also Ford et al., 2008). Rethinking resistance as subtle and diverse responses to ongoing organizational change processes would involve employees within organizational change processes, rather than marginalising them as resistant bystanders.

Ethics, power, politics and organizational change: In *Leading Change,* Kotter (1996/2012) at best minimises ethical concerns, whereas by contrast critical scholars foreground ethical approaches, towards leading change (see for example Wall, 2007; Rhodes et al., 2010 and By and Burnes, 2011). *Leading Change* (Kotter, 1996) depicts leaders as the powerful ones explaining its enduring popularity, yet failing really to

Table 10.4 Failings in Kotter's (1996/2012) transformation explanations (summarised)

- Employees depicted as change resisters
- Ethics, power and politics underplayed
- Overemphasis upon a sequence of linear steps
- Disparaging history limits learning and an appreciation of incremental change
- Leader and leader communications overemphasised
- Underemphasis on unique cultural contexts
- Rhetorical treatment of organizational success/failure

deal theoretically with power and politics. Use of management power in times of organizational change is logical and inevitable, recognised as far back as the early 1970s (see Bradshaw and Boonstra, 2004; Hardy and Clegg, 2004; Buchanan and Badham, 2008 for discussion). Rethinking ethics, power and politics would introduce important dynamics and choices often absent within typical explanations of leading change.

Process thinking and organizational change: There are similarities between Kotter's (1996/2012) eight steps and Lewin's (1947) unfreeze, change and refreeze, indicative of sequential temporality common within change explanations (Hendry, 1996; Cummings, 2002; Burnes, 2004; Cummings et al., 2016). However, Kotter (1996/2012) billed his approach at the time of writing as a new approach to leading change. Rethinking in terms of process thinking disrupts the sequentialism and linearity currently evident within leading change explanations.

Learning and organizational change: Kotter (1996/2012) in looking forward, neglects temporal dimensions of organizational change (Ybema, 2010) and contributions of learning theory (Starkey et al., 2002). Ongoing learning is believed to be the best preparation for the future (Lakomski, 2001; Sugarman, 2001). Rethinking organizational learning acknowledges the past, as well as, the future and the often evolutionary/incremental nature of strategic change, potentially involving employees within processes of organizational change.

Agency, discourse and organizational change: In *Leading Change*, Kotter (1996/ 2012) depicted leaders/powerful guiding coalitions as the agents of change. Caldwell (2003) was sceptical about claims made for change leaders; over-emphasising leaders transforming organizations, failure to differentiate leaders and managers, underestimating leadership at different organizational levels and conflating leadership with change. Caldwell (2003) highlighted change agency being located within leadership, management, consultants and teams (see also Caldwell, 2005 and Caldwell, 2006). Kotter's (1996/2012) depiction of leader/powerful guiding coalitions as change agents privileges one-way communication at the expense of listening to or engaging with employees. Rethinking agency challenges belief in a change leader's exclusive agency highlighting choices with regard to where change agency is located, dispersal of power and construction of change discourses.

Contextualising organizational change: In *Leading Change,* Kotter's (1996/2012) transformation cases lack context. He never discloses the names of the companies, their histories or their sectors. Hope Hailey and Balogun (2002) warned against descriptive contingency models offering 'recipes' for making complex business simpler and more manageable. They cited Kotter and Schlesinger (1979) as illustrative of such formulaic recipes. Instead, they encourage: rigorous analysis of context, consideration of the different implementation options, being aware of personal preferences and how this limits options considered, and the development of change judgement. Rethinking a-contextual accounts of leading change, in favour of acknowledging unique contexts and cultures encourages movement away from formulaic recipes and refocuses upon the diverse choices reflexive change leaders have to make.

Evaluating organizational change: Leading change is depicted as either failing with improved leadership the solution (Kotter, 1995) or leading change will be successful if leaders follow eight successful transformation steps (Kotter, 1996/2012). However, the evaluation of the success of change initiatives is practically very difficult as success may be related to notions of quantity, quality, and pace of change all giving different outcomes (Pettigrew et al., 2001). Rethinking academic evaluations of organizational change evaluation offers an antidote to simplistic generalisations that transformations fail or succeed exclusively as a consequence of leaders and leadership.

Critique of transformational leadership

Bass and Riggio's (2006) *Transformational Leadership* was the most cited transformational leadership publication (please see Hughes, 2016). The preface by James McGregor Burns and Georgia Sorenson explicitly acknowledged their endorsement of *Transformational Leadership*. However, commentators critically questioned if transformational leadership, which Burns (1978) envisaged in his book *Leadership*, was really being realised within Bass's conceptualisations. Carey (1992) critically questioned the shift from change towards higher values which Burns (1978) encouraged as opposed to the change leadership which Bass encouraged. Carey (1992) differentiated Burn's (1978) view of transforming leadership from Bass (1985) in three ways. First, for Burns the transforming leader raises followers' needs levels, whereas for Bass the leader expands the needs and wants of followers. Second, Burns regarded moral leadership as essential to transforming leadership, whereas 'Bass removes the variables of moral good and evil and simply views transformational leadership as producing change' (Bass, 1990) (Carey, 1992: 220). Third, there is divergence regarding how transactional and transformational leadership are related.

While moral leadership does imply a change in both leaders and followers as Burns (1978) states, change per se is not always moral, since it does not invariably result in a 'relationship of mutual stimulation and elevation' (Burns, 1978: 4) for both leader and follower. There also appears to be confusion around the treatment of charisma within transformational leadership theories. Beyer (1999) was particularly prominent criticising an emphasis upon psychological explanations at the expense of sociological explanations (such as Weber, 1947). Beyer (1999) wanted a clear differentiation between charismatic leadership and transformational leadership, which would have been beneficial, but which Bass was unable to provide (Diaz-Saenz, 2011).

Yukl's (1999) influential critique of transformational leadership acknowledged Burns's (1978) emphasis upon the importance of collective leadership within transforming leadership, but that other accounts of transformational leadership neglected the importance of distributed and shared leadership. In identifying conceptual weaknesses with transformational leadership, Yukl (1999) regarded Bass (1985) as generating the most research at the time of his critique (please see Table 10.5).

In their critical review, Tourish and Pinnington (2002) highlighted transformational leadership potentially encouraging authoritarian forms of organization, which may be related back to Yukl's (1999) concerns about transformational leadership working with a stereotype of a historic leader. Tourish and Pinnington's (2002) critique was not with leadership per se, but that dominant transformation leadership models were fundamentally flawed. Instead, they offered an alternative model which emphasised

Table 10.5 Conceptual weaknesses of transformational leadership (Yukl, 1999)

1	Ambiguity about underlying influence processes
2	Overemphasis on dyadic processes
3	Ambiguity about transformational behaviours
4	Ambiguity about transactional leadership
5	Omission of important behaviours
6	Insufficient specification of situational variables
7	Insufficient identification of negative effects
8	Heroic leadership bias

key elements of transactional leadership. They acknowledged the ubiquity of workplace power differentials and the need to look again to democratic and stakeholder perspectives for organizational restructuring. Currie and Lockett's (2007) critique narrowed the focus to questioning the applicability of transformational leadership to English public services, noting that transformational leadership as promoted through government policy diverged from its academic conception (Bryman, 1992). However, in reviewing transformational leadership literature, they found it to be strong on rhetoric and advocacy, yet weak on evidence. For Tourish (2013) transformational leadership as traditionally envisaged had become part of the problem, rather than the solution.

The dark side of leading organizational change

The dark side of organizations is the focus of Chapter 16. However, given its relevance to explanations of leading organizational change, it is introduced here. Linstead et al. (2014: 165) in their editorial introducing a Special Issue of *Organization Studies* focussed upon the dark side highlighting 'frustrations with the tendencies of mainstream work to overlook, ignore or suppress difficult ethical, political and ideological issues, which may well mean life or death to some people, has in recent years led to a research that self-identifies its concerns as being with the dark side'.

The dark side of leadership has been recognised (see for example Conger, 1998 Judge et al., 2009 and Vince and Mazen, 2014). In the following discussion, the focus is on the dark side of leadership with specific reference to organizational change through visiting Higgs (2009), Fyke and Buzzanell (2013) and Tourish (2013). In "The Good, the Bad, and the Ugly: Leadership and Narcissism", Higgs (2009) encouraged greater engagement with the dark side of leadership literature and change implementation. He cited Rowland and Higgs (2008) demonstrating strong relationships between leadership behaviours and change success, highlighting that '...leaders were behaving in a way that focussed on meeting their own goals and needs rather than serving the purpose of the change' (Higgs, 2009: 166). Higgs (2009) reviewed the bad leadership literature. He highlighted that there was a bias towards good leadership, but also highlighted literature focussed on bad leadership, including leadership derailment, toxic leadership, negative leadership, evil leadership, abusive leadership and destructive leadership. He identified central themes within this bad leadership literature as: abuse of power, inflicting damage on others, over the exercise of control to satisfy personal needs and rule breaking to serve own purposes. Higgs (2009) highlighted an emerging interest in understanding narcissistic leadership, although he warned that this debate had been strong on assertion and argument, but limited in terms of empirical research.

In "The Ethics of Conscious Capitalism: Wicked Problems in Leading Change and Changing Leaders", Fyke and Buzzanell (2013) took a discursive approach in engaging with a consulting and leadership development firm with a focus on conscious capitalism. They believed that ethical business is achieved through leaders being increasingly conscious and self-reflexive, a belief which has proved popular with practitioners, but which has received little scholarly attention. The pseudonym Devenir is used for the management consulting firm they studied. They describe what the firm does as follows:

> Devenir provides a unique element in the change management/leader development industry; namely, having CC as the foundation and target of their efforts, and integrating cognitive, moral, and spiritual elements for requisite development and change.

(Fyke and Buzzanell, 2013: 1625)

The authors pragmatically argued that the value of conscious capitalism went beyond organizational change and leader development and could potentially be used to facilitate social change in the community, although this was not what Devenir were doing. Their summary is quite critical.

> …'The Work' of Devenir's everyday leadership development practices differs little from other leader/organization change efforts – there are inspirational talks, telelessons, group work, practice sessions, prereadings, and other activities. The training is long-term, developmental, and embodied – one is encouraged to live, breathe, speak, and feel the power of CC in all aspects of life, but particularly in business settings.
>
> (Fyke and Buzzanell, 2013: 1637)

In reading these findings, there are echoes of Tourish and Pinnington's (2002) account of transformational leadership and corporate cultism. However, it is Tourish's (2013) *The Dark Side of Transformational Leadership* which concludes this discussion. As the title suggests, this book brings together interest in the dark side within leadership studies and interest in transformational leadership. The book benefits from case-study based chapters which illustrate the dark side within Enron, Militant Tendency, Jonestown, Heaven's Gate and the banking sector.

> In good times or bad, it appears that most of us remain fascinated by leadership and enthralled by leaders…Ultimately, this book challenges our enduring preoccupation with leader agency…
>
> (Tourish, 2013: 5)

This quotation brings us full circle. From Storey's (2011) opening quotation, this fascination appears to be enduring and it appears to become magnified when leadership is associated with change/transformation, the theme of this chapter. Tourish's (2013) concerns with excessive leader agency in the context of transformation are shared with change agency discussed further in Chapter 14. In ending this discussion of the dark side a little more positively, Tourish's (2013) final chapter reimagines leadership and followership with an emphasis upon a processual, communication perspective. Tourish (2013: 210) suggests that 'leadership is less one person doing something to another (with their more or less willing compliance). Rather, it is a process whereby leaders and non-leaders accomplish each other through dynamics of interaction in which mutual influence is always present'. He concludes with the following implications for practice: the context in which leadership is practised is critical. More emphasis upon followership is required and leaders, as well as non-leaders, need to embrace uncertainty, rather than going for discursive closure.

Summary

The chapter may be succinctly summarised through answering the questions posed in the chapter's introduction. The original questions are restated in italics.

How do practitioners lead organizational change? Buchanan and Macaulay's (2014) article – "How to be a Successful Change Leader" was highlighted as offering prescriptions for practitioners grounded in research and scholarship. Kotter's (1996/2012) *Leading Change* and Bass's (1985) transformational leadership were introduced as two of the most influential practitioner oriented approaches.

What challenges impede theorising leading organizational change? There are competing and contradictory definitions of leadership and definitions of organizational change. It is difficult to develop theory when the subject of theorising is so variable. Researching leadership and organizational change raise significant research design challenges particularly in terms of ambiguity, contexts, dynamism and evaluation.

How might organizational change leadership bricolage inform understanding? Weick (1993) favoured more fluid recipes as opposed to static blueprints, attention rather than intention and bricolage with its acknowledgement of the flexible use of repertoires and resources. In this spirit, the research informed insights of Denis et al. (2001); Paglis and Green (2002); Higgs and Rowland (2005); Tyler and De Cremer (2005) and Battilana et al. (2010) offer ways forward.

How does a mythical change leadership narrative impede our understanding? A mythological story of leadership has been told over and over again and that almost everyone believes (Rost, 1993 see also Gemmill and Oakley, 1992 and Kelly, 2014).

Whilst, Rost, Gemmill and Oakley and Kelly were writing about leadership in general, their writings appear to be highly applicable to leading organizational change.

What are the criticisms of Kotter's (1996/2012) Leading Change? The following criticisms were identified: employees being depicted as change resistors, ethics, power and politics underplayed, an overemphasis upon a sequence of linear steps, disparaging history limiting learning and an appreciation of incremental change, leader and leader communications overemphasised, under emphasis of unique cultural contexts and rhetorical treatment of organizational success/failure.

What are the criticisms of transformational leadership? Yukl (1999) offered the most famous critique of transformational leadership highlighting ambiguity about underlying influence processes, overemphasis upon dyadic processes, ambiguity about transformational behaviours, ambiguity about transactional leadership, the omission of important behaviours, the insufficient specification of situational variables and identification of negative effects and a heroic leadership bias.

How does the concept of the dark side inform our understanding of the leadership of organizational change? There is a tendency in mainstream work to overlook, ignore or suppress difficult ethical, political and ideological issues (Linstead et al., 2014). The dark side of leadership has been recognised (see for example Conger, 1998; Judge et al., 2009; and Vince and Mazen, 2014). In "The Good, the Bad, and the Ugly: Leadership and Narcissism", Higgs (2009) encouraged greater engagement with the dark side leadership literature and change implementation. In Tourish's (2013) *The Dark Side of Transformational Leadership,* he brings together interest in the dark side within leadership studies and interest in transformational leadership.

Research case study showcase: leading change within integrated offender management (IOM)

King et al.'s (2017) case study research focussed on evaluating two IOM schemes reported in *Criminology & Criminal Justice* is showcased here. For full details and further analysis, please visit the original source.

Case study source

King et al.'s (2017) evaluation of two IOM schemes involved interviewing 25 prac-titioners. These included: probation officers, police officers, the judiciary, mem-bers of the criminal justice boards, and drug support workers. In the interviews, topics explored included the design, implementation and delivery of the schemes.

King, S., M. Hopkins., and N. Cornish. 2017. "Can Models of Organizational Change Help to Understand 'Success' and 'Failure' in Community Sentences? Applying Kotter's model of Organizational Change to an Integrated Offender Management Case Study." *Criminology & Criminal Justice* (online first).

The case study

In terms of UK criminal justice, there have been significant changes in the frame-work of community sentences for service users. These nationally driven change initiatives have required agencies to work in 'joined-up' multi-agency offender management arrangements. Most notably, this has involved increased emphasis on police and probation working relationships, central to the concept of IOM. The success/failure of these new initiatives within community sentencing de-pends among other things on how processes of organizational change are man-aged. King et al. (2017) innovatively applied Kotter's (1996/2012) eight steps for leading change to data generated from their evaluation of two IOM schemes in England (please see Table 10.1 in this chapter for Kotter's (1996) eight steps and Kotter's (1995) reasons why transformations were failing). The case study revis-its each step as a means of evaluating changes arising out of two IOM schemes.

Step one: establish a sense of urgency

Evaluations revealed discrepancies in how IOM schemes were initially perceived by practitioners. Police and probation tended to be positive, whereas other agen-cies appeared more sceptical. It was apparent that not all partners 'bought into' either the philosophy or the objectives of these schemes. This may explain why subsequent phases of change were not successfully achieved.

Step two: form a powerful guiding coalition

King et al.'s (2017) interview data revealed that, over time, governance struc-tures of the schemes became unclear with uncertainties about the nature of leadership in the IOM schemes. There was a stark contrast amongst practi-tioners in terms of different perceptions of leadership. A potential difficultly in establishing a guiding coalition within IOM schemes related to cultural clashes, for example, between police cultures and probation cultures.

> It may be the case that successful change management in criminal justice is dependent on there being multiple coalitions at various levels within rele-vant organizations.
>
> *(King et al., 2017: 7)*

(Continued)

Step three: create a vision

Participants unanimously recognised the need to change, and by association the need for a shared vision of an alternative approach to offender management. However, there were concerns about the lack of a clear strategic vision.

Step four: communicate the vision

The interviews revealed a lack of communication about these schemes to the wider police and probation personnel. In particular, non-IOM officers were sometimes ignorant about the schemes with negative implications for the treatment of service users by uniformed officers. Ineffective communication potentially undermined the credibility of these schemes and their outcomes.

Step five: empower others to act on the vision

The schemes brought together small teams of police officers, probation officers and a drugs support worker. What was crucial in the schemes was the co-location of various partners. However, the evaluations identified some psychological barriers to realising change amongst practitioners. These were particularly related to cultural differences between police and probation and perceptions of different benefits for organizations arising out of the schemes. The existence of these psychological barriers was likely to be detrimental to schemes achieving their goals.

Step six: plan for and create short-term wins

A challenge with this step is that goals for police and probation differ even though IOM encourages multi-agency integration. This is particularly problematic when different partners work towards discrete goals, with no overarching strategic objective. Inevitably multi-agency schemes will result in different goals that each agency sets out to achieve. However, where a goal results in a significant increase in the number of service users without additional resources, this may undermine achieving other goals.

Step seven: consolidate performance and produce still more change

The danger with not achieving short-term goals is that it makes consolidating performance difficult. The original intention of IOM schemes was crime reduction through the intensive reform and rehabilitation of prolific acquisitive offenders. However, findings from the Crime Reduction Programme suggested the impetus to consolidate performance through short-term wins should be tempered with realism. Realism about what could be achieved and clarity about what initiatives intended to achieve.

Step eight: institutionalise new approaches

The challenge for IOM was that new approaches needed to become rooted in norms and values of the wider organizations, not only within the small teams operating the schemes. If this didn't happen, then it was less likely that they would continue to be supported, particularly when new pressures, objectives or priorities emerged requiring different approaches to community justice.

King et al. (2017) acknowledge that IOM schemes have achieved only modest improvement in terms of reducing reoffending. They conclude that part of the explanation might lie in the approach adopted to managing change. They concluded that Kotter's model could provide a framework to manage organizational change in an iterative process with consideration given to the specific contextual factors that might affect change.

Case study questions

In answering these case study questions, please put to one side your like/dislike for Kotter's (1996/2012) eight steps for leading change.

1   What are the advantages of applying Kotter's (1996/2012) framework in King et al.'s (2017) evaluation of two IOM schemes?
2   What are the disadvantages of applying Kotter's (1996/2012) framework in King et al.'s (2017) evaluation of two IOM schemes?

Discussion questions

1   Why has leadership terminology and organizational change terminology been so ambiguous?
2   What is the potential appeal of transformational leadership for senior managers?
3   Do you believe that Kotter's (1996/2012) *Leading Change* has been beneficial or detrimental to leading organizational change theories and practices?
4   Why do we prefer to engage with the bright side of leading organizational change, rather than the dark side?

Navigating the leading organizational change literature

Leadership studies and organizational change studies reflect two independent and robust fields of study. The first challenge in navigating the leading organizational change literature is understanding a literature review which reflects the union of these two fields. Theories could be generated from an exclusively leadership studies perspective or an exclusively organizational change perspective, but ideally, they draw upon both. The second challenge is that both leadership studies and organizational change studies draw upon a range of academic disciplines, each informed by competing paradigms, philosophies, and perspectives. The practical orientation of leading organizational change becomes blurred when you look to the literature for explanations.

It is important to acknowledge that this chapter draws heavily upon my scholarly monograph *The Leadership of Organizational Change* (Hughes, 2016). It reviews the literature informing this subfield over the past 35 years. In Hughes (2017), I offer guidance on studying organizational change leadership as a subfield.

The coverage of *Leading Change* (Kotter, 1996/2012) in this chapter has been critical, but it is worthwhile reading this book and drawing your own conclusions given the influence of this book upon the leadership of organizational change. If you are interested in exploring the dark side further the Linstead et al. (2014) editorial offers an extensive and relatively up-to date-overview of literature informing this developing field of study. In a similar way, Tourish (2013) provides the resources for a critical literature review of transformational leadership.

References

Bandura, A. 1986. *Social Foundations of Thought and Action: A Social Cognitive Theory.* Englewood Cliffs, NJ: Prentice Hall.

Bass, B.M. 1985. *Leadership and Performance Beyond Expectations.* New York: Free Press.

Bass, B.M., and R.E. Riggio. 2006. *Transformational Leadership.* Mahwah, NJ: Lawrence Erlbaum Associates Inc/Psychology Press.

Battilana, J., M. Gilmartin, M. Sengul, A.C. Pache, and J.A. Alexander. 2010. "Leadership Competencies for Implementing Planned Organizational Change." *The Leadership Quarterly* 21(3): 422–438.

Beyer, J.M. 1999. "Taming and Promoting Charisma to Change Organizations." *The Leadership Quarterly* 10(2): 307–330.

Bradshaw, P., and J. Boonstra. 2004. "Power Dynamics in Organizational Change: A Multi-Perspective Approach." In *Dynamics of Organizational Change and Learning,* edited by J. J. Boonstra, 279–299. Chichester: John Wiley & Sons.

Bryman, A. 1992. *Charisma and Leadership in Organizations.* London: Sage Publications.

Buchanan D., and R. Badham. 2008. *Power, Politics and Organizational Change: Winning the Turf Game.* London: Sage Publications.

Buchanan, D., and S. Macaulay. 2014. "How to be a Successful Change Leader." *The Training Journal,* 1 January available at https://www.trainingjournal.com/articles/feature/how-be-successful-change-leader.

Burnes, B. 2004. "Kurt Lewin and the Planned Approach to Change: A Re-appraisal." *Journal of Management Studies* 41(6): 977–1002.

Burns, J.M. 1978. *Leadership.* New York: Harper Row.

By, R.T., and B. Burnes. 2011. "Leadership and Change: Whatever Happened to Ethics?" In *The Routledge Companion to Organizational Change,* edited by D.M. Boje, B. Burnes., and J. Hassard, 295–309. London: Routledge.

Calas, M.B., and L. Smircich. 1991. "Voicing Seduction to Silence Leadership." *Organization Studies* 12(4): 567–602.

Caldwell, R. 2003. "Change Leaders and Change Managers: Different or Complementary?" *Leadership & Organization Development Journal* 24(5): 285–293.

Caldwell, R. 2005. "Things Fall Apart? Discourses on Agency and Change in Organizations." *Human Relations* 58(1): 83–114.

Caldwell, R. 2006. *Agency and Change.* Abingdon: Routledge.

Carey, M.R. 1992. Transformational Leadership and Fundamental Option for Self-transcendence." *The Leadership Quarterly* 3(3): 217–236.

Collins, D. 2000. *Management Fads and Buzzwords: Critical-Practical Perspectives.* London: Routledge.

Conger, J.A. 1998. "The Dark Side of Leadership." In *Leading Organizations: Perspectives for a New Era,* edited by G.R. Hickman, 250–260. Thousand Oaks: Sage Publications.

Cummings, S. 2002. *Recreating Strategy.* London: Sage Publications.

Cummings, S., T. Bridgman, and K.G. Brown. 2016. "Unfreezing Change as Three Steps: Rethinking Kurt Lewin's Legacy for Change Management." *Human Relations* 69(1): 33–60.

Currie, G., and A. Lockett. 2007. "A critique of transformational leadership: Moral, professional and contingent dimensions of leadership within public services organizations." *Human Relations,* 60(2): 341–370.

Dawson, P. 2014. "Reflections: On Time, Temporality and Change in Organizations." *Journal of Change Management* 14(3): 285–308.

Denis, J. L., L. Lamothe, and A. Langley. 2001. "The Dynamics of Collective Leadership and Strategic Change in Pluralistic Organizations." *Academy of Management Journal* 44(4): 809–837.

Diaz-Saenz, H.R. 2011. "Transformational Leadership." In *The Sage Handbook of Leadership*, edited by A. Bryman, D. Collinson, K. Grint, B. Jackson, and M. Uhl-Bien, 299–310. London: Sage Publications.

Downton, J.V. 1973. *Rebel Leadership: Commitment and Charisma in a Revolutionary Process*. New York: Free Press.

Ford, J.D., and L.W. Ford. 2012. "The Leadership of Organization Change: A View from Recent Empirical Evidence." In *Research in Organizational Change and Development (Research in Organizational Change and Development, Volume 20)* edited by B. Abraham, (Rami) Shani, W.A. Pasmore, and R.W. Woodman, 1–36. Bingley: Emerald Group Publishing.

Ford, J.D., L.W. Ford., and A. D'Amelio. 2008. "Resistance to Change: The Rest of the Story." *Academy of Management Review* 33(2): 362–377.

Fyke, J.P., and P.M. Buzzanell. 2013. "The Ethics of Conscious Capitalism: Wicked Problems in Leading Change and Changing Leaders." *Human Relations* 66(12): 1619–1643.

Gemmill, G., and Oakley, G. 1992. "Leadership: An Alienating Social Myth." *Human Relations* 45(2): 113–129.

Grint, K. 2005. *Leadership: Limits and Possibilities*. Houndmills: Palgrave Macmillan.

Hardy, C., and S. Clegg. 2004. "Power and Change: A Critical Reflection." In *Dynamics of Organizational Change and Learning*, edited by J.J. Boonstra, 343–370. Chichester: John Wiley and Sons.

Haslam, S.A., S.D. Reicher, and M.J. Platow. 2011. *The New Psychology of Leadership: Identity, Influence and Power*. Hove: Psychology Press.

Hendry, C. 1996. "Understanding and Creating Whole Organizational Change Through Learning Theory." *Human Relations* 48(5): 621–641.

Higgs, M. 2009. "The Good, the Bad and the Ugly: Leadership and Narcissism." *Journal of Change Management* 9(2): 165–178.

Higgs, M., and D. Rowland. 2005. "All Changes Great and Small: Exploring Approaches to Change and Its Leadership." *Journal of Change Management* 5(2): 121–151.

Hope Hailey, V., and J. Balogun. 2002. "Devising Context Sensitive Approaches to Change: The Example of Glaxo Wellcome." *Long Range Planning* 35(2): 153–178.

Huczynski, A. 2006. *Management Gurus*, revised edition. London: Routledge.

Hughes, M. 2016. *The Leadership of Organizational Change*. London: Routledge.

Hughes, M. 2017. "Reflections: Studying organizational change leadership as a subfield." *Journal of Change Management* (online first).

Judge, T.A., R.F. Piccolo, and T. Kosalka. 2009. "The Bright and Dark Sides of Leader Traits: A Review and Theoretical Extension of the Leader Trait Paradigm." *The Leadership Quarterly* 20(6): 855–875.

Kelly, S. 2014. "Towards a Negative Ontology of Leadership." *Human Relations* 67(8): 905–922.

King, S., M. Hopkins, and N. Cornish. 2017. "Can Models of Organizational Change Help to Understand 'Success' and 'Failure' in Community Sentences? Applying Kotter's Model of Organizational Change to an Integrated Offender Management Case Study." *Criminology & Criminal Justice* (online first).

Kotter, J.P. 1990. *A Force for Change: How Leadership Differs from Management*. New York: The Free Press.

Kotter, J.P. 1995. "Leading Change: Why Transformation Efforts Fail." *Harvard Business Review* 73(2): 59–67.

Kotter, J.P. 1996/2012. *Leading Change*. Boston, MA: Harvard Business School Press.

Kotter, J.P., and D.S. Cohen 2002. *The Heart of Change: Real-life Stories of How People Change their Organizations*. Boston, MA: Harvard Business School Press.

Kotter, J.P., and J.L. Heskett. 1992. *Corporate Culture and Performance*. New York: The Free Press.

Kotter, J.P., and L.A. Schlesinger. 1979. "Choosing Strategies for Change." *Harvard Business Review* 57(2): 106–114.

Lakomski, G. 2001. "Organizational Change, Leadership and Learning: Culture as Cognitive Process." *The International Journal of Educational Management* 15(2): 68–77.

Lewin, K. 1947. "Frontiers in Group Dynamics." In *Field Theory in Social Science*, edited by D. Cartwright, 188–237. London: Social Science Paperbacks.

Linstead, S., G. Marechal, and R.W. Griffin. 2014. "Theorizing and Researching the Dark Side of Organization." *Organization Studies* 35(2): 165–188.

March, J.G. 1981. "Footnotes to Organizational Change." *Administrative Science Quarterly* 26(4): 563–577.

Merton, R. 1968. "The Matthew Effect in Science." *Science* 159: 56–63.

Merton, R. 1988. "The Matthew Effect in Science, II: Cumulative Advantage and the Symbolism of Intellectual Property." *ISIS* 79: 606–623.

Nadler, D.A., and M.L. Tushman. 2004. "Beyond the Charismatic Leader: Leadership and Organizational Change." In *Managing Strategic Innovation and Change: A Collection of Readings*, edited by M.L. Tushman and P. Anderson. New York: Oxford University Press.

Paglis, L.L., and S.G. Green. 2002. "Leadership Self-Efficacy and Managers' Motivation for Leading Change." *Journal of Organizational Behavior* 23(2): 215–235.

Parry, K.W. 2011. "Leadership and Organization Theory." In *The Sage Handbook of Leadership*, edited by A. Bryman, D. Collinson, K. Grint, B. Jackson, and M. Uhl-Bien, 53–70. London: Sage Publications.

Pettigrew, A.M., R.W. Woodman, and K.S. Cameron. 2001. "Studying Organizational Change and Development: Challenges for Future Research." *Academy of Management Journal* 44(4): 697–713.

Piderit, S.K. 2000. "Rethinking Resistance and Recognizing Ambivalence: A Multidimensional View of Attitudes Towards an Organizational Change." *Academy of Management Review* 25(4): 783–794.

Rhodes, C., A. Pullen, and S.R. Clegg. 2010. "'If I Should Fall from Grace...': Stories of Change and Organizational Ethics." *Journal of Business Ethics* 91(4): 535–551.

Riggio, R.E. 2011. "The Management Perspective: Engineering Effective Leadership in Organizations." In *Leadership Studies: The Dialogue of Disciplines*, edited by M. Harvey and R.E. Riggio, 119–128. Cheltenham: Edward Elgar.

Rost, J.C. 1993. *Leadership for the Twenty-First Century*. Westport, CT: Praeger Publishers.

Rowland, D., and M. Higgs. 2008. *Sustaining Change: Leadership that Works*. Chichester: Jossey Bass.

Starkey, K., S. Tempest, and A. Mckinlay. 2002. "Introduction." In *How Organizations Learn: Managing the Search for Knowledge*, edited by. K. Starkey, S. Tempest, and A. Mckinlay, 13–15. London: Thomson Learning.

Storey, J. (Ed.). 2011. *Leadership in Organizations: Current Issues and Key Trends*. London: Routledge.

Sugarman, B. 2001. "A Learning-Based Approach to Organizational Change: Some Results and Guidelines." *Organizational Dynamics* 30(1): 62–76.

TIME. 2016. *The 25 Most Influential Business Management Books*. Available at http://content.time.com/time/specials/packages/completelist/0,29569,2086680,00.html.

Tourish, D. 2013. *The Dark Side of Transformational Leadership*. London: Routledge.

Tourish, D., and A. Pinnington. 2002. "Transformational Leadership, Corporate Cultism and the Spirituality Paradigm: An Unholy Trinity in the Workplace?" *Human Relations* 55(2): 147–172.

Tyler, T.R., and D. De Cremer. 2005. "Process-Based Leadership: Fair Procedures and Reactions to Organizational Change." *The Leadership Quarterly* 16(4): 529–545.

Van de Ven, A.H., and M.S. Poole. 2005. "Alternative Approaches for Studying Organizational Change." *Organization Studies* 26(9): 1377–1404.

Vince, R., and A. Mazen. 2014. "Violent Innocence: A Contradiction at the Heart of Leadership." *Organization Studies* 35(2): 165–188.

Wall, S. 2007. "Organizational Ethics, Change and Stakeholder Involvement: A Survey of Physicians." *HEC Forum* 19(3): 227–243.

Weber, M. 1947. *The Theory of Social and Economic Organization.* Glencoe, IL: Free Press.

Weick, K.E. 1993. "Organizational Redesign as Improvisation." In *Making Sense of the Organization*, edited by K.E. Weick, 57–91. Oxford: Blackwell.

Ybema, S. 2010. "Talk of Change: Temporal Contrasts and Collective Identities." *Organization Studies* 31(4): 481–503.

Yukl, G. 1999. "An Evaluation of Conceptual Weaknesses in Transformational and Charismatic Leadership Theories." *The Leadership Quarterly* 10(2): 285–305.

Chapter 11

Power, politics and organizational change

Introduction and chapter questions

> In leading change I confront the organization rather than serve it. In order to moti-vate me confront the organization [*sic*] I need freedom associated with 'brutality'.
>
> (Espedal, 2017: 158)

> In leading change I must perform and get results. Thus, I need power to secure compliance to my domination through the shaping of beliefs and desires and through commitment to common goals.
>
> (Espedal, 2017: 158)

The two opening quotations are taken from Espedal's (2017) interviews with 15 leaders with reputations as good and efficient change agents. They offer us a rare explicit glimpse into the exercise of power and politics with regards to leading organizational change. Power and politics potentially informs many of the debates featured in this textbook. Despite this, power and politics are largely unacknowledged in organizational change theories and practices. Instead, an apolitical view of shared/unified interests characteri-sing organizations tends to be assumed and encouraged (please see McMillan, 2016 for further discussion). Fineman and Gabriel (1996) regarded the image of an organization which had been cultivated over decades as one in which everyone collaborates towards a common objective. One consequence of the rhetoric of common objectives was that power and politics were perceived as irrelevant or even taboo paraphrased as 'there is no place for power and politics in this organization'. Against such a backdrop, behav-iours may be deemed 'political', with political considered inappropriate in most or-ganizations. This set of beliefs more subtly '...supports reliance on making the case for change through top-down initiatives' (Marshak, 2006: 7). Unfortunately, such organi-zational beliefs appear to have restricted interest in power and politics in management and organization studies, although in recent decades there have been signs of greater engagement with power and politics as the chapter will highlight.

The following definitions of power and politics are taken from Buchanan and Badham (2008: 11) *Power, Politics and Organizational Change: Winning the Turf Game,* which when the first edition was published in 1999 gave impetus to engaging with power and politics with regard to organizational change theories and practices.

Power = the ability to get other people to do what you want them to do.
Politics = power in action, using a range of techniques and tactics.

The questioning section will suggest that the exercise of power may be more subtle than these definitions imply, but these definitions are helpful in navigating a debate which in the literature can appear to oscillate between power and politics. Another way to think about such oscillations is politics as the practical domain of power. This chapter is organized around and provides answers to the following power, politics and organizational change questions:

- What are practitioners doing in terms of power and politics?
- How have power and politics informed organizational studies?
- What faces of power and perspectives on power exist?
- What do we know about power, politics and organizational change?
- How does power inform understanding discourses of organizational change?
- How does power inform understanding resistance to change?
- How does power inform understanding managing/leading organizational change?

In the next section, political games in organizations (Mintzberg, 1989) are highlighted as a means of illustrating practitioner involvement in politics and case studies of practitioners as change agents acting politically are featured. In terms of theories of power, politics and organizational change, a selected chronology of power and politics theories informing organization studies is presented. What is apparent is that power has multiple faces and may be understood from multiple perspectives. Understanding about power, politics and organizational change is informed by the writings of Hardy (1996), Buchanan and Badham (1999/2008), Marshak (2006) and Hope (2010). The questioning section takes the analysis of power further in terms of how power informs discourses and resistance to organizational change, with a more critical account of how power informs managing/leading organizational change. Finally, the chapter is summarised, discussion questions raised and guidance offered with regards to navigating the power, politics and organizational change literature.

What are practitioners doing in terms of power and politics?

Power and politics pervade our organizations regardless of sector or national boundaries and during times of organizational change, power and politics are likely to be more prevalent. However, documented accounts of such power and politics are far less evident. Imagine interviewing or surveying people in a particular department about exercising power and politics in their organizations.

- Who are the most political players in your department?
- How have you used power to gain promotion?
- How does your department ensure you receive the most resources?

Interview subjects are likely to be evasive or sanitise their behaviours. Whilst, this chapter will introduce a range of relevant theories, practical illustrations are less evident. Mintzberg's (1989) famous account of political games and Buchanan and Badham's (1999) account of the political behaviours of change agents are featured as well as, Auster and Ruebottom's (2013) five practical steps to navigate the politics of change.

In *Mintzberg on Management: Inside Our Strange World of Organizations*, Mintzberg (1989) challenged traditional assumptions about the apolitical nature of

Table 11.1 Political games in organizations (based on Mintzberg, 1989)

Political game	Description
Insurgency game	Resisting authority or effecting change in an organization.
Counter-insurgency game	Those in authority fighting back with political means.
Sponsorship game	Individuals attach themselves to someone with more status.
Alliance building game	Negotiating implicit contracts of support for each other.
Empire building game	Building power bases not cooperatively with peers, but with subordinates.
Budgeting game	The prize becomes resources, not positions or units per se.
Expertise game	Use of expertise to build a power base, either by flaunting expertise or feigning expertise.
Lording game	'Lording' legitimate power over those without it or with less of it.
Line versus staff game	A game of sibling rivalry, line managers pitted against staff advisers and specialised expertise.
Rival camps game	Two major power blocks arise out of an alliance or empire building game with a view to defeating a rival.
Strategic candidates game	Groups promote through strategic means their favoured candidates.
Whistle blowing game	Privileged information used by an insider to 'blow the whistle'.
Young Turks game	'Young Turks' close to the centre but not at the centre of power seek to reorient the organization.

organizational life from a 'grass roots' point of view. The political games he identified in organizations are featured in Table 11.1.

The political games featured in Table 11.1 offer us a window on potential political behaviours of practitioners from an authoritative source (a highly respected professor of management). Anyone with experience inside organizations will be able to identify with such games which are likely to still be played out to this day. Certainly, all of these games are evident in the setting of a single south coast university to a greater or lesser degree. In reflecting upon these political games, we witness the complexities and subtleties of politics in organizations, which are likely to be magnified at times of organizational change.

Buchanan and Badham (1999) feature prominently in this chapter and their paper "Politics and Organizational Change: The Lived Experience" offered a very vivid and very real account of the political behaviour of change agents in the roles of management consultant, head of school, hospital manager and project manager. Case studies of each of these change agents offered real life examples of the lived experience of political behaviours. Authors demonstrate that political behaviour was an accepted and pervasive dimension of the role of change agents who adopted creative approaches to their different contexts. Auster and Ruebottom (2013) have offered practitioners five steps to navigate the politics of change. They argue that the five steps offer an action-oriented and easy to navigate approach for working with the political and emotional dynamics of organizational change.

Step one – map the political landscape: The focus here is on the stakeholders in a process of organizational change. These stakeholders may be internal/external, product/service oriented, geographic or regional, regardless of whether their interests and influence need to be mapped.

Step two – identify the key influencers within each stakeholder group: In each group, there will be key influencers who potentially marshal resources and can enrol others. They potentially can win over the hearts and minds of the larger group.

Step three – assess influencers' receptiveness to change: Organizational change will generate a range of reactions from eager and excited through to angry and uncertain. The authors offer their own categorisation of receptiveness to change: sponsors, promoters, indifferent fence-sitters, cautious fence-sitters, positive sceptics and negative sceptics.

Step four – mobilise influential sponsors and promoters: These change champions are believed to have the insight, energy and passion to aid the content, culture and momentum for change.

Step five – engage influential positive and negative sceptics: Working with sceptics early on is believed to be time well invested.

In Auster and Ruebottom's (2013) five steps to help practitioners navigate the politics of change, we witness recognition of the centrality of power and politics at times of organizational change.

Theories of power, politics and organizational change

Whilst, the focus of this chapter is power, politics and organizational change, developments in theorising power and politics within organization studies and acknowledging the multiple faces of power informs understanding.

Power, politics and organizational studies

The following selective chronology highlights famous theories of power and politics with the potential to inform organizational studies (please see Table 11.2).

Whilst, in the introduction, it was suggested that acknowledgement of the role of power and politics in organizational change was a fairly recent phenomenon Table 11.2 demonstrates interest in power and politics informing organizational studies stretching back to the middle of the last century. The selected theories in Table 11.2 potentially inform organizational studies, with the origins of these theories going back to sociology, political science and industrial relations. The selected theories have become the orthodoxy when studying power and politics. More radical and more recent accounts of power and politics will be introduced in the questioning section.

Bottlenecks in organizational processes presented opportunities for lower-level employees to have power disproportionate to their level in the organizational hierarchy.

Table 11.2 Understanding power and organizational studies – a selective chronology

Author	Year	Elements of theory
Crozier	1964	Understanding power through bottlenecks – the case of the tobacco factory maintenance workers
French and Raven	1968	Understanding power in terms of power bases: reward, coercive, referent, legitimate and expert power
Fox	1974	Understanding power through: unitarist, pluralist, interactionist and radical frames of reference on conflict
Etzioni	1975	Understanding power in terms of compliance through coercive, remunerative and normative power

Crozier (1964) drew attention to this phenomenon in his study of maintenance workers working in a French tobacco factory. Whilst, maintenance workers were perceived as being peripheral to production processes in the factory, they were very powerful when machinery broke down. This was because production workers depended upon maintenance workers to repair machines, as, when machines were not operating, their earnings and bonuses were curtailed. The contemporary equivalent would be an IT department in a bank. Whilst market traders and senior managers may earn far more than IT staff, these staff are dependent upon IT staff to ensure that IT systems operate effectively and with no bottlenecks in these systems.

French and Raven (1968) favoured a resource-based view in order to understand power in terms of the power holder and their subordinates with five power bases identified: reward power, coercive power, referent power, legitimate power and expert power. It was the subordinate's perception of the power holder regardless of the accuracy of the perception, which was important. So you might buy somebody in the HR Department a coffee in the belief that it might help with your promotion or pay rise (reward power), although this might not be the case, but their power is a consequence of your perception. Power bases were regarded as interrelated, rather than being separate with different power bases used in different situations.

Fox's (1974) framework for differentiating perspectives on industrial relations with reference to conflict offers different ways to think about organizations highlighting assumptions informing such thinking. The four frames of reference on conflict were: unitarist, pluralist, interactionist and radical.

1   A *unitarist frame* of reference assumes that common interests are shared within an organization. The implication is that working relations are harmonious and that there is an absence of conflict.
2   A *pluralist frame* of reference assumes that organizations are comprised of different groups with differing interests which result in conflicts. These conflicts are managed through negotiation and compromise.
3   An *interactionist frame* of reference regards conflict as inevitable, however regarding such conflict as positive and essential for effective performance.
4   A *radical frame* of reference perceives conflict as an inevitable consequence of capitalist employment and organization.

The influence of unitarist assumptions in organizations should not be underestimated, particularly during processes of organizational change. These assumptions are most tangible in annual reports of companies when the chair or chief executive talks in terms of shared visions which everyone works towards. This is an exercise of power in that competing frames of reference (2, 3 and 4) often go unacknowledged.

Etzioni (1975) offered another famous contribution to contemporary understanding of power. His typology had three components: power, involvement, and relations between power and involvement. He was subsequently able to explain compliance in terms of these three dimensions highlighting the existence of coercive power, remunerative power, and normative power. Coercive power involved threats and physical sanctions, in colloquial terms 'just do it!' Remunerative power involved material resources and rewards, so if coercive power was the stick, remunerative power was the carrot. Normative power was the most subtle involving symbolic rewards, for example, the metaphorical arm around the shoulder by your line manager. Etzioni (1975) highlighted three forms of involvement: alienative (employees involved against their wishes), calculative (employees motivated by extrinsic rewards) and moral (employee's belief in their organization's goals). These different emphases did not preclude the use of all three.

Theories just discussed were drawn from academic disciplines and fields of study broader than management and organization studies. It was Pfeffer (1981, 1992a, 1992b) who gave impetus to management and organization studies scholars engaging with power. Pfeffer (1992b) considered how we get things done in organizations. Choices include getting things done through hierarchical authority and getting things done through developing a strongly shared vision or organizational culture and getting things done through power and influence. These choices in themselves are political. Pfeffer (1992b) made the case for managing with power in that there was a need to acknowledge varying interests existing inside organizations and that this political landscape needed to be diagnosed. This is a direct challenge to a unitarist frame of reference (Fox, 1974). Pfeffer (1992b) highlighted a need to establish how power differed between positions and between individuals. Pragmatically, he acknowledged that to accomplish things, there was a need to have more power than those in opposition. Managing with power required understanding strategies and tactics, using structures, understanding commitment and different forms of interpersonal influence.

Multiple faces of power and perspectives on power

Transformational change can be more fully understood and enabled through recognising the tensions between different perspectives on power (Bradshaw and Boonstra, 2004). In seeking to understand power, politics and organizational change, it is necessary to recognise the existence of different faces of power and perspectives on power. Bradshaw and Boonstra (2004) highlight four different perspectives on power which they related to organizational change: manifest-personal power, manifest-structural power, latent-cultural power and latent-personal power.

Manifest-personal power reflected person X having more power than person Y, resulting in person X having the potential ability to influence person Y. Manifest-structural power explains power as residing in a position or location emphasising organizational structures rather than personal traits. Latent-cultural power relates to creating and reproducing latent or unconscious shared meanings. Power is maintained by those who set agendas and manage meaning in that power relations are regarded as natural and unquestionable. Latent-personal power relates to how individuals limit themselves in obeying others. This perspective has its roots in psychoanalytic, postmodern and feminist theories embedding latent or unconscious power in the psyche of individuals.

Fleming and Spicer (2010) drew upon Bachrach and Baratz (1970) highlighting four different faces of power. First, coercion as a face of power involved one individual getting another to follow his/her orders. Second, manipulation as a face of power involves behind-the-scenes politics. Third, domination as a face of power is concerned with the domination of the preferences and opinions of others. Fourth, subjectification as a face of power is concerned with actors being constituted as subjects, understanding themselves and the world around them in certain ways. In a manner similar to Fleming and Spicer (2010), Buchanan and Badham (2008) acknowledged that there was no agreed framework highlighting three broad perspectives on power: power as a personal property, power as a relational property and power as an embedded property. These three perspectives offer us different ways to think about power which may be applied to hypothetical organizational change scenarios.

Power as a personal property regards power as something that you can accumulate and possess, with Pfeffer (1992a) cited as a good illustration of such a perspective. For example, Barry was chosen to review why this change initiative had failed because of his personal qualities in asking awkward questions and his ability to bring powerful stakeholders together in discussions. Power as a relational property looks for power within different relationships with Crozier (1964) and French and Raven (1968) cited as good illustrations of this perspective. For example, the Head of Finance turned down our request for funding for focus groups which were integral to our participative approach to managing change. Power as an embedded property highlights the influence of culture upon power relations. For example, the absence of any women in the change agency working group was never discussed and appeared to be non-discussable. Power and politics in organizations have multiple faces with Hardy and Clegg (2004) highlighting one of the more coercive faces. If employees do not want to change, managers must use power to make them change despite their disinclination, against their resistance.

Power, politics and organizational change

The previous subsection considered studies of power and politics potentially informing management and organization studies. These studies have the potential to inform organizational change studies, but also a more narrowly focussed power, politics and organizational change literature has developed. Since the 1970s, the role of power in organizational change initiatives has been recognised with conceptual thinking evolving in parallel to this recognition (Bradshaw and Boonstra, 2004). The following discussion features the writings of Hardy (1996), Buchanan and Badham (1999/2008), Marshak (2006) and Hope (2010).

In a famous account of power and strategic change, Hardy (1996) drew upon Lukes (1974) and other radical writers to demonstrate how power informed strategic change. Hardy's goal was to acknowledge that power was multi-dimensional and to offer managers ways to move from strategic intent through alignment to realisation. Her concerns echoed (Buchanan and Badham, 1999) with regards to political implications of organizational change, previously being neglected in the literature.

> Hence power is an integral part of strategic change, regardless of whether the organization is a political cauldron of conflicting interests and power is a way to combat resistance to strategic intentions, or whether it is united by common goals and power is required to facilitate collaborative action.
>
> (Hardy, 1996: S6)

Hardy's (1996) model encompassed four dimensions of power: the power of resources, the power of processes, the power of meaning and the power of the system (please see Table 11.3). Hardy (1996) argued that managers attempting strategic change must use the first three dimensions of power to modify the existing system (please see Table 11.3). The strategic change would be achieved when the power of resources, processes and meaning converged.

Organizational change, and the uncertainty which results, heightens the intensity of political behaviour (Buchanan and Badham, 1999). Buchanan et al. (1999: 29) in

Table 11.3 Four dimensions of power (based on Hardy, 1996)

Dimensions of power	Explanation
Power of resources	The traditional conceptualisation linking power to an ability to control scarce resources. Power may influence behaviours through rewarding scarce resources or punishing through withholding scarce resources.
Power of processes	Power of processes acknowledges that power resides in decision-making processes, particularly the power of 'non-decision-making'. Through non-decision-making, the status quo may be protected as actors determine outcomes behind the scenes through procedures and political routines.
Power of meaning	Power of meaning is the most subtle and the least tangible. Citing Lukes (1974), this is about how power shapes perceptions, cognitions, and preferences.
Power of the system	Power of the system refers to taken for granted power deeply embedded within organizational systems.

surveying management organizational development and change experiences and attitudes offered empirical insights into managers' perceptions of the political aspects of managing change 'this evidence suggests that about one-third of managers enjoy the politics game, one-third do not, and one-third are neutral on the issue'. *Power, Politics and Organizational Change: Winning the Turf Game* (Buchanan and Badham, 1999/2008) gave impetus to academic engagement with the power and politics of organizational change. Four underlying beliefs informed Buchanan and Badham's (1999/2008) position.

1 Political behaviour was more prevalent than was commonly recognised or admitted with such behaviour heightened at times of significant organizational change.
2 Managerialist literature underplayed political behaviour and when connections between political behaviour and organizational change were acknowledged, it was with the caveat that political behaviour would ethically be unacceptable.
3 Engaging with political behaviour in the context of organizational change revealed both positive and negative features of such behaviour, rather than the common stereotype that organizational politics was to be avoided.
4 The implication of 1, 2 and 3 is that political behaviour needs to be actively incorporated into management education, training and development.

Marshak (2006) cited Ostrom (1967) when he offered a diagnostic framework to work with the political dimensions of organizational change (please see Table 11.4). Marshak's (2006) framework featured in Table 11.4 synthesises many of the earlier discussions about locating power and the faces of power and how it is exercised through politics. What is insightful about the framework is that it offers a means to navigate the politics of organizational decision making, heightened at times of organizational change. The framework highlights how decision making around an organizational change may be invisible (decision arenas), how involvement in decision making may be limited (participation, rounds, the degree of agreement), how regardless of

Table 11.4 Politics, decision making and organizational change (based on Marshak, 2006)

	Political decision making diagnostic factors	Framework questions
1	Decision arenas	Where are decisions made inside an organization?
2	Degree of participation	Who is invited to participate in decisions?
3	Decision rounds	How many rounds of decision making before implementation?
4	Required degree of agreement	How many actors/offices must agree for a decision to proceed?
5	Access to information	Who has access to information related to a particular decision?
6	Reciprocity	Is reciprocity expected in organizational decision making?
7	Expected styles	What are the expected behaviours in a particular organization's decision-making process?
8	Types of sanctions	How are violations of the organization's political norms policed and punished?

the visibility of decision making and involvement in decision-making access to information about an organizational change may be limited. And that expectations may exist about reciprocity arising out of decisions, styles of behaviour and expectations for policing violations.

In considering power, politics and organizational change, it is easy to perceive power as being located exclusively at the top of an organizational hierarchy. However, Hope's (2010) account of sensemaking and sensegiving offers insights into the political activities of middle managers when top management implements organizational change. The research findings were based on a Nordic insurance company. Middle managers played an important role in implementing organizational change with their actions either convergent supporting the change goals or divergent in seeking to move in a different direction. In the case of the Nordic insurance company, the middle managers took a deliberately divergent direction. The middle managers mobilised different sources of power and relied on a variety of tactics in influencing others. Through mobilising process power and reward power (Hardy, 1996) several middle managers were able to influence meaning making with regard to organizational change.

Questioning theories of power, politics and organizational change

Marshak (2006: 148) when discussing politics as a covert process at work, cited an old superstition 'to say the name of an evil spirit is to invoke its presence'. In this sense, earlier discussions naming power and politics may be regarded as invoking the presence of evil spirits. However, for critical scholars, these invocations have not gone far enough. Yes, power and politics have been discussed, but discussion of power, discourse and resistance remain largely invisible within these discussions. Power in this questioning section offers a means to challenge orthodox accounts of power, politics and organizational change, and to potentially rethink organizational change. Overlapping themes of discourse, resistance and power are discussed with a view to informing a different understanding about managing/leading organizational change related to power. In order to aid exposition, these themes are discussed separately through answering the following questions.

How does power inform understanding discourses of organizational change?
How does power inform understanding the resistance to change?
How does power inform understanding managing/leading organizational change?

How does power inform understanding discourses of organizational change?

Whilst discourse is discussed further in the next chapter, for Hardy and Thomas (2014), discourses are saturated with power relations potentially constraining and enabling individuals. In this way, for example, recent discourses explaining organizational change as a consequence of national austerity or organizational efficiency may be read as discourses of power. Hardy and Thomas (2014) acknowledge and cite the writings of Michel Foucault as influencing their thinking about discourse and power, regarding a Foucauldian approach as raising the following awkward questions about power:

1   Rather than asking who has power, how does power circulate through discourses in shaping strategy?
2   Rather than resistance being regarded as an adversarial response to power, how are power and resistance adaptive responses to each other?
3   How does power through discourse produce subjects and subjectivities?

These questions may be applied illustratively to organizational change, with numbers in brackets relating back to Hardy and Thomas's (2014) questions. In seeking to understand organizational change, rather than focussing on the activities of change agents organizational discourses about what is changing and why it is changing are more informative (1). This approach would sceptically regard this textbook as a discourse (1) that change can be led and managed. Resistance to a change initiative is as much a consequence of the actions of the change agents as the resistors (2) as they adaptively respond to each other. Discourses of overcoming resistance to change produce resistors as problematic subjects in a process of organizational change and the change agents as heroic subjects in a process of organizational change (3). These attributions arise out of discourses of organizational change, rather than the inherent characteristics of individuals. This is similar to Fleming and Spicer's (2010) subjectification as a face of power discussed earlier.

McMillan (2016) offers a thought-provoking account of how business oriented discourses of organizational change may be exclusionary in healthcare settings potentially limiting individuals and groups of individuals contributing to change discourses and processes. One of the problems of exploring organizational change in healthcare is that what '…has historically informed what is deemed correct and desirable does not reflect what is known about nurses' experiences of organizational change' (McMillan, 2016: 224). The danger is that nurse's voices may reflect concepts which have not been linked to organizational change because the dominant discourses are managerial and organizational.

How does power inform understanding the resistance to change?

Fleming and Spicer (2008) in their editorial for a special issue of *Management Communication Quarterly* encouraged moving beyond power and resistance, offering an alternative account of interrelationships between power and resistance. They regarded power and resistance as knitted together closely in a complex and often contradictory manner. They recount a historical shift away from resistance amongst sociologists who had been fascinated by the subject up to the late 1970s and early 1980s when it became marginalised. It was interest in the writings of Michel Foucault on power/ knowledge which informed this shift. However, Fleming and Spicer (2008: 304) in their special issue on reframing power and resistance maintained that 'our current vocabulary of power and resistance is rather limiting given the way it draws a strict contrast between the diabolic world of power and the liberating world of resistance'.

Vince (2002) offers a very different framing of power and resistance creatively bringing together psychodynamics, power and politics, emotion and organizational change. He (2002: 1194) noted '...that people in organizations desire and encourage change whilst also avoiding and resisting it. The act of organizing involves attempts to make change happen at the same time as creating ways to contain or control it'. He coined the phrase for this 'imagined stability' which highlighted the fantasy of stability that organizational change potentially creates.

How does power inform understanding managing/leading organizational change?

In questioning accounts of power, politics and organizational change, the danger is that an emphasis upon critique limits practical implications/prescriptions for managing and leading organizational change differently. Morgan and Sturdy (2000: 8) differentiated the organizational change literature in terms of three approaches: managerialist, political and social approaches, explaining the political approach as acknowledging '...greater recognition that actors within organizations bring different sets of values and interests into any change context. Political conflict, bargaining, and negotiation become the central elements of analysis and the key managerial skill is that of political manipulation.' However, for Morgan and Sturdy (2000) and other critical scholars, the political approach did not go far enough, merely promoting more sophisticated 'cultural engineering'. Hardy and Clegg (2004) subsequently warned that the organizational change literature assists change management failure due to a lack of pragmatism about power. Clegg et al. (2016: 294) in their textbook treatment of managing power and politics offer seven steps for managing power which is worth restating.

Clegg et al. (2016) in Table 11.5 (after summary) echo earlier discussions about power and politics. However, importantly they offer managers/leaders a way to openly engage with power, in a transparent and ethical manner.

Summary

The chapter may be succinctly summarised through answering questions posed in the chapter's introduction. The original questions are restated in italics.

What are practitioners doing in terms of power and politics? It is difficult to highlight practitioner engagement in power and politics in that it is often covert and/ or unacknowledged. Identifying political games (Mintzberg, 1989) helps to make the intangible tangible and Buchanan and Badham's (1999) account of the lived experience of change agents offers case studies of the political behaviours of change agents.

How have power and politics informed organizational studies? Theories of power and politics have informed organizational studies since the middle of the last century. Crozier (1964) highlighted how disproportionate power could arise around bottlenecks in organizational processes. French and Raven (1968) highlighted how perceptions of power bases influenced subordinates. Fox (1974) highlighted the existence of different frames of reference with regards to conflict and Etzioni (1975) highlighted compliance being achieved through coercive, remunerative and normative power.

What faces of power and perspectives on power exist? Power does not have a single face or reflect a single perspective. Bradshaw and Boonstra (2004) highlighted four different perspectives; manifest-personal power, manifest-structural power, latent-cultural power and latent-personal power. And Fleming and Spicer (2010) highlighted four different faces of power: coercion, manipulation, domination and subjectification.

What do we know about power, politics and organizational change? Hardy (1996) highlighted how managers engaging in strategic change could draw upon the power of resources, processes, meaning and the system. Buchanan and Badham (1999/2008) encouraged greater engagement with power and politics in the context of organizational change. Marshak (2006) drew attention to the visible and invisible political aspects of organizational decision making and Hope (2010) highlighted the political activities of middle managers.

How does power inform understanding discourses of organizational change? Hardy and Thomas (2014) acknowledged and cited the writings of Michel Foucault as influencing their thinking about discourse and power and McMillan (2016) warned that business oriented discourses of organizational change may be exclusionary in healthcare settings.

How does power inform understanding the resistance to change? Fleming and Spicer (2008) encouraged reframing power and resistance with its strict contrast between diabolic power and liberating resistance. Vince (2002) illustrated such a reframing of power creatively bringing together psychodynamics, power and politics, emotion and organizational change.

How does power inform understanding managing/leading organizational change? Clegg et al. (2016) in their textbook treatment of managing power and politics offered seven steps for managing power (please see Table 11.5) which openly engage with power, in a transparent and ethical manner.

Table 11.5 Managing with power – seven steps to its effective use (based on Clegg et al., 2016)

1   Establish goals and what you are trying to accomplish, consulting with direct stakeholders in your organization.
2   In terms of patterns of dependence and interdependence, who inside and outside the organization are important/influential in achieving these goals?
3   What are the points of view of important people and how do they feel about what you are doing?
4   What are the important people's power bases and which are most influential in the decision?
5   Identify your own power bases/influence and the influence you can develop in gaining more positive control over a situation?
6   Which strategies and tactics for the exercise of power is most appropriate and likely to be effective?
7   Based on steps 1 to 6, choose an ethical course of action.

Research case study showcase: the politics of imagined stability at Hyder PLC

Vince's (2002) research case study based on the Hyder PLC and reported in *Human Relations* is showcased here. For full details and further analysis, please visit the original source.

Case study source

Vince (2002) undertook action-research in Hyder PLC interviewing seven senior managers from different parts of Hyder over two months (28 interviews in total).

Vince, R. 2002. "The Politics of Imagined Stability: A Psychodynamic Understanding of Change at Hyder PLC." *Human Relations* 55 (10): 1189–1208.

The case study

Hyder PLC developed from Welsh Water into a multi-utility and infrastructure management company. This change from a Welsh public utility company to a global private company was initiated in 1997. At the height of its development, Hyder was representative of something referred to in the Welsh media as 'the new Wales'. This was a time when the new Welsh Assembly government gave the country increased political autonomy from the British Parliament. As well as global aspirations, Hyder was unique in being the biggest private company in Wales.

How the enterprise was seen both from outside and imagined from within was informed by a national and social projection of power and confidence. The social function of being Wales' largest private company made an emotional and political connection with how Hyder undertook organizational change and development. Hyder was symbolic of anxieties and desires to ensure that the first home rule in 600 years was successful in demonstrating that the new Welsh Assembly government was making a positive difference to Wales. Because of the size and significance of Hyder particularly in terms of numbers of people employed, any threats to the organizational stability of Hyder were linked to the political and economic stability of Wales. Ambition was conditional on development as a global company, but tempered with powerful, national, social and economic responsibilities to Wales.

The chief executive gave a keynote speech to senior staff of Hyder on 6 October 1997 marking the rebranding of Welsh Water to Hyder. The speech utilised imaginary newspaper clippings highlighting news stories five years in the future. This creative communication of the vision the chief executive had for Hyder included, doubling market capitalisation to just over £2 billion and a further round of price cuts was imagined as Hyder reaped benefits from the strategy to create the UK's first truly integrated utility.

In the new company, there was an emphasis on creating greater collegiality responding to previous conflicts between organizational subsystems, particularly the former electricity and water companies and between the combined utilities company and the management of infrastructure. This desire for greater collegiality was captured in the new company slogan 'One Hyder: Altogether

Stronger'. However, in interviews the slogan was not believed to represent the divided and fragmented nature of Hyder. Unfortunately, organizational changes arising out of the creation of Hyder sharpened past conflicts and problems, rather than creating the new desire for collegiality. The existence of 'empires' and different views on strategy, such as stay as a 'core' utility business or grow into a global infrastructure company surfaced. Senior managers did not engage with conflicts highlighted through the rebrand. Instead the rebrand was believed to have wall-papered over the actual identity of Hyder.

One specific aspect of organizational change in Hyder called the 'learning journey', was developed by human resource development. This was a process available to all staff, which linked mandatory appraisal processes and various different approaches to training and development (including formal and informal training, on-the-job learning strategies, mentoring and fast-track programmes). The 'learning journey' recognised a need for the gradual management of organizational change. However, interviewees felt that change initiatives in Hyder inevitably tended to 'sink into the sand', and rarely had significant impact on behaviours.

An expectation that Hyder's high share price/commercial success would enable the organization to pull together as a whole was not met and between September 1998 and January 2000 the share price dropped by more than 50 per cent. A growing lack of internal confidence was reinforced through a growing lack of external confidence in Hyder. A complex and drawn-out takeover battle was resolved in August 2000. Hyder was taken over by an American-owned company Western Power Distribution and by the third anniversary of his speech, the chief executive left the company which was now being broken up. The chief executive's vision was not realised and the demise of Hyder was critically reported in the media with the mixing of water and electricity through a multi-utility strategy now critically questioned.

Vince (2002) discussed and analysed the learning from the Hyder case. Some of the key insights may be summarised here. Interviews with the senior managers revealed three general fantasies about the organization. Hyder was imagined to be a global company, one company and a learning company. This was collectively depicted by interviewees in terms of imagined stability of the organization. Interviewees were unable to separate their perception of the company from the national dynamics related to the company's significant position in Wales and the Welsh economy. Interviewees were well aware that Hyder represented the aspirations of Wales in the global economy. The new Welsh Assembly government brought increased political and economic independence from Britain.

Hyder was Welsh for confidence as well as representing the confidence of Wales in the global business community. However, the Hyder 'branding booklet' required the anglicised pronunciation of the company's name (High-der), rather than the Welsh pronunciation (Her-der). Anglicising the word removed both the emotional and political connection to Wales fuelling resistance to change.

(*Continued*)

Despite an imagined and espoused commitment to 'One Hyder', the idea of being one coherent company was an institutionalised fantasy of oneness. Two different organizations of Hyder Utilities (the former public sector part of the company) and the new businesses of Hyder Infrastructure Management rarely worked well together. There was considerable senior manager denial around the power of long-standing conflicts between different organizational 'empires'. Partnerships and alliances required to enable 'One Hyder' to succeed were unlikely to emerge.

'One Hyder' communicated a confusing message, in terms of strategic politics. The organization was meant to be collegial, involving and confident, but beneath the surface it was controlling, cautious and risk averse. Owing to a fear of the consequences of failure for Hyder and Wales, there was fear amongst managers, despite strategic communications stating otherwise. Fear of failure and risk reinforced a fear of conflicts and manifested in a fear of things getting personal. A consequence of this was undermining the extent of managerial authority in acting corporately.

The learning journey as a corporate change initiative was meant to successfully underpin learning in the new company. However, senior managers in the company were not part of the learning journey themselves, regarding it as a training and development intervention for others, rather than as a strategic initiative informing the Hyder rebrand. Identification of clear corporate learning objectives focussed on company growth, would have provided senior management with a process to transcend fears of conflict and communication problems between different empires. However, successful implementation would have had implications for existing power relations. In the absence of senior management support, changes tended to 'sink into the sand'.

> The key proposition in this article is that the management of change involves the identification of the politics of imagined stability that characterize and inform the limitations and possibilities of change in a specific organizational context.
>
> *(Vince, 2002: 1205)*

The corporate fantasy was constructed around an interaction between three linked ideas: Hyder as a confident organization, as one coherent organization, and as an organization that could change. This case study highlights tensions between the fantasy of stability and the internal/external politics of maintaining and challenging this stability.

Case study questions

1   Which political games (Mintzberg, 1989) are most evident in the Hyder PLC case study?
2   Which of Hardy's (1996) dimensions of power is most applicable in explaining what is happening at Hyder PLC?
3   In terms of power and politics, why did the creation of Hyder PLC eventually fail?

Discussion questions

1 Why are power and politics not discussed more openly inside organizations?
2 What are the advantages and disadvantages of political games inside organizations?
3 What are the implications for academic study of power having multiple faces?
4 How is power embedded in contemporary discourses of organizational change?

Navigating the power, politics and organizational change literature

Academic studies relating organizational change to power and politics are prefaced by earlier and broader interest in power and politics. It is within academic disciplines such as sociology and political science that the foundations of studying power and politics are located. *Power in Organizations* (Pfeffer, 1981) encouraged studying power and politics within organizations. In 1999, the first edition of *Power, Politics and Organizational Change: Winning the Turf Game* was published, with the second edition (Buchanan and Badham, 2008) featured in this chapter. The implication is that in reviewing literature informing power, politics and organizational change, earlier accounts of power and politics will play a role and that literature specifically focussed on power, politics and organizational change will be drawn from the last two decades.

Power, Politics and Organizational Change: Winning the Turf Game (Buchanan and Badham, 2008) highlights the centrality of power and politics both to organizational change theories and practices, with the caveat that often power and politics remain hidden within the literature, practices and how leaders and managers are developed.

In reviewing the literature for this chapter, the application of power and politics to organizational change appears to have particularly caught the imagination of critical scholars. A good way into what can sometimes be discursive debates is through Duarte's (2010) account of teaching the subject, in which she offers a means of navigating what at times can be an intellectually and practically challenging literature.

References

Auster, E.R., and T. Ruebottom. 2013. "Navigating the Politics and Emotions of Change." *MIT Sloan Management Review* 54(4): 31–36.

Bachrach, P., and M.S. Baratz. 1970. *Power and Poverty: Theory and Practice*. New York: Oxford University Press.

Bradshaw, P., and J. Boonstra. 2004. "Power Dynamics in Organizational Change: A Multi-Perspective Approach." In *Dynamics of Organizational Change and Learning*, edited by J.J. Boonstra, 279–300. Chichester: John Wiley & Sons.

Buchanan, D., and R. Badham. 1999. "Politics and Organizational Change: The Lived Experience." *Human Relations* 52(5): 609–629.

Buchanan D., and R. Badham. 1999/2008. *Power, Politics and Organizational Change: Winning the Turf Game*. London: Sage Publications.

Buchanan, D., T. Claydon, and M. Doyle. 1999. "Organizational Development and Change: The Legacy of the Nineties." *Human Resource Management Journal* 9(2): 20–37.

Clegg, S.R., M. Kornberger, and T. Pitsis. 2016. *Managing and Organizations: An Introduction to Theory and Practice*. London: Sage Publications.

Crozier, M. 1964. *The Bureaucratic Phenomenon*. Chicago, IL: University of Chicago Press.

Duarte, F. 2010. "Teaching Organizational Power and Politics Through a Critical Pedagogical Approach." *Journal of Management & Organization* 16(5): 715–726.

Espedal, B. 2017. "Understanding How Balancing Autonomy and Power Might Occur in Leading Organizational Change." *European Management Journal* 35(2): 155–163.

Etzioni, A.A. 1975. *Comparative Analysis of Complex Organizations: On Power, Involvement and their Correlates*, Revised Edition. New York: Free Press.

Fineman, S., and Y. Gabriel. 1996. *Experiencing Organizations*. London: Sage Publications.

Fleming, P., and A. Spicer. 2008. "Beyond Power and Resistance: New Approaches to Organizational Politics." *Management Communication Quarterly* 21(3): 301–309.

Fleming, P., and A. Spicer. 2010. *Contesting the Corporation: Struggle, Power and Resistance in Organizations*. Cambridge: Cambridge University Press.

Fox, A. 1974. *Beyond Contract, Work, Power and Trust Relations*. London: Faber and Faber.

French, J.R.P., and B.H. Raven. 1968. "The Bases of Social Power." In *Group Dynamics*, edited by D. Cartwright and A. Zander, 150–167. New York: Harper & Row.

Hardy, C. 1996. "Understanding Power: Bringing About Strategic Change." *British Journal of Management* 7 (special issue), S3–S16.

Hardy, C., and S. Clegg. 2004. "Power and Change: A Critical Reflection." In *Dynamics of Organizational Change and Learning*, edited by J.J. Boonstra, 343–370. Chichester: John Wiley & Sons.

Hardy, C., and R. Thomas. 2014. "Strategy, Discourse and Practice: The Intensification of Power." *Journal of Management Studies* 51(2): 320–348.

Hope, O. 2010. "The Politics of Middle Management Sensemaking and Sensegiving." *Journal of Change Management* 10(2): 195–215.

Lukes, S. 1974. *Power: A Radical View*. London: Macmillan.

Marshak, R.J. 2006. *Covert Processes at Work: Managing the Five Hidden Dimensions of Organizational Change*. San Francisco, CA: Berrett-Koehler Publishers.

McMillan, K. 2016. "Politics of Change: The Discourses that Inform Organizational Change and their Capacity to Silence." *Nursing Inquiry* 23(3): 223–231.

Mintzberg, H. 1989. *Mintzberg on Management: Inside Our Strange World of Organizations*. New York: Free Press.

Morgan, G., and Sturdy, G. 2000. *Beyond Organizational Change: Structure, Discourse and Power in UK Financial Services*. London: Macmillan.

Ostrom, E. 1967. *Strategy and Structure of Interdependent Decision Making Mechanisms*. Worskhop in Political Theory and Policy Analysis, Indiana University, Bloomington, IN Series: Workshop Working Paper, W67-3.

Pfeffer, J. 1981. *Power in Organizations*. Boston, MA: Pitman.

Pfeffer, J. 1992a. *Managing with Power: Politics and Influence in Organization*. Boston, MA: Harvard Business School Press.

Pfeffer, J. 1992b. "Understanding Power in Organizations." *California Management Review* 34(2): 29–50.

Vince, R. 2002. "The Politics of Imagined Stability: A Psychodynamic Understanding of Change at Hyder PLC." *Human Relations* 55(10): 1189–1208.

Chapter 12

Communicating organizational change

Introduction and chapter questions

As well as an extensive literature on organizational change, there is an extensive literature on organizational/corporate communications. The focus of this chapter is the overlap between these literatures. Communicating change is particularly significant for leaders, hence its inclusion in Part III, but equally it is important for everyone and at all organizational levels. Gabriel (2008) captures the slipperiness of communications when he refers to it as a protean term, highlighting that this term can have multiple meanings and that these meanings are variable. Accepting this slipperiness, Clampitt's (2013: 4) definition is utilised in this chapter:

> Communication is the transmission and/or reception of signals through some channel(s) that humans interpret based on a probabilistic system that it is deeply influenced by context.

Clampitt (2013) unpacks this definition by highlighting seven communication propositions (please see Table 12.1) which provides an introduction to studying communications.

Each of the propositions featured in Table 12.1 merits clarification as they speak to the importance of communication meaning and context, but also they are relevant to organizational change (numbering refers to proposition numbers in Table 12.1). Proposition 1 highlights the ambiguities which exist within language, reminding us that it is probable that messages will be interpreted in very different ways. Proposition 2 reminds us that particular contexts will influence the probabilities of how a message is interpreted, with interpretation further influenced by assumptions people tend to default to. Proposition 3 relates to the dynamic nature of context warning against assuming that a common context is shared, fixed and static. Proposition 4, with its reference to black holes, is concerned with the influence context may exert and even severely warp interpretation. Proposition 5 relates to message order in emphasising that each message forms the context for the next message. Proposition 6, speaks to multiple messages being contained within a single communication event. And finally, proposition 7 acknowledges that it is the interaction between content and context which produces meaning.

These propositions appear to be an obtuse means to introduce communications, but their strength is that they highlight how something which initially appears straightforward is far more subtle when we begin to study it. Each proposition echoes the complexities of organizational change and when we combine communications and organizational change, we have a chapter focus which on one level is functional and straightforward and on another level is intangible and ambiguous.

Table 12.1 Communications propositions (based upon Clampitt, 2013)

No	Proposition
1	Communication can be described in terms of probabilities.
2	Context shapes the probabilities by creating default assumptions.
3	Context building is a dynamic process.
4	The context may act like a black hole.
5	Context construction is uniquely sensitive to time sequencing.
6	There are multiple messages in each communication event.
7	Content and context interact to produce meaning.

In this chapter, the focus is on communicating change, but it is worth acknowledging that the absence of employee communication can itself be highly problematic. Morrison and Milliken (2000: 707) introduced the concept of organizational silence as follows 'the possibility that the dominant choice within many organizations is for employees to withhold their opinions and concerns about organizational problems – a collective phenomenon that we have termed organizational silence...' Organizational silence is particularly problematic during organizational change, with Daly et al. (2003: 161) warning that: 'change initiatives will disappear into the cracks if management is not careful...' The concept of organizational silence offers another rationale for effective two-way communications in times of change. It is also worth acknowledging that whilst the focus of this chapter is upon change communications within organizations, there are many further change communications with external stakeholders, such as governments, customers and clients and shareholders.

This chapter is organized around and provides answers to the following communicating organizational change questions:

- What are practitioners doing with regards to communicating change?
- What are corporate communications and how has this function developed?
- What change communication theories exist?
- How do the writings of Barrett (2014) on leader communications and the writings of Lewis (2011) on creating change through communications inform our understanding?
- What is social constructionism and how does it inform understanding change communications?
- What are discourses and how do they inform understanding change communications?
- How does the concept of framing offer a new perspective on leader's change communications?

The chapter commences with a practically oriented discussion of communicating change which helps to introduce the highly applied nature of such activities. Theories are next introduced incrementally, first looking to the concept of corporate communications, before looking to theories specifically informing change communications. The work of two academics who have been influential in this field is showcased, the writings of Deborah Barrett (2014) on leadership communications and Laurie Lewis's (2011) writings on creating change through communications. In the questioning section, the focus shifts to thinking differently about change communications and the subtleties alluded to in the introductory propositions (please see Table 12.1).

In particular, notions of reality being a social construction, the persuasive nature of discourses and thinking about leadership regard communications as framing, similar to the way a photographer frames a photograph. The chapter concludes with a summary, research case study and guidance on further reading.

Communicating change: what are practitioners doing?

In answering this question, a good starting point is to look for the practical guidance on employee communications offered by a respected professional body – the Chartered Institute of Personnel and Development (CIPD, 2015). They highlight the following principles of an effective employee communication strategy as:

> built on a shared sense of purpose and aligned with business strategy,
> receives attention and support from senior leadership,
> is driven by genuine dialogue,
> is part of the expectation of good people management,
> draws on a range of digital channels and tools and
> is reviewed and assessed for effectiveness.

This guidance offers an indication of what is involved, highlighting that there will be overlaps between communication and strategy, leadership, people management and technology. In this practical guidance, senior leadership engagement is seen as integral, but the involvement of everyone and the two-way nature of communications is equally emphasised. The need to assess communications is regarded as important to an overall culture of communication within an organization and with success gauged in terms of specific objectives. Other issues highlighted include the development of specific communication strategies, appropriate communication channels and message selection, the tailoring of communications for particular audiences and consideration of roles and responsibilities within a communications strategy.

Moving into the practicalities of communicating change, Jackson (2016) offered a fascinating first-hand account of his own experiences of being a recipient of change communications as well as his involvement in crafting change communications.

> If the communication of change is done well, you will gain the overriding enthusiasm and cooperation of those affected; and if the communication is done badly, you will create resistance and opposition.
>
> (Jackson, 2016: 128)

For Jackson communication is integral to and essential for effective organizational change. His discussion of leaders and communicating change is pertinent to the leadership focus of Part III. Jackson (2016) regards the mindset of the change leader as determining their behaviour, which determines the employees' mindset and their behaviour. Consequently, communications are crucial in conveying the mindset of a leader with regard to a change. He places great emphasis upon mindsets and the way that the mindset informs a negative or positive perception of an organizational change. He offers two reasons why change is poorly communicated. First, it can be a consequence of the change leader's attitude with the leader becoming immersed in the substantive change and immersed in their own self-importance. Second, the reason for change is under-communicated. Senior managers invariably understand the why of a change initiative, but this is often not so well understood by employees. Jackson makes a strong case for involving and engaging employees early on. He acknowledges that leaders often use the defence of confidentiality/sensitivity at an early stage of a change initiative, but he regards this often as an excuse for not involving employees.

Johnson (2017) on the hbr.org website recently offered practical guidance on communicating clearly during an organizational change. She highlights how leaders are far more visible than they realise and that this is very important at times of strategic change. She offers three ways in which leaders can effectively signal strategic change to their organizations, informed by working with leaders and asking followers.

No.1 – Tell your organization what you want, too often leaders weren't clear enough about what they wanted or what it would entail.

No.2 – Personally living the change you have asked for, making decisions that support the change.

No.3 – Resourcing and measuring the change you have asked for. How an organization spends resources and what it chooses to measure are critical ways for signposting what is important.

Theorising change communications

This section commences with an overview of corporate communications as communicating change is a subset of this wider body of knowledge, it then narrows to theories speaking specifically to communicating change before narrowing further to the writings of two influential authors. These are Barrett's (2014) writings on leadership communication and Lewis's (2011) writings on creating change through strategic communication.

Corporate communications

This introduction draws upon Cornelissen's (2017) *Corporate Communication: A Guide to Theory and Practice*. He acknowledges, that up to the 1970s, practitioners referred to communications with stakeholders as 'public relations'. The new function came to incorporate far more than communicating with the press, with change communications included within this widening remit. The new function focused upon the organization as a whole, addressing how the organization presented itself to key stakeholders both internally and externally. Cornelissen acknowledges that the word 'corporate' does have origins in business settings, but also has a second meaning, in terms of the Latin 'corpus' meaning 'body'. So, corporate communications look at the organization as a body which includes internal and external communications. He regards corporate communication as a management function offering a framework for effectively coordinating all internal and external communication with the purpose of establishing and maintaining favourable reputations with stakeholders upon which the organization depends.

There is an acknowledgment that these characteristics make the function quite complex and in this way there are echoes of Clampitt's (2013) propositions cited earlier. In beginning to focus upon corporate communications, a number of terms are prevalent in the literature and in the vocabulary of practitioners: mission, vision, corporate objectives, strategies, corporate identity, corporate image, corporate reputation, stakeholder, market, communication, integration (Cornelissen, 2017). The emphasis upon these key concepts has shifted over time. Consequently, it is informative to look at trends and developments in corporate communications over time. Between the 1900s and the 1970s, emphasis was upon publicity, promotions and information dissemination with communication regarded as tactical support. Between the 1980s and the 2000s, there was an emphasis on positioning. Since 2000, the emphasis has been on stakeholder engagement with communication no longer regarded as tactical support but instead regarded as a strategic tool.

Change communications

Corporate communications as discussed in the previous subsection provides both a rationale for change communications and a framework within which to undertake change communications. In a manner similar to corporate communications, there is a strong practitioner influence upon this field of study. It is worth acknowledging that whilst communicating change implies something universal and consistent, this is not the case. As Chapters 2 and 3 explained, there are many different explanations of change, ranging from a humanistic initiative, such as *Investors in People* through to a radical technology oriented approach such as *Business Process Reengineering*. The implication is that communication will vary considerably in terms of the type of change, but also communications will be influenced by the context of the change and the stage of the change process. Accepting these significant caveats, the intention here is to signpost contributions made to this field with references offering a means of further exploring these contributions.

The reason why leadership is so closely aligned with change communications is captured in Garvin and Roberto (2005), Fox and Amichai-Hamburger's (2001) and Ford et al.'s (2002) contributions. Johansson and Heide (2008), Clampitt et al. (2000) and Clampitt (2013) offer insights into change communication strategy choices. Armenakis et al. (1999) and Balogun et al. (2015) offer guidance on crafting change messages and Salem (2008) warns of the communication reasons why change can fail.

Change communications may be understood as emotional appeals and persuasion. Fox and Amichai-Hamburger (2001: 84) focused on how emotional appeals may be used in order to promote change initiatives addressing the following questions:

> Why is it the case that managers and workers sometimes respond more strongly to an emotional appeal than to a rational one?
> What is it in the emotional message that gives it this power?

Five domains pertinent to these emotional appeals were identified: the core messages, the packaging of messages, change leader characteristics, change leader interaction with their audience and the setting in which interactions take place. For Garvin and Roberto (2005), leaders can only make change happen when they have a coherent strategy of persuasion. In their *Harvard Business Review* article, they highlight four phases of a persuasion campaign. Phase 1 involves convincing employees that radical change is imperative and demonstrating why the new direction is the right one. Phase 2 involves positioning and framing the preliminary plan, gathering feedback and announcing the final plan. Phase 3 involves managing employee moods through a process of constant communication. Finally, phase 4 is concerned with reinforcing behavioural guidelines in order to avoid backsliding. Whilst, leaders through positional power can appeal to and persuade employees, there is a need to recognise that background conversations take place amongst employees. Ford et al. (2002) offered an influential account of the role that such background conversations play during times of change. They argued persuasively that resistance to change is a product of the background conversations being spoken at times of change, creating the context for the change initiative and determining the responses to a change initiative.

As already implied, communicating change raises choices for leaders in terms of choosing the most appropriate communication strategy. Whilst, Johansson, and Heide (2008) is far less applied than some of the other citations in this subsection, their paper is informative in its mapping of three communication approaches evident when studying organizational change. Through reviewing literature published between 1995 and 2007 they were able to identify three different approaches to communication during organizational change: communication as a tool, communication as a socially constructed process, and communication as social transformation. Social construction and transformation processes are discussed further in the questioning section. In their review of communication as a tool, they do highlight criticisms of such literature, but they also identify three themes evident within this literature, in terms of the importance of:

1   wide participation in the change process to make organizational members feel more included, committed and in control of the situation;
2   wide dissemination of information together with openness, early notification and discussion possibilities; and
3   communication about vision and purpose of the change process in order to provide justification.

In terms of communication as a tool, Clampitt et al. (2000) highlight typical organization communication strategies as: spray and pray, tell and sell, underscore and explore, identify and reply and withhold and uphold. Each strategy offers a different way of communicating change which may be more or less appropriate, contingent on the change and the context in which it is being communicated.

Clampitt (2013) offers further guidance on choices with regards to the degree of communication employed. He highlights how changes may be located on a continuum in terms of the initiator's perspective from routine to non-routine and equally how receivers may perceive a change as routine or as non-routine. The implication here is that these perceptions may differ with the goal being to avoid either under-communicating or over-communicating. This differentiation allows him to highlight four zones (approaches) for change communications. The first is under-communicating when there is an under-estimation of the impact a change will have. There can be extensive planning/preparation for a change initiative without proportionate communications. The second zone is over-communicating, as Clampitt warns more information does not necessarily equate to better communication. He refers to the other two zones as the 'Goldilocks' zones, with routine changes located in the routine 'Goldilocks' zone and non-routine changes in the other 'Goldilocks' zone. The implication being the routine or non-routine nature of the change will determine the balance between over and under-communicating, but, in a manner similar to Goldilocks being unable to choose a particular bowl of porridge, communicators may not be able to choose.

As well as choices around communicating a change strategy, there are choices around crafting the change message. Armenakis et al. (1999) identified five key components of change messages: discrepancy, efficacy, appropriateness, principal support and personal valence. They related discrepancy to the need for a change and they related efficacy to confidence that a change would succeed. Appropriateness was related

Table 12.2 Communication reasons organizations do not change (based upon Salem, 2008)

Reason		Description
1	Insufficient communication	Not enough communication.
2	Local identification	Without communication building global/shared identification members will resort to local/ independent identities.
3	Global distrust	If organizational members distrust the agents of change or each other change initiatives fail.
4	Lack of productive humour	Organizational members can encourage and discourage change by how they use humour.
5	Poor interpersonal communication skills	Lack of interpersonal communication skills.
6	Conflict avoidance	Despite confronting difference being important in times of change.
7	An inappropriate mix of loose and tight coupling	Organizational members may resist transformational change through loosening couplings between each other.

to if a change was perceived to be the correct change and principal support spoke to the level of institutional resources and commitment with valence concerned with the question 'What is in it for me?'

Balogun et al. (2015) offered guidance on the timing of change communications with employees. Employees prefer hearing about the change from management, rather than through rumours. Communicating early allows employees time to understand and adjust to changes. Employees prefer honest and even incomplete announcements, rather than information being covered-up and, despite policies of silence, employees inevitably learn about change initiatives.

Finally, Salem (2008) highlighted seven communication reasons why organizations do not change. His paper integrated the learning from three recent communication and organizational change studies with recent change theory and complexity theory developments with his results summarised in Table 12.2.

Change communications are often couched in terms of a change initiative being successful or the need to avoid a change initiative failing. But even notions of change failure/success are not as black and white as the literature often implies (please see Chapter 17 for further discussion).

Leadership communications

Deborah Barrett has worked as an academic and consultant in the field of leadership communications for many decades. In this subsection, her contribution is revisited with a particular focus on leaders communicating change. "Change Communication: Using Strategic Employee Communication to Facilitate Major Change" (Barrett, 2002) offered insights into communicating change practices grounded in her experiences of working as a change communications consultant. She suggested that the communication of a major change required an 'MoT' of organizational communication processes. An MoT is a test of the road worthiness of a vehicle, with the implication that all communication processes required testing before communicating change.

Table 12.3 Basic objectives of employee communications (Barrett, 2014: 349–350)

No	Employee communication objective
1	Educate employees in the organization's culture, vision, and strategic goals.
2	Motivate employee support for the organization's goals.
3	Encourage higher performance and discretionary effort to achieve those goals.
4	Limit misunderstandings and rumours that may damage morale and productivity.
5	Align employees with the organization's performance objectives and position them to help achieve them.

She recognised that a failure to effectively communicate a change may really reflect a failure of broader organizational communication processes. Subsequently, she developed her textbook *Leadership Communication* (Barrett, 2014). In developing any communication strategy, it is necessary for the manager/leader to address a series of key questions (Barrett, 2014) relating to purpose, message, medium/forum, communicator, timing, audiences and feedback. The basic objectives of employee communications are summarised in Table 12.3.

Barrett (2014) favoured the *Strategic Employee Communication Model* first presented in her 2002 paper, which emphasised a supportive management, targeted messages, effective media and forums, well-positioned staff with a requirement for ongoing assessment with a balanced scorecard of current employee communications favoured. The scope of change communications needs to be determined in terms of the scale of the change. Three potential levels of change communication effort are proposed: basic, strategic and major change with a three-phased change communication plan for a major change.

Phase 1 – design change communication strategy and plan

Barrett warns against initiating changes without establishing how to communicate them. A change communication team (CCT) is favoured in order to analyse needs and implement the change communication programme.

Phase 2 – launch change communication and ensure employee understanding

Allowing employee involvement in the creation of the vision during major change will increase their understanding and acceptance of the new direction and what the changes mean to them.

(Barrett, 2014: 369)

All employees need to feel that they are involved in the change process. The more they contribute, the more they will internalise the changes.

Phase 3 – monitor results and make adjustments

Once changes have been communicated, leaders should stop and plan to assess employee understanding. Surveying a cross-section of employees will help to determine if communications are effective.

Creating change through strategic communication

The title *Organizational Change: Creating Change Through Strategic Communication* (Lewis, 2011) effectively communicates what this book is all about. A communications perspective on change is adopted similar to Barrett (2014). Communications are not just an extra task, but instead they are perceived as integral to change processes.

> ...organizational change is accomplished or not accomplished through implementers' interactions with stakeholders, and stakeholders' interactions with each other.
>
> (Lewis, 2011: 12)

In this subsection, the focus is on the book (Lewis, 2011), but Lewis has made many influential contributions to communicating change debates, through journal papers including: Lewis and Seibold, 1998; Lewis, 2000; Lewis et al., 2006; Lewis and Truss, 2012. Lewis (2000) offered four case studies of communicating change on quality programmes revealing how communication failures contributed to stalled and/or failed programmes of change. In Lewis and Truss (2012), the focus was upon participative communication processes, studying 26 human resource specialists involved in introducing/implementing specifically planned change within the past five years. Two research questions were posed:

- What criteria are used to select input providers?
- What considerations do implementers make in the use of stakeholders' input during the change?

Their research revealed practitioners adopting four approaches which they labelled: open, political, restricted and advisory. The open approach involved implementers inviting people to volunteer input. The political approach involved 'important' individuals being sought out regardless of the relevance/usefulness of their inputs. The restricted approach involved seeking input from select stakeholders in order to confirm choices already made. The advisory approach involved a wide array of stakeholders providing supportive input. Lewis and Truss (2012) suggested that '...many organizations will have their own preconceived idea of how a change should be installed and be unwilling or highly reluctant to alter it through implementation adjustments'. These findings are intriguing in that what appears to be a participative approach towards communicating change may prove really to be window dressing.

In the introduction to her book, Lewis (2011) identifies three weaknesses that she perceives in current approaches to change implementation. First, there has been an over-emphasis on implementers' strategies and recipients' responses.

> We ascribe 'resistance' behaviors or attitudes as a mere reaction rather than as an affirmative, principled perspective of stakeholders who care about their organizations and a wide array of stakes held by various stakeholders, and whom in their resistance can bring much to enhance and inform change processes.
>
> (Lewis, 2011: 4)

Instead of the crude caricature of leader change communications seeking to overcome resistance to change, the quotation opens up a different way of thinking about resistance (please see Chapter 13 for further discussion). The second weakness, which is related to the first is the danger of ascribing reactions stakeholders have to change efforts. In essence, we assume how individuals will react to change initiatives. The third weakness is gauging the success of implementing a change against what the implementers initially desired, as there is no scope to acknowledge that what the change implementers originally desired may have been flawed. In creating change through strategic communications, Lewis distinguishes between formal and informal communications, identifying three key processes in communication during planned change: dissemination of information, soliciting input, and socialization. Implementers, as well as other stakeholders, have to make strategic decisions about how to engage in such processes. A strong case for change through communications is made, although with the caveat of avoiding the notion that 'communication is everything'.

Her concluding chapter draws upon earlier chapters in order to offer a model which applies ideas in the book to practices of communicating change. Instead of depicting change as stages or steps, a more fluid notion of activities is employed with actions and reactions during change implementation running along three 'meta-tracks': managing meaning, managing networks and managing practice. These tracks are regarded as competing for our attention and the attention of others. Managing meaning is concerned with enacting realities of what is going on in a change process, for example, who is resisting, but equally, what resistance means. Managing networks refer to stakeholders and implementers involved in shaping relationships with those impacted by and/or witnessing change. Managing practice refers to more physical and material considerations when bringing about change. Practice may or may not reflect the desired results implementers have in mind. All three activity tracks occur during a process of changing, but there may be different emphases at different times. Failing to monitor or misreading an activity track may potentially lead to problems.

The three activity tracks have implications for the tools of practice: monitoring and articulating goals, developing the strategic communication plan and messages, analysing input (USER) and influencing the implementation climate. The first two tools of practice are self-explanatory, but the USER acronym requires clarification (please see Table 12.4).

The acronym is a reminder to use input as a resource, rather than mere symbolic references to input. The fourth tool of practice is influencing implementation climate. Communications are not everything, with physical, material, financial and other resources requiring allocation and management. The model encourages thinking in terms of three activity tracks in terms of each of the four tools of practice. So for example, thinking in terms of the managing networks track might have the following implications for the four numbered tools of practice. Highlighting the need to map out how different stakeholders goals conflict/overlap (1). Raising those strengths and weaknesses which speak to stakes of important stakeholders (2). Monitoring the way in which the network is reshaped around interpretations (3). Monitoring the key resources that various stakeholders are able/willing to bring to the change effort (4).

Table 12.4 Clarifying the USER acronym (based on Lewis, 2011: 273)

Use input as a resource in the decision making and adjustments.
Systematically collect input.
Evaluate the process by which input is collected to ensure it is working.
Rigorously drill down and examine the input that is collected.

Questioning explanations of change communications

In the previous section, the focus was on the practical and functional requirements of communicating organizational change and those theories which serve this function. In this section, the focus shifts to understanding the role communications in general and language in particular plays in influencing people to change. In the following quotation from Charles Allen the then Chief Executive of Granada, a far more subtle approach than a transmission model of communication is illustrated.

> I always brand the change programmes. Then people associate the negatives of the restructuring with the brand, and once you've made the reorganization, you shut the brand down.
>
> (Conner, 1998: xiv)

The unifying notion within this questioning section is highlighting approaches which better explain the subtle influences and inferences of communications such as the Charles Allen quotation. As Palmer and Dunford (2008: S26) suggested 'communication, and language more specifically, is central not just to conveying or transmitting required changes; it is the medium through which change itself occurs'. In this section, three related approaches are introduced and explained: the notion of reality as a social construction, the notion of discourses seeking to persuade and influence us and the concept of framing. These approaches offer us different ways of thinking about organizational change communications. Initially, they may appear as academic abstractions, but they do have considerable potential to inform practices. Consciously or unconsciously change agents do employ language and metaphor to galvanise change (Johnson et al., 2013).

Social constructionism

Berger and Luckmann (1966) gave impetus to understanding reality as socially constructed and this line of reasoning remains influential to this day. They identified three basic processes within the social construction of reality: externalisation, objectification, and internalisation. Externalisation refers to when we act on the world, such as painting a picture or writing an annual report. Objectification is when that act is widely talked about and/or engaged with, such as many people viewing the painting or the annual report being published and widely read. Internalisation is when people subsequently take on board new ways of acting such as painting in a certain way or writing and publishing annual reports. Whilst, social constructionism as part of the sociology of knowledge initially appears remote from the practicalities of communicating change, it offers a framework for rethinking change communications.

Change initiatives such as total quality management, business processing re-engineering or benchmarking initially appear very real and tangible in their impact upon organizations and their members. However, what is happening may be viewed as a social construction in that for each of these initiatives, there was a process of externalisation as new ways of working were introduced. Each of these initiatives then went through a process of objectification as these new ways of working were translated into policies and procedures. Subsequently, at least, for a time new ways of working became internalised within organizations. Interest in discourse and framing which feature later in this section are highly compatible with social constructionism.

If we look for a moment specifically to leaders, the notion of socially constructing reality offers a different way of thinking about what leaders do and the centrality of communications to processes of leading. Pondy (1989) famously highlighted leaders as managers of meaning and Smircich and Morgan (1982: 258) elaborated this position as follows:

> Leadership is realized in processes whereby one or more individuals succeed in attempting to frame and define the reality for others, leadership situations are those in which there exists an obligation or a perceived right on the part of certain individuals to define the reality of others.
>
> (Smircich and Morgan, 1982: 258)

More recently Bryman (2004: 754) highlighted '...the importance and significance of the leader as a manager of meaning who actively manipulates symbols in order to instill a vision, manage change, and achieve support for his or her direction'. These leadership acts may be benign, but equally, they can be malicious with Grint and Case (1998) writing specifically about business process re-engineering and its rhetoric taking a violent turn. Collins (2000) in his account of management fads and buzzwords warned that a grammar based upon commands and imperatives developed which could not countenance dissent.

The social construction of leadership literature is now extensive having grown rapidly over the past 15 years (Fairhurst and Grant, 2010). This literature possesses two interrelated characteristics: first, eschewing a leader-centric approach in which the leader's personality, style and/or behaviour are the primary determining influences on follower's thoughts and actions. Second, there is an emphasis on leadership as a co-constructed reality and as an outcome of interaction between and among social actors. Social constructionist perspectives question common assumptions that leaders inside organizations respond to their external environment (context). Instead, Grint (2005), for example, favoured a social constructionist perspective suggesting that leaders may construct a context and that '...we should pay more attention to the role of leaders and decision-makers in the construction of contexts that legitimates their intended or executed actions and accounts' (Grint, 2005: 1472). In Chapter 10, Kotter's (1996/2012) emphasis upon creating a sense of urgency when leading change, may involve a leader socially constructing a sense of urgency as much as, the leader reporting reality.

Discourse centred understanding of change

The discourse literature itself can be quite discursive. In the following quotation, Gabriel (2008: 78) offered an accessible introduction to the relevance of discourse:

> Currently, discourse stands at the centre of what is known as the "linguistic turn" in the human sciences, a trend which views language not as a passive medium reflecting or describing the world, but as an active entity through which the world becomes meaningful to us.

In this way, discourse is very relevant to this chapter but very different from the discussion of communications in the first half of this chapter. One of the challenges of engaging with discourse is that the term can mean different things to different people. Alvesson and Kärreman (2000) spoke to this challenge in their influential account of discourse differentiating discourse with a small 'd' from discourse with a capital 'D'. The former speaks to micro- and meso-level discourse of texts as empirical material and the latter speaks to grand and mega level discourses, such as a discourse of performance management. Writing more specifically with regard to organizational change, Caldwell (2006) acknowledged that there were, at least, four meanings of discourse: as rule-bound systems, as discursive practices, as 'power/knowledge' and discourse as discourse (a grand meta-narrative).

Tsoukas (2005) made a very good case for adopting a discourse analytic approach when studying the language of change, contrasting behaviourist, cognitivist and discursivist approaches and the way that each approach places a different emphasis on explaining how change is communicated. Grant and Marshak (2011: 206) captured the essence of discourse as follows 'in essence, discourses shape how people think about things (how they "talk to themselves") and therefore how they act, and how people act and think about things shape their discourses'. Management and organization studies discourse literature is large and is growing.

The strength of Grant and Marshak's (2011) paper was focussing specifically upon advancing and encouraging discourse centred understanding of organizational change which they believed had the potential to inform both scholars and practitioners. They identified three benefits of a discourse centred approach to understanding organizational change. First, the approach encourages a focus on communicative practices and discursive practices such as conversations. Second, the approach highlights processual and temporal aspects of organizational change. Third, the approach has the potential to develop further theory and research. They identified four concepts as central to a discourse centred approach towards understanding organizational change: discourse, text, context, and conversation. They cite Hardy, Lawrence and Grant (2005: 59) asserting that 'a discursive approach to organizational phenomena is more than a focus on language and its usage in organizations. It highlights the ways in which language constructs organizational reality, rather than simply reflecting it.' In this quotation, we see both an articulation of social constructionism discussed earlier and a critical counterpoint to discussions in the first half of this chapter. Through reviewing research literature, Grant and Marshak identified five levels of discourse relevant to understanding organizational change: intrapsychic, micro, meso, macro and meta.

Framing leadership change communications

The concept of framing has caught the imagination of theorists for many decades and offers an insightful perspective on the change communications of leaders. In this subsection, the concept of framing and its background is introduced and illustrated through its application to leaders.

> In today's new market economies, recall that leaders are the architects of change while managers are the everyday problem solvers.
>
> (Fairhurst, 2011: 51)

This quotation illustrates framing at work with leaders framed as the 'architects of change' and managers framed as the 'everyday problem solvers'. This framing is probably undertaken knowingly given its context within a book on framing. Leaders and managers are respectively contrasted and privileged as 'architects of change' and as 'everyday problem solvers'. It is very apparent that such framing is closely aligned with social constructionism and discourse discussed earlier in this section. Cornelissen et al. (2011) in reviewing the framing and legitimisation of strategic change, highlighted the development of framing and its different applications in different fields and institutional settings tracing the basic idea of framing back to Bateson (1955/1972).

Gail Fairhurst's (Fairhurst and Sarr, 1996; Fairhurst, 2011) practically oriented books on framing leadership have been influential. In the groundbreaking, *The Art of Framing: Managing the Language of Leadership,* Fairhurst and Sarr (1996: 3) described framing as an essential tool for the manager of meaning, 'to determine the meaning of a subject is to make sense of it, to judge its character and significance'. The book benefited from Gail Fairhurst being an established academic researching inside an organization in which Bob Sarr (her co-author) worked. They used an analogy of a gifted photographer focussing their camera and framing their subject so that a person viewing the photograph knew what the photographer intended. They identified three components of framing: language thought and forethought. The cautionary note here is that 'as photographers decide what lies inside the frame, authors decide which information to present' (Buchanan and Dawson, 2007: 677).

Their discussion of goals is pertinent to the change theme of this textbook in that they suggest that '...ambiguous language and generally framed goals often help facilitate organizational change' (Fairhurst and Sarr, 1996: 37). Fairhurst and Sarr (1996) identified tools used to design memorable frames: metaphors, jargon, and catchphrases, contrast, spin and stories. When Fairhurst (2005) revisited *The Art of Framing* and its critical and practitioner reception, she acknowledged that practising managers either really embraced the concept or struggled with it. In terms of those practising managers embracing the concept she noted that they '...seem to place a premium on communication especially regarding its role in organizational change' (Fairhurst, 2005: 167). *The Power of Framing: Creating the Language of Leadership* (Fairhurst, 2011) built upon *The Art of Framing* (Fairhurst and Sarr, 1996), but went into framing more deeply and consequently it particularly informs the potential of frames explained here. Fairhurst (2011: 2) presented six rules guiding the relationship between leadership and reality construction (please see Table 12.5).

Table 12.5 Reality construction rules (Fairhurst, 2011)

No	Reality construction rule
1	Leaders often cannot control events, but they can control the context under which events are seen if they recognise a framing opportunity.
2	At its most basic level, framing reality means defining 'the situation here and now' in ways that connect with others.
3	'Reality' is often contested. Framing a subject is an act of persuasion by leaders, one imbued with ethical choices.
4	It is the uncertainty, confusion and undecidability of 'the situation here and now' that opens it up for interpretation and provides an opportunity for the more verbally skilled among us to emerge as leaders.
5	Ultimately, leadership is a design problem. Leaders must figure out what leadership is in the context of what they do and, through the framing and actions, persuade themselves and other people that they are doing it.
6	Effective framing requires that leaders be able to control their own spontaneous communications.

The rules of reality construction (please see Table 12.5) provide a helpful and succinct way into leadership reality construction. More specifically, Fairhurst (2011) highlighted framing skill components related to cultural discourses, mental models and core framing tasks, focussing on five types of memorable frame commonly used by leaders: metaphorical, master, simplifying, gain and loss and believability. In terms of the leadership context of framing, Fairhurst (2011: 184) offered the following guidance 'first, you must focus on the "who, what, when, where, why" details of the situation at hand to discern framing at work. Second, you must figure out the design problem of the leader or leaders involved.' Through the concept of framing, we are offered insights into the change communications of leaders which go beyond viewing communications as merely the transmission of information and highlight how communications may influence the thinking and behaviour of recipients.

Summary

The chapter may be succinctly summarised through answering the questions posed in the chapter's introduction. The original questions are restated in italics.

What are practitioners doing with regards to communicating change? The CIPD's (2015) practical guidance on employee communications offered insights into the principles of an effective employee communication strategy, highlighting that there will be overlaps between communication and strategy, leadership, people management and technology. Jackson's (2016) own experiences of being a recipient of change communications as well as his involvement in crafting change communications offered a first-hand practitioner account.

What are corporate communications and how has this function developed? Cornelissen (2017) regarded corporate communications as developing out of what had been referred to up to the 1970s as 'public relations', but which was developing into addressing how the organization presented itself to key stakeholders both internally and externally. Today, corporate communications embrace mission, vision, corporate objectives, strategies, corporate identity, corporate image, corporate reputation, stakeholder, market, communication, integration.

What change communication theories exist? The following theories were highlighted: Garvin and Roberto (2005), Fox and Amichai-Hamburger's (2001) and Ford et al.'s (2002) theories relating to persuasion and emotional appeals, Johansson and Heide (2008), Clampitt et al. (2000) and Clampitt's (2013) insights into change communication strategy choices, Armenakis et al. (1999) and Balogun et al.'s (2015) guidance on crafting change messages and Salem's (2008) warning about the communication reasons why change initiatives fail.

How do the writings of Barrett (2014) on leader communications and the writings of Lewis (2011) on creating change through communications inform our understanding? Managers/leaders need to address a series of key questions (Barrett, 2014) relating to purpose, message, medium/forum, communicator, timing, audiences and feedback. Barrett (2014) favoured the Strategic Employee Communication Model emphasising a supportive management, targeted messages, effective media and forums, well-positioned staff with a requirement for ongoing assessment with a balanced scorecard of current employee communications. Lewis (2011) adopts a communication perspective similar to Barrett (2014). Communications are not just an extra task, but are perceived as being integral to change processes. Three weaknesses perceived in current approaches to change implementation are highlighted, first, the over emphasis upon implementers' strategies and recipients' responses; second, the danger of ascribing re-actions where stakeholders have to change efforts and third, the danger of gauging the success of implementing a change against what the implementers initially desired.

What is social constructionism and how does it inform understanding change communications? Berger and Luckmann (1966) gave impetus to understanding reality as socially constructed, highlighting three basic processes of: externalisation, objectification, and internalisation. Pondy (1989) famously highlighted leaders as managers of meaning, with the social construction of leadership literature now extensive having grown rapidly over the past 15 years (Fairhurst and Grant, 2010).

What are discourses and how do they inform understanding change communications? Discourse is part of what is known as the 'linguistic turn' viewing language as an active entity through which the world becomes meaningful to us (Gabriel, 2008). Grant and Marshak (2011) identified three benefits of a discourse centred approach to understanding organizational change; encouraging a focus on communicative practices and discursive practices such as conversations, highlighting processual and temporal aspects and third, having the potential to develop further theory and research. Four concepts central to a discourse centred approach towards understanding organizational change were identified as: discourse, text, context, and conversation.

How does the concept of framing offer a new perspective on leader's change communications? Cornelissen et al. (2011) in reviewing the framing and legitimisation of strategic change, highlighted the development of framing and its different applications in different fields and institutional settings tracing the basic idea of framing back to Bateson (1955/1972). Gail Fairhurst's practically oriented books on framing leadership have been influential; *The Art of Framing: Managing the Language of Leadership* (Fairhurst and Sarr, 1996) and *The Power of Framing: Creating the Language of Leadership* (Fairhurst, 2011).

Research case study showcase: communicating change in Brazil's Organization X

Simões and Esposito's (2014) research case based on a pharmaceutical company in Brazil reported in the *Journal of Management Development* is showcased here. For the full case and further analysis please visit the original source.

Case study source

Simões and Esposito's (2014) qualitative research focused on Organization X (a pseudonym for the real company name). In researching corporate communications, they collected data through observation, semi-structured interviews and questionnaires with Organization X's change leaders and communication managers. They also undertook document analysis, making direct observations in order to check the data. As well as the views of managers, group discussions were carried out in order to elicit employee understanding about the changes in terms of feelings and beliefs about how change communications were being conducted.

Simões, P.M.M., and M. Esposito. 2014. "Improving Change Management: How Communication Nature Influences Resistance to Change." *Journal of Management Development* 33(4): 324–341.

The case study

Organization X had been a market leader in the production of generic medi-cines in Brazil since 2002. They had a portfolio of more than 150 products and were the third largest pharmaceutical company in Brazil. However, in 2009, Organization X found itself in financial difficulties, owing money to the bank. Suppliers became increasingly concerned about the finances of Organization X and employees became concerned about being paid and their job security. There had been rumours over the past year that the company was going to be sold.

When on 9 April 2009 the acquisition of Organization X by The Group (a pseudonym) was announced, the announcement was greeted with a sense of relief. For both employees and the board, strong financial support from a re-spected global pharmaceutical group, would be beneficial in the short term and long term. The Group as a global company had operations in over 100 countries employing over 100,000 people. It is one of the world's largest pharmaceutical companies and a leading company in the so-called 'emerging countries'. The Group as a world leader in the production and marketing of vaccines has its shares traded on the Paris and New York stock exchanges.

How was the acquisition announced to employees?

There was both formal (written) and face-to-face communications announcing the acquisition. In a letter signed by Organization X's President to employees, they were informed about the ending of hard times for the company and the beginning of a new stage of development for the company.

The President dedicated 8–9 April to explaining the immediate consequences of the acquisition and to addressing common employee doubts about the ac-quisition. Face-to-face meetings for all shifts in both plants were organized. The focus was addressing items such as whether the acquisition was partial or complete, would planned investment change, would the board change and would employee benefits change. These face-to-face communications were put together by human resources and the President himself. They followed an es-tablished tradition of openness in Organization X with regards to major facts involving the organization. The organization favoured open, direct and frank communications.

How did The Group communicate with Organization X employees post-acquisition?

By the end of April 2009, a team from The Group were working at Organization X sites. This team included the new Finance Director in order to address the cash-flow problems of the company, people from human resources and business support directors. In the following quotation, Interviewee G, recalls the brief given by The Group's President in Brazil (Simões and Esposito, 2014: 333).

> We received three messages: 'Open the drawers, look at everything and find out how the business works', the first point. Second point, 'preserve the

(Continued)

culture, though you are from the Group, preserve Organization X's culture because it has a very strong thing there and that has to be preserved'. And the third point, 'protect the people.'

The goal of The Group in acquiring Organization X was to maintain the existing culture with the objective of maintaining separate business models and structures, whilst ensuring the integration of back office operations. The intention was to respect Organization X's expertise and success in the generic market as The Group did not have expertise and success in generic medicines. Simultaneously, the intention was to ensure that The Group's management style was adopted. The preservation of the existing culture was reinforced more than a year later by the incoming General Director of Organization X when the process of integration was believed to have been successful.

Interviewees favourably evaluated the quality of information provided about the change, although there was room for improvement in terms of the detail and timing of information provided. Communication challenges related to the speed of change, the creation of new initiatives and adjustments to existing projects, this required care in terms of the quality of information provided. However, no new communication processes were initiated after the acquisition with an emphasis on preserving existing processes. Organization X had always favoured an informal and open internal climate which had helped the flow of information during the change process and this was maintained post acquisition.

> In terms of the environment of support and trust that must exist for dialogue to succeed (empathy) it is clear this was largely facilitated by the informal atmosphere that already existed in Organization X before the acquisition.
>
> *(Simões and Esposito, 2014: 335)*

There was an appreciation post acquisition amongst employees that they had to adjust due to now being part of a multinational corporation with global standards and procedures to follow. There was also appreciation of benefits arising out of integration, specifically in terms of management and exposure to global experiences and professional opportunities for growth. There was a realisation that The Group had the management know-how and Organization X had the generic market know-how. When Organization X's General Director was interviewed about communications the importance of identity symbols was emphasised. An illustration of this was offered in maintaining the famous June Festival of Organization X post acquisition.

Case study questions

1   What was positive about how The Group engaged with Organization X?
2   How did The Group go about communicating change compared with Barrett's (2014) objectives of employee communications (please see Table 12.3)?
3   How might the concept of framing offer a different perspective on the case study of Organization X?

Discussion questions

1 Why do you think the concept of change communications is often omitted from managing and leading change textbooks?
2 How does the concept of corporate communications offer a rationale for change communications?
3 Do leaders in organizations really exist?
4 What is appealing in the concept of framing to a change leader?

Navigating the communicating change literature

There is certainly no shortage of communications literature in general and literature specifically relating communications to organizational change. The cautionary note relates to the quality of this literature, particularly in terms of the evidence base and if it is research informed. Two disciplines are particularly evident within this area of study. Psychology offers insights into how individuals, groups, and teams process communications and sociology looks to the social shaping of communications. In critical accounts of communications focussing upon discourse, these boundaries between psychology and sociology blur. However, more generally, communication is influenced by competing schools of thought each with assumptions embedded within these different ways of thinking. This is reflected in the particular journals where you are likely to find papers published. Journals such as *Human Relations*, *Journal of Management Studies* and the *British Journal of Management* will often include papers on communications. More specifically, *Management Communications Quarterly* and *Corporate Communications: An International Journal* as their titles suggest, concentrate upon themes within this chapter. In terms of the leadership aspects of communications, *Leadership* and *The Leadership Quarterly* frequently publish papers with a communications perspective.

Many of the issues raised in *Management Fads and Buzzwords: Critical-practical Perspectives* (Collins, 2000) remain pertinent to this day. The challenge in engaging with change communications is the faddish and rhetorical nature of much of the literature. Collins (2000) offered a means of dealing with this challenge through acknowledging the critical-practical aspects of fads and fashions.

It is always good when literature reviewing to go back to journal papers and original sources, but anyone seeking a textbook overview of themes covered in the chapter is recommended to look at the following. Cornelissen's (2017) *Corporate Communication*, benefits from being written by a highly respected communications scholar who regularly publishes in respected journals. The chapter 'Leadership and change communication' is particularly pertinent to themes in this chapter. Similarly, *Communicating for Managerial Effectiveness* (Clampitt, 2013) is recommended, with his chapter 'Communicating about change', particularly informative. In terms of leadership oriented textbooks, Barrett's (2014) *Leadership Communication*, brings together leadership and communication in a practical and pragmatic manner. As mentioned previously, organizational change textbooks often omit covering change communications. However, a notable exception is Palmer et al. (2016) *Managing Organizational Change: A Multiple Perspectives Approach* with Chapter 6 focused upon change communication strategies.

References

Alvesson, M., and D. Kärreman. 2000. "Varieties of Discourse: On the Study of Organizations Through Discourse Analysis." *Human Relations* 53(9): 1125–1149.

Armenakis, A.A., S.G. Harris, and H.S. Field. 1999. "Making Change Permanent: A Model for Institutionalizing Change." In *Research in Organization Change and Development*, Volume XII, edited by W. Pasmore and R. Woodman, 97–128. Greenwich, CT: JAI Press.

Balogun, J., V. Hope Hailey, and S. Gustafsson. 2015. *Exploring Strategic Change.* Harlow: Pearson Education.

Barrett, D.J. 2002. "Change Communication: Using Strategic Employee Communication to Facilitate Major Change." *Corporate Communications: An International Journal* 7(4): 219–231.

Barrett, D.J. 2014. *Leadership Communication.* New York: McGraw-Hill Education.

Bateson, G. 1955/1972. *Steps to an Ecology of Mind.* New York: Ballantine.

Berger, P.L., and T. Luckmann. 1966. *The Social Construction of Reality: A Treatise in the Sociology of Knowledge.* Garden City, NY: Anchor Books.

Bryman, A. 2004. "Qualitative research on leadership: A critical but appreciative review." *The Leadership Quarterly*, 15(6): 729–769.

Buchanan, D., and P. Dawson. 2007. "Discourse and Audience: Organizational Change as a Multi-Story Process. *Journal of Management Studies* 44(5): 669–686.

Caldwell, R. 2006. *Agency and Change.* London: Routledge.

Chartered Institute of Personnel and Development. 2015. Employee Communication Fact Sheet. Available at http://www.cipd.co.uk/hr-resources/factsheets/employee-communication.aspx. CIPD: London.

Clampitt, P.G. 2013. *Communicating for Managerial Effectiveness: Problems, Strategies and Solutions.* Thousand Oaks, CA: Sage Publications Inc.

Clampitt, P.G., R.J. Dekoch, and T. Cashman. 2000. "A Strategy for Communicating About Uncertainty." *Academy of Management Executive* 14(4): 41–57.

Collins, D. 2000. *Management Fads and Buzzwords: Critical-practical Perspectives.* London: Routledge.

Conner, D.R. 1998. *Managing at the Speed of Change.* Chichester: John Wiley and Sons.

Cornelissen, J. 2017. *Corporate Communication: A Guide to Theory and Practice.* London: Sage Publications.

Cornelissen, J.P., R. Holt, and M. Zundel. 2011. "The Role of Analogy and Metaphor in the Framing and Legitimization of Strategic Change." *Organization Studies* 32(12): 1701–1716.

Daly, F., P. Teague, and P. Kitchen. 2003. "Exploring the Role of Internal Communication During Organisational Change." *Corporate Communications: An International Journal* 8(3): 153–162.

Fairhurst, G.T. 2005. "Reframing the Art of Framing: Problems and Prospects for Leadership." *Leadership* 1(2): 165–185.

Fairhurst, G.T. 2008. "Discursive Leadership: A Communication Alternative to Leadership Psychology." *Management Communication Quarterly* 21(4): 510–521.

Fairhurst, G.T. 2011. *The Power of Framing: Creating the Language of Leadership.* San Francisco, CA: Jossey Bass, Wiley Imprint.

Fairhurst, G.T., and D. Grant. 2010. "The Social Construction of Leadership: A Sailing Guide." *Management Communication Quarterly* 24(2): 171–210.

Fairhurst, G.T., and R.A. Sarr. 1996. *The Art of Framing: Managing the Language of Leadership.* San Francisco, CA: Jossey Bass Inc.

Ford, J.D., L.W. Ford, and R.T. McNamara. 2002. "Resistance and the Background Conversations of Change." *Journal of Organizational Change Management* 15(2): 105–121.

Fox, S., and Y. Amichai-Hamburger. 2001. "The Power of Emotional Appeals in Promoting Organizational Change Programs." *Academy of Management Executive* 15(4): 84–94.

Gabriel, Y. 2008. *Organizing Words: A Critical Thesaurus for Social and Organization Studies*. Oxford: Oxford University Press.

Garvin, D.A., and M.A. Roberto. 2005. "Change Through Persuasion." *Harvard Business Review* 83(2): 104–112.

Grant, D., and R.J. Marshak. 2011. "Toward a Discourse Centred Understanding of Organizational Change." *The Journal of Applied Behavioral Science* 47(2): 204–235.

Grint, K. 2005. "Problems, problems, problems: The social construction of leadership." *Human Relations*, 58(11): 1467–1494.

Grint, K., and P. Case. 1998. "The Violent Rhetoric of Re-engineering: Management Consultancy on the Offensive." *Journal of Management Studies* 35(5) 557–577.

Hardy, C., T.B. Lawrence, and D. Grant. 2005. "Discourse and Collaboration: The Role of Conversations and Collective Identity." *Academy of Management Review* 30(1): 58–77.

Jackson, P. 2016. "Change into Practice: Communicating Change." In *Perspectives on Change: What Academics, Consultants and Managers Really Think About Change*, edited by B. Burnes and J. Randall, 128–143. New York: Routledge.

Johansson, C., and M. Heide. 2008. "Speaking of Change: Three Communication Approaches in Studies of Organizational Change." *Corporate Communications: An International Journal* 13(3): 288–305.

Johnson, E. 2017. "How to Communicate Clearly During Organizational Change." *Harvard Business Review*, Online article posted 13 June. Available at https://hbr.org/2017/06/how-to-communicate-clearly-during-organizational-change.

Johnson, G., R. Whittington, K. Scholes, D. Angwin, and P. Regner. 2013. *Exploring Strategy*. Harlow: Pearson Education.

Kotter, J.P. 1996/2012. *Leading Change*. Boston: Harvard Business School Press.

Lewis, L.K. 2000. "Communicating Change: Four Cases of Quality Programs." *The Journal of Business Communication* 37(2): 128–155.

Lewis, L.K. 2011. *Organizational Change: Creating Change Through Strategic Communications*. Chichester: Wiley.

Lewis, L.K., and D.R. Seibold. 1998. "Reconceptualizing Organizational Change Implementation as a Communication Problem: A Review of Literature and Research Agenda." In *Communication Yearbook Vol.21*, edited by M.E. Roloff, 93–151. Thousand Oaks, CA: Sage Publications.

Lewis, L.K., and T.L. Truss. 2012. "Soliciting and Using Input during Organizational Change Initiatives: What are Practitioners Doing?" *Management Communication Quarterly* 26(2): 267–294.

Lewis, L.K., A.M. Schmisseur, K.K. Stephens, and K.E. Weir. 2006. "Advice on Communicating during Organizational Change: The Content of Popular Press Books." *Journal of Business Communication* 43(2): 113–137.

Morrison, E.W., and F.J. Milliken. 2000. "Organizational Silence: A Barrier to Change and Development in a Pluralistic World." *Academy of Management Review* 25(4): 706–725.

Oswick, C., D. Grant, G. Michelson, and N. Wailes. 2005. "Looking Forwards: Discursive Directions in Organizational Change." *Journal of Organizational Change Management* 18(4): 383–390.

Palmer, I., and R. Dunford. 2008. "Organizational Change and the Importance of Embedded Assumptions." *British Journal of Management* 19: S20–S32.

Palmer, I., R. Dunford, and G. Akin. 2016. *Managing Organizational Change: A Multiple Perspectives Approach*. Boston, MA: McGraw-Hill International Editions.

Pondy, L.R. 1989. "Leadership is a Language Game." In *Readings in Managerial Psychology*, edited by H.J. Leavitt, L.R. Pondy, and D.M. Boje, 224–233. Chicago, IL: University of Chicago Press.

Salem, P. 2008. "The Seven Communication Reasons Organizations do not Change." *Corporate Communications: An International Journal* 13(3): 333–348.

Simões, P.M.M., and M. Esposito. 2014. "Improving Change Management: How Communication Nature Influences Resistance to Change." *Journal of Management Development* 33(4): 324–341.

Smircich, L., and G. Morgan. 1982. "Leadership: The Management of Meaning." *The Journal of Applied Behavioral Science* 18(3): 257–273.

Tsoukas, H. 2005. "Afterword: Why Language Matters in the Analysis of Organizational Change." *Journal of Organizational Change Management* 18(1): 96–104.

Tsoukas, H., and R. Chia. 2002. "On Organizational Becoming: Rethinking Organizational Change." *Organization Science* 13(5): 567–582.

Chapter 13

Resistance and organizational change readiness

Introduction and chapter questions

Belief in 'overcoming resistance to change' has been integral to the development of organizational change theories and practices. Many debates featured in other chapters start with a perception of resistance to change as the major organizational change problem which has to be overcome. Organizational members are frequently depicted as resisting organizational change emphasising and justifying the role of change leaders/managers in overcoming such resistance. In Kotter's (1996/2012) *Leading Change*, which has been cited over 6000 times (Hughes, 2016), resistors are repeatedly critically disparaged, for example:

> the key lies in understanding why organizations resist needed change... (page 16),
> Colin was typical of the foot draggers (page 104),
> these blockers stop needed action (page 114),
> ...quick performance improvements undermine the efforts of cynics and major league resisters (page 123).

However, are these stereotypes of individuals and organizations resisting the changes a leader proposes still relevant today? In order to answer this question, the focus is on two closely related themes of resistance to change and readiness for change. The initial focus of the chapter is the evolution of thinking about resistance to change and change readiness, followed by critical questioning of belief in resistance and change readiness. This chapter is organized around and provides answers to the following questions:

> How are practitioners engaging with resistance and readiness to change?
> How have studies into resistance to change chronologically evolved?
> What is change readiness and how does it inform theories and practices of organizational change?
> Have we underestimated the role of stability and continuity in organizational change?
> Does the language of resistance to change and change readiness impede understanding organizational change?
> How do critical scholars understand resistance to organizational change?

In the next section, practitioner oriented accounts of engaging with resistance to change and change readiness are featured by way of introducing the applied nature of these debates. The understanding section focuses on two themes of resistance to change and change readiness with the former dealt with chronologically and the latter as an organizational change concept which appears more recently to have caught the academic and practitioner imagination. The critical questioning section questions resistance to change and change readiness, asking if we have underestimated the role of stability and continuity in organizational change. Does the language of resistance and readiness impede understanding organizational change and how do critical scholars understand resistance to organizational change? Finally, the chapter is summarised, discussion questions raised and guidance offered with regard to navigating literature informing understanding about resistance to change and change readiness.

Resistance and organizational change readiness: what are practitioners doing?

An internet search reveals a large volume of guidance on how to overcome/manage resistance to organizational change (please see Table 13.1).

The practitioner guidance featured in Table 13.1 is just a small sample of the guidance available on the internet. The guidance in Table 13.1 illustrates belief in responding to resistance to change through the way that change is managed/led, but also

Table 13.1 Practitioner guidance on overcoming and managing resistance to organizational change

Five tips for managing resistance	Seven strategies for overcoming resistance to change in the workplace	How to overcome resistance to change in an organization
1 Get change management right the first time	1 Structure the team to maximise its potential	1 Create a way to communicate with employees about new initiatives
2 Expect resistance to change	2 Set challenging, achievable and engaging targets	2 Market the new strategy to each group
3 Address resistance formally	3 Resolve conflicts quickly and effectively	3 Invite a team member from each functional group to participate in meetings
4 Identify the root causes of resistance	4 Show passion	4 Select a group of change agents from key positions to help
5 Engage the right 'resistance' managers	5 Be persuasive	5 Develop key deliverables for each, department, organization and person
	6 Empower innovation and creativity	6 Tie successful implementation to compensation. Create at least four key milestones and goals to measure success
	7 Remain positive and Supportive	

Five tips for managing resistance: Source: www.prosci.com/.
Seven strategies for overcoming resistance to change in the workplace: Source: www.forwardfocusinc.com/inspire-leaders/7-strategies-for-overcoming-resistance-to-change-in-the-workplace/change-management/thought-leadership-library/managing-resistance-to-change.
How to overcome resistance to change in an organization: http://smallbusiness.chron.com/overcome-resistance-change-organization-154.html.

through cultivating certain behaviours and emphasising certain traits. There is also a suggestion in the third column that resistance can be overcome through group work (please see Chapter 8 for discussion about group dynamics).

Erwin and Garman (2010: 41) explicitly attempted to link research into resistance to organizational change with practice through reviewing research published in peer review journals since 1978. They posed the question 'What practice guidance does the findings of recent research provide to organizational change agents and managers in addressing individual resistance to organizational change?' They found that individual resistance to change was influenced by individual predispositions with regard to openness and resistance to change: how individuals considered the threats and benefits of change; communication, understanding, participation, trust in management, management styles, as well as, the nature of relationships with the change agents.

In terms of change readiness, the practitioner oriented *Harvard Business Review* website, highlighted four ways to know whether you are ready for change (Musselwhite and Plouffe, 2010). The authors believed that successful companies no longer regarded change as a discrete event to be managed, but rather as an opportunity to constantly evolve the business. Their implication was that all employees needed to be ready for change with change readiness now perceived as the new change management. Change readiness required a new mindset informed by change awareness, change agility, change reaction and change mechanisms. The requirements of the new mindset may be defined as follows. First, *change awareness* relates to how able the company is to reinvent itself through scanning the environment focusing on emerging trends and planning for the future. Second, *change agility* is about the ability of the company to engage people in pending changes. A company should have the capacity and commitment to carry a change initiative through. Third, *change reaction* is concerned with managing the reactions of employees. The authors ask, 'How does your organization react and respond to the crisis?' Fourth, *change mechanisms* are concerned with encouraging goal alignment, accountability for results and reward systems which reinforce change behaviours.

Theories of resistance to change and organizational change readiness

In reviewing the literature about attitudes towards change, Bouckenooghe (2010) found that 92 per cent of this literature was limited to two constructs: resistance to change and readiness for change. These two themes are the focus of this section with resistance explained chronologically in terms of how theories have evolved and readiness for change explained as a phenomenon gaining prominence since the 1990s.

The chronological evolution of resistance to organizational change studies

The study of resistance to organizational change commenced with the pioneering research of Coch and French (1948) at the Harwood Manufacturing Corporation in the United States. At this plant, new production methods were being introduced in response to increased post-World War II demand for consumer goods. Women mainly were employed to produce pyjamas. When they resisted the new production methods being introduced, plant management wanted to know why they were resisting change so strongly and what could be done to overcome this resistance. At the Harwood plant, researchers were able to experiment with varying group methods in order to test how methods impacted the reception of changes. Their first variation tested group participation through involvement of representatives in designing changes to jobs. Their second variation tested groups totally participating in designing changes and their third group was a control group.

> It is possible for management to modify greatly or to remove completely group resistance to changes in methods of work and the ensuing piece rates. This change can be accomplished by the use of group meetings in which management effectively communicates the need for change and stimulates group participation in planning the changes.
>
> (Coch and French, 1948: 531)

The write-up of this research appeared in one of the earliest issues of *Human Relations* at a time when studies of organizational change were just commencing. The research findings supported adopting a participative approach towards the implementation of organizational change. However, it was the paper's title 'overcoming resistance to change' which subsequently framed the debate. This wasn't the major learning from the research, but instead, the original problem which had concerned the Harwood plant management. Whilst Coch and French (1948) is still frequently cited, Burnes (2015) warns that the paper is frequently cited without being read. He highlighted Coch and French's (1948) work being part of a long-running series of experiments conducted by Kurt Lewin in the 1930s and 1940s. He provided a broader context to these developments and background information about Lester Coch who studied engineering before joining the US infantry and John French who received his PhD from Harvard University.

In seeking to understand resistance to change, it is important to understand the work of Kurt Lewin. In 1947, he established the National Training Laboratories yet died prematurely the same year (Burnes, 2004). Field theory, group dynamics, action research and the 3-step model in combination informed Lewin's approach to planned change. However, in terms of this chronology of resistance to change Lewin's contribution in terms of field theory is pertinent. Lewin highlighted individual behaviour as being a function of the group environment referred to as the 'field' (Burnes, 2004).

> Lewin argued that changes in behaviour only occur when the field changes, either by a decrease in the power of restraining forces or an increase in the power of driving forces.
>
> (Burnes, 2015: 99)

Coch and French's (1948) examination of resistance to change sought to identify/reduce forces acting to increase worker's resistance and promote those acting to reduce it and in changing workers' behaviour Coch and French had to ensure that Harwood's leaders modified how they managed change situations (Burnes, 2015). Burnes (2015) critically reflected upon why Coch and French's (1948) message and Lewin's situational perspective on resistance did not have greater influence. He argued that organizational development scholars chose to focus upon individuals as the source of change problems, largely ignoring the organizational context. The tool of a force field analysis is often attributed to the work of Kurt Lewin and the NTL researchers at this time. However, there is a need for caution. Swanson and Creed (2014) concluded after reviewing Kurt Lewin's writings that his intention was never to condense field theory into a modernistic map of external and internal organizational factors, although they acknowledge that this is how the change management literature has depicted and applied force field theory.

> The field is not a straight line with barriers, constraints, and enablers, as indicated in far too many articles, lectures slides and textbooks. Change does not occur unless the right combination of forces running in the right directions emerges in the individuals of a group in complex space–time configurations.
>
> (Swanson and Creed, 2014: 32)

Kotter (1996/2012) has featured prominently in this part of the textbook giving impetus to leading change. However, one of his earliest publications was co-authored (Kotter and Schlesinger, 1979). The article published in the practitioner magazine, *Harvard Business Review*, encouraged diagnosing resistance to change and the need to choose methods to overcome it. Kotter and Schlesinger (1979) identified what they believed to be the four most common reasons why employees were resisting change: a desire not to lose something of value, misunderstanding change and the implications of change, believing that a change did not make sense for an organization, and the existence of a low tolerance for change within certain individuals. Diagnosing reasons for resisting change subsequently informed the methods of dealing with resistance to change. The authors prescribed six potential approaches: education and communication, participation and involvement, facilitation and support, negotiation and agreement, manipulation and co-optation and explicit and implicit coercion. They acknowledged that different approaches could be used at different stages in a change process with potentially more than one approach used.

Ford and Ford (1994) made an important contribution to the debate, pulling together earlier strands of the debate. They revisited notions of resistance as based on forces for change and forces against change which they referred to as a dialectical view and revisited Kotter and Schlesinger's (1979) encouragement to overcome resistance to change. However, they chose to highlight resistance as an interpretation which an observer gave to a particular event or circumstance, rather than being some 'thing' to be overcome. This insight allows leaders/managers to adopt a very different strategy from that proposed by Kotter and Schlesinger (1979). Instead for those not engaged in a particular strategy, it may be fruitful to create a future strategy which they are attracted to and that they can relate to, rather than attempting to overcome their resistance.

Dent and Goldberg (1999: 26) explicitly challenged the concept of resistance to change and the misrepresentation of Kurt Lewin's writings '...the best way to challenge the conventional wisdom is to suggest that people do not resist change, per se'. They noted Kotter (1995) himself acknowledging that individual resistance was rare which was intriguing given his (Kotter, 1996/2012) later emphasis on resistance as problematic (please see the introduction to this chapter). They offered a critical review of the literature commencing with Coch and French (1948) tracing the ascendance of what they referred to as a 'bankrupt mental model'.

Oreg (2006) regarded resistance as a multi-faceted construct in his study of 177 largely male employees working within the defence industry as two core units merged. Primary data was collected via surveys with Oreg (2006) testing a set of hypotheses and developing a theoretical model of resistance to change. He found that some employees were more likely to experience negative emotions and act against organizational changes because of their dispositional inclination, rather than the particular nature of the change. He also found that an organization's leadership could negatively impact organizational change.

> ...lack of faith in the organization's leadership was strongly related to increased reports of anger, frustration, and anxiety with respect to the change, to increased actions against it, and in particular to negative evaluations of the need for, and value of, the organizational change.
>
> (Oreg, 2006: 93)

Oreg's (2006) empirical findings have far-reaching implications for managers and change agents meriting a synthesis of the learning from the research. First, employees' sense of challenge, autonomy and stimulation and trust in management were the most meaningful antecedents of resistance to change. Second, in terms of the atmosphere in which change was implemented trust in management was the dominant variable. Third, rather than thinking in terms of resistance versus acceptance, there is a need to consider ambivalence (Piderit, 2000) as a response. Fourth, given resistance to change is often based on valid concerns, resistance should be used to improve organizations and decision making. Finally, how employees feel about change predicts how they feel about their jobs.

In "Resistance to Change: The Rest of the Story", Ford et al. (2008) highlighted how prevailing views of resistance to change told a one-sided story favouring change agents and disparaging change recipients. They challenged the resistance to change story in three ways. First, they regarded resistance to change as a potentially self-serving and self-fulfilling label. Second, they highlighted how change agents contribute to the occurrence of the reactions labelled as resistance. Third, they highlighted such occurrences potentially being positive contributions to change. Their second way merits clarification as it initially appears paradoxical that change agents could contribute to resistance to change. However, resistance may occur as a consequence of change agents breaking agreements and violating trust. Resistance may occur through change agents' communication breakdowns, such as failing to legitimise change, misrepresenting participation and an absence of a call to action. Imagine your reaction to men and women in expensive designer suits coming into your workplace with their stopwatches and laptops. Ford et al. (2008) highlighted resistance as a resource with the value of resistance being to keep conversations about change ongoing, encouraging engagement with change processes and strengthening and improving the quality of decisions.

Thomas and Hardy (2011) in revisiting many of the references cited here detected two contrasting approaches to resistance: demonising resistance versus celebrating resistance to change. However, they regarded both approaches as problematic, instead arguing that power and resistance constituted organizational change, requiring the adoption of a critical approach to resistance to change (see questioning section for a discussion of such a critical approach).

Jones and Van de Ven (2016) researched change resistance in 40 healthcare clinics undergoing significant organizational change over three years, with a real strength of this research being its extended nature. They found that resistance to change had important consequences for employees' commitment to the organization and perceptions of organizational effectiveness. These relationships became stronger (rather than weaker) suggesting that effects of resistance to change festered. More positively, they found that over time supportive leadership increasingly impacted reducing change resistance. Practice implications were that change agents needed to address employee resistance because left unchecked, it could fester and cause harm. Supportive leadership behaviours helped to ameliorate resistance to change.

Change readiness for organizational change

Bouckenooghe (2010) highlighted Jacobson (1957) first coining the term readiness for change. However, it was Armenakis et al. (1993) who appear to have fuelled and given impetus to current interest into readiness for change. Armenakis et al. (1993) likened change readiness to Lewin's (1951) concept of unfreezing and revisited Coch and French's (1948) study and their emphasis upon participation in processes of change. Change readiness was described 'as organizational members' beliefs, attitudes and intentions regarding the extent to which changes are needed and the organization's capacity to successfully make those changes' (Armenakis et al., 1993: 681). The primary mechanism for creating change readiness was the message for change, which they argued needed to incorporate the need for change and the perceived ability to change. This allowed them to develop a typology of four change readiness programmes using the change readiness of employees and the urgency of the change as the means of differentiation.

1   *Low readiness/Low urgency (aggressive)* – When employees are not ready for change and there is ample time to create readiness a comprehensive readiness programme is required.
2   *Low readiness/High urgency (crisis)* – When employees are not ready for change, but there is great urgency the system needs a jolt.
3   *High readiness/Low urgency (maintenance)* – When employees are ready for change, but there is little urgency the emphasis should be on maintaining change readiness.
4   *High readiness/High urgency (quick response)* – When employees are ready for change and the time for implementation is short, the challenge is to maintain change readiness energy.

Armenakis et al. (1993) regarded the readiness concept as complementing rather than replacing Kotter and Schlesinger's (1979) account of resistance to change and other accounts of resistance to change. They felt that it was important to build readiness within the context facing the organization. In implementing readiness programmes,

Table 13.2 Key change beliefs (based on Armenakis and Harris, 2009)

Change belief	Definition
Discrepancy	The belief that a change is required (the gap between the current state and as it should be).
Appropriateness	The belief that the change designed to address the discrepancy is the correct choice.
Efficacy	The belief that the organization and the change recipient can implement the change effectively.
Principal support	The belief that formal leaders (vertical change agents) are committed to the success of the change.
Valence	The belief that the change will be beneficial for the change recipient.

they argued that these should be guided by the readiness of employees and the urgency of the changes. They used Whirlpool's aggressive change readiness programme as an illustrative case study, regarding change readiness as a cognitive precursor to potential resistance to change.

Subsequent academic accounts of change readiness have studied different aspects of it. Rafferty et al. (2013) presented an informative multilevel theoretical review of the change readiness literature highlighting two limitations in this literature. First, whilst key cognitions underlying change readiness were understood, the affective element was not understood. Second, a multilevel perspective had not been adopted. They were able to present a multilevel perspective identifying the antecedents and consequences for individual, work group, and organizational change readiness.

A common question raised when organizations change – is what is in it for me? Vakola's (2014) research with 183 employees in a Greek technological company examined individual readiness to change and the impact of the perceived impact of organizational change on personality and context characteristics. The perceived impact of the change was found to mediate relations between the pre-change conditions, work attitudes and individual readiness to change.

Armenakis and Harris (2009) reflected upon their 30 years of researching organizational change. They contrasted their favoured change recipient, employee-centric approach with a leader-centric approach such as Kotter (1996/2012). Armenakis and Harris (2009: 128) highlighted the central question which had interested them in their studies: 'What do change recipients consider when making their decision to embrace and support a change effort or reject and resist it?' In revisiting Armenakis et al. (1993), they identified five key change beliefs underpinning change recipients' motives to change (please see Table 13.2).

In Table 13.2, a positive approach to change recipients' beliefs in change is evident, which is very different from depictions of change recipients resisting change. Armenakis and Harris (2009: 132), make this contrast in the following quotation 'we prefer using the term readiness instead of resistance because readiness is more congruent with the roles that coaches and champions play in introducing change. In other words, it fits better with a positive approach to framing change' (please see discussion of framing in the previous chapter). The literature featured here has reflected an apparent shift from negative depictions of employees resisting change towards positive depictions of employees being change ready. However, in thinking critically about organizational change how might such beliefs be questioned?

Questioning resistance and organizational change readiness

The title of Coch and French's (1948) paper 'overcoming resistance to change' subsequently framed debates featured here, both in terms of resistance and change readiness. However, theories and practices of organizational change need to be as dynamic and open to change as the changes that they seek to inform. In critically reflecting back on these debates, three questions merit further consideration:

- Have we underestimated the role of stability and continuity in organizational change?
- Does the language of resistance to change and change readiness impede understanding organizational change?
- How do critical scholars understand resistance to organizational change?

Have we underestimated the role of stability and continuity in organizational change?

Organizational change offers societies and organizations the potential for improvement and development, for example, improving the quality of care at a hospital, avoiding redundancies through turning around a failing supermarket chain and enabling multi-agency working amongst voluntary organizations. However, the danger inherent within such celebrations is potentially that we underestimate the importance of stability at the individual level and continuities at the organizational level. These themes will be revisited in Part IV in terms of managing and leading change and the sustainability of change initiatives (please see Chapter 18).

Individuals, groups, and teams are likely to experience a degree of stability even in organizations undergoing significant organizational change. For example, workplace friendships can be sustained over decades even with a high staff turnover. An office may remain largely the same despite the introduction of innovative new technology. Stability in our lives may be perceived in a manner similar to the stabilisers on a child's bicycle. They allow the child to move forwards whilst simultaneously maintaining the child's stability. Change is frequently depicted as the only constant and in terms of the human lifecycle we do experience constant change, but we also experience elements of stability in our work, rest and play. Alvin Toffler (1990) in *Future Shock* suggested that we are reliant upon stability zones with an implication that we can deal with change in certain aspects of our life, but not all aspects of our lives. A partner challenging another late night at the office, or a child objecting to a new babysitter (Conner, 1998) may be depicted as resisting change, but may not necessarily be irrational (see Marris's, 1974 acknowledgement of the impulse of conservatism). At an individual level, maintaining stability may be a rational response to change rather than irrational resistance.

At an organizational level, attempts to overcome resistance to change imply that change is beneficial, underestimating continuities which inevitably exist within any organization. For example, a successful hospital delivering health services even if it is undergoing significant change will seek to maintain continuities in terms of the existing quality of healthcare. Whilst, UK universities are beginning to experience significant organizational change particularly in terms of digital transformation, they still consciously choose to celebrate continuities with the past, exemplified through graduation ceremonies with caps, gowns and ancient rituals. If stability acts as stabilisers for individuals experiencing organizational change, acknowledging continuities may act as a handbrake for organizations preoccupied with constantly changing everything.

This is not a new argument in the hype of leading and managing organizational change. Eccles and Nohria (1992) found arguments for maintaining the status quo hard to find and hard to defend. However, organizations, do not necessarily need to change all the time (Abrahamson, 2000). Reed (2001) suggested that belief in constantly re-engineering existing processes raised anxiety levels and ignored good practices which may have gone before. For Sturdy and Grey (2003), change and continuity were not alternative states, but instead, they were coexistent and coterminous, with what constitutes a change or continuity perspective dependent. Success and failure breed new demands for organizational change with only the absence of change perceived as a deficiency (Sorge and van Witteloostuijn, 2004). Abrahamson (2000: 76), even subversively, coined a new phrase 'dynamic stability', which he defined as 'a process of continual but relatively small change efforts that involve the reconfiguration of existing practices and business models rather than the creation of new ones'.

Perhaps, we really do need more messages about old-fashioned stability (Mintzberg et al., 2009). The role of stability and continuities in organizational change does appear to have been underestimated in attempts to overcome resistance to change and encourage change readiness.

Does the language of resistance to change and change readiness impede understanding organizational change?

In this chapter, interest in resistance to change has been depicted as being superseded by change readiness. Resistance to change implies a negative individualistic orientation which should be discouraged, whereas change readiness implies a positive individualistic orientation which should be encouraged. In many ways, these approaches are opposite sides of the same coin, with Armenakis et al. (1993) regarding change readiness as a cognitive precursor to dealing with resistance to change.

The language of resistance to change and change readiness is far from neutral with assumptions embedded in such language. Turning to national politics, we do not talk about the government and the resistance. We talk about the government and the opposition with resistance only referred to in times of war. Embedded in the language of resisting organizational change are notions that such activities are dysfunctional and unacceptable. Even the language of government in terms of 'opposition' would be more honest and constructive, than 'resistance to change'. The language of resistance to change attributes the blame for rejection (or even delay in acceptance) onto the potential recipients of the proposed change. Whereas change readiness attributions praise the recipients of a proposed change for being ready for a change allowing individuals, groups and teams to be evaluated in terms of their apparent change readiness. Positive attributions of employees being change ready signal to other employees what is expected of them. The language may appear positive, but the intent is highly normative. The language of resistance to change and change readiness focusses upon individuals as change recipients. However, Ford et al. (2002: 106) challenged individual-based explanations of resistance to organizational change 'resistance, therefore, is not to be found "in the individual" but in the constructed reality in which individuals operate'. In critically questioning the language in use, simplistic dualisms of resisting/not resisting and change ready/not change ready are encouraged which misrepresent and misunderstand the subtleties and complexities of organizational change as featured in earlier chapters.

Whilst it is apparent why such biased language might be adopted, such manipulative language may not serve the best interests of organizations or individual leaders/ managers. In Chapter 12, Morrison and Milliken's (2000) concept of organizational silence was introduced in terms of organizational members withholding opinions and concerns about organizational problems. One implication of the problematic language of resistance to change and change readiness is that organizational members are discouraged from expressing their resistance to particular changes and encouraged to express their readiness for particular changes. However, this artificial compliance may not be in anyone's best interests. For Piderit (2000) resistance to change terminology had taken us as far as we could go, and she encouraged retiring the phrase 'resistance to change' (see also Merron, 1993, and Dent and Goldberg, 2000 and Ford et al., 2008). The language of resistance to change and change readiness through explicit biases and implicit assumptions impedes understanding organizational change.

How do critical scholars understand resistance to organizational change?

This chapter has focussed chronologically on the evolution of thinking about resistance to change. Resistance was initially depicted as dysfunctional and something which had to be overcome. However, subsequently there was an acknowledgement that recipient responses potentially played a role in change initiatives as recipients became change ready. In questioning resistance to change, the final contribution is far more radical. The focus now shifts towards challenging organizational change and celebrating the resistance of change recipients. Ybema et al. (2016) in their contribution to *The Sage Handbook of Resistance* (Courpasson and Vallas, 2016) were particularly interested in identity and how debates featured here created very different identities for 'change agents', 'change recipients' and 'resistant subjects'.

They presented three different approaches to resistance and organizational change as:

- promoting change/demonising resistance,
- promoting change/celebrating resistance and
- challenging change/celebrating resistance.

They referred to the first approach as traditional, in that it demonised resistance and adopted an unequivocal managerial orientation towards organizational change. They regarded the second approach as also having a managerial orientation although now regarding resistance positively. This would be compatible with many accounts of resistance to change from the mid-1990s onwards. The third critical approach celebrated resistance through challenging managerialism and change. The first two approaches which have featured prominently throughout the chapter do not require restating. The third critical approach offers a different and far more radical way to think about resistance and organizational change.

Instead of following a managerial agenda, the third approach is critical about organizational change and the oppressive nature of contemporary work practices (see Chapter 16 for further discussion about the dark side of change and transformation). The critical approach regards resistance to changes as legitimate and desirable, given the exploitative nature of organizational change. Critical scholars understand the employee no longer as a willing change recipient, but as a resistant subject, obliged to resist those changes being imposed.

Summary

The chapter may be succinctly summarised through answering the questions posed in the chapter's introduction, the original questions are restated in italics.

How are practitioners engaging with resistance and readiness to change? The practitioner guidance encouraged responding to resistance to change through the way that change was managed/led, but also through cultivating certain behaviours and emphasising certain traits. There was also a suggestion that resistance could be overcome through group work.

How have studies into resistance to change chronologically evolved? The study of resistance to organizational change commenced with the pioneering research of Coch and French (1948). Their research findings supported adopting a participative approach towards the implementation of organizational change. However, it was the paper's title 'overcoming resistance to change' which subsequently framed the debate.

In 'Resistance to Change: The Rest of the Story', Ford et al. (2008) highlighted how prevailing views of resistance to change told a one-sided story favouring change agents and disparaging change recipients. Ford et al. (2008) highlighted resistance as a resource with the value of resistance being to keep conversations about change going, encouraging engagement with change and strengthening and improving the quality of decisions.

What is change readiness and how does it inform theories and practices of organizational change? Jacobson (1957) first coined the term readiness for change. However, Armenakis et al. (1993: 681) fuelled and gave impetus to current interest in readiness for change, describing it 'as organizational members' beliefs, attitudes and intentions regarding the extent to which changes are needed and the organization's capacity to successfully make those changes'.

Have we underestimated the role of stability and continuity in organizational change? The danger inherent in celebrating organizational change is underestimating the importance of stability at the individual level and continuities at the organizational level. Individuals, groups, and teams are likely to experience a degree of stability even in organizations undergoing significant organizational change. At an organizational level, attempts to overcome resistance to change imply that change is beneficial underestimating continuities which inevitably exist within any organization.

Does the language of resistance to change and change readiness impede understanding organizational change? Resistance to change implies a negative individualistic orientation which should be discouraged, whereas change readiness implies a positive individualistic orientation which should be encouraged. The language of resistance to change and change readiness is far from neutral with assumptions embedded in the language in use.

How do critical scholars understand the resistance to organizational change? The third approach is critical about organizational change and the oppressive nature of contemporary work practices, regarding resistance to change as legitimate and desirable, given the exploitative nature of organizational change.

Research case study showcase: resisting change in a New South Wales credit union

Cutcher's (2009) research case study of resisting change in a New South Wales credit union reported in the *Journal of Organizational Change Management* is showcased here. For the full case study and further analysis, please visit the original source.

Case study source

The case study of Coast (a pseudonym) was part of a larger study into changing relationships between banks and their customers. Coast was a medium-sized credit union servicing rural and regional communities in New South Wales, Australia.

The focus of the case study was the resistance to change by Coast's front-line employees. Coast employed approximately 100 people located in 15 branches at the time of the research. The branch network was made up of three regions: Northern, Central and Southern with the Southern region the focus for the case study. The general manager had provided research access to the Southern region as he was keen to learn why staff in this region were having so much trouble adapting to a new sales strategy. Five managers, all of whom were male, and 15 front-line service employees all of whom were female were interviewed in Coast. The names of staff in the case study are pseudonyms. Interviews were carried out at four branches, all interviews were semi-structured ranging from 45 minutes to 90 minutes.

Cutcher, L., 2009. "Resisting Change from Within and Without the Organi-zation." *Journal of Organizational Change Management* 22(3): 275–289.

Case study

For Cutcher (2009) it was important that the reader understood the context of the changes happening at Coast before attempting to understand the resistance to these changes. This is mirrored in the following discussion, first, focusing on organizational change in context at Coast, and second, focusing on resisting organizational change at Coast.

Organizational change in context at Coast

The management of Coast were largely responding to deregulation of financial services which had begun in Australia in the 1980s and continued throughout the 1990s. This deregulation resulted in credit unions facing more regulatory change than for-profit banks, which was a consequence of the government wanting to 'create a level playing field' for deposit-taking institutions. In par-ticular, this meant the removal of special provisions for credit unions, which included losing their tax-exempt status. Credit unions such as Coast had to adopt strategies of the large for-profit competitors. A 'discourse of enterprise' which privileged competitiveness and individuality was introduced in order to move away from the co-operativeness and mutuality of the traditional values of credit unions.

In Southern region towns, Coast was the only financial institution offering a branch facility for residents. Large retail banks closed during the bank closures which took place in the 1990s with the closure of more than 7,000 branches. The southern branches of Coast were small shop-front offices on shopping strips of towns. Coast maintained branches when other bank branches closed. This was because as a not-for-profit credit union, they did not have to make returns to shareholders, instead returning surpluses to providing services for members. However, as a consequence of the deregulation mentioned earlier, Coast had to move its emphasis from service to sales, reimagining its members through the concept of 'customer as member'. Coast as a credit union now mimicked large retail bank practices. There was a contradiction between these practices based on sales targets and customer segmentation and the principles of a not for-profit organization with a philosophy of mutuality.

(Continued)

Table 13.3 Two perspectives on the new sales strategy at Coast (based on Cutcher, 2009)

If their performance doesn't improve they won't be staying here for very much longer. It is either improve and we give them all the resources and all the help, or go. (p. 281)	*There is the stress from the sales; we have to be thinking, thinking. Then we get stressed, if we get sick. Who can cover us? No-one. It really scared me and I haven't been right and I kept getting sick all the time. I feel like I need to go to the toilet all the time. I would think about work and almost start crying (p. 281).*
John (Branch manager)	Ruth (Front-line employee)

It was not just that the relationship between the credit union and its members changed. The role of front-line employees also changed from providing customer service to selling financial products. Front-line employees in the Southern region were expected to meet the same sales targets as those for employees working in towns in the more affluent central and northern regions. Interviews with branch managers revealed their impatience with employees in not making changes required by the new sales strategy (please see Table 13.3).

In Table 13.3, two very different perspectives are apparent. For the general manager and branch managers the assumption was that employee resistance to change was due to uneasiness with sales which resulted in front-line employees 'non-coping'. However, Cutcher's (2009: 281) research revealed that 'it was not that the employees could not make the shift from service to sales; they would not make the shift'.

Resisting organizational change at Coast

In credit unions, the word 'member', rather than 'customer' was used in order to reflect that as a mutual they were owned by their members. Front-line service employees never referred to customers, reiterating the importance of the distinction between 'members' and 'customers', whereas branch managers did use 'customer' and 'member' interchangeably.

> Well, it is interesting because we have always said members, always, always, and our General Manager released some articles sometime ago and said, 'Our customers'. And we brought it up in a meeting and asked our manager why is he calling them customers? And he said 'Well everyone is a customer'. And I was like that is totally changing the whole philosophy that I joined a credit union for.
>
> *(Anne cited by Cutcher, 2009: 281)*

Employees realised the significance of a changing discourse of 'customers', as well as, the significance of changes to their job titles. Whilst, job titles were changed to 'Sales Consultants', employees resisted in continuing to refer to themselves as 'Member Service Officers'.

I always thought credit unions were there for their members. I would never sell or push a product onto somebody that wouldn't help them and if that means I don't meet sales targets then I don't meet sales targets.

(Ruth cited by Cutcher, 2009: 281)

The new sales strategy was resisted by employees, not only because it required them to think about 'members' more instrumentally, but because it also threatened their self-identity as helping, caring individuals. Self-identification was important allowing them to project an alternative identity drawing on a 'discourse of mutuality' in identifying themselves as service workers. They also resisted attempts by the branch manager encouraging them to compete with each other over sales targets. They had grown up with each other and did not want to compete against each other. They entered the daily sales figures so that rewards were evenly shared.

> The tactics of resistance they employed drew on a solidarity forged with each other both inside and outside the workplace. They were friends, they lived in the same communities, and their resistance was aimed at protecting those friendships and a sense of belonging to a community.
>
> *(Cutcher, 2009: 284)*

Case study questions

1   Why does Cutcher (2009) emphasise understanding the credit union's context in order to understand this example of resistance to change?
2   How might Armenakis and Harris's (2009) key change beliefs (please see Table 13.2) offer an explanation of why the changes were being resisted?

Discussion questions

1   Is it possible to live a fulfilling life without resisting everyday changes?
2   Why is resistance to change problematic for those managing change?
3   Why was there a shift from 'resistance to change' to 'change readiness'?
4   Why is organizational change more fashionable than organizational stability?

Navigating the resistance and organizational change readiness literature

Debates featured in this chapter draw on a wide range of academic disciplines and fields of study. In particular, psychology helps us to understand individual attitudes and behaviours and group dynamics with regards to organizational change. Sociology and political science speak to societal beliefs in conformity and change, as well as, how social movements resist or embrace change. The organizational change literature in this area has a distinctly functionalist/rational perspective with debates often framed in terms of overcoming resistance to change. However, in recent times, academics have encouraged a shift in thinking towards understanding the diversity of responses to organizational change.

Any review of this literature should start with "Overcoming Resistance to Change" (Coch and French, 1948). This is where the debate began and unfortunately too often the debate doesn't gain any more sophistication than the title of this paper. "Choosing Strategies for Change" (Kotter and Schlesinger, 1979) reinforced this framing in terms of managers diagnosing resistance and then choosing strategies to deal with this resistance. This article was published in the practitioner magazine *Harvard Business Review*. Whilst the magazine is highly influential, it does not benefit from the peer review of an academic journal. For example, Kotter and Schlesinger (1979: 107) acknowledged 'the methods described are based on our analyses of dozens of successful and unsuccessful organizational changes'. The warning when navigating this literature is that practitioner concerns often prevail over research informed accounts. The debate has evolved through coverage in peer-reviewed journals with papers benefiting from critical peer-review. The *Journal of Change Management* and the *Journal of Organizational Change Management*, as organizational change focussed journals, have published papers relevant to themes in this chapter. Less obvious is *The Journal of Applied Behavioral Science*, founded by the NTL Institute where Kurt Lewin and colleagues undertook their pioneering work and the journal in recent years has published influential studies of change readiness.

In the 1990s and 2000s, substantial critical questioning of resistance to change was published. This literature appears to have influenced the orthodoxy of organizational change studies to such an extent that far less has been written about resistance to change in the current decade. The concept of change readiness is a far more recent development and to date, it hasn't come under the same critical scrutiny as resistance to change. Published literature reviews can help navigate the literature featured here, with Oreg et al.'s (2011) review of quantitative studies into change recipients' reactions to organizational change particularly informative.

In terms of books, whilst the title suggests innovation studies, *Resistance to Innovation: Its Sources and Manifestations* (Oreg and Goldenberg, 2015) offers an overview and commentary on Shaul Oreg's contribution to debates about resistance to organizational change. *The Sage Handbook of Resistance* (Courpasson and Vallas, 2016) is far broader than the organizational change focus of this chapter, but in offering theoretical essays by leading scholars, debates are located in wider societal concerns. This handbook is divided into six sections: foundations, sites of resistance, technologies of resistance, languages of resistance, geographies of resistance and consequences of resistance.

References

Abrahamson, E. 2000. "Change Without Pain." *Harvard Business Review* 78(4): 75–79.

Armenakis, A.A., and S.G. Harris. 2009. "Reflections: Our Journey in Organizational Change Research and Practice." *Journal of Change Management* 9(2): 127–142.

Armenakis, A.A., S.G. Harris, and K.W. Mossholder. 1993. "Creating Readiness for Organizational Change." *Human Relations* 46(6): 681–703.

Bouckenooghe, D. 2010. "Positioning Change Recipients' Attitudes Toward Change in the Organizational Change Literature." *The Journal of Applied Behavioral Science* 46(4): 500–531.

Burnes, B. 2004. "Kurt Lewin and the Planned Approach to Change: A Re-appraisal." *Journal of Management Studies* 41(6): 977–1002.

Burnes, B. 2015. "Understanding Resistance to Change – Building on Coch and French." *Journal of Change Management* 15(2): 92–116.

Coch, L., and J.R.P. French (Jr). 1948. "Overcoming Resistance to Change." *Human Relations* 1(4): 512–532.

Conner, D.R. 1998. *Managing at the Speed of Change*. Chichester: John Wiley and Sons.

Courpasson, D., and S. Vallas (Eds). 2016. *The Sage Handbook of Resistance*. Thousand Oaks, CA: Sage Publications.

Cutcher, L. 2009. "Resisting Change from Within and Without the Organization." *Journal of Organizational Change Management* 22(3): 275–289.

Dent, E.B., and S.G. Goldberg. 1999. "Challenging 'Resistance to Change'." *Journal of Applied Behavioral Sciences* 35(1): 25–41.

Eccles, R.G., and N. Nohria. 1992. *Beyond the Hype: Rediscovering the Essence of Management*. Cambridge, MA: Harvard Business School Press.

Erwin, D.G., and A.N. Garman. 2010. "Resistance to Organizational Change: Linking Research and Practice." *Leadership and Organization Development* 31(1): 39–56.

Ford, J.D., and L.W. Ford. 1994. "Logics of Identity, Contradiction, and Attraction in Change." *Academy of Management Review* 19(4): 756–785.

Ford, J.D., L.W. Ford, and R.T. McNamara. 2002. "Resistance and the Background Conversations of Change." *Journal of Organizational Change Management* 15(2): 105–121.

Ford, J.D., L.W. Ford, and A. D 'Amelio. 2008. "Resistance to Change: The Rest of the Story." *Academy of Management Review* 33(2): 362–377.

Hughes, M. 2016. *The Leadership of Organizational Change*. London: Routledge.

Jacobson, E.H. 1957. "The Effect of Changing Industrial Methods and Automation on Personnel." Paper presented at the *Symposium on Preventive and Social Psychiatry*. Washington, DC.

Jones, S.L., and A.H. Van de Ven. 2016. "The Changing Nature of Change Resistance: An Examination of the Moderating Impact of Time." *The Journal of Applied Behavioral Science* 52(4): 482–506.

Kotter, J.P. 1995. "Leading Change: Why Transformation Efforts Fail." *Harvard Business Review* 73(2): 59–67.

Kotter, J.P. 1996/2012. *Leading Change*. Boston, MA: Harvard Business School Press.

Kotter, J.P., and L.A. Schlesinger. 1979. "Choosing Strategies for Change." *Harvard Business Review* 57(2): 106–114.

Lewin, K. 1951. *Field Theory in Social Science*. New York: Harper and Row.

Marris, P. 1974. *Loss and Change*. London: Routledge and Kegan Paul.

Merron, K. 1993. "Let's Bury the Term 'Resistance'." *Organizational Development Journal* 11(4): 77–86.

Mintzberg, H., B. Ahlstrand, and J. Lampel. 2009. *Strategy Safari: The Complete Guide Through the Wilds of Strategic Management*. London: FT Prentice Hall.

Morrison, E.W., and F.J. Milliken. 2000. "Organizational Silence: A Barrier to Change and Development in a Pluralistic World." *Academy of Management Review* 25(4): 706–725.

Musselwhite, C., and T. Plouffe. 2010. "Four Ways to Know Whether you are Ready for Change." Article published online at *Harvard Business Review* website. Available at https://hbr.org/2010/06/four-ways-to-know-whether-you. Accessed 28 April 17.

Oreg, S. 2006. "Personality, Context, and Resistance to Organizational Change." *European Journal of Work and Organizational Psychology* 15(1): 73–101.

Oreg, S., and Goldenberg, J. 2015. *Resistance to Innovation: Its Sources and Manifestations*. Chicago, IL: University of Chicago Press.

Oreg, S., M. Vakola, and A. Armenakis. 2011. "Change Recipients' Reactions to Organizational Change: A 60-Year Review of Quantitative Studies." *The Journal of Applied Behavioral Science* 47(4): 461–524.

Piderit, S.K. 2000. "Rethinking Resistance and Recognizing Ambivalence: A Multidimensional View of Attitudes Toward an Organizational Change." *Academy of Management Review* 25(4): 783–794.

Rafferty, A.E., N.L. Jimmieson, and A.A. Armenakis. 2013. "Change Readiness: A Multilevel Review." *Journal of Management* 39(1): 110–135.

Reed, P.J. 2001. *Extraordinary Leadership: Creating Strategies for Change.* London: Kogan Page.

Sorge, A., and A. van Witteloostuijn. 2004. "The (Non) sense of Organizational Change: An Essay About Universal Management Hypes, Sick Consultancy Metaphors and Healthy Organization Theories." *Organization Studies* 25(7): 1205–1231.

Sturdy, A., and C. Grey. 2003. "Beneath and Beyond Organizational Change Management: Exploring Alternatives." *Organization* 10(4): 651–662.

Swanson, D.J., and A.S. Creed. 2014. "Sharpening the Focus of Force Field Analysis." *Journal of Change Management* 14(1): 28–47.

Thomas, R., and C. Hardy. 2011. "Reframing Resistance to Organizational Change." *Scandinavian Journal of Management* 27(3): 322–331.

Toffler, A. 1990. *Future Shock.* New York: Bantam.

Vakola, M. 2014. "What's in There for Me? Individual Readiness to Change and the Perceived Impact of Organizational Change." *Leadership and Organization Development Journal* 35(3): 195–209.

Ybema, S., R. Thomas, and C. Hardy. 2016. "Organizational Change and Resistance: An Identity Perspective." In *The Sage Handbook of Resistance*, edited by D. Courpasson., and S. Vallas, 386–404. London: Sage Publications.

Part IV

Managing and leading organizational change

Chapter 14

Managers, leaders and the agents of change

Introduction and chapter questions

The central theme of this chapter is who makes change happen. Is it leaders, or managers, or is change agency dispersed amongst organizational members? The chapter features a debate which is more contested than might initially be imagined: who makes change happen closely relates to culture (Chapter 6), power and politics (Chapter 11) and communications (Chapter 12). The most appropriate means of making change happen will vary between organizations and between change initiatives (please see Chapter 2). In one of the earliest accounts of planned change, *The Dynamics of Planned Change*, Lippitt et al. (1958: 10) discussed professional change agents with a footnote introducing change agents to their readers.

> The term was adopted by the National Training Laboratory staff in 1947 to facilitate discussions among heterogeneous groups of professional helpers. It is a term which has since proved very useful.

This term has subsequently proved useful. However, in beginning to study change agents, there is a need to clarify competing terminology of change agents, agency and champions and the meanings of such terminology. There isn't a consensus definition of a change agent, but Wylie et al.'s (2014: 100) definition of a change agent is favoured here '...specialist staff who provide change advice, facilitation and management, typically on a project/programme basis'. Straightaway, we see the breadth of activities which may be included or excluded. Also, the definition in referring to specialist staff highlights other staff whom may be involved, such as organizational development, human resource management and project management staff. In this chapter, sometimes 'agent' is referred to and at other times 'agency'. Agency acknowledges the plurality of actors or players involved in change processes (Buchanan and Badham, 2008). Another term sometimes used in the context of change agency is 'change champion'. Schon (1963), in focussing upon innovation studies in his contribution, referred to champions with practitioners often favouring 'champion' terminology. Academics appear to favour 'agent/agency' terminology, although there is no consistency in how these competing terms are applied.

This chapter is organized around and provides answers to the following questions about managers, leaders and the agents of change:

> In terms of making change happen – what are practitioners doing?
> What are the potential roles for leaders, managers, consultants and teams in change agency?

What do we know about the dispersal of change agency?

How do different discourses inform change agency?

Is the differentiation between managing change and leading change a false dichotomy?

Why is change agent-centric thinking problematic?

What challenges do dispersing change agency and change agency discourses raise?

In the next section, accounts of how practitioners make change happen are featured. This is followed by a section focussed on understanding agency and change informed by three sub-sections. First, Caldwell's (2003) classification in terms of leadership, management, consultancy and team based change agency roles is featured. Second, issues raised by dispersing change agency are featured and third, how different discourses inform change agency are discussed. It is necessary to critically question explanations of agency and change with such questioning focussing upon a potential false dichotomy between leaders and managers, the problematic nature of change agent-centric thinking and the challenges of dispersed change agency and discourses of change agency. Finally, the chapter is summarised, discussion questions raised and guidance offered with regards to navigating the change agency literature.

Making change happen: what are practitioners doing?

In reviewing the literature, the practitioner literature often appears more engaged with change agency than the academic literature, although prescriptions for what works can be many and varied. This literature is featured as a means of introducing change agency practices and academic debates informing such processes.

In Table 14.1, website guidance on making change happen is featured. In each instance, the guidance is positive and encouraging, favouring step-based approaches which require managers to take steps.

Table 14.1 Practitioner guidance on making change happen

Making change happen, and making it stick (Harshak et al., 2010)	Five steps to successful change (NCVO, 2014)	All talk, no action? A 5-step guide to make change happen within your organization (Cozad, 2016)
The five success factors:	1 Acknowledge and understand the need for change	1 Understand what you want
1 Understand and spell out the impact of the change on people	2 Communicate the need and involve people in developing the change	2 Test the waters
2 Build an emotional and rational case for change		3 Build your plan
3 Ensure that the entire leadership team is a role model for the change	3 Develop change plans	4 Anticipate resistance
4 Mobilise your people to "own" and accelerate the change	4 Implement change plans	5 Give a great presentation
5 Embed the change in the fabric of the organization	5 Evaluate progress and celebrate success	

Table 14.2 Practitioner accounts of change champions

Make change sustainable with change champions (Pickering, 2009)	10 characteristics of a change champion (Gordon, 2015)	8 traits of a change management champion (Portier, 2016)
1 Change programmes fail because people do not change their behaviour 2 Change champions can make change a success 3 Identifying the right change champions is one of the secrets of success 4 Don't leave change to chance	1 A willingness to listen to new ideas 2 They are good networkers 3 A focus on solutions 4 Understanding of the organization 5 Not afraid to take risks 6 Able to communicate the positives 7 Not afraid to ask for help 8 They are people focussed 9 Not afraid to speak up 10 They are values-driven	1 Enthusiasm and willingness to learn new things! 2 Excellent communication skills, both written and verbal! 3 Coaching and facilitation skills – like a superhero! 4 Interpersonal skills; the ability to build rapport and motivate individuals! 5 Effective listening skills! 6 Ability to represent the needs and interests of all functional or business areas! 7 Unwavering energy and leadership efforts throughout the change cycle! 8 Ability to plan and execute activities with creativity and specificity!

Table 14.3 Competencies of effective change agents (Buchanan and Boddy, 1992)

Goals
  i Sensitivity to change in key personnel, top management perceptions and market conditions.
  ii Clarity in specifying goals, in defining the achievable.
  iii Flexibility in responding to changes with the control of the project manager.

Roles
  iv Team-building activities, to bring together key stakeholders and establish effective work groups.
  v Networking skills in establishing and maintaining appropriate contacts within and outside the organization.
  vi Tolerance of ambiguity, to be able to function comfortably.

Communication
  vii Communication skills to transmit effectively to colleagues and subordinates.
  viii Iterpersonal skills.
  ix Personal enthusiasm, in expressing plans and ideas.
  x Stimulating motivation and commitment in others involved.

Negotiation
  xi Selling plans and ideas to others, by creating a desirable and challenging vision of the future.
  xii Negotiating with key players for resources or for changes in procedures and to resolve the conflict.

Managing Up
  xiii Political awareness, in identifying potential coalitions and in balancing conflicting goals and perceptions.
  xiv Influencing skills, to gain commitment to project plans and ideas.
  xv Helicopter perspective, to stand back from the immediate project and take a broader view of priorities.

In Table 14.2, website guidance for change champions is featured. In the first column, positive encouragement for change champions is offered. In the second and third columns, the characteristics and traits of change champions are featured. Whilst, again these job profiles are encouraging, they may pay insufficient attention to change agency requirements of different types of organization and change. In a now out-of-print book, *The Expertise of the Change Agent,* Buchanan and Boddy (1992) highlighted the requirements of a change agent informed by a systematic review of the 15 competencies of effective change agents. However, they knowingly warned about the dangers of following such a prescriptive path (please see Table 14.3).

In Table 14.3, we begin to appreciate the type of practical challenges change agents/champions are likely to encounter, although again there is a need for caution here. If we could build a super change agent/champion, it is doubtful that she/he would be super for all changes and for all scenarios. For example, a change agent working on the relocation of the head office of a voluntary sector organization would face very different challenges from a change agent seeking to redesign business processes of the IT department of a global bank. In seeking to understand change agency, the next section presents an overview of advances in academic thinking.

Understanding change agency

In this section, three themes will be developed: first, revisiting Caldwell's (2003) four models of change agency, second, considering the dispersal of change agency both in terms of how it might be dispersed throughout an organization and how it might be dispersed through particular specialisms such as human resources, and third, considering change agency as four competing discourses (Caldwell, 2005, 2006).

Four models of change agency

This subsection is organized around Caldwell's (2003) influential fourfold classification of change agent roles covering leadership, management, consultancy and team models. Caldwell (2003) did not regard these roles as mutually exclusive and acknowledged that during a process of change, change agency might move between roles. His goal was to synthesise and re-conceptualise the nature of change agency, through emphasising that there was no universal model of change agency or a single type of change agent with a fixed set of competencies. The classification draws attention to different locations of change agency and the ways in which change agency may be located at different hierarchical levels.

First, leaders may be regarded as change agents, 'change agents are identified as leaders or senior executives at the very top of the organization who envision, initiate or sponsor strategic change of a far-reaching or transformational nature' (Caldwell, 2003: 140). In Part III, leading change was featured and many of the debates featured there were predicated on a belief that leaders were and should be the change agents. As Caldwell's (2003) quote suggests, this model emphasises change agency being located at the highest level.

> ...the terms "leadership" and "change agency" are often used interchangeably. While leaders are typically regarded as agents of change, change agents are not always seen as leaders.
>
> (Buchanan et al., 2007a: 248)

Second, managers may be regarded as change agents, 'change agents are conceived as middle-level managers and functional specialists who adapt, carry forward or build support for strategic change within business units or key functions' (Caldwell, 2003: 140). Caldwell (2003) discusses the emphasis upon managerial competencies (please see Table 14.2 for typical illustrations), warning that considerable confusion and controversy surrounds the idea of such competencies. Whereas a perceived shift from managing change to leading change was discussed in Chapter 10, Caldwell (2003: 135) is referring to a broader dispersal of change agency.

> In this way, responsibility for managing change is devolved to the local level and becomes an intrinsic requirement for all employees. Moreover, managers are increasingly expected to display a positive or exemplary 'change orientation' as demonstrated by personal flexibility, the competence to deal with uncertainty or ambiguity and the ability to take risks.

Heyden et al. (2017) in a recent research study were able to demonstrate how change initiated by top managers did not engender above-average levels of employee support, whereas change initiated by middle managers did engender above-average levels of employee support.

Third, consultants may be regarded as change agents, 'change agents are conceived as external or internal consultants who operate at a strategic, operational, task or process level within an organization, providing advice, expertise, project management, change programme coordination, or process skills in facilitating change' (Caldwell, 2003: 140). The notion of consultants taking on change agent roles speaks to issues of power and politics featured in Chapter 11. McCalman et al.'s (2015) textbook treatment of change agency is a bit different from the norm in that they make a strong case for consultants as objective outsiders, balancing theories of change agency with practical challenges of change agency. In considering using consultants as change agents, there are choices around internal and external consultants with pros and cons for each choice. They cite Lippitt (1959) offering four golden rules for such change agents (please see Table 14.4).

Fourth, teams may be regarded as change agents, 'change agents are conceived as teams that may operate at a strategic, operational, task or process level within an organization and may include managers, functional specialists and employees at all levels, as well as internal and external consultants' (Caldwell, 2003: 140). The advantage of this approach is potentially in the mix of the team covering different specialisms such as projects and human resources and potentially engaging with perceptions at different organizational levels, rather than a top-down approach. Caldwell (2003) and Charles and Dawson (2011) highlighted the paucity of empirical research into the role of change teams managing large-scale change. Caldwell (2003) regarded Senge's

Table 14.4 The golden rules of consultants as change agents (McCalman et al., 2015)

Rule 1:   The nature of the relationship – this has to be seen as a voluntary one.
Rule 2:   To action a change process within any organization the change agent has to help solve a current or potential problem.
Rule 3:   The relationship is a temporary one and the change agent and organization must accept the temporary nature of the assistance being provided.
Rule 4:   The change agent must be an outsider who is not part of the hierarchical power system in which the client organization is located.

(1990/2006) concept of the 'learning organization' as the most influential model of a team based approach to change agency. However, more recently Caldwell (2012a) has become sceptical about the usefulness of the concept.

Caldwell (2003) highlighted reasons why there had been increasing interest in change agency as a team process. First, change initiatives were often based on reducing hierarchical control placing greater emphasis on teamworking. Second, team coordination was important because change in one area potentially impacted other areas. Third, large-scale changes require risk and complexity to be shared. Fourth, there was growing disillusionment with heroic and individual leaders. Fifth, consulting teams present an opportunity to combine external and internal knowledge. Sixth, dispersing change agency through teams has the potential to institutionalise behavioural change more deeply.

Dispersing change agency

Two closely related themes are discussed here, first, notions of dispersing change agency throughout organizations and second, how change agency might be dispersed through particular specialisms such as human resource management. The previous subsection which drew upon Caldwell's (2003) classification of change agency roles highlights choices and these choices closely relate to not dispersing change agency or dispersing change agency. Paraphrasing the debate, the senior leaders/figures initiate and drive the change with the majority of organizational members following this initiative (not dispersing change agency). Or everyone is a change agent responsible for making change happen in their respective part of the organization. There are strengths and weaknesses in dispersing and not dispersing change agency.

Doyle's (2001) account of dispersing change agency was informed by collaboration with a forum of public and private sector organizations. In his paper he focussed upon a UK privatised water utility and a large regional NHS teaching hospital. He identified the following messages the dispersal and management of change agency might send to strategic leaders in 'high velocity' organizations. First, there is considerable ambiguity with regards to terms such as 'empowerment' and 'change agency'. In the NHS teaching hospital, there was concern that the dispersal of change agency was impacting negatively on patient care. Second, those who led change in organizations appeared to make oversimplified assumptions about the dispersal of change agency in organizations. Third, strategic leaders may lose a degree of control over the people change agency is dispersed to. Fourth, problems of control may relate to the perceptions and management styles of those seeking to exert control.

Meyerson (2001) coined the phrase 'tempered radicals' based upon 15 years of research and observation into family-friendly and socially responsible workplaces. She found that such workplaces were developed not by revolutionaries, but by tempered radicals walking a tightrope between conformity and rebellion. In Buchanan et al.'s (2007b) account of change agency in an acute hospital, rather than referring to 'dispersal' they referred to 'distributed change agency'. They demonstrated how, despite literature often encouraging centralised or leadership-based change agency, distributed change agency appeared to work.

> The change process in some contexts may benefit from being dispersed, fluid, migratory, and influence-based, rather than well-defined, planned, and stable in definition and location. The corollary is that change in some settings may be less

effective where a small number of formally appointed change agents with defined roles follow standard procedures.

(Buchanan et al., 2007b: 1081)

They found distributed change agency to be very effective in the healthcare setting that they were researching, but as the quotation highlights, this may not be applicable in all contexts. Charles and Dawson (2011) studied notions of change agency and its dispersal to change teams during the process of an enterprise resource planning (ERP) transformation in a multinational corporation. They were able to demonstrate how dispersed teams of change agents facilitated improvisations in ERP software and strategies which accomplished complex large-scale change.

Another way of thinking about the dispersal of change agency is in terms of the functional specialists seeking to deliver change agency. Change agency has been studied and practised by different specialists including innovation studies (Schon, 1963; Francis et al., 2010), project management (Turner et al., 1996) and organizational development (OD) (Cummings and Worley, 2014). Wylie et al. (2014) regarded change agency as a 'congested domain' with operations management, OD, project management and programme management professionals all claiming change agent expertise within organizations.

In *Human Resource Champions: The Next Agenda for Adding Value and Delivering Results*, Ulrich (1997) gave impetus to the concept of HR professionals becoming change agents. Ever since this rhetorical encouragement, attempts have been made to establish whether HR professionals had become change agents. The dilemma is that it is difficult to generalise across organizations, hierarchical levels and different types of organizational change initiative. The studies of Caldwell (2001) and Alfes et al. (2010) are two of the more insightful accounts of HR change agency. Caldwell (2001), based upon his survey findings and interview evidence, depicted change agents as champions, adapters, consultants and synergists. Change champions were directors or executives at the highest level of the organization envisioning, leading and implementing strategic HR policy changes. Change adapters were middle-level HR generalists and personnel specialists carrying forward and building support for change. Change consultants were specialist personnel professionals or external consultants with expertise or experience to implement discrete change projects or key stages of HR change initiatives. Change synergists as senior personnel managers or high-level external HR consultants were capable of coordinating, integrating and delivering complex, large-scale changes across the whole organization. Caldwell (2001) concluded that the HR change agent role had grown in significance and complexity.

Alfes et al. (2010) undertook qualitative case study research in a UK general hospital and a borough council. They highlighted four potential roles for HR professionals; change driver, responsive, change focussed and human resources focussed. Change drivers were actively involved in all stages of change programmes. Responsives were potentially neither involved in processes of managing change, nor the deployment of HR interventions in support of change. HR focussed were proactive in how HR could support the change but largely reactive in driving the change. Change focussed HR played an active role in supporting the change but did not engage in developing HR initiatives to create/embed change. In the council, the HR function reflected a responsive role and in the hospital, the HR function reflected a change driver role.

Discourses and change agency

On a practical level, senior management can talk the talk of change agency 'for example, managers espouse rational theories of strategic action and open dialogue, but they engage in processes of collusion, self-deception and cover-up that subvert rationality' (Caldwell, 2006: 38). In parallel to such developments, academic understanding is informed by competing discourses and in order to fully understand change agency, we need to acknowledge these different discourses. As discussed in Chapter 12, discourses are not 'mere' words. They help us to appreciate how language shapes our thinking. Caldwell (2005, 2006) developed a classification around four discourses he identified when reviewing the agency and organizational change literature; rationalist, contextualist, dispersalist and constructionist. The implication of these discourses is not just that they offer a means of classification, but that they highlight four different ways of thinking about change agency. Each discourse is briefly introduced and an illustrative example of a different way of thinking about change agency offered for each discourse.

Rationalist discourses prioritise centred agency. They emphasise the concepts of planned change and the possibilities of strategic action. Lewin's (1947) promotion of planned change is cited as an example of a rationalist discourse on change agency. Contextualist discourses focus on processes of 'emergent' change and the bounded nature of centred agency in organizations. Pettigrew's (1985) longitudinal research into ICI is cited as an example of a contextualist discourse on change agency. Dispersalist discourses focus predominantly on systemic or self-organizing processes of learning in organizations, while giving autonomy to new forms of 'conjoint agency', 'sensemaking', 'distributed leadership' and 'communities of practice'. Wenger's (1998) interest in communities of practice is cited as an example of dispersalist discourse on change agency. Constructionist discourses decentre human agency within discursive practices over which human actors appear to have little rational or intentional control. Caldwell (2005) acknowledged that it was almost impossible to disentangle the strands of constructionist discourses, but he highlights four themes: anti-rationalism, anti-scientism, anti-essentialism and anti-realism.

Questioning explanations of agency and change

In the earlier 'making change happen' section, practitioner interest in change agency was highlighted, whereas academics have often appeared suspicious of change agency claims. Caldwell (2006) warned that the history of the concept of change agency in organizational theory over the past 50 years made dismal reading (please see also Hartley, Benington and Binns, 1997). In this section, four closely related critical change agency debates are featured: managing and leading change as a false dichotomy, the problematic nature of change agent-centric thinking and challenges arising out of dispersing change agency and change agency discourses.

Managing or leading change as a false dichotomy

A perceived shift from managing change towards leading change has been highlighted in earlier chapters, although the evidence informing such a shift is questionable. The implication of such a shift is that there is a choice between change agency being located in management or leadership, which may be a false dichotomy.

Many of the debates featured in this textbook suffer through the influence of artificial dualisms, such as change versus stability, managing versus leading, succeeding versus failing. However, a dualities aware approach might be more fruitful:

> Effective change leadership means appreciating how dualistic forces can shape and enable change. By adopting a dualities aware perspective, leaders can come to terms with the intuitive desire to resolve contradiction by instead managing the complementarities within contradictory forces.
>
> (Sutherland and Smith, 2013: 220)

The implication is that rather than trying to locate change agency within a leadership role or a management role, managers may move between managing and leading in the space of a single meeting and may have to deal with change, but equally stability within their organizations.

The problem with change agent-centric thinking

Remember the caricatured stereotype of a change agent, smart suit, clip board and stop watch, you begin to appreciate the problem with change agent-centric thinking. Ford et al. (2008) highlighted that the change agent rather than facilitating change may contribute to the occurrence of resistance to change, as discussed in Chapter 13. Potentially, change agent-centric thinking can contribute to communication breakdowns through failing to legitimise change, misrepresenting the chances of success and failing to call people to action. They emphasised the centrality of conversations, discourses and texts in processes of changing.

> Change agents, therefore, must provide discursive justifications that establish the appropriateness and rationality of change adoption, create readiness for change, and increase not only the likelihood of recipient acceptance and participation in the change but also the speed and extent of that acceptance.
>
> (Ford et al., 2008: 366)

The concern here is that change agents through preoccupations with overcoming resistance to change may fail to engage in the type of conversations which enable change to happen. Another way to think about change agent-centric thinking is in terms of the way we depict either leaders or managers as change agents, when change agency may be inherent within all managerial work. As Buchanan and Badham (2008) suggested, most functional and general managers typically combine change responsibilities with their day job. In hyping up the leader or manager as change agent, we may be misrepresenting or misunderstanding processes of changing.

Things fall apart – dispersing change agency

Dispersed change agency is appealing in terms of potentially embedding change initiatives deeply and throughout an organization. However, such dispersal has to be reconciled with each individual maintaining their personal interpretation of change and its meaning to them (Doyle, 2001). The dilemma becomes how you manage a multiplicity of change agents working with different interpretations of a change initiative. Disparate and unconnected change initiatives may potentially undermine the coherence and control of change initiatives. Doyle (2001: 326) offered a warning based upon his research 'in the case of the Water Company, senior managers became alarmed when a spot check revealed 147 separate change initiatives were operating simultaneously'. This warning is echoed by Caldwell (2006: 160) when he warns that '...empowering new and sometimes "unaccountable" collective leaders and teams, often with no clear focus or agenda for change can disempower or undermine the fragile interventions of more conventional forms of expert knowledge'. Another dilemma with dispersed change agency becomes apparent in Buchanan et al.'s (1999: 26) findings. Whilst change agency was widely distributed in organizations, it was potentially problematic, with 80 per cent agreeing that 'we don't seem to have enough people with the right change management expertise'. Although senior managers may favour the dispersal of change agency, employees may not have the experience/expertise to act as change agents. These research findings highlight the tensions between top-down management and popular notions of dispersing change agency throughout organizations. Dispersal of change agency discussions can become polarised in terms of either top-down change agency or bottom up change agency (see Sminia and Van Nistelrooij, 2006 and Heyden et al., 2017).

Things fall apart – discourses of change agency

The writings of Raymond Caldwell have featured prominently in this chapter and so it is appropriate to conclude with his insights. In his review of discourses on agency and change in organizations over the past 50 years, he was able to identify four discourses: rationalist, contextualist, dispersalist and constructionist. Whilst acknowledging early optimism that organizational change could be managed as a planned or rational process, he believed that the growing plurality of discourses challenged the ambitions for the field to be objective, cumulative or unified (Caldwell, 2005). He offered four major reasons for his sceptical conclusion. First, despite decades of empirical research and theoretical discussion on organizational change a cumulative logic was lacking. Second, there had been a failure of synthesis with no successful attempts to link micro-level understanding of agency to macro-level structural/institutional change. Third, change agents as subjects have been central to this chapter, but discourses of power/knowledge may eclipse the subject. Fourth, there are paradoxes of practice in that the ideal of the 'change agent' as an 'unbiased' facilitator of planned change may be an intellectual and moral illusion.

Summary

The chapter may be succinctly summarised through answering the questions posed in the chapter's introduction. The original questions are restated in italics.

In terms of making change happen – what are practitioners doing? Approaches to making change happen are many and varied with an emphasis on positive and proactive approaches. Processes of changing were typically broken down into proactive steps with ideal competencies, characteristics of change agents/champions specified.

What are the potential roles for leaders, managers, consultants and teams in change agency? Caldwell (2003) offered an influential classification for locating change agency in different roles. This has implications for theory in terms of authors focussing on different roles, but also for practice in terms of choices made about locating change agency.

What do we know about the dispersal of change agency? One of the major choices is with regards to dispersing/distributing change agency or not, as there are advantages and disadvantages inherent in such processes. Another more subtle form of dispersal is through different specialisms informing organizational change processes such as OD, project management and HRM.

How do different discourses inform change agency? Competing explanations of change agency may be understood in terms of different discourses. Caldwell (2005/2006) highlighted four which he identified in his review of the change agency literature: rationalist, contextualist, dispersalist and constructionist with each reflecting different ways of thinking about change agency.

Is the differentiation between managing change and leading change a false dichotomy? Potentially change agency has moved from the change managers to change leaders, but there is a need for caution as this may be a false dichotomy. Instead, a dualities aware approach (Sutherland and Smith, 2013) was favoured.

Why is change agent-centric thinking problematic? We think of change agents as being a solution to problems of changing, but for Ford et al. (2008) change agents rather than facilitating change may contribute to the occurrence of resistance to change.

What challenges do dispersing change agency and change agency discourses raise? The answer to this question may best be paraphrased as: things fall apart. Through dispersing change agency, organizations may lose their favoured sense of strategic direction and discourses of change agency may never reach a cumulative logic.

Research case study showcase: leading change through turbulence in an English school

Rayner's (2017) case study of leading change in an English school reported in *Educational Management Administration & Leadership* is showcased here. For the full case and further analysis please visit the original source.

Case study source

This case study is drawn from Rayner's (2017) doctoral research which studied academisation in English schools.

> I use the term academisation to refer to the process whereby a school in England changes its legal status, so that it is no longer maintained by its local authority, but by an Academy Trust, which is a company that has charitable status and that holds control over the land and other assets of the school. The name of the school is usually, but not necessarily, changed to include the word Academy.
>
> *(Rayner, 2017: 2)*

In the featured paper, Rayner (2017) looks at this process of academisation in one particular school referred to by the pseudonym St Clement's. The school was a Church of England (C of E) school, maintained by the local education authority (LEA). In early 2014, the school was one of only five in the local authority which

(Continued)

was not an academy. The governors and the Head Teacher began a process of consultation on converting the school to academy status. Subsequent discussions continued for 18 months. However, after 18 months of consultation, academisation as a proposal was dropped. Instead it was proposed that the school change its governance arrangements to become a Voluntary-Aided C of E school and this was agreed by the LEA in July 2015. What is interesting, as Rayner (2017) acknowledges, is that the case was neither a story of success, in which the school became an academy through visionary leadership. Nor was it a story of failure with the school saved from academy status due to school leaders mobilising a campaign of resistance. Instead, the case offers insights into how change leaders respond to contradictions and complexities which inevitably accompany systemic change, put more succinctly how they deal with turbulence in their environment.

The case study reported here is informed in particular by interviews about the actions and views of three staff with leadership roles at the school: Martin (Head Teacher), Carol (Deputy Head Teacher) and Lesley (Head of a Large Subject Department). These names are pseudonyms. Martin and Carol were senior leaders, whereas Lesley was a middle-level leader. A strength of Rayner's (2017) research was that he interviewed these leaders at different stages of the academisation process.

Rayner, S.M. 2017. "Leaders and Leadership in a Climate of Uncertainty: A Case Study of Structural Change in England." *Educational Management Administration & Leadership* (online first).

Case study

Martin, Carol and Lesley represented different views, positions and professional dilemmas in English schools particularly at a time of change. Each of these leaders stated that education provision was harmed through continual politically motivated change. However, on academisation, their views differed even though they all worked at St Clement's. For Carol, this policy change was a welcome necessity, with St Clement's on a journey to hopefully becoming an academy. Whilst Carol was disappointed when St Clement's didn't become an academy, she still expected the school eventually to become an academy, regarding Voluntary-Aided status as a stepping stone towards becoming an academy. In contrast, Lesley stated that she would not work for an academy and that she would resign if St Clement's became an academy 'I will not work for an academy, because it would be hypocritical of me, because I do not agree with the philosophy at all' (Lesley, interview 1, cited in Rayner, 2017: 5). Martin had opposed in principle the Academies Programme, but now regarded it as irresistible. He believed that he had a responsibility to make these inevitable structural changes work in benefiting pupils and staff.

> So, if we are going to become an academy, I think what's incumbent upon myself as somebody leading an organization is to look at a provider that would give equitable opportunities to staff, the best they possibly can for kids, and has a high degree of moral integrity.
>
> *(Martin, interview 1 cited in Rayner, 2017: 6)*

The challenge for Martin in leading this potential change to the status of St Clement's was not to represent or mediate policy, but instead to explain to staff what the change would mean for them and the school. He perceived his role as reassuring the school, staff and pupils that they would suffer no harm and that they might even benefit from the change.

Local context and competition

Rayner's (2017) wider research study revealed that, during the first interviews, only the Head Teacher and senior leaders made reference to local competition. However, during second interviews, almost all participants made reference to competition.

> There's an awful lot of competition in the area, and especially from the larger academy chains, where they are heavily focussed on marketing…and I do think as a school we feel that pressure.
>
> *(Carol, interview 1 cited in Rayner, 2017: 6)*

In responding to this competition, three crucial factors for St Clement's were highlighted. First, they needed to have a reputation for high standards, evidenced by published inspection reports and performance tables. Second, they required the ability to recruit pupils who would contribute to maintaining these outcomes. Third, a strong and distinctive brand was required to aid market-positioning.

The school's history

Local context and competition are closely related to the history of the school. Academy status for a school being scrutinised as a result of poor examination results with a low Ofsted (government school inspectors) rating, becomes a threat. On the contrary, it becomes an opportunity for a school with a good Ofsted rating, whose results are improving. St Clement's institutional narrative articulated by senior leaders and echoed by staff was that, five years earlier, St Clement's had been a warm and caring school which was recognised locally for its inclusive approach, although standards evidenced by public examination results were low. However, after the school moved to a new campus and Martin was appointed Head Teacher, examination results had improved. The institutional narrative changed with the school increasingly appealing to families due to its new buildings, improved results and the new location.

External accountability

This new narrative was also informed by a good Ofsted rating. However the inspection regime remained a potential threat to the school and its leaders and staff. If the school did not maintain its good Ofsted rating, it might revert to its insecure position of five years earlier. It was this external accountability which underpinned

(Continued)

maintaining the reputation of the school and its market-position through controlling recruitment of pupils and through links with other primary schools.

Staff wellbeing

Throughout Rayner's (2017) research, Martin's concern was the care, welfare and development of pupils and staff at St Clement's. He used sayings, such as to 'keep the wolves from the door', helping colleagues in 'a siege mentality', and 'to create a raft of stability' to convey this care. Martin communicated frequently and frankly about academisation. So, when the original proposal for structural change was dropped, this was not regarded as contradictory and there was no loss of confidence in Martin's leadership of the school.

Leaders, leading and leadership

In seeking to understand these school leaders as change agents, Carol, Lesley and Martin each adopted differing positions. Even though Carol's position on academisation differed from Martin's she expressed trust in, and loyalty towards senior colleagues, especially Martin. She recognised the importance of speaking collectively as the school's leadership team. However, on a personal level she maintained her favourable view of academisation and her resistance to criticism of academisation.

> Untroubled by doubts about government policy, Carol had a clear vision for the future of St Clement's as an academy. The delay over conversion was disappointing, but 'in the interim, I think Voluntary-Aided status is one way that we can go part of the way'.

> *(Carol, interview 2 cited in Rayner, 2017: 9)*

Lesley had diverse and contradictory loyalties. Ideologically, she opposed government policy, but trusted her Head Teacher implementing this policy. She had introduced herself as a 'middle leader' and consciously differentiated herself from the school senior leadership team. Her main commitment as a leader was to her immediate colleagues in the subject team engaging particularly with the curriculum in her subject, changes to examination requirements and potential interference from policy-makers.

For Martin, steering the school through these uncertain times was a responsibility that was dependent upon himself. He did not mean this arrogantly or heroically. He had no aspiration to be a 'system leader' or a chief executive officer. However, he could protect pupils and staff from risks such as: a corporatised agenda, a profit-making organization take over, the loss of staff employment rights and restrictions to curriculum opportunities for vulnerable groups of children. Martin's focus as a school leader was not translating, interpreting, or mediating government policy. In interviews, he expressed reservations about these policies. He was not enthusiastic about the concept of inter-school competition in pupil recruitment, aggressive marketing, corporatisation, private finance, being a 'system leader' for 'weaker' schools, or LAs being marginalised.

Martin exercised leadership through being open with his colleagues. He secured their confidence and influenced their thinking and positioning.

> Confidence in Martin's vision for the future of the school endured, even when the practical manifestation of that vision differed from his original articulation of it…Martin practised leadership in a manner that, as all the staff agreed, was reliable and predictable, bringing stability amid the political turbulence.
>
> *(Rayner, 2017: 11)*

Case study questions

1   In this case study where was change agency located?
2   Compare and contrast the leadership of change in this case with Kotter's (1996/2012) eight steps to lead change (featured in Chapter 10).
3   Do you regard the shifting positions on academisation of leaders in this case study positively or negatively?

Discussion questions

1   Change agents and change champions, are these mere words or something deeper?
2   What is the problem with these debates focussing upon individual agents/champions?
3   Why do organizations sometimes locate change agency in external consultants?
4   What are the strengths and weaknesses of dispersed change agency?

Navigating the change agency literature

Three challenges arise which may be apparent from earlier discussions in this chapter when reviewing this literature relating to semantics, theory and practices and fields of study. A broad definition of a change agent (Wylie et al., 2014) has been favoured, but in reviewing this literature there was no consensus around defining change agents. The implication of this is that the activities of change agents may be very broad or very narrow with implications for understanding. The second challenge relates to tensions between practitioner interest in change agency and academic indifference. There are many practical prescriptions about making change happen, but far less evidence based/research informed accounts. However, sometimes, the differentiation between theory and practice is blurred. Finally, the focus of this textbook has been organizational change as a field of study, but in engaging with this literature it quickly becomes apparent that other fields make claims to change agency, such as HRM, project management, and OD. The implication is that change agency literature may not necessarily be bounded within the organizational change field of study. Caldwell's work has featured prominently in this chapter. A personal favourite is *Agency and Change* (Caldwell, 2006) which was organized around a review of the literature over the past 50 years. It needs to be acknowledged that it is a very academic book. His journal papers are far more concise and accessible. In reviewing literature for this chapter, it was apparent that interest in change agency, particularly the dispersal/distribution of agency, peaked in the late 1990s/early 2000s. It may be that the notion of change agents and dispersing/distributing change agency were no longer subtle enough to deal with the complexities and ambiguities of organizational life. Certainly, if you look at Caldwell's later writings he moved away from the change agency focus reported here, focussing more on systems thinking (see Caldwell, 2012a) and practice theory (see Caldwell, 2012b).

References

Alfes, K., C. Truss, and J. Gill. 2010. "The HR Manager as Change Agent: Evidence from the Public Sector." *Journal of Change Management* 10(1): 109–127.

Buchanan, D., and D. Boddy, 1992. *The Expertise of the Change Agent.* Hemel Hempstead: Prentice Hall (out of print).

Buchanan, D., and R. Badham. 2008. *Power, Politics and Organizational Change: Winning the Turf Game.* London: Sage Publications.

Buchanan, D., R. Caldwell, J. Meyer, J. Storey, and C. Wainwright. 2007a. "Leadership Transmission: A Muddled Metaphor?" *Journal of Health Organization and Management* 21(3): 246–258.

Buchanan, D., T. Claydon, and M. Doyle, 1999. "Organisation Development and Change: the Legacy of the Nineties." *Human Resource Management Journal* 9(2): 20–37.

Buchanan, D.A., R. Addicott, L. Fitzgerald, E. Ferlie, and J.I. Baeza, 2007b. "Nobody in Charge: Distributed Change Agency in Healthcare." *Human Relations* 60(7): 1065–1090.

Caldwell, R. 2001. "Champions, Adapters, Consultants and Synergists: The New Change Agents in HRM." *Human Resource Management Journal* 11(3): 39–52.

Caldwell, R. 2003. "Models of Change Agency: A Fourfold Classification." *British Journal of Management* 14(2): 131–142.

Caldwell, R. 2005. "Things Fall Apart? Discourses on Agency and Change in Organizations." *Human Relations* 58(1): 83–114.

Caldwell, R. 2006. *Agency and Change.* London: Routledge.

Caldwell, R. 2012a. "Leadership and Learning; A Critical Re-examination of Senge's Learning Organization." *Systemic Practice and Action Research* 25(1): 39–55.

Caldwell, R. 2012b. "Reclaiming Agency, Recovering Change? An Exploration of the Practice Theory of Theodore Schatzki." *Journal for the Theory of Social Behaviour* 42(3): 283–303.

Charles, K., and P. Dawson. 2011. "Dispersed Change Agency and the Improvisation of Strategies during Processes of Change." *Journal of Change Management* 11(3): 329–351.

Cozad, L. 2016. "All Talk, No Action? A 5-Step Guide to Make Change Happen Within your Organization." Available at www.business.com/articles/all-talk-no-action-your-5-step-guide-to-make-change-happen-within-your-organization/

Cummings, T.G., and C.G. Worley. 2014. *Organization Development and Change.* Stamford, CT: Cengage Learning.

Doyle, M. 2001. "Dispersing Change Agency in High Velocity Change Organisations: Issues and Implications." *Leadership and Organization Development Journal* 22(7): 321–329.

Ford, J.D., L.W. Ford, and A. d'Amelio. 2008. "Resistance to Change: The Rest of the Story." *Academy of Management Review* 33(2): 362–377.

Francis, D., H. Rush, and M. Parejo, 2010. *The Innovation Change Agent's Manual.* Brighton: Report for the United Nations Educational, Scientific and Cultural Organization.

Gordon, J. 2015. "10 Characteristics of a Change Champion." The People Development Network. Available at http://peopledevelopmentmagazine.com/2015/10/12/10-characteristics-of-a-change-champion/

Harshak, A., D. Aguirre, and A. Brown. 2010. "Making Change Happen, and Making it Stick." *Strategy + Business.* Available at www.strategy-business.com/article/00057?gko=39ed2

Hartley, J., J. Benington, and P. Binns. 1997. "Researching the Roles of Internal-change Agents in the Management of Organizational Change." *British Journal of Management* 8(1): 61–73.

Heyden, M.L., S.P. Fourné, B.A. Koene, R. Werkman, and S.S. Ansari. 2017. "Rethinking 'Top-Down' and 'Bottom-Up' Roles of Top and Middle Managers in Organizational Change: Implications for Employee Support." *Journal of Management Studies* 54(7): 961–985.

Kotter, J.P. 1996/2012. *Leading Change*. Boston, MA: Harvard Business School Press.

Lewin, K. 1947. "Frontiers in Group Dynamics." *Human Relations* 1(1): 5–41.

Lippitt, R. 1959. "Dimensions of the Consultant's Job." *Journal of Social Issues* 15(2): 5–12.

Lippitt, R., J. Watson, and B. Westley. 1958. *The Dynamics of Planned Change*. New York: Harcourt, Brace and Company.

McCalman, J., R. Paton, and S. Siebert. 2015. *Change Management: A Guide to Effective Implementation*. London: Sage Publications.

Meyerson, D. 2001. *Tempered Radicals*. Boston, MA: Harvard Business School.

NCVO. 2014. "Five Steps to Successful Change." The National Council for Voluntary Organisations. Available at https://knowhownonprofit.org/leadership/change/basics-on-managing-change/fivesteps/five-steps-to-successful-change-1#

Pettigrew, A. 1985. *The Awakening Giant: Continuity and Change in Imperial Chemical Industries*. Oxford: Blackwell.

Pickering, B. 2009. "Make Change Sustainable with Change Champions." The HR Zone. Available at www.hrzone.com/lead/change/make-change-sustainable-with-change-champions

Portier, C. 2016. "8 Traits of a Change Management Champion." Paragon Solutions. Available at www.consultparagon.com/blog/change-management-champion

Rayner, S.M. 2017. "Leaders and Leadership in a Climate of Uncertainty: A Case Study of Structural Change in England." *Educational Management Administration & Leadership*, (online first).

Schon, D.A. 1963. "Champions for Radical New Inventions." *Harvard Business Review* 41(2): 77–86.

Senge, P. 1990/2006. *The Fifth Dimension: The Art and Practice of the Learning Organization*. New York: Doubleday.

Sminia, H., and A. Van Nistelrooij. 2006. "Strategic Management and Organization Development: Planned Change in a Public Sector Organization." *Journal of Change Management* 6(1): 99–113.

Sutherland, F., and A.C.T. Smith. 2013. "Leadership for the Age of Sustainability: A Dualities Approach to Organizational Change." In *Organizational Change, Leadership and Ethics: Leading Organizations Towards Sustainability*, by R.T. By and B. Burnes, 216–239. London: Routledge.

Turner, J.R., K.V. Grude, and L. Thurloway (Eds). 1996. *The Project Manager as Change Agent: Leadership, Influence and Negotiation*. New York: McGraw-Hill.

Ulrich, D. 1997. *Human Resource Champions: The Next Agenda for Adding Value and Delivering Results*. Cambridge, MA: Harvard Business School Press.

Wenger, E. 1998. *Communities of Practice: Learning, Meaning and Identity*. Cambridge: Cambridge University Press.

Wylie, N., A. Sturdy, and C. Wright. 2014. "Change Agency in Occupational Context: Lessons for HRM." *Human Resource Management Journal* 24(1): 95–110.

Chapter 15

Management and leadership tools and techniques

Introduction and chapter questions

Whilst this textbook informing study has majored upon theories, models and concepts, the focus for practitioners is more likely to be tools and techniques used in the context of organizational change. It was originally envisaged that this chapter would address three very straightforward questions:

Q1. What organizational change tools and techniques are used,
Q2. Why are they used?
Q3. How are they used?

However, when you attempt to study organizational change tools and techniques challenges quickly become apparent. First, (Q1), the identification of organizational change tools and techniques, requires differentiation from other tools and techniques. However, it is almost impossible to identify those tools and techniques specifically for organizational change given the many tools and techniques managers and leaders use. Tools and techniques favoured within specific fields of study and practice, such as strategy, leadership, quality management, project management and organizational development raise questions about their transferability to organizational change. Have you identified a strategy tool or an organizational change tool or both? Second, (Q2), tools and techniques may be used superficially to manage and lead organizational change. However, have the rationales for tool usage espoused the real reasons or are tools and techniques being used because they are fashionable and have legitimacy in a particular sector and at a particular time? Do managers and leaders base their choices on empirical evidence? Can empirical evidence even exist given the diverse contexts in which organizational change takes place? Third, (Q3), the usage of particular tools and techniques is likely to be highly variable. The philosophy of a technique such as lean management with its emphasis on eliminating systematic waste may be fully embraced or the language may be invoked whilst the technique is undertaken in a fairly instrumental manner. Tools and techniques may be used on a long-term basis or fleetingly. As far as possible, questions Q2 and Q3 will be addressed. However, in terms of Q1, it has been necessary pragmatically to broaden the chapter focus to management and leadership tools and techniques given the difficulty of differentiating tools and techniques specifically for organizational change. The assumption is that many management and leadership tools and techniques may be used for organizational change.

Lightening the tone, Burke (2009) used a helpful cooking analogy to differentiate tools, skills, techniques, and processes in the context of project management and this differentiation appears to be equally applicable to organizational change.

Table 15.1 A cookery analogy to explain project management tools and techniques (based on Burke, 2009)

	Cookery	Project management
Tools	Pots, pans and utensils	Work breakdown structure (WBS) or planning software
Skills and techniques	How you use the utensils; chopping, carving and frying	How WBS or planning software is used in preparing a project management plan
Processes	Transformation of food through cooking, to produce something edible, such as a cake	Collecting raw data and transforming it into meaningful reports

The cultural web, featured in Chapter 6 may be used to illustrate the cookery analogy (please see Table 15.1) when applied to organizational change. The cultural web itself may be considered as a tool in a manner similar to a pot or a pan. The focus then shifts to how it is used (skills and techniques). The cultural web could be used with regard to two organizational groups merging. Facilitation skills and techniques would be used to assist each group in drawing a cultural web of their respective cultures. The two groups would then share their respective cultural webs as part of a transformation (process) forming a single group.

This chapter is organized around and provides answers to the following questions about understanding management and leadership tools and techniques.

What are practitioners doing, in terms of their tools and techniques usage?
What do we know about change management tools and techniques?
How might tools and techniques from different fields of study inform our understanding?
What questions need to be raised about the utility of tools and techniques?

In the next section, studies of management and leadership tools and techniques usage are considered in order to gain an understanding of what practitioners are doing. In the understanding section, the tools and techniques of change management (Hughes, 2007) are revisited as a means of addressing issues relating to classifying tools and techniques. The tools and techniques of project management, organizational development and strategy are highlighted as potentially informing organizational change processes. Academics have traditionally had reservations about practitioner belief in tools and techniques with the questioning section looking at the utility of tools and techniques.

Management and leadership tools and techniques: what are practitioners doing?

The mundane example of cookery (please see Table 15.1) takes us back to Peters' (1978) clever highlighting of how effective change tools were embedded into the daily message sending and receiving activities of managers. He characterised these tools as symbols (raw materials), patterns (systematic use of the raw materials) and settings (the showcase for the systematic use). In this way, mundane tools could be used practically as follows: calendars, reports, and agendas as examples of symbols, their usage (patterns) acting as a positive reinforcement for ensuring consistent and frequent behaviour. Settings for using these symbols could include deadline management, presentation format and agenda control. Forty years later, Peters (1978) highlighting such mundane use of tools appears arcane. However, the implication for this chapter is that in terms of what practitioners are doing, they are likely to use many tools and techniques on a daily basis which we wouldn't even register as tools and techniques. For example today, smartphones may be regarded as change tools with different techniques of usage. Accepting this acknowledgment, the following discussion revisits literature focused upon practitioner utilisation of tools and techniques.

What quickly becomes apparent is that many tools and techniques might be utilised when managing and leading organizational change with varying degrees of usefulness. A reasonable quest evident in the practitioner oriented literature is establishing the most popular tools and techniques and practitioner satisfaction with these tools and techniques. There is a need for caution as the usability and satisfaction with tools and techniques may vary from context to context. It is informative to chronologically revisit practitioner oriented literature on tool and technique usage.

Clark (1997) undertook an exploratory comparative study of strategic management tool usage by practitioners in the UK and New Zealand. He was interested in tool usage during the different phases of; situation assessment, strategic analysis, and strategic implementation. Strengths, Weaknesses, Opportunities and Threats analysis was dominant during the situation assessment phase. Focus groups were prominent in all three phases and budgeting was dominant in the strategic implementation phase. In terms of country-specific differences, core competencies were prominent during the first phase in New Zealand. Multiple tools of different types were often used for each strategic task. Whilst, this study is now dated, it draws attention to different tools being used during different phases and potential geographical variations in tool usage.

Cullen et al. (2004) reported on two research projects into Irish business practices in 2002 and 2003. The first study focused on usage, satisfaction and attitudes to 31 management tools and techniques. The second study looked at top management challenges. In terms of the second study, the highest ranked management challenge was reducing costs, followed by maintaining/increasing profits and then managing change. So, going back to the first study, what management tools and techniques were favoured? In terms of usage, strategic planning, performance management and key performance indicators (KPI) were ranked joint first. In terms of satisfaction, KPI's and supply chain integration achieved the highest satisfaction scores. So here we see practitioner usage being differentiated from practitioner satisfaction.

Rigby (2001) publicised the annual survey of management tool usage initiated by Bain & Company in 1993. They surveyed executives around the world about their management tool usage and how effectively those tools performed, highlighting different usage of management tools and techniques in different parts of the world (please see Table 15.2).

Bain & Company focused on 25 tools, with revisions to their list each year. At the time of the fifteenth survey, they had a database of more than 13,000 respondents drawn from North America, Europe, Asia, Africa, the Middle East and Latin America. The 25 tools with a bibliographical guide to resources for each tool is contained in *Management Tools 2015: An Executive's Guide* available at the time of writing at the website www.bain.com.

Table 15.2 Top five management tools by region (based upon Rigby, 2001)

Rank	North America	Europe	South America
1st	Strategic planning	Benchmarking	Strategic planning
2nd	Mission and vision statements	Mission and vision statements	Benchmarking
3rd	Benchmarking	Strategic planning	Customer satisfaction measurement
4th	Customer satisfaction measurement	Customer satisfaction measurement	Pay-for-performance
5th	Growth strategies	Outsourcing	Mission and vision statements + total quality management

Whilst, annual surveys offer useful indications of which management tools are gaining popularity/losing popularity, there is a need for caution in terms of the reliability and validity of the findings. Rigby (2001: 160) acknowledged '...the sample is largely drawn from new respondents each year, so true time cohorts are not possible'. Today, Bain & Company appear to place less emphasis upon management tools and techniques. Umbeck and Bron (2017) in a recent Bain Briefing encouraged readers to resist the urge to make change management a separate work stream or a standalone activity, advising that it is not just a collection of tools and techniques or an HR-led exercise.

Understanding management and leadership tools and techniques

In this section, two themes are developed: first, how we might begin to classify tools and techniques in deepening understanding about their usage, and second, how different fields of study encourage using different tools and techniques. These different emphases are highlighted through reference to project management, organizational development, and strategy.

The tools and techniques of change management redux

"The Tools and Techniques of Change Management" (Hughes, 2007) benefited from a catchy title, but unfortunately, the paper hasn't really stood up to the test of time. In this subsection, the paper is revisited as its classifications help us to understand that different tools and techniques and developments are gauged with regard to three groups of stakeholders: practitioners, professionals and their representative bodies and academics. The paper began with a quotation from Salaman and Asch (2003) highlighting consultants selling tools and techniques beautifully presented and forcefully marketed, contrasted with academics pointing out inconsistencies, contradictions, and simplifications in the tools and techniques literature.

Over a decade later, this tension is still apparent. The paper (Hughes, 2007) highlighted four challenges which again still appear to be relevant: defining tools and techniques, the nature of tools terminology, tools and techniques choices, and credibility. The suggestion was that the tools and techniques terminology was inconsistent.

A way forward was differentiating tools from techniques, so a tool is a standalone application and a technique is an integrated approach. For example, a quality circle might be labelled as a tool, which is used as part of a quality management integrated approach (technique). There is still a need for choices in using tools and techniques which are contingent on a particular situation. For example, my lawn mower is an effective tool for cutting the grass, but useless as a tool for tidying crumbs on my carpet. Finally, we need to consider the objectivity of those promoting tools and techniques and those critiquing tools and techniques. A consultant may be biased in the favourable way that they present tools and techniques, but equally academics in their critiques are influenced by their favoured paradigms and perspectives.

Hughes (2007) majored on classification questions for classifying tools and techniques in order to advance theory and practice. Classification questions in Table 15.3 are potentially useful for anyone academically or practically studying tools and techniques who wants to go beneath the superficial and often 'sexy' rhetoric. The first four questions should resonate with earlier discussions in this chapter. Questions 5 and 6 offer a useful differentiation between tools and techniques used for diagnostic purposes and for intervention purposes. Certain tools may be used for both purposes, such as the cultural web which potentially informs the diagnosis of a culture and informs an intervention in terms of changing a culture. Questions 7 and 8 were inspired by Peters (1978) and again his differentiation of tools in terms of degree of control and speed of implementation still feels relevant today (please see Table 15.4).

Table 15.4 introduces a subtle differentiation (control/speed) often missing from tools and techniques debates. Tool and technique choices are inevitably informed by choices relating to how much control individuals have and the speed of implementation required.

Hughes (2007) concluded by asking how understanding about change management tools and techniques could be advanced in the future? In reflecting back on the paper,

Table 15.3 Classifying change management tools and techniques (based on Hughes, 2007)

Classification questions

1 Is it a change management tool (standalone application) or a change management technique (integrated approach)?
2 How popular is this change management tool or technique? (Potential indicators include: references in the business press, academic citations, survey evidence and research studies.)
3 How satisfied are users with the change management tool or technique? (Potential indicators include: references in the business press, academic citations, survey evidence and research studies.)
4 At which level/s is the change management tool or technique applicable? (individual, group and organizational)
5 Does the change management tool or technique seek to diagnose a change problem?
6 Does the change management tool or technique seek to inform a change intervention?
7 Does the change management tool or technique require high or low levels of control? (for example, levels of managerial intervention required to facilitate the change)
8 Does the change management tool or technique aim to deliver change at high or low speed?

Table 15.4 Control over change and the speed of change
(based on Peters, 1978)

Category	Control	Speed	Example
1	High	Low	Planning
2	High	High	Divisionalisation
3	Low	High	Changing structure or senior managers for change's sake
4	Low	Low	Team building

what is immediately apparent is an emphasis upon static management in 2007, rather than a more fluid process of managing. Also, there were no references to leaders/ leadership in the body of the paper. Today there is a considerable emphasis upon leaders/leadership with regards to organizational change.

In terms of considering the future, the paper highlighted three groups of stakeholders: practitioners, professional and representative bodies and academics. Today, there is still ongoing interest in tools and techniques, although shifts in Bain & Company's engagement with tools and techniques suggests either less interest or more sophisticated interest. The interests of practitioners are often represented through professional and representative bodies and project management features in the next subsection. In *The Effective Change Manager's Handbook*, Smith et al. (2014) seek to develop a body of knowledge in a manner similar to the project management bodies of knowledge (please see Morris et al., 2000 for further discussion of such bodies of knowledge). In this way, certain tools and techniques are given legitimacy and backing by professional bodies and potentially become part of the body of knowledge.

Finally, academics still appear to be suspicious of tools and techniques, as will be demonstrated in the questioning section. Personally, the goal of bridging the 'gap' between theories and practices (see Hughes, 2007) oddly seems less relevant today. Practitioners use tools and techniques and academics develop theories, models and concepts. We need to respect the knowledge and experience of both groupings, even if we favour and align ourselves with one group or the other. Critical literature on tools and techniques today feels rather patronising and condescending. A practitioner studying for a business degree may move between theory and practice, but that still does not mean that we need to bridge a 'gap'. Hopefully, this chapter demonstrates that understanding tools and techniques may be informed by a practitioner perspective and an academic perspective. They really do not have to be merged.

Project management, organizational development and strategy tools and techniques

Organizational members may learn about tools and techniques through business school courses, social media, business biographies, television shows, etc. In engaging with processes of organizational change, they may use tools and techniques from fields other than organizational change, such as quality management and human resource management. In this subsection, the fields of project management, organizational development (OD) and strategy will be featured.

Project management theories and practices place an emphasis on tools and techniques (Burke, 2009; Tayntor, 2010). Hornstein (2015) didn't favour applying project management tools and techniques to organizational change, but did favour integrating project management and organizational change. For Crawford and Nahmias (2010) organizational changes may be viewed as a specific project type benefiting from the application of project management skills, tools and techniques (see also Smith et al., 2014). In *The Handbook of Project-based Management: Leading Strategic Change in Organizations* (Turner, 2014), the whole handbook encouraged the use of project-based management tools and techniques with a view to leading change.

OD has a long and successful history, with the origins of OD tools and techniques being traced back to the pioneering work of Kurt Lewin (Burnes and Cooke, 2012). In Table 15.5, the differentiation between diagnostic and intervention tools and techniques is very evident (please see questions 5 and 6 in Table 15.3). Also, particular themes are related to particular tools and techniques. Even within the bounded context of the NHS in the North West, choosing the right tools for the right theme and activity is important.

In terms of strategy, Tassabehji and Isherwood (2014) highlighted the use of strategic tools for innovation during turbulent times. Although a plethora of strategy tools exist, the lack of a definitive summary of tools was acknowledged (Clark, 1997). The best-known strategy tools are featured in Table 15.6.

Tassabehji and Isherwood (2014) cite Gunn and Williams (2007) highlighting how professional and educational backgrounds may influence strategic tool preferences. They found that academically trained managers favoured Porter's five forces, whereas professionally trained managers favoured SWOT analysis. Wright et al. (2013) highlighted

Table 15.5 OD diagnostics tools and techniques (the North West NHS Leadership Academy toolkit). www.nwacademy.nhs.uk/developingtogether/od-diagnostics-tools-techniques. Accessed 28 September 2017

Themes	OD diagnostic tools and techniques (examples)	OD intervention (examples)
Service improvement	Focus groups	Force field analysis
	Benchmarking	Stakeholder analysis
Staff engagement and consultation	Knowledge management	Appreciative inquiry
	Staff survey	Facilitated events
Culture	Organizational metrics	SWOT
	7 S model	Training needs analysis
Leadership development	Self-evaluation against the NHS leadership framework	360 degree feedback
		Coaching or mentoring
Team development	Interviews, observation, and questionnaires	Team building exercises
		Personality testing

Table 15.6 Common strategy tools (based upon Tassabehji and Isherwood, 2014)

Tool	Description
SWOT analysis	Strengths, weaknesses, opportunities, and threats in a 4 × 4 matrix
PEST or PESTEL	Mnemonic for analysis of the external environment
Porter's five forces	Analysis of existing industry and competition
Scenario planning	Creating scenarios to compare and contrast different options
Boston Consulting Group Matrix	Analysis of product portfolios

the most popular tools taught on strategy capstone courses included Porter's five forces model and generic strategies; SWOT; the resource-based view of the firm; value chain; Boston Consulting Group (BCG) Matrix; McKinsey 7S framework; balanced scorecard; Bowman's strategy clock; strategic group maps; strategic factor analysis summary (SFAS); and Blue Ocean four action framework.

Questioning the utility of tools and techniques

In this questioning section, the emphasis upon management and leadership tools and techniques featured in earlier sections will be questioned. Whilst tools and techniques may be perceived as facilitating organizational change, they may also impede dynamic and often complex ongoing processes of changing. Questioning is undertaken from four related perspectives. These subsections are more philosophical than the practical emphasis of the previous section with each subsection answering a specific question:

> How does the notion of management fashions inform our understanding of tools and techniques?
> Is practical judgement more important than rational notions of tools and techniques?
> What happens when theories become tools?
> How useful are the strategic tools taught in business schools?

How does the notion of management fashions inform our understanding of tools and techniques?

In *Management Fads and Buzzwords*, Collins (2000) offered a different way of thinking about tools and techniques. His chapters are organized around themes such as total quality management, business process re-engineering, and knowledge work. In terms of earlier discussions, we can then think of each management fad as using particular tools and techniques. This encourages us to think in terms of the transitory nature of the appeal of tools and techniques, just like the fashion for hair length and dress length might oscillate over time between short and long, so there may be variations in which tools and techniques are in or out of fashion. Collins (2000) encourages us to think about how critical thinking can inform the practical application of tools and techniques. His favoured critical-practical perspective, recognises practical challenges that managers and leaders encounter but tempers this through the application of critical thinking. Abrahamson and Fairchild (1999) explained quality circles in terms of a problem discourse, a solution discourse and a bandwagon discourse. Quality circles were very fashionable a few decades ago, yet they are rarely mentioned today. In this instance, the bandwagon moved elsewhere.

Is practical judgement more important than rational notions of tools and techniques?

Stacey (2012: 40) offers a very insightful and very different perspective on tools and techniques informed by his interests in complex responsive processes.

> In essence, all of these tools and techniques are prescriptions that are supposed to make it possible to choose improved organizational outcomes and results well

in advance of acting. In other words, they are instruments for choosing and controlling the future of an organization, for choosing and realizing its aims, and they have been developed through rational analysis and measurement.

There is a challenge here to tools and techniques, which could be applied to many of the debates featured in this textbook. The idea that we can choose and control organizational futures with the right methodologies, tools, and techniques is highly seductive but questionable. Stacey (2012) describes the thinking that informed the first half of this chapter as 'instrumental rationality'. Whilst, he concedes that it is the dominant discourse in organizations and society, he is very sceptical that tools and techniques can control future outcomes and he offers four reasons for this scepticism.

First, tools and techniques suggest efficient causality which is too simplistic to explain human interaction. Second, tools and techniques as abstractions have to be particularised to unique contexts, resulting in the loss of instrumental rationality. Third, tools and techniques require rule following and again rule following varies with context. Fourth, experts do not follow the rules of tools and techniques but exercise practical judgement. Stacey (2012: 108) reminds us that those who are proficient in and expert at performing an activity do not use rules or tools. Instead, they exercise practical judgement 'practical judgement is the experience-based ability to notice more of what is going on and intuit what is most important about a situation'.

What happens when theories become tools?

In Chapter 1, tensions between the practical requirements of organizational change and academic emphasis on theory and research were introduced. Worren et al. (2002) creatively speak to such tension in explaining three different ways in which academic theories can become management tools. They highlight three modes: propositional, narrative and visual representation which make very different appeals to different audiences in different scenarios.

First, there is the propositional mode of representation involving prescriptions about potential managerial actions and outcomes, for example, Japanese manufacturing practices leading to higher quality and productivity. In this way, specific tools and techniques, such as quality circles, are represented as propositions. Second, there is the narrative mode of representation relying on stories and anecdotes as illustrations of courses of action. Using Japanese manufacturing again, the influential book *The Machine that Changed the World* (Womack et al., 1991) illustrates a narrative mode of representation and the use of tools and techniques is exemplified in that book. Third, there is the visual mode of representation, such as diagrams and conceptual models, which simplify complex information into meaningful patterns. For example, the intent of Japanese manufacturing principles may be conveyed through four boxes. The first box 'Japanese manufacturing principles' feeds into two separate boxes, 'productivity' and 'quality' and these feed into 'competitive advantage'. Each mode of representation has strengths and weaknesses. As with the Japanese manufacturing illustrative example cited here, all three modes of representation could be drawn upon. The learning is that they highlight ways in which theories such as those emanating from Japanese manufacturing might be communicated as tools through very different modes of representation.

How useful are the strategic tools taught in business schools?

The final question raises an awkward concern that an emphasis on tools and techniques in many business schools may not be that useful. Sturdy et al. (2006: 851) (as discussed in Chapter 7) studied what MBAs learnt from their MBAs at an anonymous business school finding that 'overall then, despite forming the bulk of the MBA syllabus and lying at the heart of student expectations and business school promises, specific and applicable managerial tools and techniques were largely dismissed as an outcome of the learning process for these managers and part-time students'. However, this did not equate to dissatisfied students as their studies contributed to increased self-confidence and legitimised their identities as managers.

Sturdy et al.'s (2006) finding about tools and techniques leads into Wright et al. (2013) considering the use of strategic tools taught in business schools. They were interested in managers' internal logic as they put these tools into practice. Their research respondents were 46 full-time managers enrolled on capstone strategy courses, they had an average of 15 years' work experience.

> ...our findings show that managers do in fact look for tools that provide multiple perspectives, help users to come up with new ideas and perform analysis from different angles, show interconnectivity between entities, divide areas to give a clearer picture, and guide the thinking process in ways that foster complex and connected thinking.
>
> (Wright et al., 2013: 114)

The implications of this research for practitioners were a need to develop capabilities for paradoxical thinking, peripheral vision, connected thinking and learning to see things from different perspectives. Skill in differentiating and integrating complex interconnected issues for clearer thinking was required. Although Wright et al.'s (2013) study focused on strategic tools, it offers a positive conclusion to this chapter suggesting that tools and techniques potentially do have a role to play, but that their utility is contingent on their use being informed by subtle and critical thinking.

Summary

The chapter may be succinctly summarised through answering the questions posed in the chapter's introduction with the original questions restated in italics.

What are practitioners doing, in terms of their tools and techniques usage? Practitioners are likely to use mundane tools every day, which we do not even think about as tools (Peters, 1978). There has been ongoing practitioner interest in establishing the most popular tools and levels of practitioner satisfaction (Clark, 1997; Cullen et al., 2004; Rigby, 2001).

What do we know about change management tools and techniques? In answering this question, Hughes (2007) was revisited and his classification questions were still felt to be useful. These included differentiating tools from techniques, the popularity, and satisfaction with tools and techniques, the levels of use, use for diagnosis or intervention and choices about levels of control and speed of implementation.

How might tools and techniques from different fields of study inform our understanding? Tools and techniques from the fields of project management, organizational development (OD) and strategy were featured. Burke (2009), Tayntor (2010), Turner (2014) and Smith et al. (2014) all placed emphasis upon the use of project management tools and techniques in implementing organizational change. OD utilises particular tools and techniques and this was illustrated through their usage by the North West NHS Leadership Academy (2017) using a mix of OD diagnostic and intervention tools and techniques for particular themes such as service improvement and staff engagement. In a similar manner Tassabehji and Isherwood (2014) highlighted the use of strategic tools for innovation during turbulent times. Although acknowledging a lack of a definitive summary of tools (Clark, 1997), the best-known strategy tools included SWOT analysis and PESTEL.

What questions need to be raised about the utility of tools and techniques? Potentially notions of management fashions inform our understanding of tools and techniques, highlighting their transitory nature (please see Collins, 2000 and Abrahamson and Fairchild, 1999). Practical judgement may be more important than instrumental rationality of tools and techniques (Stacey, 2012). We need to understand what happens when theories become tools. Worren et al. (2002) highlight three modes of representation: propositional, narrative and visual representation which make very different appeals to different audiences in different scenarios. Finally, the usefulness of the strategic tools taught in business schools was questioned. Sturdy et al. (2006) in their study of MBA students found managerial tools and techniques largely dismissed, whereas Wright et al.'s (2013) study of student use of strategic tools, suggested that tools and techniques potentially had a role to play.

Research case study showcase: scenario planning at Rolls-Royce and the Royal Society of Chemistry

Ramirez et al.'s (2017) scenario planning case studies reported in the *MIT Sloan Management Review* are showcased here. For full analysis and further details, please visit the original source.

Case study source

Scenario planning offers organizations an approach to deal with uncertainties in framing long-term strategies. The lead author is a professor of practice and director of the Oxford Scenarios Programme at the University of Oxford's Said Business School and the second and third authors work for Rolls-Royce and the Royal Society for Chemistry respectively.

Ramirez, R., S. Churchhouse, J. Hoffman, and A. Palermo. 2017. "Using Scenario Planning to Reshape Strategy." *MIT Sloan Management Review* 58(4): 31–37.

The case study

The Oxford scenario planning approach encourages collaboration between individuals and groups at different levels and from different functions within an organization. They examine factors potentially contributing to the future as a means of reframing collective understanding of the present. The Oxford scenario planning approach focuses upon what is plausible, rather than the focus of other scenario planning approaches which is what is probable. They use the mnemonic TUNA to refer to turbulence, unpredictable uncertainty, novelty and ambiguity, regarding TUNA conditions as unsettling and destabilising for organizations. The Oxford approach focuses on two layers, first the immediate business environment including the company's suppliers, customers, competitors, partners, and other stakeholders. The second layer is all the factors which are beyond an organization's direct influence. Ramirez et al. (2017) share how the Oxford approach to scenario planning was put into practice at Rolls-Royce and the Royal Society of Chemistry.

Rolls-Royce PLC

The organization was founded in 1906 in order to produce quality cars in the United Kingdom. Today, it is a leading supplier of power systems for aircraft and marine and energy markets and Rolls-Royce Holdings PLC is no longer in the automobile business. Rolls-Royce designs, manufactures and distributes power systems for aviation and other industries employing about 50,000 employees, with an underlying revenue of £13.8 billion.

During the 2008 financial crash, the company benefited from a substantial order book and the quality of its aftermarket service business. However, in early 2014, the company was involved in the cyclical decline in wide-body airliner orders. Also, there was a slowdown in Chinese economic growth and an end to the boom in commodities impacted airline businesses. The decline in oil prices affected marine and energy markets, and the accident at Fukushima in Japan impacted the company's civil nuclear power business. These unrelated events affected most aspects of Rolls-Royce's business. The share price fell more than 50 per cent as management issued five profit warnings during 2014 and 2015.

A new CEO arrived in July 2015, with the company searching for new ways to do business. Their top managers participated in an Oxford University executive education course during this summer. One session featured scenario planning and the managers subsequently lobbied Rolls-Royce for this scenario planning to be introduced company wide. The focus was on cataloguing significant factors potentially affecting Rolls-Royce by the year 2040 and developing a set of strategic questions. Management in conversation with board members and some authors of the Ramirez et al. (2017) paper designed and ran a programme to develop and review a set of future scenarios. The process began at Rolls-Royce with about 25 mid/senior-level executives being selected from different business units, different functions, and different locations. In preparation for the three-day workshop, the group studied a wide range of topics relating to the company's future.

Day one: Participants presented posters summarising the research that they had undertaken. Then, in four small groups, they were tasked with creating scenarios for Rolls-Royce in 2040. These scenarios had to be plausible and relevant and to challenge assumptions in current strategies of the company.

Day two: The small groups shared draft scenarios with the whole group, enabling the development of three draft scenarios.

(Continued)

Table 15.7   Four Rolls-Royce strategic questions (Ramirez et al., 2017: 34)

What would digitization look like in the future?
What factors would affect relations between employees and companies in 2040?
What conditions will determine the future of emerging markets?
How might technology pathways develop?

i   The world is characterised by high connectivity in which efficiency and collaboration were the norm.
ii   A new world order emerges where India and China leverage technology to rival the United States with other countries having to adjust to this new world order.
iii A highly divided digital future benefits some groups and not others.

Day three: Workshop participants reviewed and critiqued the three scenarios and considered four strategic questions (please see Table 15.7).

Post workshop, the scenarios informed Rolls-Royce management's 2016 strategic planning process. Scenarios were shared with the wider strategy community and senior executives. The implication was that investment proposals had to account for each of the three scenarios in order to mitigate or exploit the three scenarios, with proposals not meeting these criteria being rejected. The three scenarios helped to determine the selection of investment initiatives emerging through the 2016 strategy development process and the scenarios provided a backdrop for developing the company's 2017 strategy.

The Royal Society of Chemistry (RSC)

The RSC is an international organization based in London seeking to advance the field of chemical sciences. The goal of scenario planning for the RSC was to understand how chemical sciences might evolve over the next 10 or 20 years, and how these changes would impact industry, academia and society. The scientific, social and technological trends which are changing the lives and work of people are also changing the nature and practice of chemistry and the roles of chemists. Chemistry plays a key role in solving practical problems relating to: disease, sustainable energy, food, water, and creating new industries. The fundamental question was: "How should people think about the future of chemistry?" The RSC's mission is to advance excellence in the chemical sciences. Its roots go back to the 1840s, when a group of scientists including doctors, academics, manufacturers, and entrepreneurs, formed the Chemical Society of London. Today the RSC has more than 55,000 members and a reputation for championing the chemical sciences.

A long-range planning initiative was launched by the RSC in December 2014 with broad goals. The initiative did not use the language of scenario planning, but did aim to identify possible future directions and anticipate, plan, and prepare for advances in the field over the next 10 to 15 years. Ramirez et al. (2017: 35) highlighted some of the big questions the RSC leadership wanted to be considered:

How might the identity of chemistry change?

Could chemistry be facing a future in which academic chemistry departments disappear altogether?

If public funding is not available to support the type of blue-skies research that has traditionally produced the next major advances, how will future research be funded?

And how will increasingly sophisticated technology and computational techniques change the way new hypotheses are analysed and tested?

A one-day workshop was convened for the RSC leadership team with selected senior managers considering a wide range of factors. The workshop encouraged senior staff from throughout the RSC to look broadly at how the field was changing. The workshop set the stage for a new role the RSC could play. A multi-phase scenario planning programme was developed. The first phase ran for three months. About 50 stakeholders from industry, government, and academia selected by RSC leaders were interviewed by phone in order to identify possible trends. Follow-up in-person interviews with certain stakeholders aimed to understand controversies and in some instances secure buy-in from key leaders in the chemical industry.

During this process, themes began to emerge and these themes informed three one-day scenario planning workshops run by the RSC in London and Boston. The intention was to encourage future oriented conversations which would help executives, academics and policy-makers act proactively. As a means of challenging assumptions of chemistry leaders, four scenarios were developed by the RSC (please see Table 15.8).

The scenarios in Table 15.8 helped the RSC develop its long-term strategy. The process nudged chemical science leaders in planning for the future to move beyond conventional thinking.

The long-range planning team at the RSC encourages the wider community to reflect on opportunities and challenges with the scenario planning process findings broadening engagement with RSC communities. The RSC leadership

Table 15.8 Chemistry science scenarios developed by the RSC and reported by Ramirez et al. (2017: 35)

1   The first scenario focused on the benefits chemistry brings to the world – its ability to provide answers to global challenges, such as climate change, water shortages, natural resources scarcity, and providing healthcare for an aging population.
2   The second scenario focused on changes in the way chemistry is done and how it is organized, envisioning a world where the chemical sciences are increasingly automated and decentralized.
3   The third scenario spoke to the growing separation of chemistry into subdisciplines and how that might negatively impact the pipeline of future chemists.
4   And the fourth scenario explored the impact of reduced public funding for the chemical sciences.

(Continued)

wants to initiate new scenario-based activities, including the launch of new programmes advancing chemistry education and scholarly communication into the future. All elements of the RSC's new strategy, which the governing board was due to approve in July 2017 were tested against the scenario planning opportunities and challenges.

Case study questions

1   How can Oxford scenario planning be explained using Burke's (2009) differentiation between tools, skills, techniques and processes?
2   How can Oxford scenario planning be explained in terms of Worren et al.'s (2002) differentiation between propositional, narrative and visual representation of tools?

Discussion questions

1   Why do practitioners turn to tools and techniques?
2   Why are academics suspicious of tools and techniques?
3   What are the strengths and weaknesses of a professional body promoting tools and techniques?
4   Why is it difficult to evaluate the strengths and weaknesses of particular tools and techniques?

Navigating the tools and techniques literature

In writing this chapter literature has been reviewed from the previous two decades. The impression gained is that there is still a strong practitioner interest in tools and techniques. However, the beliefs of a decade ago (please see Hughes, 2007) that a gap between theories and practices could be bridged appears less realistic. This is possibly due to a greater acknowledgement of the challenges and complexities of organizational change processes. These processes require more than selecting the correct tools from the manager/leader toolbox.

The journal *Strategic Change* has been cited in this chapter, although please note that the journal now focusses on finance with a new strapline – *Briefings in Entrepreneurial Finance*. Qehaja et al.'s (2017) recently published literature review was helpful in writing this chapter and whilst it focusses upon strategy tools it is a good starting point for anyone undertaking their own review of the literature. Wright et al. (2013) in their paper offer a short literature review on strategic tools, which is very useful for anyone who wants to think more deeply about the debates featured here.

The Bain & Company website (www.bain.com) is worth visiting as there are many free management tools and techniques trends, satisfaction and usage rates documents which can be downloaded. However, post-2015, their coverage of tools and techniques notably lessened. The challenge in writing this chapter for an organizational change textbook is that a bounded organizational change tools and techniques literature does not exist. Consequently, for anyone undertaking a review of this literature, it is necessary to cross boundaries around fields of study such as 'strategy' and 'organizational development'. Also, it is necessary to acknowledge variables discussed in earlier chapters. Differences in terms of types of change, sector and the geographical area may influence the appropriateness of particular tools and techniques.

References

Abrahamson, E., and G. Fairchild. 1999. "Management Fashion: Lifecycles, Triggers, and Collective Learning Processes." *Administrative Science Quarterly* 44(4): 708–740.

Burke, R. 2009. *Fundamentals of Project Management: Tools and Techniques*. London: Burke Publishing.

Burnes, B., and B. Cooke. 2012. "The Past, Present and Future of Organization Development: Taking the Long View." *Human Relations* 65(11): 1395–1429.

Clark, D.N. 1997. "Strategic Management Tool Usage: A Comparative Study." *Strategic Change* 6(7): 417–427.

Collins, D. 2000. *Management Fads and Buzzwords: Critical-Practical Perspectives*. London: Routledge.

Crawford, L., and A.H. Nahmias. 2010. "Competencies for Managing Change." *International Journal of Project Management* 28(4): 405–412.

Cullen, J., M. O'Connor, and J. Mangan, 2004. "Matching Management Tools and Techniques with Management Challenges." *Strategy and Leadership* 32(3): 27–30.

Gunn, R., and W. Williams. 2007. "Strategic Tools: An Empirical Investigation into Strategy in Practice in the UK." *Strategic Change* 16(5): 201–216.

Hornstein, H.A. 2015. "The Integration of Project Management and Organizational Change Management is now a Necessity." *International Journal of Project Management* 33(2): 291–298.

Hughes, M. 2007. "The Tools and Techniques of Change Management." *Journal of Change Management* 7(1): 37–49.

Morris, P.W.G., M.B. Patel, and S.H. Wearne. 2000. "Research into Revising the APM project Management Body of Knowledge." *International Journal of Project Management* 18(3): 155–164.

Peters, T.J. 1978. "Symbols, Patterns, and Settings: An Optimistic Case for Getting Things Done." *Organizational Dynamics* 7(2): 3–23.

Qehaja, A.B., E. Kutllovci, and P.J. Shiroka. 2017. "Strategic Management Tools and Techniques: A Comparative Analysis of Empirical Studies." *Croatian Economic Survey* 19(1): 67–99.

Ramirez, R., S. Churchhouse, J. Hoffman, and A. Palermo. 2017. "Using Scenario Planning to Reshape Strategy." *MIT Sloan Management Review* 58(4): 31–37.

Rigby, D. 2001. "Management Tools and Techniques: A Survey." *California Management Review* 43(2): 139–160.

Salaman, G., and D. Asch. 2003. *Strategy and Capability: Sustaining Organizational Change*. Oxford: Blackwell.

Smith, R., D. King, R. Sidhu, and D. Skelsey (Eds). 2014. *The Effective Change Manager's Handbook: Essential Guidance to the Change Management Body of Knowledge*. London: Kogan Page Publishers.

Stacey, R.D. 2012. *Tools and Techniques of Leadership and Management: Meeting the Challenge of Complexity*. London: Routledge.

Sturdy, A., M. Brocklehurst, D. Winstanley, and M. Littlejohns. 2006. "Management as a (self) Confidence Trick: Management Ideas, Education and Identity Work." *Organization* 13(6): 841–860.

Tassabehji, R., and A. Isherwood. 2014. "Management use of Strategic Tools for Innovating during Turbulent Times." *Strategic Change* 23(1–2): 63–80.

Tayntor, C.B. 2010. *Project Management Tools and Techniques for Success*. London: CRC Press.

Turner, R.J. 2014. *The Handbook of Project-based Management: Leading Strategic Change in Organizations.* London: McGraw-Hill Education.

Umbeck, T. and A. Bron. 2017. "Change Management in Merger Integration." Bain Brief, June 14, 2017. Available at www.bain.com/publications/articles/change-management-in-merger-integration.aspx

Womack, J.P., D.T. Jones, and D. Roos. 1991. *The Machine that Changed the World.* London: Simon and Schuster.

Worren, N.A., K. Moore, and R. Elliott. 2002. "When Theories Become Tools: Toward a Framework for Pragmatic Validity." *Human Relations* 55(10): 1227–1250.

Wright, R.P., S.E. Paroutis, and D.P. Blettner. 2013. "How Useful are the Strategic Tools we Teach in Business Schools?" *Journal of Management Studies* 50(1): 92–125.

Chapter 16

The dark side of organizations

Introduction and chapter questions

This chapter draws on earlier chapters, particularly debates featured in the questioning sections in order to highlight dark side activities which all stakeholders in organizations need to challenge. Crude J.D.I. (Just Do It!) exhortations are indicative of a breakdown in communications often accompanied by physical or verbal violence. These exhortations have created an ugly stereotype of managing/leading change which needs to be actively challenged. This chapter focuses on the dark side of organizations as another perspective on theories and practices of managing and leading change and transformation.

Kotter's (1996/2012) encouragement of managers to manipulate and to create artificial crises in order to create the sense of urgency which would enable leading change was highlighted in Chapter 10. These dark side activities were unacceptable at the time and they are certainly out of date today with regards to attitudes, values, and beliefs in organizations and societies. Future managers need to appreciate the need to use power ethically in acknowledging the growing demands of civil society for ethical standards in management (Duarte, 2010). McMillan (2016) encourages a shift of focus from standardised and scientifically oriented knowledge (McKinlay and Starkey, 1998). Rather than regarding organizational change as apolitical, measurable and predictable, she encourages us to think about moral, political and ethical aspects of organizational change, recognising how organizational change impacts individuals.

Whilst, this textbook has focussed upon organizational change, there are signs of broader changes in organizations and societies with regards to what is acceptable and unacceptable. As this chapter will highlight, concerns about the dark side of organizations are not exclusive to critical academics (please see the what practitioners shouldn't be doing section). However, the approach unifying this chapter is critical in focussing upon issues of power, domination, exploitation and resistance resulting in implicit/explicit concerns with emancipation (Linstead et al., 2014). This chapter is organized around and provides answers to the following questions about the dark side of organizations:

What shouldn't practitioners be doing?
What can we learn from the study of coercive persuasion?
Why is understanding the dark side of behaviour at work believed to be informative?
What can we learn from the study of corporate psychopaths?
What can we learn from the dark side of organizations in different contexts?
What do we need to question in current accounts of the dark side of organizations?
What do we know about management's dark side?
What do we know about the dark side of transformational leadership?

Other chapters have been designed to contrast the orthodoxy of practices and theories in the first half of the chapter with questioning in the second half of the chapter. In this chapter, the whole chapter largely questions dark side activities of organizations.

In the next section, what shouldn't practitioners be doing highlights the dark side of corporate scandals. The understanding section is organized around four themes: the often-neglected notion of coercive persuasion, the dark side of employee behaviour, the existence of corporate psychopaths at senior levels inside organizations and three accounts of the dark side in different contexts. The questioning section is organized around Linstead et al.'s (2014) account of the dark side of organizations, Hanlon's (2015) account of the dark side of management and Tourish's (2013) account of the dark side of transformational leadership.

What shouldn't practitioners be doing?
Examples of the dark side at work

By definition dark side activities of organizations tend to lurk in the shadows. However, authors (Furnham and Taylor, 2004; Nguyen et al., 2015; Ward and McMurray, 2015) have increasingly begun to illuminate previously undisclosed activities. It is a sad indictment of the state of business that 'Fortune' a leading business magazine is able to publish a listing of the biggest corporate scandals of the year (please see Table 16.1).

Table 16.1 The five biggest corporate scandals of 2016 as reported by Fortune in 2016

	Title	Description
1	Wells Fargo's fake accounts	Wells Fargo grew its profits by cross-selling more profitable products to its customers. Employees were pressurised to hit sales quotas, resulting in employees fraudulently opening customer accounts. The bank was forced to repay fees to customers and fines to the government.
2	Roger Ailes's sexual-harassment scandal	Gretchen Carlson (Fox News anchor) made public her lawsuit against the chairman and CEO of Fox News, Roger Ailes, which resulted in further allegations of harassment. Ailes finally settled with Carlson for $20 million with further lawsuits pending at the time of writing.
3	Mylan's EpiPen price gouging scandal	The EpiPen administers epinephrine to those suffering anaphylactic shock. Since acquiring the device in 2007, Mylan increased the price by 400 per cent. The CEO, Heather Bresch, had to answer for Mylan's pricing decisions to the House Oversight Committee and subsequently, there were investigations into antitrust violations.
4	Samsung battery recall	Batteries in Samsung Galaxy Note 7 smartphones exploded. The Federal Aviation Administration and the Consumer Product Safety Commission urged consumers not to use these particular smartphones, and the batteries were recalled.
5	The Panama Papers	11.5 million documents were stolen from Panamanian law firm Mossack Fonseca. The documents exposed wealthy people hiding their wealth and income from tax authorities and other interested parties.

Source: http://fortune.com/2016/12/28/biggest-corporate-scandals-2016/. Accessed 21 November 2017.

Table 16.1 highlights dark side activities, although sadly these are only the corporate scandals which had come to light. Wells Fargo pressurised employees to meet sale quotas. Women were sexually harassed. EpiPen's price rose by 400 per cent. Samsung was encouraged to recall its batteries and the Panama Papers revealed the scale on which the wealthy hide their wealth and income from tax authorities. Unfortunately, these scandals have become far too common in the current decade. Raufflet and Mills (2009) in *The Dark Side: Critical Cases on the Downside of Business*, brought together cases of the dark side and subsequently, further volumes have been published.

Understanding the dark side of organizations

There has been a growth in interest in studying the dark side of organizations. The dark side appears to be a container concept, in that many unacceptable activities in organizations may be discussed under this label. Also, in the questioning section, an even darker side of organizations will be highlighted. In this understanding section, many illustrations could have been offered, but four have been chosen which are particularly pertinent to organizational change and its management and leadership. First, the concept of coercive persuasion is introduced which for Schein (1985) underpinned his influential work on organizational culture and leadership. Second, Furnham and Taylor's (2004) account of the dark side behaviours of employees is introduced. Third, Boddy (2011) shifts the focus to how certain managers and leaders act as corporate psychopaths. Fourth, the dark side of organizations in different contexts is highlighted through accounts published in particular journals.

Coercive persuasion

Organizational Culture and Leadership (Schein, 1985) was an important milestone in studying organizational culture and change leadership. However, what is often overlooked is Schein's (1985) honest and open acknowledgement that such cultural change would require coercive persuasion. Cooke (1999) in his historiography of the management of change is one of the few scholars to highlight what has been written out of accounts of Edgar Schein's work. In a section subtitled *Managerial Attitude Change as Maoist Brainwashing*, Cooke (1999) highlights how Schein's research into the Chinese Communist Party (CCP) informed the writing of his book *Coercive Persuasion* (Schein, 1961). It was this now out-of-print book which subsequently informed Schein's (1985) influential account of organizational culture and leadership. Cooke (1999) highlighted that Schein's (1961) interest in coercive persuasion is rarely acknowledged in the management literature except by Schein himself.

Ofshe (1991 in his overview of coercive persuasion and attitude change revisited Schein's (1961) work on coercive persuasion. Coercive persuasion is synonymous with brainwashing. However, coercive persuasion may be differentiated from other forms of training and socialization in four ways. First, there is an intense interpersonal and psychological attack which seeks to destabilise an individual's sense of self in promoting compliance. Second, there is the use of an organized peer group. Third, the interpersonal pressure is applied to promote conformity and fourth, the totality of the person's social environment is utilised in stabilising behaviour once modified. Schein (1961) separated the behavioural sequence of coercive persuasion into the three subphases: unfreezing, change and refreezing utilising persuasive, influencing and coercive tactics.

Unfreezing – destabilising a person's sense of identity, diminishing confidence in prior social judgments and fostering a sense of powerlessness.

Changing – offers a chance to escape punishing destabilisation by demonstrating that the preferred ideology has been learned, demonstrating zeal through displays of commitment.

Refreezing – promoting and reinforcing behaviour acceptable to the controlling organization; the target is encouraged to understand the errors of his or her former life.

Schein (1961) developed his understanding of coercive persuasion through studying the treatment of prisoners of war by the CCP during the Korean War. This may appear tangential to the discussions about organizational change in this textbook. However, Schein (1985) regarded coercive persuasion as integral to changes in organizational culture and leadership. In Chapter 6, theories and practices of cultural change were highlighted and in Chapter 10, leading organizational change theories and practices were highlighted. These significant organizational change debates underpinned by the brainwashing of coercive persuasion may be regarded as illustrative of the dark side at work.

The dark side of behaviour at work

Furnham and Taylor's (2004) thesis is captured in the subtitle of their book *Understanding and Avoiding Employees Leaving, Thieving and Deceiving*. Their position is atypical of most of the dark side literature, but in the context of a textbook offers a different perspective on the chapter theme.

> Whistle-blowers these days almost have hero status. Their motive is clearly to expose a wrong, but few stop to think if there might be some other reason for their action. Fewer, have tried to analyze their motivation. Could it be that to question the motive of a whistle-blower is not politically correct?
>
> (Furnham and Taylor, 2004: xi)

Whilst, this is a contentious preface to their book, it does signal one of their concerns, that in order to understand dark side behaviours at work we need to understand what motivates these behaviours. They highlight cultural, economic and political forces, as well as organizational factors and individual factors. In particular, at the individual level, they highlight how a breakdown in psychological contracts may be a motivation for dark side behaviours at work.

> The road from hopeful candidate to disenchanted employee is a long one. The ideal fit between employer and employee may not last and the psychological contract is easily broken.
>
> (Furnham and Taylor, 2004: 25)

Whilst, their book majors on managers and leaders dealing with the potential leaving, thieving and deceiving of employees, the presence of bad bosses is acknowledged in terms of narcissism, bullying bosses and toxic bosses.

In *Bad Apples: Identify, Prevent & Manage Negative Behavior at Work*, Furnham and Taylor (2011) develop themes from the earlier book. The book is organized around the metaphor of an apple as featured in the title. The implication is that one bad apple can spoil the other apples through close contact. Consequently, managers and leaders need to identify these so-called bad apples (bad employees) lest they contaminate other employees. The author's concern is that bad people affect those around them. Consequently, the way people are organized can strengthen or weaken such a process. Positively, they believe that if people are managed in a just, open and aligned organization, they will perform better.

Corporate psychopaths

As a counterpoint to the leaving, thieving and deceiving of bad apple employees, we can point the critical spotlight towards senior management. In *Corporate Psychopaths: Organisational Destroyers*, Boddy (2011) draws attention to large corporations being destroyed by their senior directors. Potential consequences of such corporate psychopaths are employees losing their jobs and capitalism losing some of its credibility. He notes these corporate collapses gathering pace culminating in the global financial crisis (2007/2008). However, senior directors have frequently failed to take responsibility instead blaming others. He suggests that some of these directors display the characteristics of psychopaths, and he labels them corporate psychopaths 'psychopaths are the 1 percent of people who have no conscience or empathy and who do not care for anyone other than themselves' (Boddy, 2011: 1).

Boddy (2011) revisits the literature on the negative effects leaders with personality disorders can have on their organizations with the book underpinned by his own empirical studies, as well as, the studies of others. This allows him to highlight six effects of corporate psychopaths on corporate outcomes (please see Table 16.2).

Another troubling finding from Boddy's (2011: 103) research and other studies is that the higher up the organization you go, the more likely you are to encounter corporate psychopaths, 'corporate psychopaths seek leadership positions because of their desire to access the prestige, power, control of others and financial rewards that are associated with senior management'. However, troublingly, corporate psychopaths may be encouraged by their respective organizations to rise up the organizational hierarchy as many of their traits are the traits organizations desire, such as determination, dynamism, and ambition (see Boddy, 2015 for an update of his earlier work).

Table 16.2 Effects of corporate psychopaths on corporate outcomes (based on Boddy, 2011)

Effects of corporate psychopaths on corporate outcomes

1   Heightened level of conflict
2   Perceptions that an organization does business in a socially responsible manner and in a way that shows commitment to employees plummet dramatically
3   There are heavier than necessary organizational constraints in workplaces where corporate psychopaths are present
4   Neglect of managerial and leadership responsibilities, others blamed for mistakes and omissions
5   Significant negative impacts on multiple aspects of job satisfaction
6   Employees experiencing corporate psychopaths withdraw from the organizational environment

The dark side of organizations in different contexts

Reviewing accounts of the dark side reported in management and organization studies journals illustrates contextual differences in studies of the dark side. Lips-Wiersma et al. (2009) focus on the dark side of workplace spirituality (WPS). Baruch and Vardi (2016) explore the darker dynamics of careers and Yagil (2017) the dark side of customer aggression. In each instance, the researchers are looking at different aspects of organizational life under the broader umbrella concept of the dark side.

Initially, it feels counterintuitive to seek out the dark side of WPS. However, Lips-Wiersma et al. (2009) effectively highlight WPS's dark side specifically in terms of seduction, evangelisation, manipulation, and subjugation.

> WPS is an organizational phenomenon describing employees' spiritual or religious expressions and experiences in the workplace.
>
> (Lips-Wiersma et al., 2009: 288)

There is often an emphasis on meaningful work, with employees regarded as bringing physical, intellectual, emotional and spiritual attributes to the workplace. WPS seeks to utilise such resources in making organizations more productive and innovative. Lips-Wiersma et al. (2009) encountered a win-win orthodoxy around WPS, but they wanted to critically explore the management of the soul which WPS requires. Their critical focus is not WPS, but how WPS may be misused or misappropriated.

In studying WPS in organizations, Lips-Wiersma et al. (2009) were interested in control in terms of the degree of direction exercised over members and instrumentality the extent to which employees are treated as a means to an end. In organizations which exhibit low instrumentality and low levels of control, WPS is achieved through seduction. They cite pharmacists refusing to prescribe contraceptives due to such WPS seduction.

Organizations with low instrumentality and high control practise evangelisation. In such organizations, spirituality is not regarded as a tool to improve performance. However, how WPS is incorporated into the organization is highly specified by management, with the organization in many ways displaying informal and formal characteristics of a religious cult.

Organizations with high instrumentality and low control practise manipulation with spirituality a tool for improving performance. In this instance, WPS becomes another tool to potentially manipulate employees in order to improve productivity. Finally, organizations exhibiting high instrumentality and high control practise subjugation. In this instance, WPS is a tool to improve performance and the form and nature of WPS are highly specified by management.

> WPS literature errs in its tendency to portray the benefits of the movement as all light and joy for individuals without acknowledging ever-present dark-side manifestations. Ultimately, we must examine organizations and the individuals who inhabit them, at the intersection of control and instrumentality if we are going to achieve a realistic understanding of the WPS movement.
>
> (Lips-Wiersma et al., 2009: 295)

Baruch and Vardi (2016) explore the darker dynamics of careers which they regard as almost untouched. Instead, they encountered careers literature which tends to be euphemistic and normatively biased. In engaging with the darker dynamics of careers, they encourage accounts grounded in reality.

One cannot comprehend the true nature of careers by employing constructs and measures that presume positivity without at least considering notions of failure, job insecurity, unfair treatment, harassment and incivility in the same analysis.

(Baruch and Vardi, 2016: 355)

Their argument is that acknowledging the inevitable dark side of careers will offer a more balanced account of careers. They acknowledge the thrill of embarking on contemporary careers, but also that there is likely to be some agony along the way for most of us. Their paper is organized around prominent career concepts of the boundaryless career, protean career, career resilience, intelligent career, post-corporate career, multidirectional career, and kaleidoscope career. They highlight dark side arguments relating to each of these concepts. Baruch and Vardi (2016) warn that most career-oriented (management-anchored) people plateau at mid-career with their earlier career expectations a broken dream which may lead to counterproductive conduct in this phase of their career.

Acknowledging the negative aspects of careers and accepting the dark sides as significant and salient components of organizations can serve to encourage a balanced perspective in the study of careers and the complex interaction between person, work, and organization.

(Baruch and Vardi, 2016: 369)

Furnham and Taylor's (2004, 2011) interest in the misbehaviour of employees by definition does not focus upon the misbehaviour of customers, begging the question what do we know about customer misbehaviour particularly in service settings involving customer/employee interaction? For Yagil (2017), there is no dark side of customer aggression. It is all dark. She is interested in studying customer aggression both physical and verbal and cites high levels of verbal aggression in a range of different service settings. Yagil (2017: 1415) cites Bitner et al. (1994) acknowledging the impossibility of flawless performance.

Maintaining perpetual service perfection is impossible, not just because mistakes happen, but also because service quality is ultimately determined by customers' subjective evaluation, as reflected in the notion that flawless performance is meant to imply completely satisfying performance from the customer's point of view.

The danger inherent within such notions of flawless performance is that customer expectations are implausible with service employees constantly violating these expectations resulting in potential aggressive reactions from customers. Customer aggression is supported by a power differential between employees and customers with the ideology of customer sovereignty resulting in the customer becoming a second manager. The employee-customer power gap limits the freedom of employees to express anger and react to aggression. Normal coping strategies of fight or flight are not available in these service encounters where the goal is a flawless performance. Yagil (2017: 1417) cites Grandey et al. (2004).

Aggression is therefore less inhibited when directed towards service employees than in other contexts because there is lower perceived danger from abuse enacted by customers towards employees than in other contexts, such as in relationships with supervisors and co-workers.

Yagil (2017) attempts to end her account of the dark side of customer aggression positively by acknowledging how sexual harassment and workplace bullying have been challenged through legislation and how legislation could be introduced to limit customer aggression.

Questioning the dark side, the darker side of organization, management and transformational leadership

The debates featured in the previous section encouraged questioning dark side behaviours and activities in organizations. However, the danger is that some of the radical intent may be lost as the dark side becomes another label, similar to 'employee engagement', 'meaningfulness' or 'appreciative inquiry'. In the case of Furnham and Taylor (2011), employees were even depicted as 'bad apples' which need to be removed from organizations. Dark side conference streams and special issues of journals have appeared. You are reading a chapter on the dark side of organizations in this textbook.

However, the darker intent of the dark side literature is to question organizational, economic and societal structures which result in significant inequalities, rather than encouraging more benign management and leadership. This questioning section is informed by a paper (Linstead et al., 2014) and two books (Hanlon, 2015 and Tourish, 2013). Linstead et al. (2014) present a review of literature informing understanding about the dark side of organizations. They major on more radical/critical accounts of the dark side and, in particular, highlight Hanlon (2015) featured in the next subsection. The final subsection introduces Tourish's (2013) *The Dark Side of Transformational Leadership*, a book organized around real-life case studies of the damage transformational leadership does to organizations and the wider society.

The dark side of organizations

In theorising and researching the dark side of organization, Linstead et al. (2014: 165) couch their interest in the dark side in terms of their frustrations with orthodox accounts of organization studies.

> ...the tendencies of mainstream work to overlook, ignore or suppress difficult ethical, political and ideological issues, which may well mean life or death to some people, has in recent years led to a research that self-identifies its concerns as being with the dark side.

In this way, it could be argued that acknowledging the dark side has now become part of management and organization studies orthodoxy, rather than a challenge to orthodoxy. So how does Linstead et al.'s (2014) account of the dark side differ from such orthodoxy? They highlight early organizational behaviour research looking at the dark side from the perspective of workplace violence and aggression, viewing such behaviours as abnormal or deviant. Dark side focus then broadened to cover all workplace behaviours. Dark side behaviours which harmed individuals were differentiated from those which harmed organizations. They highlighted how the dark side may be deeply rooted in the inner darkness of the individual psyche.

However, Linstead et al. (2014) favoured a more critical approach to the dark side in focussing on issues of power, domination, exploitation, and resistance with an implicit or explicit concern with emancipation. They draw two insights from Marx. First, capitalism needs ideology such as commodity fetishism, nationalism or corporate culture to obscure from the exploited the nature of their oppression, impelling them away from collaboration. Second, capitalism constantly needs to creatively destroy itself, at the extreme end of entrepreneurship, sometimes referred to as the creative gales of destruction (please see Schumpeter, 1942 for further discussion). Current dark side orthodoxy may obscure the destructive dark side of capitalism, whilst purporting to offer to management and organization studies a critical perspective. Linstead et al. (2014) regard Gerard Hanlon as an exemplar of the truly critical dark side of management studies.

Management's dark side

Hanlon (2015) subtitles his *The Dark Side of Management* as a secret history of management theory. The subtitle acknowledges that his account of the history of management theory is very different from the history found in most textbooks and taught on most management/leadership courses (please see also Cummings et al.'s, 2017 recent historiography of management for further discussion). Hanlon (2015) regards management as constantly encouraging competition among labour and re-engineering employees as subjects, with these processes regarded as being inherently violent.

His secret history highlights certain groups such as children, women and migrants being particularly vulnerable to the early brutality of factories and capitalism. An emphasis on deskilling and the division of labour is highlighted in the nineteenth-century as a precursor to the management control which characterises organizations today. The secret history depicts how management became more subtle moving away from an early emphasis on coercion (J.D.I.) through to techniques of manipulation (such as cultural change). In the final chapter, he (2015: 22) argues '... that management is fundamentally a tool for delivering neo-liberalism through the competition of the managed work organization. Both share the following: a belief in active intervention, the prioritisation of competition, and the necessity of elite leadership.' Hanlon's (2015) focus is management rather than leadership in his secret history. Concerns have equally been raised about the dark side of organizational leadership.

Transformational leadership's dark side

The Dark Side of Transformational Leadership (Tourish, 2013) offers a critical perspective again in the spirit of the critical perspective on the dark side which Linstead et al. (2014) favour. The book is illustrated with troubling contemporary case studies of dark side behaviours with the second part of the book focussing on Enron, Militant Tendency, Jonestown, Heaven's Gate and the 2008 banking crisis. The book challenges preoccupations with leadership agency with regards to transformation and change, particularly pertinent to themes in this textbook. There is currently a preoccupation with leaders as the solution to a host of organizational problems, but Tourish (2013: 199) reverses this logic '...leadership, as traditionally envisaged, is a key part of the problems we now face, rather than the solution. This is particularly true of transformational leadership in its various guises.'

Tourish (2013) revisited Enron as one of his case studies of the dark side of leadership in corporate America. Enron's 2001 bankruptcy was the largest in US corporate history. Enron's intention had been to become the world's leading company, but since its demise, it has been remembered as an anecdote for corporate greed and corruption (Turnage, 2010). It is too easy to think of Enron's demise as a consequence of the dark side behaviours of its leaders Kenneth Lay and Jeffrey Skilling. Enron, until its bankruptcy, was celebrated as an exemplar of the orthodoxy troubling Linstead et al. (2014).

> Faculty at the prestigious Harvard Business School produced 11 case studies into Enron, uniformly lauding its 'successes' and commending its business model to others. All of them have since been discretely withdrawn.
>
> (Tourish, 2013: 120)

As Tourish (2013) acknowledged Enron is a complex story. The 'rank and yank' appraisal system illustrates one cultural aspect of the larger story. 'Rank and yank' was very similar to the appraisal system of Jack Welch at General Electric. Employees were rated twice a year and then divided into three groups. The 'As' were challenged and given large rewards. The 'Bs' were encouraged and affirmed and the 'Cs' were told to shape up or ship out. The 'Cs' were given six months to improve. Although as it was almost impossible to improve sufficiently to move to the 'B' category, most staff left quickly.

> The rank-and-yank system, therefore, pitted employees against each other. It was clearly in every individual's interest that someone other than themselves received a poor rating. This created a strong incentive to provide poor evaluations for others while seeking positive evaluations for oneself.
>
> (Tourish, 2013: 127)

This is just a small example of transformational leaders seeking to engineer a cut-throat culture. It makes explicit the dark side which must be deeply troubling for those working in such organizations. Tourish (2013) highlights implications for practice arising out of his critical account of the dark side of transformational leadership. Potentially, the dark side content and mood of this chapter may be lightened through acknowledging how transformational leadership could be very different (please see Table 16.3).

Table 16.3 Reimagining transformational leadership, implications for practice (based on Tourish, 2013)

1   The context in which leadership is practised is critical – avoid generic leadership development.
2   Leadership is inherently complex, contradictory, iterative, adaptive and contested.
3   Understand the limitations inherent in the agency of leaders and acknowledge the agency of others.
4   Leaders need to be more willing to share the spoils of victory/pain of defeat with followers.
5   More emphasis on the role of followership, rather than an infatuation with leadership.
6   Leaders and non-leaders need to embrace uncertainty renouncing the mutual quest for discursive closure.

These implications for practice (please see Table 16.3) have resonance with debates featured in Chapters 9 and 10. Personal experience of higher education suggests a growing infatuation with dark side transformational leadership, despite the wisdom of Table 16.3 and its grounding in learning from the dark side of transformational leadership. There is hope that history will not repeat itself, although the trajectory of management history (see Linstead et al., 2014 and Hanlon, 2015) does not provide reasons to be optimistic.

Summary

The chapter may be succinctly summarised by answering the questions posed in the chapter's introduction. The original questions are restated in italics.

What shouldn't practitioners be doing? Fortune's top five corporate scandals of 2016 (please see Table 16.1) offered illustrations of dark side activities in the public domain. These were Wells Fargo employees creating fake accounts, Roger Ailes sexual-harassment scandal, Mylan increasing the price of the EpiPen by 400 per cent, the recall of Samsung smartphone batteries and revelations contained in the Panama Papers.

What can we learn from the study of coercive persuasion? Schein (1961) learned about coercive persuasion through studying the treatment of prisoners of war by the Chinese Communist Party during the Korean War. For Schein (1985), coercive persuasion is integral to changes in organizational culture and leadership though very rarely acknowledged.

Why is understanding the dark side of behaviour at work believed to be informative? For Furnham and Taylor (2004), in order to understand dark side behaviours at work, we need to understand what motivates these behaviours, in particular how a breakdown in psychological contracts may be a motivation for dark side behaviours at work.

What can we learn from the study of corporate psychopaths? Boddy (2011) highlighted the existence of corporate psychopaths seeking leadership positions because of their desire to access the prestige, power, control of others and financial rewards. They may be encouraged by their respective organizations to rise up the organizational hierarchy as many of their traits are the traits organizations desire, such as determination, dynamism and ambition.

What can we learn from the dark side of organizations in different contexts? Researchers looking at different aspects of organizational life under the umbrella concept of the dark side reveal different aspects of the dark side of workplace spirituality (Lips-Wiersma et al., 2009), careers (Baruch and Vardi, 2016) and customer aggression (Yagil, 2017).

What do we need to question in current accounts of the dark side of organizations? The mainstream dark side of organization work may overlook, ignore or suppress difficult ethical, political and ideological issues, which may well mean life or death to some people (Linstead et al., 2014). They favoured a more critical approach to the dark side in focussing on issues of power, domination, exploitation, and resistance with an implicit or explicit concern with emancipation.

What do we know about management's dark side? Hanlon (2015) regards management as constantly encouraging competition among labour and re-engineering employees as subjects, with these processes regarded as being inherently violent. An emphasis on deskilling and the division of labour was highlighted in the nineteenth-century as a precursor to the management control which characterises organizations today.

What do we know about the dark side of transformational leadership? In *The Dark Side of Transformational Leadership,* Tourish (2013) offers a critical perspective illustrated with troubling contemporary case studies of dark side behaviours in Enron, Militant Tendency, Jonestown, Heaven's Gate and the 2008 banking crisis. The book challenges preoccupations with leadership agency with regards to transformation and change.

Research case study showcase: a UK charity's corporate psychopath leader

As Boddy's (2011) highlighting of corporate psychopaths featured prominently in this chapter, it is relevant to showcase his case (Boddy, 2017) of a corporate psychopath chief executive officer (CEO) at a UK charity reported in the *Journal of Business Ethics*. For the full case study and further analysis please visit the original source.

Case study source

The case study features a UK charity which gained a new CEO who was reported by two middle managers, who worked at the charity, as embodying (respectively) all or most of the ten characteristics used to measure corporate psychopathy. The main respondent met Boddy (2017) at a networking event in 2013 and agreed to be interviewed. Certain details about the charity had to be changed in order to protect the charity's name and reputation, as well as, the identity of the respondent and the psychopathic CEO. In the case study, the current CEO is contrasted with the charity's previous CEO, but that contrast is not made here. Two separate interviews were undertaken with the respondent and these informed the development of the case study, as well as, two follow-up sets of questions by email. The respondent was shown an advanced copy of Boddy (2017) and agreed that it was a true and valid account of the experience of working for a psychopathic CEO. A second manager at the charity judged the CEO as psychopathic enough to be rated as a corporate psychopath. Boddy (2017) acknowledges potential limitations of what is an unusual piece of research. It is shared here as potentially throwing light onto a psychopathic leader and the issues such leaders raise for individuals and organizations as a whole.

Boddy, C.R. 2017. "Psychopathic Leadership a Case Study of a Corporate Psychopath CEO." *Journal of Business Ethics*, *145*(1): 141–156.

Case study

The following extracts from Boddy's (2017) case study are inevitably selective, but hopefully, they will encourage you to read further, although such rich depictions of psychopathic organizational leaders are less common than you might imagine. The psychopathic CEO ruled through fear and intimidation denying any real voice to those working under him. Questioning of the psychopathic CEO's decision making was discouraged.

> Another example of a diminution of voice among senior managers was that shortly after appointment the CEO convened a working group to look at

organizational strategy. However, instead of appointing a variety of staff including senior directors to the group he only asked junior staff and middle managers. These junior employees were reported to be easy to manipulate towards the CEO's point of view.

(Boddy, 2017: 144)

The respondent believed that the CEO had been given advice about his undemocratic management style. This had resulted from employee complaints made about the CEO.

(With) One female…director…he walked (all) over her in meetings, wouldn't allow her to speak to other directors when they had board meetings and so on and talked over her and made her life a living hell until, bless her, she decided the best thing for her to do was to sign a compromise agreement and leave.

(First in-depth interview 2013 cited in Boddy, 2017: 146)

The psychopathic CEO reportedly discouraged discussion through pre-arranged 'discussion' papers which people agreed with at various meetings including board meetings and staff meetings. Reportedly, the need for control of the psychopathic CEO was so great that he could not tolerate a manager disagreeing with him, even though this manager agreed to the CEO's plans. The leadership ability of the psychopathic CEO was so lacking, that the organization was described as being without leadership and as a lost organization. Staff became too scared to challenge the aggressive, psychopathic CEO, although they had no faith in his leadership abilities.

A consequence was that competent directors were replaced by the psychopathic CEO, or they left. Also, experienced senior managers left, leaving few experienced managers able to lead. After three years of the psychopathic CEO's tenure, employees were reported as being cynical about the organization and its leadership. Employees lost their enthusiasm for their jobs. They became aimless and directionless, abandoning the leaderless organization as quickly as they could.

At the time of the second in-depth interview, turnover which included the imminent departure of the respondent was reported to have exceeded 100 per cent, as recently hired employees left once they realised the type of leadership and lack of direction of the organization. According to the respondent, about one third of employees left without work to go to, at a time of relative economic stagnation in the UK economy. Absence due to illness went from a once-a-month occurrence for a single employee under the previous CEO to a daily occurrence for four employees under the psychopathic CEO.

Under the current CEO, people reportedly spent up to 30% of their time at work undertaking personal activities such as playing internet games, sending text messages to their friends and drinking coffee in local cafes. There was reportedly no discouragement from the organizational leadership for undertaking such activities.

(Boddy, 2017: 149)

In this instance, the normal case study questions are inappropriate. Hopefully, this case study speaks for itself.

Discussion questions

1   Do you agree or disagree with coercive persuasion being used in organizations?
2   What has informed the appeal of studying the dark side of organizations?
3   Why is the dark side of transformational leadership which Tourish (2013) highlights so problematic for individuals, organizations and societies?
4   What would be the advantages and disadvantages of focussing on the bright side of organizations?

Navigating dark side of change and transformation literature

In beginning, to engage with dark side literature, you quickly realise that interest in the dark side is not limited to management and organization studies. The dark side has become a focus for many academic disciplines and fields of studies over the last two decades. In navigating this literature, you may need to cross boundaries between disciplines and between fields of study.

In navigating this literature, you also realise that there are shades of darkness which vary considerably. Furnham and Taylor (2004) use the dark side label when referring to employees lying and deceiving, whereas for Hanlon (2015) lying and deceiving are consequences of a capitalist economic system. Whilst the dark side label is used for both books the authors have very different conceptions of what the label means. More generally, the label dark side was regarded as a container concept, with very different focuses evident.

Linstead et al.'s (2014) introduction to the Special Issue they edited on the dark side of organizations was the most informative source encountered when reviewing the literature and whilst, at times, quite theoretical, it is recommended to anyone seeking to seriously engage with the dark side. Their review raises a question for anyone navigating this literature, which may be paraphrased as how dark do you want to go? Tourish's (2013) book is a personal favourite in that he manages to make his critical account of transformational leadership highly accessible, whilst raising important questions for individuals, organizations and societies.

References

Baruch, Y., and Y. Vardi. 2016. "A Fresh Look at the Dark Side of Contemporary Careers: Toward a Realistic Discourse." *British Journal of Management* 27(2): 355–372.

Bitner, M.J., B.H. Booms, and L.A. Mohr. 1994. "Critical Service Encounters: The Employee's Viewpoint." *The Journal of Marketing* 58(4): 95–106.

Boddy, C. 2011. *Corporate Psychopaths: Organisational Destroyers*. Houndmills: Palgrave Macmillan.

Boddy, C.R. 2015. "Organisational Psychopaths: A Ten Year Update." *Management Decision* 53(10): 2407–2432.

Boddy, C.R. 2017. "Psychopathic Leadership a Case Study of a Corporate Psychopath CEO." *Journal of Business Ethics* 145(1): 141–156.

Cooke, B. 1999. "Writing the Left out of Management Theory: The Historiography of the Management of Change." *Organization* 6(1): 81–105.

Cummings, S., T. Bridgman, J. Hassard, and M. Rowlinson. 2017. *A New History of Management*. London: Cambridge University Press.

Duarte, F. 2010. "Teaching Organizational Power and Politics Through a Critical Pedagogical Approach." *Journal of Management and Organization* 16(5): 715–726.

Furnham, A., and J. Taylor. 2004. *The Dark Side of Behaviour at Work: Understanding and Avoiding Employees Leaving, Thieving and Deceiving*. Houndmills: Palgrave Macmillan.

Furnham, A., and J. Taylor. 2011. *Bad Apples: Identify, Prevent & Manage Negative Behavior at Work*. Houndmills: Palgrave Macmillan.

Grandey, A.A., D.N. Dickter, and H.P. Sin. 2004. "The Customer is not Always Right: Customer Aggression and Emotion Regulation of Service Employees." *Journal of Organizational Behavior* 25(3): 397–418.

Hanlon, G. 2015. *The Dark Side of Management: A Secret History of Management Theory*. London: Routledge.

Kotter, J. 1996/2012. *Leading Change*. Boston, MA: Harvard Business School Press.

Linstead, S., G. Maréchal, and R.W. Griffin. 2014. "Theorizing and Researching the Dark Side of Organization." *Organization Studies* 35(2): 165–188.

Lips-Wiersma, M., K. Lund Dean, and C.J. Fornaciari. 2009. "Theorizing the Dark Side of the Workplace Spirituality Movement." *Journal of Management Inquiry* 18(4): 288–300.

McKinlay, A., and K. Starkey (Eds). 1998. *Foucault, Management and Organization Theory: From Panopticon to Technologies of Self*. London: Sage Publications.

McMillan, K. 2016. "Politics of Change: The Discourses that Inform Organizational Change and their Capacity to Silence." *Nursing Inquiry* 23(3): 223–231.

Nguyen, B., L. Simkin, and A.I. Canhoto (Eds). 2015. *The Dark Side of CRM: Customers, Relationships and Management*. London: Routledge.

Ofshe, R. 1991. "Coercive Persuasion and Attitude Change." In *Encyclopedia of Sociology*, edited by E.F. Borgatta, 212–224. New York: Macmillan Library Reference.

Raufflet, E., and A.J. Mills. 2009. *The Dark Side: Critical Cases on the Downside of Business*. London: Routledge.

Schein, E.H. 1961. *Coercive Persuasion*. Norton: New York.

Schein, E.H. 1985. *Organizational Culture and Leadership*. San Francisco, CA: Jossey Bass.

Schumpeter, J.A. 1942. *Capitalism, Socialism and Democracy*. New York: Hamper Brother.

Tourish, D. 2013. *The Dark Side of Transformational Leadership: A Critical Perspective*. London: Routledge.

Turnage, A. 2010. Identification and Disidentification in Organizational Discourse: A Metaphor Analysis of E-Mail Communication at Enron. PhD thesis, North Carolina State University.

Ward, J., and R. McMurray. 2015. *The Dark Side of Emotional Labour*. London: Routledge.

Yagil, D. 2017. "There is No Dark Side of Customer Aggression – It's All Dark." *Journal of Marketing Management* 33(15–16): 1413–1420.

Chapter 17

Evaluating organizational change

Introduction and chapter questions

It is perverse that the evaluation of organizational change processes and outcomes does not feature prominently in organizational change textbooks with Graetz et al. (2015) a notable exception. The applied and practitioner oriented nature of many of the debates featured in this textbook would suggest that evaluating processes and outcomes would be an integral debate, so the omission of organizational change evaluation from other textbooks initially appears to be an anomaly. However, there are mitigating circumstances. First, evaluating organizational change is more complicated and contested than might be imagined. Second, given the career and power implications of a negative outcome, it is difficult to quantify, as managers and leaders may not welcome explicit evaluations of their change facilitation. Third, inside organizations the outcomes of organizational changes may be less closely scrutinised than decisions to embark on the organizational change initiatives.

Academics face different challenges around what is being evaluated and how it is being evaluated. In the questioning section, it will even be suggested that organizational change is reified (made into something real), when it is better understood as a process of becoming. Even before such philosophical debates, academics will have different evaluation preferences, with different evaluation methodologies resulting in different evaluation outcomes. For example, a quantitative survey of the experience of organizational change restructuring is likely to result in a different emphasis to a qualitative study into the lived experience of an organizational change restructure. More pragmatically, there is particular interest in evaluating organizational change in specific sectors such as health and education. Even within these broad sector boundaries, differences in what is evaluated and how it is evaluated will vary considerably. Consequently, a favoured evaluation methodology in for example American clinical care may be inappropriate for evaluating the implementation of digital technology in German universities. Any search for an approach to organizational change evaluation needs to be tempered with the contextual factors discussed in Chapter 2.

The more that you begin to seriously reflect upon evaluating organizational change, the more you appreciate that it is one of the central conundrums of this field of study. The implication is that it may never be satisfactorily/universally resolved and that any universal explanation such as the pronouncement by *Harvard Business School* professors (Beer and Nohria, 2000) that '70% of all change initiatives fail' should be treated with suspicion.

In these ways, it is easier to appreciate why the coverage of organizational change evaluation is less prominent in textbooks than you might anticipate. Despite these significant caveats a real need for debate around evaluating organizational change initiative processes and outcomes still remains. Pettigrew et al. (2001) famously advised that, despite organizational change evaluation being a notably difficult research area, this should not deter us from the challenge. In studying evaluations of organizational change, two themes are addressed throughout the chapter:

> processes of changing and their facilitation and
> outcomes (successful and unsuccessful) of these processes.

In engaging with the literature, evaluations of change outcomes often appear to be privileged over evaluations of change processes, but in terms of advancing theory and practice, both are important. Evaluations of change processes are informed by implicit and explicit choices about facilitating organizational change. These choices have featured in previous chapters, particularly in the questioning sections. For example, if you favour a group/team based approached towards changing (please see Chapter 8), your evaluation needs to address such factors. Earlier discussions will not be repeated, but they do have a bearing on evaluation choices.

Over the past decade the sustainability of organizational change outcomes has gained increasing attention. For example, senior figures in an organization may champion cultural change with a view to developing an entrepreneurial culture, the sustainability issue relates to maintaining such an entrepreneurial culture given that an old culture might resurface. These concerns are very real given earlier discussions in chapters about individuals, groups and teams, relating to psychodynamic issues and issues of identity. The sustainability of organizational change outcomes is addressed in the concluding chapter. Also, for some critical scholars (Grey, 2003; Sturdy and Grey, 2003) even the notion of managing change is regarded as fatally flawed and again in the concluding chapter the sustainability of different organizational change theories, models and concepts will be addressed.

This chapter is organized around and provides answers to the following questions about evaluating organizational change initiative processes and outcomes.

> What are practitioners doing? How is the success and failure of organizational change processes and outcomes typically evaluated?
> What do we know about the why, who, what, how and when of evaluating organizational change?
> What can we learn from academic accounts of evaluating organizational change?
> What critical questions help to advance understanding about evaluating organizational change?

In the next section, practitioner oriented accounts of evaluating organizational change are featured by way of introducing the applied nature of these debates. The understanding section focuses on answering five questions relating to the why, who, what, how and when of evaluating organizational change. The implication here is that different answers to these questions will result in different evaluations of the processes and outcomes of organizational change. In engaging with the evaluation of organizational change, it is necessary to engage with and understand the limitations of these approaches. Also, earlier academic accounts of evaluating organizational change are revisited. Finally, the chapter is summarised, discussion questions raised and guidance offered with regards to navigating the diverse literature which informs evaluations of organizational change.

What are practitioners doing? How is the success and failure of organizational change processes and outcomes typically evaluated?

Prosci (2016), a change management oriented consultancy, offer an informative practitioner oriented answer to this question. They work with corporations, governments and not-for-profit organizations with an emphasis on the application of scientific principles and research. They regularly survey change practitioners, sharing this information with their clients. Their website offers selected insights into the *Best Practices in Change Management – 2014 Edition* (please note that more recent insights are available to purchase). They acknowledge that there can be difficulties in implementing measurement systems and metrics in terms of the provision of solid data. However, they claim that they found practitioners leading the way and share the type of metrics being used in organizations to evaluate change management effectiveness under three headings.

1   Individual employee assessments were used to demonstrate change management effectiveness, such as adoption metrics, usage and utilisation reports, observations of behavioural change and employee satisfaction surveys.
2   Project performance metrics, such as project key performance indicator measurements, benefit realisation and return on investment and adherence to a timeline.
3   Tracking change management activity effectiveness such as training tests and effectiveness measures, training participation and attendance numbers and communication effectiveness.

In these three approaches, we see different ways of evaluating organizational change. There is a similar diversity of approaches in *The Effective Change Manager's Handbook* (Smith et al., 2014). The aim of this handbook is to help practitioners, employers and academics practise change management successfully. The 'essential guidance' which this practitioner oriented handbook offers provides an informative window on current organizational change evaluation practices. Contributions to the handbook are made by different authors (Jenner, 2014; Perkins, 2014; and Busby, 2014) offering very different perspectives on evaluating organizational change. In Jenner's (2014: 132) chapter, the focus is on benefits defined as '...the measurable improvement from change, which is perceived as positive by one or more stakeholders, and which contributes to organizational (including strategic) objectives'. A benefits management process is encouraged comprised of: identify and quantify, value and appraise, plan, realise and review. Jenner (2014: 137) encourages '...benefits-led change initiatives that "start with the end in mind", where the scope of the initiative is determined by the benefits required'.

In the chapter by Perkins (2014), the focus shifts to change impact with impacts being positive and negative, affecting individuals, teams, business units, the whole organization, customers and other external groups.

> Identifying and analysing the impact of change is one of the keys to effective change management planning and helps to avoid or at lease minimize, the disruptive effects and support the positive aspects of the change.
>
> (Perkins, 2014: 258)

In organizations, there is the danger of a 'Pollyanna' effect in which only good things are imagined as happening or only the 'good' aspects are focussed upon (Perkins, 2014). However, the change impacts approach encourages paying attention to change impacts, change risks and business continuity. The implication is that all three are important, as well as, the interplay between them.

In Busby's (2014) chapter, the focus shifts to preparing the organization for the changes it is facing, in the belief that an organization ready for change will be better able to implement and sustain new ways of working. Busby (2014) concedes that measuring change is not simple, highlighting four aspects which could be measured:

engagement with the change,
feelings about the change,
readiness for the change and
progress with change activities.

She suggests that commonly used techniques for measuring change are pulse surveys (survey of employees/customers gauging climate/performance), one-off surveys, focus groups and individual interviews. Each of the practitioner oriented approaches featured in this section could be used in isolation or in conjunction with the other approaches. Each approach encourages a different emphasis with benefits realisation speaking particularly to financial benefits, impacts speaking to the interplay between impacts, risks and continuities and change readiness focussing upon the human aspects. The implication is that there is no one best way to evaluate organizational change. Choices are very contingent upon the organizational change context and the type of change with evaluation choices influencing the outcome of the evaluation.

Understanding organizational change evaluation

Understanding is informed from two different perspectives. First, focussing on the questions which evaluating organizational change raises, and second, extracting the learning from earlier academic accounts of evaluating organizational change.

The why, who, what, how and when of evaluating organization change

This subsection is organized around five closely related questions:

1   Why evaluate organizational change processes and outcomes?
2   Who should evaluate organizational change processes and outcomes?
3   What should organizational change evaluations focus upon?
4   How should organizational change evaluations be undertaken?
5   When should organizational change evaluations be undertaken?

Why evaluate organizational change processes and outcomes?

The rationales for evaluation are many and varied. However, the rationale for evaluation will determine those organizational processes which are focussed on and consequently the outcomes of the evaluation. An evaluation may be undertaken to ensure that an organization is gaining value for money in terms of resources expended, or an evaluation may seek to inform learning with a view to future change initiatives. There may be a publicly espoused rationale for an evaluation such as ensuring optimum customer service, whereas the latent rationale may be to identify cost cutting opportunities.

Who should evaluate organizational change processes and outcomes?

Buchanan et al. (2007) argue that the 'effectiveness' of organizational change is socially constructed. For example, closing local hospitals and moving to a large 'super' hospital may in financial terms be an effective change. Whereas for service users in a local community where their hospital has been closed down, the initiative may have failed to serve their needs. The potential agency of managers and leaders in processes of changing has featured prominently in this textbook implying that they are well placed to evaluate processes and outcomes of organizational change. However, there are many other stakeholders in processes of organizational change and these stakeholders may offer different evaluations from those of managers and leaders. Stakeholders in a change initiative may include shareholders in private sector organizations and governance boards in public and voluntary service organizations. Employees are likely to be involved in processes of changing. Outside of organizations, service users and product consumers will be well placed to evaluate the outcome of service/product oriented changes. Alternatively, all of these stakeholders may be regarded as lacking objectivity in their evaluations and instead the evaluations of external consultants as objective outsiders may be favoured (please see McCalman et al., 2015 for further discussion about objective outsiders).

What should organizational change evaluations focus upon?

Focussing on processes and outcomes was highlighted in the chapter introduction. This relates closely to the rationales featured earlier. If the rationale for evaluation is learning, then focussing upon processes becomes the emphasis. In essence, given that the change was managed this way this time, what does this evaluation tell us about managing future changes? Whereas, if the rationale is financial, then focussing upon outcomes becomes the emphasis. Learning and financial rationales and process and outcome evaluations may potentially be combined.

   There are also choices around gathering quantitative data or qualitative data with each form of data having strengths and weaknesses suggesting a combination of data might be beneficial. The advantage of quantitative data is that it can cover a breadth of views within an organization, for example, 37 per cent of employees favoured the way in which the change process was being managed. Whereas qualitative data covers different views in depth, so for example, Irene felt there was no acknowledgement of her disability in the office relocation.

How should such organizational change evaluations be undertaken?

Evaluations imply objectivity, yet evaluation choices are inevitably subjective with how an evaluation is undertaken impacting upon evaluation findings. Graetz et al. (2015) highlighted measures and means of monitoring organizational change (please see Table 17.1).

The measures and means of monitoring organizational change in Table 17.1 each have strengths and weaknesses. In relying on quantitative or qualitative data or a combination of data, they focus on different aspects of changing. They appear to bring science and objectivity to often irrational processes of changing. However, such claims of objectivity are questionable, particularly given that choices about evaluation are highly subjective. Whilst, financial measures can accurately gauge share price, cash flow and profitability attributing this to an organizational change and then using this to determine the success/failure of a change initiative is problematic. Graetz et al. (2015) highlighted three concerns about popular financial indicators of change. First, long term financial data is required when measuring and evaluating organizational change. Second, financial performance arising from an effective change initiative cannot be differentiated from that arising from improvements in the economy. Third, financial indicators in isolation are believed to be inadequate in evaluating an organizational change initiative.

When should organizational change evaluations be undertaken?

This is an odd question to ask in the final subsection. Surely evaluation is undertaken after the organizational change has happened? However, gauging when a process of changing has been completed, is more difficult than might be imagined and evaluations during a process of change might potentially inform the process. Action research (please see Table 17.1) even works with an assumption that evaluation is an integral aspect of the ongoing organizational change process. Burke's (2014) discussion of the leader's role and function in organizational change during four phases: pre-launch, launch, post-launch and sustaining is informative. At the pre-launch phase, there is an opportunity for evaluation in terms of change readiness. At the launch phase, there is an opportunity to gauge expectations and the effectiveness of change communications. At the post-launch phase, there are opportunities for more traditional organizational change evaluations. In tandem, evaluating at different phases potentially

Table 17.1 Measuring and monitoring organizational change (based on Graetz et al., 2015)

Conventional financial measures	• Share price performance • Market share • Overall performance measures • Profitability measures • Cash flow • Internal targets or budgets
Strategy – driven measures	• Critical success factors • Key performance indicators
Benchmarking	• A process of comparing and measuring with other organizations and other parts of the organization
Total quality management analytical tools	• Improving quality, measurement to identify origins of quality problems, involving employees in the process
The HR scorecard	• Measuring how human resource management affects strategic performance
Action research	• An approach in which the researcher is an integral part of shaping the change

informs processes of changing. Ongoing constructive organizational change evaluations have the potential to motivate. For example, imagine a weight loss or fitness programme without reoccurring measurements which could be gauged and shared with others (Deetz et al., 1999). In this example, it is the (hopefully positive) reoccurring measurements which help you towards your goal.

Another way to think about when to evaluate organizational change is in terms of boiled/drowned frog analogies (Villiers, 1989), popular in the 1980s. Richardson et al. (1994) subsequently applied the analogy to understanding the causes of business failures. Boiled frog relates to how successful organizations drift progressively towards failure and drowned frog relates less to managerial complacency and more to managerial ambition and hyperactivity. Richardson et al. (1994) highlighted causes of why managers may be excessively complacent (boiled frog) or hyperactive (drowned frog) which still appear to be relevant today. The implication is that at times of complacency or hyperactivity, evaluating organizational change takes on added significance.

Academic accounts of evaluating organizational change

> Billions of dollars have been spent in the last two decades on management activities purportedly designed to change organizations. Virtually none of these efforts has any systematic monitoring or evaluation associated with it.
>
> (Tichy, 1983: 363)

The following academic accounts of evaluating organizational change are organized chronologically, although as Tichy (1983) warned, evaluation was not necessarily the norm on organizational change initiatives and this may still be the case. Doyle et al. (2000), in their report surveying 92 managers from 14 public and 14 private sector organizations in terms of their experiences of organizational change, addressed change evaluation as one of their themes. They acknowledged that whilst evaluation was often prescribed, it was technically difficult in terms of appropriate measures, timescales and comparisons, and in a previous survey, they had found systematic evaluation to be rare (Buchanan et al., 1999). This was again the case in Doyle et al.'s (2000) main findings:

- change continued to resist systematic pre-planning, monitoring and assessment;
- change was subjectively evaluated by managers as beneficial;
- further radical changes were anticipated over the next five years.

Pettigrew et al. (2001) raised six challenges for future research in terms of studying organizational change and development with the challenge to link change processes and organizational performance outcomes being particularly pertinent to this chapter. They warned that (2001: 701) '...in very few empirical studies do researchers seek to link change capacity and action to organizational performance'. The goal appears to be not just evaluating organizational change, but relating these evaluations to the performance of organizations. Stated crudely, what is it that organization XYZ does in terms of managing change which enables it to achieve their successful performance? As was discussed in Chapter 6, with regards to relationships between culture and performance, it is difficult to offer convincing evidence with regards linking organizational change and performance, despite the rhetoric.

Hughes (2011) reviewed the evidence in support of Beer and Nohria's (2000: 133) *Harvard Business Review* claim that 'the brutal fact is that about 70% of all change initiatives fail'. However, the 'brutal fact' was not supported by research, although many people subsequently believed that the statistic was supported by *Harvard Business School* research. Even the idea of a single inherent failure/success rate such as 70 per cent, 39 per cent, 51 per cent, etc., misunderstands the highly context-dependent nature of organizational change. In Table 17.2, the main arguments against inherent failure rates featured in Hughes (2011) are restated.

The arguments in Table 17.2 may also be read as cautions about evaluating organizational change. Evaluating organizational change seems eminently sensible, yet it is more difficult than might be imagined to relate dynamic processes of changing to dynamic change outcomes and to isolate specifically how the change process influences the change outcomes when a series of other variables are likely to influence change outcomes.

Barends et al. (2014) encouraged the application of an evidence-based management approach when gauging the effects of change interventions. This is slightly different from the focus of the chapter on organizational change evaluations within organizations, but still very relevant. The authors (2014: 5) suggest that '... scholars and practitioners should be sceptical regarding the body of research results in the field of organizational change management published to date'. Whilst, disturbing, this is compatible with commentaries in other parts of this textbook. The implication for this chapter is that we do not empirically know the effects of different change interventions in different settings, so to expect organizations to convincingly evaluate the effectiveness of their interventions may be unrealistic (a critique of evidence-based management is offered in the next section). Thomas et al. (2016) recently explored why the perception of change failure, such as the 70 per cent change failure rate, remains strong amongst practitioners and academics despite little supporting evidence (their findings are discussed in the questioning section).

Table 17.2 Against inherent organizational change failure (success) rates (based on Hughes, 2011)

The ambiguities of organizational change	• Privileges espoused change rationales over latent change rationales • Ignores the unanticipated outcomes of organizational change • Fails to acknowledge ongoing change and improvisation
Organizational change as highly context dependent	• Disregards the unique contexts of different change initiatives
Perceptions of organizational change outcomes	• Fails to acknowledge the multiple accounts of change outcomes which exist • Neglects ontological and epistemological influences upon evaluation
Time and organizational change outcomes	• Fails to acknowledge the temporal nature of evaluating change outcomes • Downplays important debates about the sustainability of the outcomes of change initiatives
The measurability of organizational change outcomes	• Downplays any form of qualitative evaluation of organizational change • Assumes that the influence of a single change initiative can be isolated and measured

Questioning the evaluation of organizational change

In the introduction, any satisfactory/universal explanation of how to evaluate organization change was described as being likely to be flawed. The goal was depicted as being desirable, although the limitations of such evaluations were knowingly acknowledged. In this section, major limitations/challenges when evaluating organizational change are highlighted. These are evaluation delusions, ontological challenges about the reality of changing, challenging evidence-based management, ethical challenges about how change is managed/led and perception/perspective challenges. In many ways, these challenges overlap, but they are discussed separately here to aid exposition.

Evaluation delusions

In the previous section, Hughes (2011) questioned the notion emanating from Harvard Business School that 70 per cent of all change initiatives fail. The learning from that paper was that evaluating the success and failure of organizational change initiatives was far more difficult than was assumed or being reported. Rosenzweig's (2014) account of delusions he encountered in business has considerable potential to be applied to theories and practices of evaluating organizational change (please see Table 17.3).

Table 17.3 should be read as a warning for anyone studying or practising the evaluation of organizational change. Whilst, Rosenzweig's (2014) interest was focussed upon strategy and performance, each delusion can be applied to evaluating

Table 17.3 How managers let themselves be deceived (based on Rosenzweig, 2014)

Delusions	Descriptions
1 The halo effect	Many of the things claimed to drive organizational performance are simply attributions based on prior performance.
2 The delusion of correlation and causality	Despite two things being correlated, we do not know which one causes which.
3 The delusion of single explanations	Often a single factor is attributed to improved performance, whereas it is likely to be a combination of factors.
4 The delusion of connecting the winning dots	Tendency to focus upon successful organizations and attempt to establish what they have in common.
5 The delusion of rigorous research	The quality of the research data is more important than the research methodology/motivation.
6 The delusion of lasting success	All high performing organizations regress over time.
7 The delusion of absolute performance	Performance is relative not absolute, an organization can improve yet fall further behind rivals.
8 The delusion of the wrong end of the stick	Successful organizations might pursue highly focussed strategies, but that is not the same as a highly focussed strategy leading to success.
9 The delusion of organizational physics	Performance does not follow immutable laws of nature and cannot be predicted with the accuracy of science.

organizational change. The halo effect (1) regarded as the overarching delusion is very applicable to Part IV of this textbook. Belief in managing change developed in the 1980s and 1990s with performance improvements attributed to the intervention of change managers. From the 1990s onwards, there was a shift in emphasis towards leading change (please see Chapter 10) with performance improvements attributed to these change leaders. In a similar manner in the 1980s, performance improvements were attributed to cultural change (please see Chapter 6). As discussed in previous chapters, there is a need for caution when making these attributions, which is the message Rosenzweig (2014) effectively delivers.

Ontological challenges

Organizational change initiatives have been presented as being real, tangible and measurable in this chapter. This is both a pragmatic choice and reflects the ways in which practitioners engage with organizational change. However, process theorists would argue with this presentation of organizational change reality. This school of thought has been very influential amongst academics with one of the most influential accounts of process thinking and organizational change, being Tsoukas and Chia (2002: 570) in which they encouraged rethinking about organizational change (please see earlier discussion in Chapter 2).

> Change must not be thought of as a property of organization. Rather, organization must be understood as an emergent property of change. Change is ontologically prior to organization – it is the condition of possibility for organization.

Tsoukas and Chia's (2002: 570) concern with synoptic accounts of change which regard change as an accomplished event is very relevant to the evaluation focus of this chapter. Most of the discussions of change evaluation featured here are synoptic in that they assume that organizational change is an accomplished event in evaluating the change.

> Given its synoptic nature, it does not do justice to the open-ended micro-processes that underlay the trajectories described; it does not quite capture the distinguishing features of change – its fluidity, pervasiveness, open-endedness, and indivisibility.
>
> (Tsoukas and Chia, 2002: 570)

This influential yet philosophical view of organizational change may be paraphrased as in order to evaluate organizational change we make it real, yet in making change real we underestimate the processual nature of changing. The implication of this is that the quest to effectively evaluate organizational change whilst relevant, may prove elusive.

Against evidence-based management

Evidence-based management (EBM), as discussed in the understanding section, appears highly applicable to the evaluating organizational change theme of the chapter. Whilst academics such as Barends et al. (2014) have favoured EBM, it is important to temper such enthusiasm with critical academic concerns. In their opening sentence, Barends et al. (2014) cite Beer and Nohria (2000) as evidence of reportedly high failure rates. However, Beer and Nohria (2000) offer no evidence in support of their assertion (Hughes, 2011). In health studies, evidence-based medicine is established and accepted. We all benefit from research into the efficacy of different medicines and treatments with research determining which medicines/treatments are adopted. However, the concern is in applying natural science approaches to the social sciences and then assuming that ambiguity and irrationality in human activities does not exist.

> Evidence-based management sounds good, but is tough to practise in the face of too much evidence, shortages of good or relevant evidence, and the abundance of bad or misleading evidence. Nowhere is the challenge of finding the right evidence greater than in the context of measuring and monitoring change interventions.
>
> (Graetz et al., 2015: 246)

Graetz et al.'s (2015) implication that we need to treat EBM with caution is shared. Whilst, Morrell and Learmonth (2015) as academics were in favour of evidence, their concern was with the current EBM movement which may be critiqued in three ways. First, they questioned claims that all evidence was evaluated, finding this approach to be narrow and selective. Second, they found that the approach devalued narrative and story forms of knowledge. Third, the approach is managerialist as it is for management rather than about management.

Ethical challenges

A dilemma ripples throughout this chapter relating to organizational change as being successful perhaps in terms of benefits realisation (Jenner, 2014), yet against other criteria being judged as unsuccessful if gauged against ethical criteria. For example, an organizational change initiative when judged against financial criteria may be judged as successful. However, if that change results in high levels of work-related illness is the change still a success?

In the UK, in recent years, our stock markets have reached record highs. However, at the same time, record numbers of homeless people are having to sleep 'rough' in city-centre shop doorways. The statistic you chose to gauge national wealth is very contingent on the value judgements you choose to make. Tourish (2013) highlighted the dark side of transformational leadership in previous decades (please see Chapter 16). Whilst, Enron, Arthur Andersen and National Westminster Bank appeared to be exemplars of leading/managing transformation and change, it emerged subsequently that their apparent 'successes' were based upon highly unethical business practices. So when evaluating the success/failure of an organizational change initiative, this needs to be tempered with an evaluation of the ethics of the change process and the resulting change outcomes. Handy (1994: 219) famously drew attention to the McNamara Fallacy.

> The first step is to measure whatever can be easily measured. This is OK as far as it goes. The second step is to disregard that which can't be easily measured or to give it an arbitrary quantitative value. This is artificial and misleading. The third step is to presume that what can't be measured easily really isn't important.

This is blindness. The fourth step is to say that what can't be easily measured really doesn't exist. This is suicide.

This fallacy was cited in Hughes (2011) although it was only recently that I learnt the poignant meaning behind the terminology from a military historian. Robert McNamara in the late 1960s was the US Secretary of Defense. He was quantitatively very skilled and understood the world largely in quantitative terms. Unfortunately, he applied this logic to his evaluations of success/failure in the Vietnam War. His quantitative evaluations of the war (particularly body counts) missed the qualitative human costs of the war, such as the impact of casualties on families and friends. The potential danger is in quantifying the success of change initiatives without appreciating the qualitative costs of the change initiative. Conventional financial measures (please see Table 17.1) are frequently used to evaluate change initiatives, but this may be at the expense of the more human/qualitative consequences of an organizational change initiative.

Perception/perspective challenges

Balogun et al. (2015) highlight a common question which arises at times of organizational change: what are the implications of this organizational change for me? Extending this line of reasoning, the outcome of evaluating organizational change will depend very much on who you ask and the implications for themselves. Individuals, groups and teams were the focus of Chapters 7 and 8, and any organizational change is likely to result in winners and losers, regardless of the merits of the specific organizational change. Thomas et al. (2016: 286/287) indicated a paradox at play.

> All of the change projects had participants that could provide evidence for significant benefit associated with implementing the new management practices. Participants used at least one of the generic value discourses to produce narratives of success. At the same time, many, if not most, of the participants and researchers, initially evaluated these change initiatives as a failure, largely because the changes didn't deliver on what were originally identified as the valued outcomes.

This notion of perception impacting upon organizational change evaluations may be applied to the favoured perspectives of practitioners and academics. *The Effective Change Manager's Handbook* (Smith et al., 2014) had a distinct project management perspective which is neither a strength nor a weakness but suggests certain forms of evaluating organizational change will be favoured over others. It seems rather a simplistic conclusion, but the evaluation of whether an organizational change initiative was a success or a failure is very dependent upon whom you ask.

Summary

The chapter may be succinctly summarised through answering questions posed in the chapter's introduction with the original questions restated in italics.

What are practitioners doing? How is the success and failure of organizational change processes and outcomes typically evaluated? There is no one best way, but for Prosci (2016) methods included: individual employee assessments, project performance metrics and tracking change management activity effectiveness. Jenner (2014) emphasised benefits realisation. For Perkins (2014), the emphasis was on change impact and for Busby (2014) change readiness.

What do we know about the why, who, what, how and when of evaluating organizational change? There are many rationales for organizational change with different rationales encouraging different evaluations. In terms of who managers and leaders might evaluate, equally every organizational stakeholder may evaluate an organizational change initiative. What and how are highly contingent upon what is being evaluated and why the change is happening. The when would appear to suggest after the change is completed but there may be merit in evaluating during a process of changing

What can we learn from academic accounts of evaluating organizational change? An academic understanding of evaluating organizational change is still a work-in-progress. The evaluation of organizational change initiatives may not be as great as anticipated and what we know is certainly not as great as what might be anticipated.

What critical questions help to advance understanding about evaluating organizational change? First, are delusions (Rosenzweig, 2014) such as the halo effect impeding evaluations? Second, how real are the changes we seek to evaluate when viewed from an organizational becoming perspective (Tsoukas and Chia, 2002)? Third, what are the shortcomings of an EBM approach? Fourth, how do you reconcile performance expectations with ethical expectations? Fifth, how do you reconcile the different perceptions of the success or failure of an organizational change evaluation?

Research case study showcase: bankers explain banking crisis failures

Tourish and Hargie's (2012) research case study based on the testimony of four senior bankers to the Banking Crisis Inquiry reported in *Organization Studies* is showcased here. For full details and further analysis, please visit the original source. There had been significant change/transformation in the banking sector prior to the banking crisis and these testimonies offer an innovative rear view mirror on what went wrong.

Case study source

Transcripts of the testimony of four senior bankers to the Banking Crisis Inquiry, was published by the House of Commons Treasury Committee in 2009. Tourish and Hargie (2012) read the transcripts of the bankers' testimony and re-read with the intent of identifying metaphors-in-use. Several emergent categories were refined and integrated, again by the authors independently and subsequently the interpretations of metaphors throughout the 31,725-word corpus were reconciled. The process was repeated on three further occasions, until agreement was reached on the major root metaphors in use.

   Tourish, D. and O. Hargie. 2012. "Metaphors of Failure and the Failures of Metaphor: A Critical Study of Root Metaphors used by Bankers in Explaining the Banking Crisis." *Organization Studies* 33(8): 1045–1069.

The case study

The worldwide economic downturn in 2008 was widely attributed by media commentators and the public to incompetent and greedy senior executives in the major banking corporations. In the UK, four senior bankers were required to give testimony to the Banking Crisis Inquiry. They offered their own explanations for the crisis, their role within it, and responses to the torrent of criticism that they faced. Many metaphors are evident in our speech and writing, but for Tourish and Hargie (2012) they were interested in root metaphors, what might be described as the fundamental similes bankers used to explain their failures. The four root metaphors they identified were; the 'wisdom of the crowd', bankers as passive observers, bankers as victims and bankers as penitent learners.

The wisdom of the crowd

Bankers frequently used this explanation to suggest that their perception of events was largely shared amongst their peers and questioning the prevailing wisdom of the crowd would be irrational. Responsibility is minimised and actions are legitimised through the use of this metaphor. Bankers become a small part of the 'herd' which made judgement calls, although unfortunately these proved to be wrong. This raised concerns about risk management, but again risk management and scenario planning were depicted as being distributed throughout the system with responsibility again being regarded as collective. The damaging behaviour of bankers emerged directly from the pressure of others, particularly institutional investors applied pressure for greater returns. In these explanations, the agency of bankers was simultaneously affirmed and denied. They were insightful in following the herd, rather than being analytically deficient.

Bankers as passive observers

An underlying root metaphor employed by the bankers, was depicting themselves as passive observers who faced a series of rapidly cascading events, beyond anyone's control. In these instances, they had no alternatives but to observe events which had been caused by others' actions. In their testimony to the Banking Crisis Inquiry, bankers would apologise for the turn of events, rather than for their actions. Personal responsibility was avoided as the turn of events was beyond their control. This was a situation which no one could have predicted. At times, the bankers depicted themselves as passive recipients of practices largely originating elsewhere. For example, the excessive use of bonuses by the banks was regarded as being imported from the United States. Banks conceded to such 'foreign' practices as using bonuses in order to remain competitive. It would have been very difficult for an individual institution to do things differently, again suggesting that their agency was diminished. Whilst the crisis was described as something happening to the bankers, rather than being caused by them, organizational success of the leaders prior to the crisis was characterised by agent metaphors attributing responsibility for success to the role and wisdom of senior bankers.

(Continued)

Bankers as victims

We normally have sympathy for victims, rather than reproaching them. The bankers as victims metaphor attempted to frame the response of the public in a particular way through excluding the possibility that the bankers caused those economic misfortunes under investigation. In their testimonies, bankers would quantify their own personal financial losses, resulting from a dramatic drop in bank share prices.

> The dominant metaphor remains one of well-intentioned people who were victims of events beyond their control, but sufficiently moved to apologize for the effects of a crisis which had also gripped them (they too were its victims). Furthermore, a third party entity, the Board, was centrally responsible for the key decisions.
>
> (Tourish and Hargie, 2012: 1061)

Bankers as penitent learners

The testimony of the bankers depicted them as penitent and chastened learners. They were willing to acknowledge what they did not know and they were determined to learn from their experiences. Learners are less likely to be blamed for their errors and misjudgements than powerful pedagogues. The depiction of bankers as penitent learners suggests that they had full knowledge of what had happened and that they would provide a comprehensive account of what happened in order to facilitate learning.

In their final discussion and conclusions, Tourish and Hargie (2012: 1064) raise concerns particularly pertinent to this chapter, but also to the change manager/leader agency themes of this textbook.

> The metaphors of failure that we have explored are an implicit challenge to those accounts of organizational action which frame success in terms of leader action and volition. If top leaders are to present themselves as relatively passive and/or powerless in the context of adversity, they are also undermining their claims to agency in times of success.

Tourish and Hargie (2012) warned that the bankers did not claim that everything that happened was in the best interests of the banks or the wider society/economy. However, also they did not express a strong desire for remedial action.

Case study questions

1   Which of Rosenzweig's (2014) delusions are evident in the explanations of bank failure?
2   Which of the four explanations do you find most plausible and least plausible?
3   What are the implications of Tourish and Hargie's (2012: 1064) closing quotation for understanding change manager/leader agency?

Discussion questions

1 Why might different rationales be offered for organizational change and what are the implications for evaluation?
2 Why are the evaluations of the organizational change initiatives dynamic?
3 Why might managers allow themselves to be deluded?
4 What would be the generic principles of good practice when evaluating organizational change?

Navigating the organizational change evaluation literature

As the introduction to this chapter suggested, this literature is more complicated, contested and contextualised than first might be imagined. In my own teaching, prior to writing this chapter, I have used earlier editions of the Graetz et al. (2015) chapter. I have featured elements within this chapter and I recommend the chapter for anyone seeking another account of the debates featured here.

My own route into the organizational change evaluation literature was grounded in my suspicions about 70 per cent of all change initiatives failing. This statistic is frequently cited by practitioners and academics. It appears to be Beer and Nohria (2000) who gave impetus to this statistic, although I (Hughes, 2011) cite others encouraging this belief. In revisiting Beer and Nohria's (2000) original paper, it is informative how they constructed their argument and the persuasive language adopted. Their writing appealed both to practitioners and academics. It was the right message at the right time and for many, it spoke to their suspicions that managing change was flawed.

In navigating this literature, current interest in EBM was highlighted. The unifying theme of this chapter has been the quest for evidence of the success and failure of change initiatives. Evidence-based management speaks to this quest and Barends et al. (2014) were cited. ten Have et al. (2016) offer a more detailed account of the application of evidence-based management to change management.

On a more cautionary note, there appears to be more practitioner literature about evaluating organizational change than academic literature which may reflect the practical implications of success or failure for organizations. The influence of practitioner literature has featured in this chapter, but the caution is with the objectivity of consultancy firms simultaneously selling their services and seeking to inform debates about change evaluation.

References

Balogun, J., V. Hope Hailey, and S. Gustafsson. 2015. *Exploring Strategic Change*. London: Pearson Education.

Barends, E., B. Janssen, W. ten Have, and S. ten Have. 2014. "Effects of Change Interventions: What Kind of Evidence do we Really Have?" *The Journal of Applied Behavioral Science* 50(1): 5–27.

Beer, M., and N. Nohria. 2000. "Cracking the Code of Change." *Harvard Business Review* 78(3): 133–141.

Buchanan, D., T. Claydon, and M. Doyle. 1999. "Organisation Development and Change: The Legacy of the Nineties." *Human Resource Management Journal* 9(2): 20–37.

Buchanan, D.A., R. Addicott, L. Fitzgerald, E. Ferlie, and J.I. Baeza. 2007. "Nobody in Charge: Distributed Change Agency in Healthcare." *Human Relations* 60(7): 1065–1090.

Burke, W.W. 2014. *Organization Change: Theory and Practice.* Los Angeles, CA: Sage Publications.

Busby, N. 2014. "Change Readiness, Planning and Measurement." In *The Effective Change Manager's Handbook: Essential Guidance to the Change Management Body of Knowledge*, edited by R. Smith, D. King, R. Sidhu, and D. Skelsey, 290–328. London: Kogan Page Publishers.

Deetz, S.A., S.J. Tracy, and J.L. Simpson. 1999. *Leading Organizations through Transition: Communication and Cultural Change.* Thousand Oaks, CA: Sage Publications.

Doyle, M., T. Claydon, and D. Buchanan. 2000. "Mixed Results, Lousy Process: The Management Experience of Organizational Change." *British Journal of Management 11* (Special Issue): S59–S80.

Graetz, F., M. Rimmer, A. Smith, and A. Lawrence. 2015. *Managing Organisational Change*, Milton Queensland: John Wiley and Sons Australia Ltd.

Grey, C. 2003. "The Fetish of Change." *TAMARA Journal of Critical Postmodern Organization Science* 2(2): 1–18.

Handy, C. 1994. *The Empty Raincoat: Making Sense of the Future.* London: Random House.

Hughes, M. 2011. "Do 70 Per Cent of All Organizational Change Initiatives Really Fail?" *Journal of Change Management* 11(4): 451–464.

Jenner, S. 2014. "Managing Benefits: Ensuring Change Delivers Value." In *The Effective Change Manager's Handbook: Essential Guidance to the Change Management Body of Knowledge*, edited by R. Smith, D. King, R. Sidhu, and D. Skelsey, 132–170. London: Kogan Page Publishers.

McCalman, J., R.A. Paton, and S. Siebert. 2015. *Change Management: A Guide to Effective Implementation.* London: Sage Publications.

Morrell, K., and M. Learmonth. 2015. "Against Evidence-Based Management, for Management Learning." *Academy of Management Learning and Education* 14(4): 520–533.

Perkins, C. 2014. "Change Impact." In *The Effective Change Manager's Handbook: Essential Guidance to the Change Management Body of Knowledge*, edited by R. Smith, D. King, R. Sidhu, and D. Skelsey, 258–288. London: Kogan Page Publishers.

Pettigrew, A.M., R.W. Woodman, and K.S. Cameron. 2001. "Studying Organizational Change and Development: Challenges for Future Research." *Academy of Management Journal* 44(4): 697–713.

Prosci, 2016. "Change Management Measurement and Metrics." www.prosci.com/change-management/thought-leadership-library/measuring-change-management-effectiveness-with-metrics.

Richardson, B., S. Nwankwo, and S. Richardson. 1994. "Understanding the Causes of Business Failure Crises: Generic Failure Types: Boiled Frogs, Drowned Frogs, Bullfrogs and Tadpoles." *Management Decision* 32(4): 9–22.

Rosenzweig, P. 2014. *The Halo Effect: How Managers let Themselves be Deceived.* London: Simon and Schuster.

Smith, R., D. King, R. Sidhu, and D. Skelsey (Eds). 2014. *The Effective Change Manager's Handbook: Essential Guidance to the Change Management Body of Knowledge.* London: Kogan Page Publishers.

Sturdy, A., and C. Grey. 2003. "Beneath and Beyond Organizational Change Management: Exploring Alternatives." *Organization* 10(4): 651–662.

ten Have, S., W. ten Have, A.B. Huijsmans, and M. Otto. 2016. *Reconsidering Change Management: Applying Evidence-Based Insights in Change Management Practice.* London: Routledge.

Tichy, N.M. 1983. *Managing Strategic Change: Technical, Political, and Cultural Dynamics.* New York: John Wiley & Sons.

Thomas, J., S. George, and T. Rose. 2016. "Deciphering Value Discourse's Role in Explaining the Persistent Perception of Change Failure." *Journal of Change Management* 16(4): 1–26.

Tourish, D. 2013. *The Dark Side of Transformational Leadership: A Critical Perspective.* London: Routledge.

Tourish, D., and O. Hargie. 2012. "Metaphors of Failure and the Failures of Metaphor: A Critical Study of Root Metaphors used by Bankers in Explaining the Banking Crisis." *Organization Studies* 33(8): 1045–1069.

Tsoukas, H., and R. Chia. 2002. "On Organizational Becoming: Rethinking Organizational Change." *Organization Science* 13(5): 567–582.

Villiers, C. 1989. "Boiled Frog Syndrome." *Management Today*, March: 121–124.

Chapter 18

Sustaining organizational change

Introduction

This chapter addresses two closely related concerns, one practical about the sustainability of organizational change outcomes and the other academic about the sustainability of organizational change as a field of study.

The definitions in Table 18.1 will be used in this chapter with the focus here upon why outcomes are susceptible to sustainability or decay. For Buchanan et al. (2007) spread and containment were also important as they were researching into the Modernisation Agency implementation of the National Health Service (NHS) Plan in the UK. Contrast can be very useful in understanding a new concept and hopefully sustainability becomes clearer when contrasted with decay. This chapter majors on four awkward though closely related questions:

- Are the outcomes of organizational change initiatives sustainable?
- Does organizational change still have something to offer organizations?
- Is organizational change as a field of study sustainable?
- Is organizational change concerned with myth-busting or myth-understanding?

The first question addresses a phenomenon which has been referred to as 'initiative decay' and the 'improvement evaporation effect' (Buchanan et al., 2005). An assumption has rippled through earlier chapters that organizational change can be facilitated through management and leadership, but what if the outcomes of change subsequently evaporate/decay? The second question relates to a competitive marketplace for approaches to managing progress. For example, innovation management and project management make different appeals to organizations. They draw upon different academic disciplines and offer different methodologies. Any consideration of the sustainability of organizational change outcomes for organizations has to acknowledge and consider alternatives to organizational change as an approach. The third question reflects upon the credibility/legitimacy of organizational change as an academic field of study, revisiting earlier critiques of organizational change and their implications for future studies. The fourth question concludes this textbook through revisiting debates in the introductory chapter. We think of textbooks as fulfilling a myth-busting role, presenting readers with an overview of research and theories informing organizational change and that has been the intent here. However, reflecting on the sustainability of organizational change as a field of study requires acknowledgement of the mythical aspects of moving organizations from a known state to an unknown state. Anyone who talks assertively and with certainty about a future

Table 18.1 Sustainability terminology (based on Buchanan et al., 2007)

Sustainability – The process through which new working methods, performance enhancements, and continuous improvements are maintained for a period appropriate to a given context.

Spread – The process through which new working methods developed in one setting are adopted, perhaps with appropriate modifications, in other contexts.

Decay – The opposite of sustainability, where change is not maintained and benefits are lost.

Containment – The opposite of spread, where changes at one site are not adapted and adopted by others.

organizational state is a charlatan. In taking critical stock of organizational change as a field of study, myths appear to be integral to studying organizational change.

In this concluding chapter, the understanding followed by the questioning format of previous chapters is reversed. Each of the four questions provides the questioning focus for each section, with each section drawing a conclusion in terms of understanding. Wider ongoing and important ecological debates about the sustainability of the planet are outside the scope of this chapter, although organizational change has the potential to positively contribute to such processes of changing.

Questioning the sustainability of organizational change outcomes

If you have worked in an organization for a few years, you are likely to have experienced the launch of an organizational change initiative. In the past, these launches would have a party feel with food and drink provided and a speech by a senior figure positively sharing their aspirations for what the new initiative would deliver. These days, a launch may be more virtual, with perhaps a video or webinar, electronic newsletter and uplifting messages and slogans provided by the marketing and communications department. I fear we have lost something in this transition, certainly the 'food and drink'.

The concern here is not with communications (the focus of Chapter 12), but what happens after the launch (party), when the launch party is only a distant memory and the organization hits what Stephen Reeve (a colleague) calls 'the treacle'. Were the organizational aspirations realised or do organizations simply move on to a new set of aspirations? Engagement with the sustainability of organizational change outcomes has gained increasing attention over the past two decades, but it is not as straightforward as might be imagined. In this chapter, philosophical challenges similar to those in the previous chapter are raised.

Buchanan et al. (2005) undertook a review of the literature on sustaining organizational change and their significant insights are highlighted here. Buchanan et al. (2005) offered four reasons why this area of study received only limited attention. First, organizational change theories tend to emphasise adaptation and constant change, negating the need to review the sustainability of organizational change outcomes. Second, implementation can be studied over a short time horizon, whereas sustainability requires longitudinal study. Third, researching change may be more appealing than researching stability. Fourth, sustainability is regarded not as a condition to be achieved, but as a problem to be solved. They acknowledged an absence

Table 18.2 Factors affecting sustainability (based on Buchanan et al., 2005)

Category	Outline definition
Substantial	Perceived centrality, scale, fit with organization
Individual	Commitment, competencies, emotions and expectations
Managerial	Style, approach, preferences, behaviours
Financial	Contribution, balance of costs and benefits
Leadership	Setting vision, values, purpose, goals, challenges
Organizational	Policies, mechanisms, procedures, systems and structures
Cultural	Shared beliefs, perceptions, norms, values, priorities
Political	Stakeholder and coalition power and influence
Processual	Implementation methods, project management structures
Contextual	External conditions, stability, threats, wider social norms
Temporal	Timing, pacing, flow of events

of literature on sustaining organizational change. This situation hasn't really subsequently improved, but the implication of Buchanan et al.'s (2005) reasoning is that sustaining organizational change may only be significant for certain scholars.

Studies of organizational change were reviewed with specific reference to their position on sustainability. Senge and Kaeufer (2000) highlighted four categories of influence on sustainability: individual, managerial, cultural and processual. Kotter (1995) was regarded as identifying five categories of influence on sustainability: managerial, leadership, cultural, political and temporal. There is a need for caution with regards the validity and reliability of these contributions drawn from practitioner orientated magazines. More substantively, Buchanan et al. (2005) developed their own model of factors affecting the sustainability of organizational change, informed by their literature reviewing (please see Table 18.2).

Buchanan et al. (2005) wanted the model featured in Table 18.2 to meet three criteria: first, to capture the attributes and complexities of the sustainability process, second, to be able to explain a range of outcomes from sustained change to decay, third, to offer the first step towards empirical research and tabulation. Buchanan et al. (2005: 203) capture the essence of their model as follows:

> With regard to informing research, this model (a) identifies the range of potential influences, at different levels of analysis, on sustainability and decay, (b) highlights the need to consider the weighting and interaction effects among those factors, (c) emphasises the significance of contextual and temporal factors, and (d) potentially explains a range of positive and negative outcomes.

Buchanan et al.'s (2005) model offered a starting point and impetus for research studies into sustaining organizational change, but subsequent progress has been disappointing. In *The Sustainability and Spread of Organizational Change: Modernizing Healthcare*, Buchanan et al. (2007) drew upon their own experiences as researchers working in the Modernisation Agency on the NHS Plan between 2001 and 2005 and the contributions of others in their edited reader. They cite an NHS Modernisation Agency (2002: 12) document 'sustainability is when new ways of working and improved outcomes become the norm. Not only have the process and outcome changed, but the thinking and attitudes behind them are fundamentally altered and the systems surrounding them are transformed in support.' Sustainability is about far more than the superficial discourses often prevalent during times of changing. Buchanan et al. (2007) cite Lewin (1951: 228) as a reminder of the importance of group norms 'a change toward a higher level of group performance is frequently short lived; after a "shot in the arm", group life soon returns to the previous level'. Buchanan et al. (2007) offer useful practical solutions to initiative decay informed by their research.

The possible problems featured in the first column of Table 18.3 have far wider applicability than the health service. None of these problems is inevitable, but they should alert everyone involved in processes of changing to potential long-term challenges organizational change raises. The second column of Table 18.3 offers practical solutions, but the diagnosis/acknowledgement of the problem is the most important contribution here. Willis et al. (2016) in their review identified six guiding principles to assist organizing efforts and policies to sustain cultural change in health systems: align vision and action; make incremental changes within a comprehensive transformation strategy; foster distributed leadership; promote staff engagement; create collaborative relationships; and continuously assess and learn from cultural change.

Campbell (2014) looked more generically at the practicalities of sustaining change in her contribution to *The Effective Change Manager's Handbook* (Smith et al., 2014). She highlights the levers that are available in efforts to sustain a change initiative. They may be categorised as emotional, procedural and structural. Metaphorically, change recipients may be encouraged to let go of the status quo through carrot, stick and burning platforms. Potential levers which may be used are environmental (communicating challenges in the external environment), leadership (leader communications,

Table 18.3 Initiative decay: possible problems and practical solutions (based on Buchanan et al., 2007)

Possible problem	Practical solution
The initiators and drivers move on	Design career development and reward policies to motivate and retain key change agents
Accountability for development has become diffuse	Establish clear project management and line management responsibilities
Knowledge and experience of new practice are lost through staff turnover	Develop retention strategies to minimise such loss
Old habits are imported with recruits from less dynamic organizations	Strengthen the induction and training regime for new recruits
The issues and pressures that triggered the initiative are no longer visible	Launch ongoing 'public relations' scheme to keep issues visible
New managers want to drive their own agendas	Ensure new appointments have explicit remits to develop, rather than dismantling previous initiatives
Powerful stakeholders are using counter-implementation tactics to block progress	Develop a counter-implementation strategy
The pump-priming funding runs out	Start to revise budget allocations well in advance
Other priorities come on stream, diverting attention and resources	Develop a time phased change implementation strategy
Staff at all levels suffer initiative fatigue; enthusiasm for change falters	Relaunch with a new focus, clarify what is in it for them

behaviours and actions) and organizational development (such as reward systems and job design). Campbell (2014: 474) cites Gladwell's (2006) bestseller, *The Tipping Point*, as a reminder that an organizational change may reach a tipping point.

> When the groundwork for change adoption has been done, however, there comes a point – a week, a month or a year after implementation when it starts to feel easier, the change has a momentum of its own and no longer needs specific attention to make it stick – that it is just happening all on its own.

However, this is a best case scenario and she warns about vicious circles which may create an ever increasing cycle of negative reinforcement. There may be a need to measure change adoption (see previous chapter for discussion about organizational change evaluation). Also, potential barriers to adoption are acknowledged, such as change fatigue, recipients not being ready and insufficient resources, which takes us back to Chapter 13 and debates about change readiness and resistance. Stacey (2012: 89) does not follow such a rational/linear path, instead embracing the uncertainties, ambiguities and complexities of organizational life.

> Thinking together about what we are doing and why we are doing it seems to me to be the only way to produce reasonable and lasting changes in what we do. I believe that we can only address complex processes such as this if we think together about what we are doing and why we are doing it, an activity which occurs very little indeed in most organizations.

This is a profound yet troubling insight into sustaining change outcomes. Stacey (2012) isn't persuaded by the manager/leader dualism highlighted in Chapter 9. Managers telling employees what to do have simply been replaced by leaders telling employees what to do. Instead, he favours conversations which engage everyone in processes of changing. For Stacey (2012) this is how we begin to sustain change, though he believes such genuine engagement is largely lacking.

In returning to the focusing question, for this section, are the outcomes of organizational change initiatives sustainable? The contingency maxim 'it depends' is very applicable if the outcomes of an organizational change are sustained or if they decay is highly context dependent (see discussion of context variables in Chapter 2). Closely related to the outcomes of change, the experience of change is likely to influence future changes, 'employees shy away from future change when previous experiences ended badly but equally will accept change more readily if the last programme worked out well in the end' (Smith and Graetz, 2011: 117). In establishing if the outcomes of a specific organizational change initiative are sustainable, Table 18.2 offers a good starting point to consider the influencing factors.

Questioning the value of organizational change for organizations

The second question, with regards to organizational change being useful for organizations, is contingent on the sustainability of organizational change outcomes discussed in the previous section. The usefulness of organizational change for organizations will also influence sustainability in terms of the future of organizational change as a field of study. So in this sense, the question offers a bridge between the first and the third question. Put bluntly the question is concerned with whether organizations still value organizational change as an approach to changing organizations.

In the previous chapter, debates around evaluating organizational change were introduced. *Harvard Business Review (HBR)* published influential articles by Harvard Business School professors claiming that transformation efforts were failing (Kotter, 1995) and that 70 per cent of organizational change initiatives were failing (Beer and Nohria, 2000). These articles questioned the utility of how the change was being managed and encouraged a shift from managing change to leading change, a shift which has featured prominently in this textbook. However, in the context of an academic textbook, we need to be suspicious of *HBR* articles aimed primarily at practitioners. Kotter's (1995) encouragement to lead change was based upon his consultancy work, rather than an empirically tested model (please see Hughes, 2016a) and Beer and Nohria (2000) despite referring to a 'brutal fact', offered no evidence in support of their brutal fact (see Hughes, 2011).

The highly publicised *HBS* critiques of organizational change have raised questions about the utility of organizational change approaches. It is difficult to substantiate, but since Kotter (1995) and Beer and Nohria (2000), there appears to have been increased interest in innovation management and project management as methodologies for facilitating organizational change. Each approach is briefly considered here as the value of organizational change for organizations needs to be contrasted with what alternative approaches are on offer.

Innovation management

Fagerberg et al. (2006) asked where we would be without fundamental innovations such as agriculture, the wheel, the alphabet or printing. In this sense, major economic, political and social development throughout time may be explained as innovations. If we follow this logic, changes in organizations may be considered as innovations with innovation management offering theories and methodologies explaining developments and informing innovation management practices. If we look to one of the best-selling textbooks *Managing Innovation: Integrating Technological, Market and Organizational Change* (Tidd and Bessant, 2013), organizational change is referenced in the subtitle. The subtitle also highlights one of innovation management's strengths, engaging with the diffusion of technology. Innovation management draws heavily upon economics and in this sense differs from organizational change. However, innovation management can potentially deal with micro as well as macro aspects of organizations changing. Tidd and Bessant (2013) include chapters on innovation as a core business process, building an innovative organization and developing an innovation strategy. Through this lens, many of the themes of this textbook would look very different, and there would also be far more emphasis on technological change and interrelationships between technology and organizational change.

Project management

Another way to think about organizational change is in terms of project management. Morris (2011) whilst acknowledging that projects go back as far as the dawn of civilisation, suggests that the term project management first appeared in 1953. In an early, *HBR* article Gaddis (1959) introduced the project manager as somebody deserving more scrutiny from students of management and professional managers. Turner et al.

(2011) analysed the evolution of project management research through their review of three of the leading project management journals acknowledging that there is little agreement with regards to project management's heritage in terms of decision sciences, organization theory and operations research. They suggest that project management arose out of an outcropping of other fields with researchers making their homes in separate disciplines such as construction, engineering, and management science. Soderlund (2011) identified the following schools of project management research emerging between the 1950s and the 2000s: optimization, factor, contingency, behaviour, governance, relationship, and decision.

In the field of project management, professional associations have been influential particularly in their attempts to develop bodies of knowledge (please see Morris et al., 2006). The Project Management Body of Knowledge first developed by the US-based Project Management Institute in 1987 identified the following process-based knowledge areas in terms of project: integration management, scope management, time management, cost management, procurement management, quality management, risk management, human resource management and communication management (please see Hodgson and Cicmil, 2006 and Morris et al., 2006 for a critical commentary). Again, if this textbook had been written from a project management perspective, you would have been offered guidance on managing and leading organizational change, but with very different emphases and prescriptions.

The section has focussed upon the usefulness of organizational change for organizations. Whilst gauging usefulness is highly subjective, contrasting the organizational change approaches featured here with innovation management and project management highlights their respective strengths and weaknesses. Organizational change works with the ambiguities and uncertainties raised by processes of changing. Innovation management acknowledges how technology diffusion influences organizations and processes of changing. Project management offers tried and tested methodologies to systematically move through a process of changing. In an ideal world, students and practitioners of change would draw upon all three approaches, although in the real world it is unlikely that students and practitioners would have sufficient time to draw on all three approaches. This debate is ongoing and unlikely to decay in the near future.

Questioning the sustainability of organizational change as a field of study

The first question focussed on the sustainability of organizational change outcomes, raising a meta question about the status of the field of study potentially informing these organizational changes. Is organizational change as a field of study sustainable? We tend to think of academic disciplines, such as economics and psychology, as the building blocks of universities. They certainly have a role to play, but when we look to the management and organization studies focus of this textbook, it is fields of study which are far more prevalent. In the previous section, innovation management and project management were fields of study, rather than academic disciplines. We can gauge the academic health of a field of study in order to gauge its future prospects. In this questioning section, the focus is on organizational change as a field of study and its prospects. If the first section was about the outcomes of organizational change potentially decaying, this section is about organizational change as a field of study

Table 18.4 Critiques informing organizational change as a field of study

Year	Authors	Title	Journal
2003	Grey	"The fetish of change"	TAMARA
2003	Sturdy and Grey	"Beneath and beyond organizational change management: exploring alternatives"	Organization
2005	By	"Organizational change management: a critical review"	Journal of Change Management
2005	Oswick et al.	"Looking forwards: discursive directions in organizational change"	Journal of Organizational Change Management
2008	Schwarz and Huber	"Challenging organizational change research"	British Journal of Management
2008	Marshak and Grant	"Organizational discourse and new organization development practices"	British Journal of Management
2008	Palmer and Dunford	"Organizational change and the importance of embedded assumptions"	British Journal of Management
2014	Worley and Mohrman	"Is change management obsolete?"	Organizational Dynamics

potentially decaying. Will there still be organizational change papers, courses, and textbooks in 25 years or will the debate have moved elsewhere?

Memorable critiques of organizational change and its management from the past 20 years (particularly those featured in Chapter 3) are revisited in chronological order with regards to their implications for the sustainability of organizational change as a field of study. These critiques and earlier discussions are used to gauge if organizational change as a field of study is sustainable.

Many of these references featured in a critical reflection on the status of change management (Hughes, 2016b). It is important to acknowledge that they are atypical of what has been written about organizational change and its management. Organizational change literature has a tendency to be positive and prescriptive. In gauging the academic health of a field, critical inquiries are likely to be more informative than positive celebrations of a field. The papers in Table 18.4 superficially suggest that organizational change as a field of study is not sustainable. However, such challenges have informed the development of organizational change as a scholarly field of study. Critique advances a field of study, even if for some of the authors (please see Table 18.4) this wasn't their original intention.

Grey (2003) and Sturdy and Grey (2003) were very sceptical about organizational change in general and how such change was managed in particular. Grey (2003: 11) perceived change management as a troublesome fetish '…the whole business of change management should be given up on'. When Sturdy and Grey (2003) took critical stock of what they referred to as organizational change management (OCM), their critique was wide-ranging including the lack of acknowledgement of stability within organizations, the assumed manageability of change and a pro-change bias.

By (2005), in his critical review of OCM highlighted three categories of organizational change characterised by the rate of occurrence, how it comes about and by scale. He (2005: 378) warned that '…what is currently available is a wide range of contradictory and confusing theories and approaches, which are mostly lacking empirical evidence and often based on unchallenged hypotheses regarding the nature of contemporary organizational change management'. Whereas, Grey (2003) and Sturdy and Grey (2003) were sceptical about OCM and its sustainability, By (2005) appeared to constructively challenge those involved in studying organizational change. He subsequently became the editor of the *Journal of Change Management* and his paper has been by far the most downloaded paper published by the journal. In another organizational change journal, Oswick et al. (2005) encouraged scholars not to give up on organizational change, but to take a new direction, through recognising the centrality of discourse within processes of changing.

Schwarz and Huber's (2008: S1) Special Issue of the *British Journal of Management* with the aim '…to challenge the state of the field or the adequacy of current organizational change theories', was a low point in that the reviewers were only able to recommend two manuscripts for publication in the Special Issue. The two papers that were published focussed upon organizational discourse and organizational development (Marshak and Grant 2008) and the importance of embedded assumptions in managing change (Palmer and Dunford 2008). Marshak and Grant (2008, S7) highlighted '…an emerging set of new organization development (OD) practices – what we refer to collectively here as "New OD"…'.

Palmer and Dunford (2008, S22) offered a reminder about the diversity of assumptions about managing and the nature of change outcomes which were '…associated with different images of managing change: directing, navigating, caretaking, coaching, interpreting and nurturing'. They developed their argument with reference to the different ontological assumptions which relate to each of these different images of managing change illustrating their position through revisiting Sturdy and Grey's (2003) paper. They contrasted their managerialist critique of OCM with what is now known, noting that assumptions about manageability vary considerably dependent upon the image of managing change adopted.

Finally, Table 18.4 features Worley and Mohrman (2014) questioning if change management is obsolete? The paper is organized around two positions, the old normal and the new normal with regards to organizational change theories and practices. They regard organizations as having to deal with very different challenges from those of earlier decades, which is why they draw attention to a new normal, although in drawing their conclusions they do not regard organizational change as obsolete.

> This new view of change does not eliminate the value of traditional change perspectives. Traditional change management models are just one arrow in a rich and diverse quiver of approaches that will characterize the new normal.
>
> (Worley and Mohrman, 2014: 221)

In this textbook, the central focus has been on organizational change with management and leadership highlighted as a different means to facilitate organizational change. If we think of the field in these terms, it is likely to have greater longevity, than if we think of the field in terms of change management and prescriptions for managing change and change leadership and prescriptions for leading change. If we look to organizational change as a field of study, it has been very susceptible to critique, but this critique has potentially been beneficial. If you look to the quality of papers published in the *Journal of Change Management* today, compared to those published ten years ago there is a discernible improvement in the quality of papers.

In my critical reflection on the status of change management (Hughes, 2016b), the first editions of UK textbooks were highlighted; *Managing Change in Organizations* (Carnall, 1990), and *Managing Change* (Burnes, 1992). *Managing Change in Organizations* (Carnall, and By, 2014) and *Managing Change* (Burnes, 2017) are now both into sixth and seventh editions respectively. New editions only appear if there are sufficient readers to make a new edition commercially viable. Certainly, if gauged in this manner, organizational change as a field of study currently appears to be sustainable, then again as the author of this textbook I have a vested interest in claiming such sustainability.

Questioning the myth-busting or myth-understanding organizational change dualism

The answer to the fourth question about myth-busting or myth-understanding organizational change, in the final section of the final chapter of an organizational change textbook appears straightforward. The textbook has offered an informed navigation through the contradictory and at times contentious field of organizational change studies. Hopefully, you are better prepared to challenge myths such as the brutal fact that about 70 per cent of all organizational change initiatives fail (Beer and Nohria, 2000). Hopefully, you are better prepared to challenge manager or leader, change or continuity dualisms instead now favouring a dualities aware approach (Sutherland and Smith, 2013). You may in your current or future studies embrace notions of evidence-based management. All of this leads you towards becoming an organizational change myth-buster when engaging with organizational change theories and practices.

However, some of the issues raised in the first chapter of this textbook remain. Personally, I am keen to debunk myths which have misinformed organizational change studies and practices and this textbook and its extensive references should read as evidence of this intent. Over three decades, I have witnessed scholars and researchers advancing our understanding of organizational change and many of their contributions have been remembered throughout this textbook. Despite all of this, acknowledging myths for myself still has an important role to play in organizational change theories and practices. I frequently return to Dawson's (2003: 11) aside that '...change involves a movement to some future state that comprises a context and time that remains unknown'. We can forecast the future, based upon the evidence of what happened in the past, but such projections need to be treated with extreme caution.

So, let us return to the launch party for a new organizational change initiative featured at the beginning of this chapter. The senior figure shares their expectations for a positive outcome. They may have considerable past experience of managing and leading organizational change, or they may have been advised by highly qualified consultants, they may even have read this textbook. If we look to hypothetical examples, their change may be one of the following:

  A bank wants to improve the experience of customers visiting branches.
  A manufacturing business wants to successfully relocate one of its factories.
  A hospital wants to reduce the number of infections on the wards.
  A charity wants its volunteers to engage in a health and safety initiative.
  A university wants to improve its university league table ranking.

Organizational change theories, models and concepts discussed in previous chapters certainly could inform what happens in these organizations. In organizations and societies today, we know far more about managing and leading these organizational changes. Today, we also have a greater appreciation of the complexities involved, the influence of context and the processual nature of change. Despite all of this, in moving to a future unknown state, our senior figures at the launch party are undertaking a leap of faith and asking others to follow them. There must always be a mythical element to how we move into an unknown future. The importance of myth may be traced back through centuries to the beginnings of civilisation and the earliest philosophers (please see Chapter 1).

There is a danger in equating organizational change knowledge to certainty about positive outcomes for the five hypothetical examples. There is a mythical element to each of the five change examples which requires acknowledgement even for change initiatives underpinned by knowledge, research, and evidence. In the exclusively evidence-based management world some academics appear to encourage, such myth-understandings would not be permitted. If this was the case, I fear organizational change, strategy, leadership and many other fields of study would be impoverished by such a development. Myth-busting and myth-understanding is not an either/or dualism, in combination they offer a means to engage with unknown futures resulting from attempts to manage and lead organizational change.

Summary

The chapter may be succinctly summarised through answering the questions posed in the chapter's introduction with the original questions restated in italics.

Are the outcomes of organizational change initiatives sustainable? Buchanan et al. (2005) undertook a review of the literature on sustaining organizational change and offered four reasons why this area of study received only limited attention. This situation hasn't really subsequently improved, but the implication of Buchanan et al.'s (2005) reasoning is that sustaining organizational change may only be significant for certain scholars. In returning to the focusing question, are the outcomes of organizational change initiatives sustainable, the contingency maxim 'it depends' is very applicable. If the outcomes of an organizational change are sustained or if they decay is highly context dependent.

Does organizational change still have something to offer organizations? The usefulness of organizational change for organizations will also influence sustainability in terms of the future of organizational change as a field of study. Put bluntly, the question is concerned with whether organizations still value organizational change as an approach to changing organizations. It is difficult to substantiate, but since Kotter (1995) and Beer and Nohria (2000), there appears to have been increased interest in innovation management and project management as methodologies for facilitating organizational change. In an ideal world, students and practitioners of change would draw upon all the approaches, although in the real world it is unlikely that students and practitioners would have sufficient time to draw on all approaches.

Is organizational change as a field of study sustainable? If we look to organizational change as a field of study it has been very susceptible to critique, but this critique has potentially been beneficial. If you look to the quality of papers published in the *Journal of Change Management* today, compared to those published ten years ago there is a discernable improvement in the quality of papers. New editions of organizational change textbooks only appear if there are sufficient readers to make new editions commercially viable. Certainly, if gauged in this manner, organizational change as a field of study currently appears to be sustainable.

Is organizational change myth-busting or myth-understanding? Organizational change theories, models and concepts discussed in previous chapters certainly could inform what happens in these organizations. In organizations and societies today, we know far more about managing and leading these organizational changes. Today, we also have a greater appreciation of the complexities involved, the influence of context and the processual nature of change. The importance of myth may be traced back through centuries to the beginnings of civilisation and the earliest philosophers and myth-understandings still have a role to play.

Discussion questions

1   Why has the study of the sustainability of organizational change outcomes been a relatively recent phenomenon?
2   Does the sustainability of organizational change outcomes really matter or does it reflect a misunderstanding of dynamic processes of changing?
3   Do academic fields of study, such as organizational change, have life cycles similar to products?
4   What are the advantages and disadvantages of thinking in terms of organizational change myth, understandings?

Navigating organizational change sustainability literature

In engaging with this literature you will see that influential work has a distinct health service orientation. This explains the use of terminology such as decay/evaporation which reminds us that organizational change in such a setting may result in life or death. "No Going Back: A Review of the Literature on Sustaining Organizational Change" (Buchanan et al., 2005) is the logical starting point for anyone engaging with the organization change sustainability literature featured here. The paper was informed by research in the Modernisation Agency in the UK National Health Service. If you want to go deeper into this research, *The Sustainability and Spread of Organizational Change* (Buchanan et al., 2007) is recommended. The book takes the form of an edited reader offering theoretical and applied insights into organizational change sustainability. The hope was that the book and the paper, would have given impetus to further studies and literature reviews, but, at the time of writing, organizational change sustainability as a sub-field remains underdeveloped (see the earlier reasoning in the chapter).

A parallel theme of the chapter has been evaluating the sustainability of organizational change as a field of study. This theme may appear abstract, but it is integral to the ambitions of this textbook, surfacing the awkward question, are you studying a flawed and failing approach? In order to address this question, it has been necessary to take the academic inventory of organizational changes studies. If you want to undertake your own inventory, By (2005) and Hughes (2016b) offer accessible overviews of critiques of organizational change as a starting point. There is a more critical literature inspired by Critical Theory (please see Chapter 4) which critically questions notions of leading and managing as featured in this textbook (see, for example, Spicer and Levay (2012) on changing, Alvesson and Willmott (2011) on managing and Collinson (2011) on leading). Finally, if you want to explore further interrelationships between myths and organizational change, the references in the introductory chapter are worth revisiting.

References

Alvesson, M., and H. Willmott. 2011. *Critical Management Studies*. London: Sage Publications.

Beer, M., and N. Nohria. 2000. "Cracking the Code of Change." *Harvard Business Review* 78(3): 133–141.

Buchanan, D., L. Fitzgerald, D. Ketley, R. Gollop, J.L. Jones, S.S. Lamont, A. Neath, and E. Whitby. 2005. "No Going Back: A Review of the Literature on Sustaining Organizational Change." *International Journal of Management Reviews* 7(3): 189–205.

Buchanan, D.A., L. Fitzgerald, and D. Ketley (Eds). 2007. *The Sustainability and Spread of Organizational Change: Modernizing Healthcare*. London: Routledge.

Burnes, B. 1992. *Managing Change*. 1st ed. London: Pitman Publishing.

Burnes, B. 2017. *Managing Change*. 7th ed. Harlow: Pearson.

By, R.T. 2005. "Organizational Change Management: A Critical Review." *Journal of Change Management* 5(4): 369–380.

Campbell, H. 2014. "Sustaining Change." In *The Effective Change Manager's Handbook: Essential Guidance to the Change Management Body of Knowledge*, edited by R. Smith, D. King, R. Sidhu, and D. Skelsey. London: Kogan Page Publishers.

Carnall, C.A. 1990. *Managing Change in Organizations*. 1st ed. Hemel Hempstead: Prentice Hall International (UK) Ltd.

Carnall, C.A. and By, R.T. 2014. *Managing Change in Organizations*. 6th ed. Harlow: Pearson.

Collinson, D. 2011. "Critical Leadership Studies." In *The SAGE Handbook of Leadership*, edited by A. Bryman, D. Collinson, K. Grint, B. Jackson, and M. Uhl-Bien, 181–194. London: Sage Publications.

Dawson, P. 2003. *Understanding Organizational Change: The Contemporary Experience of People at Work*. London: Sage Publications.

Fagerberg, J., D.C. Mowery, and R.R. Nelson. 2006. *The Oxford Handbook of Innovation*. Oxford: Oxford University Press.

Gaddis, P.O. 1959. "The Project Manager." *Harvard Business Review* 37(3): 89–97.

Gladwell, M. 2006. *The Tipping Point: How Little Things Can Make a Big Difference*. London: Little, Brown.

Grey, C. 2003. "The Fetish of Change." *TAMARA Journal of Critical Postmodern Organization Science* 2(2): 1–18.

Hodgson, D., and S. Cicmil (Eds). 2006. *Making Projects Critical*. Houndmills: Palgrave Macmillan.

Hughes, M. 2011. "Do 70 Per Cent of All Organizational Change Initiatives Really Fail?" *Journal of Change Management* 11(4): 451–464.

Hughes, M. 2016a. "Leading Changes: Why Transformation Explanations Fail." *Leadership* 12(4): 449–469.

Hughes, M. 2016b. "Who Killed Change Management?" *Culture and Organization* 22(4): 330–347.

Kotter, J.P. 1995. "Leading Change: Why Transformation Efforts Fail." *Harvard Business Review* 73(2): 259–267.

Lewin, K. (Ed.). 1951. *Field Theory in Social Science: Selected Theoretical Papers by Kurt Lewin*. London: The Tavistock Institute.

Marshak, R.J., and D. Grant. 2008. "Organizational Discourse and New Organization Development Practices." *British Journal of Management* 19: S7–S19.

Morris, P.W.G. 2011. "A Brief History of Project Management." In *The Oxford Handbook of Project Management*, edited by P.W.G. Morris, J. Pinto, and J. Soderlund, 15–36. Oxford: Oxford University Press.

Morris, P.W.G., L. Crawford, D. Hodgson, M.M. Shepherd, and J. Thomas. 2006. "Exploring the Role of Formal Bodies of Knowledge in Defining a Profession – The Case of Project Management." *International Journal of Project Management* 24(8): 710–721.

NHS Modernisation Agency. 2002. *Improvement Leaders' Guide to Sustainability and Spread*. Ipswich: Ancient House Printing Group.

Oswick, C., D. Grant, G. Michelson, and N. Wailes. 2005. "Looking Forwards: Discursive Directions in Organizational Change." *Journal of Organizational Change Management* 18(4): 383–390.

Palmer, I., and Dunford, R. 2008. "Organizational Change and the Importance of Embedded Assumptions." *British Journal of Management* 19: S20–S32.

Schwarz, G.M., and G.P. Huber. 2008. "Challenging Organizational Change Research." *British Journal of Management* 19: S1–S6.

Senge, P.M., and K.H. Kaeufer. 2000. "Creating Change." *Executive Focus* 17: 4–5.

Smith, A.C.T., and F.M. Graetz. 2011. *Philosophies of Organizational Change*. Cheltenham: Edward Elgar Publishing.

Smith, R., D. King, R. Sidhu, and D. Skelsey (Eds). 2014. *The Effective Change Manager's Handbook: Essential Guidance to the Change Management Body of Knowledge*. London: Kogan Page Publishers.

Soderlund, J. 2011. "Theoretical Foundations of Project Management: Suggestions for a Pluralistic Understanding." In *The Oxford Handbook on the Management of Projects*, edited by P.W.G. Morris, J. Pinto, and J. Soderlund, 15–36. Oxford: Oxford University Press.

Spicer, A., and C. Levay. 2012. "Critical Theories of Organizational Change." In *The Routledge Companion to Organizational Change*, edited by D.M. Boje, B. Burnes, and J. Hassard, 276–290. London: Routledge.

Stacey, R.D. 2012. *Tools and Techniques of Leadership and Management: Meeting the Challenge of Complexity*. London: Routledge.

Sturdy, A., and C. Grey. 2003. "Beneath and Beyond Organizational Change Management: Exploring Alternatives." *Organization* 10(4): 651–662.

Sutherland, F., and A.C.T. Smith. 2013. "Leadership for the Age of Sustainability: A Dualities Approach to Organizational Change." In *Organizational Change, Leadership and Ethics: Leading Organizations Towards Sustainability*, by R.T. By and B. Burnes, 216–239. London: Routledge.

Tidd, J., and J.R. Bessant. 2013. *Managing Innovation: Integrating Technological, Market and Organizational Change*. Chichester: John Wiley and Sons.

Turner, R., J. Pinto. and C. Bredillet. 2011. "The Evolution of Project Management Research: the Evidence from the Journals." In *The Oxford Handbook of Project Management*, edited by P.W.G. Morris, J. Pinto, and J. Soderlund, 65–106. Oxford: Oxford University Press.

University of Brighton. 2016. University Strategy 2016–2021. www.brighton.ac.uk/practical-wisdom. Accessed 6 October 2017.

Willis, C.D., J. Saul, H. Bevan, M.A. Scheirer, A. Best, T. Greenhalgh, R. Mannion, E. Cornelissen, D. Howland, E. Jenkins, and J. Bitz. 2016. "Sustaining Organizational Culture Change in Health Systems." *Journal of Health Organization and Management* 30(1): 2–30.

Worley, C.G., and S.A. Mohrman. 2014. "Is Change Management Obsolete?" *Organizational Dynamics* 43(3): 214–224.

Author index

Locators in **bold** refer to tables.

Subject index

Locators in **bold** refer to tables.